Bali
Street Atlas

Published by Tuttle Publishing,
an imprint of Periplus Editions (HK) Ltd.
www.tuttlepublishing.com

©2015 Periplus Editions (HK) Ltd.
Revised Fourth Edition
18 17 16 15   5 4 3 2 1
Printed in Singapore   1503CP
All Rights Reserved
ISBN 978-0-8048-4529-8

Distributors:

North America, Latin America & Europe
364 Innovation Drive
Tuttle Publishing
North Clarendon, VT 05759-9436, USA
Tel: 1 (802) 773 8930
Fax: 1 (802) 773 6993
info@tuttlepublishing.com
www.tuttlepublishing.com

Japan
Tuttle Publishing
Yaekari Bldg, 3rd Floor
5-4-12 Osaki
Shinagawa-ku, Tokyo 141 0032
Tel: (81) 3 5437 0171
Fax: (81) 3 5437 0755
sales@tuttle.co.jp
www.tuttle.co.jp

Asia Pacific
Berkeley Books Pte Ltd
61 Tai Seng Avenue #02-12
Singapore 534167
Tel: (65) 6280 1330
Fax: (65) 6280 6290
inquiries@periplus.com.sg
www.periplus.com

Indonesia
PT Java Books Indonesia
Jl. Rawa Gelam IV No. 9
Kawasan Industri Pulogadung
Jakarta Timur 13930
Tel: 62 (021) 4682 1088
Fax: 62 (021) 461 0206
crm@periplus.co.id
www.periplus.com

Front cover photo:
© Dudarev Mikhail/ Shutterstock.com

HOW TO USE THE STREET ATLAS

The Bali Street Atlas couldn't be simpler to use. The Maps, the Map Legend and the Index have all been specially designed to make finding places quick and easy.

The Maps

Maps of three different scales are grouped into three sections, each section having its own distinctive color scheme so that it is easy to find the section you need:

1:10,000 - 1:25,000 – 31 large-scale maps covering busy Bali

1:60,000 - 1:75,000 – 26 medium-scale maps covering all of Bali including Nusa Penida

1:200,000 – 3 small-scale maps giving an overview of Bali

Using the 'Key to Maps' at the front, locate the area of Bali you wish to look at. The color scheme and easy-to-read page numbers make it simple to quickly find the right page.

Each map is also named after an important feature or locality to help you recognize where you are straight away.

If you need to turn to a neighboring page the arrows (27) around the map edge will guide you directly to the correct one.

The Map Legend

Refer to facing page for a clear explanation of all the map features used in the atlas.

The Index

There are three parts:-
Street Index a listing of all the streets in the atlas
e.g. Wibisana.................................... **28** D6
 page number ↗   ↖ grid reference

Building Index a listing of all the buildings in the atlas
e.g. Sanglah Public Hospital............. **21** K4
 page number ↗   ↖ grid reference

Places Index a listing of all the places in the atlas
e.g. Lumbung Sari............................ **29** G3
 page number ↗   ↖ grid reference

To find a desired street, building or place, locate it in the alphabetical listings then read off the page number and alphanumeric grid reference on the right.

Find the relevant page (e.g. **28**). Read across the top or bottom of the map frame to find the correct letter (e.g. **D**) and read down the left or right side of the map frame to find the correct number (e.g. **6**). Using the map grid, locate the grid square where the letter and the number meet and you will find the street, building or place you are looking for within it.

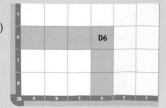

TUTTLE Publishing

Tokyo | Rutland, Vermont | Singapore

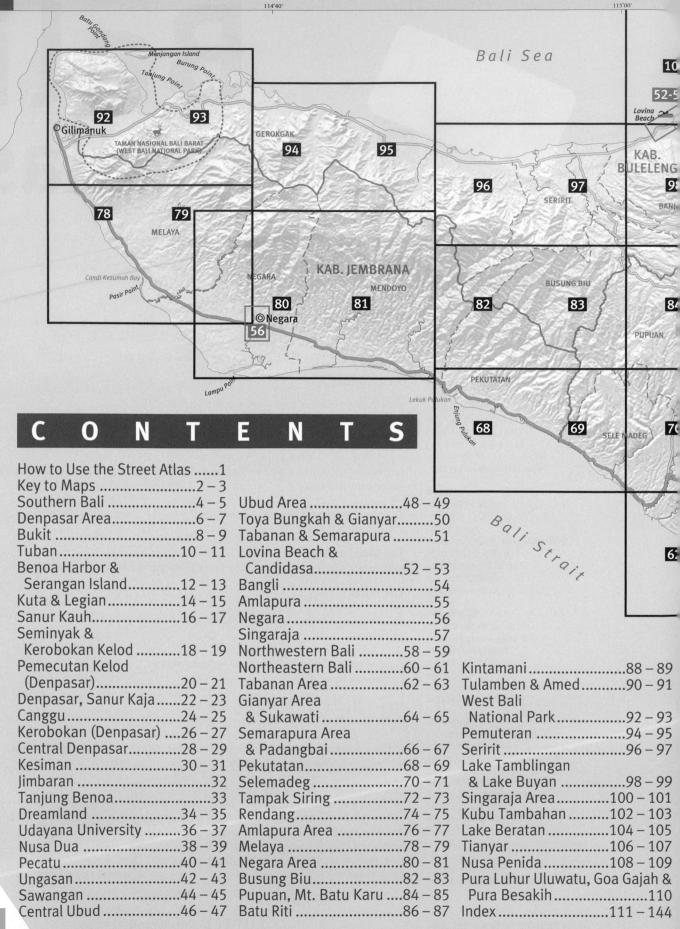

C O N T E N T S

How to Use the Street Atlas 1
Key to Maps ....2 – 3
Southern Bali ....4 – 5
Denpasar Area....................6 – 7
Bukit ....8 – 9
Tuban............................10 – 11
Benoa Harbor &
  Serangan Island............12 – 13
Kuta & Legian.................14 – 15
Sanur Kauh....................16 – 17
Seminyak &
  Kerobokan Kelod ....18 – 19
Pemecutan Kelod
  (Denpasar)..................20 – 21
Denpasar, Sanur Kaja......22 – 23
Canggu..........................24 – 25
Kerobokan (Denpasar) ....26 – 27
Central Denpasar.............28 – 29
Kesiman ....30 – 31
Jimbaran 32
Tanjung Benoa.......................33
Dreamland ....34 – 35
Udayana University ....36 – 37
Nusa Dua ....38 – 39
Pecatu............................40 – 41
Ungasan ....42 – 43
Sawangan ....44 – 45
Central Ubud ....46 – 47

Ubud Area ....48 – 49
Toya Bungkah & Gianyar.........50
Tabanan & Semarapura 51
Lovina Beach &
  Candidasa...................52 – 53
Bangli 54
Amlapura 55
Negara 56
Singaraja 57
Northwestern Bali ....58 – 59
Northeastern Bali ....60 – 61
Tabanan Area ....62 – 63
Gianyar Area
  & Sukawati ....64 – 65
Semarapura Area
  & Padangbai................66 – 67
Pekutatan.......................68 – 69
Selemadeg ....70 – 71
Tampak Siring ....72 – 73
Rendang.........................74 – 75
Amlapura Area ....76 – 77
Melaya ....78 – 79
Negara Area ....80 – 81
Busung Biu ....82 – 83
Pupuan, Mt. Batu Karu ....84 – 85
Batu Riti ....86 – 87

Kintamani ....88 – 89
Tulamben & Amed...........90 – 91
West Bali
  National Park................92 – 93
Pemuteran ....94 – 95
Seririt ....96 – 97
Lake Tamblingan
  & Lake Buyan ....98 – 99
Singaraja Area.............100 – 101
Kubu Tambahan ....102 – 103
Lake Beratan ....104 – 105
Tianyar ....106 – 107
Nusa Penida...............108 – 109
Pura Luhur Uluwatu, Goa Gajah &
  Pura Besakih.....................110
Index ....111 – 144

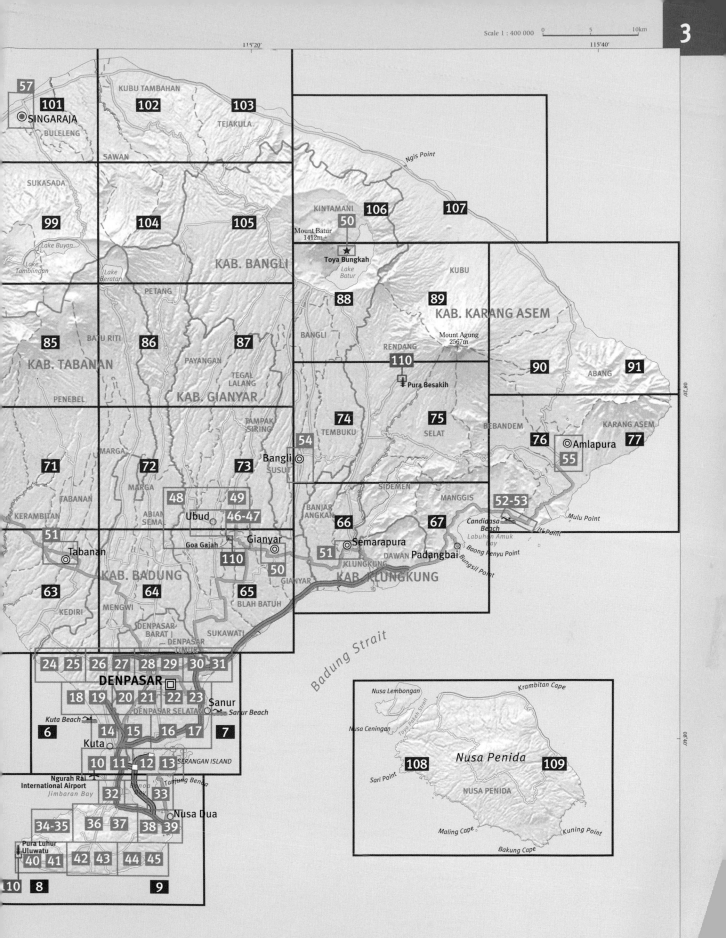

Scale 1 : 400 000 0 5 10km

115°20' 115°40'

57

101 ◎SINGARAJA

BULELENG

102 KUBU TAMBAHAN

103 TEJAKULA

SAWAN

SUKASADA

99

Lake Buyan

Lake Tamblingan

104

Lake Beratan

105

KAB. BANGLI

Ngis Point

KINTAMANI

106

50 Mount Batur 1412m +

★ Toya Bungkah

Lake Batur

107

KUBU

88

89

KAB. KARANG ASEM

Mount Agung 2567m

PETANG

85

BATU RITI

86

PAYANGAN

87

TEGAL LALANG

KAB. GIANYAR

KAB. TABANAN

PENEBEL

RENDANG

110

🏛 Pura Besakih

90

ABANG

91

08°00'

BEBANDEM

KARANG ASEM

74

TEMBUKU

75

SELAT

TAMPAK SIRING

54

73

MARGA

71

TABANAN

72

MARGA

ABIAN SEMAL

48

49

46-47

Ubud

76

55

◎Amlapura

SIDEMEN

MANGGIS

76

Bangli ◎

SUSUT

KERAMBITAN

51

Tabanan ◎

Goa Gajah

110

50

Gianyar ◎

BANJAR ANGKAN

66

67

Candidasa Beach

52-53

Iti Point

Mulu Point

Labuhan Amuk Bay

65

BLAH BATUH

51

KLUNGKUNG

DAWAN

Semarapura ◎

Padangbai

Baong Penyu Point

63

KEDIRI

64

MENGWI

KAB. BADUNG

DENPASAR BARAT

DENPASAR TIMUR

SUKAWATI

GIANYAR

KAB. KLUNGKUNG

Bungsil Point

24 **25** **26** **27** **28** **29** **30** **31**

DENPASAR ☐

18 **19** **20** **21** **22** **23**

DENPASAR SELATAN

Sanur

Sanur Beach

Kuta Beach

6

14 **15** **16** **17**

7

Kuta ◎

Badung Strait

10 **11** **12** **13** *SERANGAN ISLAND*

Ngurah Rai International Airport

Jimbaran Bay

Tanjung Benoa

32

33

◎Nusa Dua

Nusa Lembongan

Krambitan Cape

Nusa Ceningan

Toya Pakeh Strait

34-35

36 **37**

38 **39**

Pura Luhur Uluwatu

40 **41**

42 **43**

44 **45**

108

Sari Point

Nusa Penida

109

NUSA PENIDA

10 **8**

9

Maling Cape

Kuning Point

Bakung Cape

08°40'

INDIAN OCEAN

115°20' 115°40'

115°00' 115°10'

PUPUAN

Mundeh Kangin
Mundeh
Lumbung Kauh
Lumbung
Tiying Gading

Wana Giri
Pupuan Sawah
Gunung Salak

PENEBEL
Penatahan
Penebel
Pitra
Biaung
Tengkudak

Tua
BATURITI
Perean
Persiapan Pangsan
Bukian
Kedisal

PETANG
Melinggih
PAYANGAN
Kelusa
Tegal Lalang
Keliki
Rice Ter
Topeng D

Hot Spring

Jegu
Rejasa
Buruan
Tunjuk

Pura Yeh Gangga
Payangan
Petiga
Perean Tengah
Melinggih Kelod
Carangsari

MARGA
I Gusti Ngurah Rai Memorial
Sembung
Marga

Caubelayu
Pejeng Kaja
Pejeng Kang

KAB. GIANYAR
Kedewatan
Pura Telaga Wap

TAMP
SIRI
Pe

SELEMADEG

Lalanglinggah
Antosari
Bajera
Serampingan
Berembeng
Antap

Gadungan
Megati
Selemadeg
Tegal Mengkeb
Tangguntiti
Mambang
Belumbang

Kesiut
Timpag
Riang Gede
Sembung Gede
Batuan
Samsam

MARGA
Butterfly Park
Buahan
Selanbawak
Tegal Jadi
Kuwum
Werdi Bhuana
Batan Nyuh

Reptile Park
Sobangan
Ayunan
Sangeh
Taman

White Water Rafting
Monkey Forest & Pura Bukit Sari

Sayan Ridge

Ubud Village
Petulu

Holy Waringin Tree
Blahkiuh
Sayan

Ubud
Monkey Forest
Peliatan

Legong
Goa Gajah
Mas
Moon o
Pejeng

KERAMBITAN

Batuan
Kukuh
Pangkung Karung
Baturiti
Tista
Gubug

Subamia
Denbantas
Dajan Peken
Delod Reken

Monkey Forest
Beringkit
Peken
Kukuh

Cokorda's Palace Carved Bell Tower
Dauh Yehcani

ABIANSEMAL
Abian Semal
Penarungan

Singakerta
UBUD

Kemenuh
Pena T

Blah Ba

Dance Performances, Palaces
Kerambitan

Belalang
Beraban
Buwit

Tabanan
Gedong Marya Theater
Dauh Peken
Banjar Anyar
Abiantuwung

Mengwi
Gulingan
Mambal

Pura Taman Ayun

Singapadu Kaler
Lodtunduh

Pura
Hyang Tiba
Batuan Kaler

Blah Ba

TABANAN
Tibubiyu
Beraban

KEDIRI
Bongan
Kediri

Mengwi Tani
Kekeran

KAB. BADUNG

Cattle Market
Pura Sadha

Kapal
Lukluk

Sibang Kaja
Sedang
Sibang Gede

Wooden Masks

Singapadu Tengah
Singapadu

Batuan
Wood Ca

Waterfall
Craft Ma

Pasut Beach
Klating Beach
Sudimara
Bengkel
Pangkung Tibah

Kelating
Pejaten
Nyitdah

Pandak Bandung
Pandak Gede
Nyambung

Kaba-kaba
Cepaka

Abian Base
Sempidi
Sading

Pura Dalem Lukluk

Darmasaba
Agantaka

Gong Gede Music
Bali Reptile Park

Celuk
Gold/Silver Smith
Sukawa

Peguyangan Kaja
Jagapati
Bali Bird Park

Guwang
Batu Bulan
Batu Bulan Kang

SUKAWA

Enjung Kedungu
Enjung Batu Mejan
Enjung Batu Bolong
Pura Tanah Lot

Buduk
Dalung

Munggu

Kerobokan Kaja

KAB. BADUNG
KOTA DENPASAR

Padang Sambian Kaja
Ubung Kaja

DENPASAR UTARA
Peguyangan
Peguyangan Kangin

Penatih
Penatih Dangin Puri

Ketewel

Seseh Beach

Tibu Beneng
Canggu

KUTA

Kerobokan

Kerobokan Kelod

Ubung

Tonja

Gatot Subroto Bypass

Kesiman Petilan

DENPASAR TIMU

Canggu Beach

Padang Sambian

Tegal Kertha
Pemecutan

Dangin Puri Kaja
Dauh Puri Kaja

Kesiman

Kesiman Kertha Lan

Batu Belig Beach

Pemecutan Kelod
Tegal Harum

Dauh Puri Kangin
Dangin Puri Kauh
Dangin Puri

Pura Petitenget

Dauh Puri
Dauh Puri Kelod

Dangin Puri Kelod

Seminyak Beach
Seminyak

Sunset Road

Padang Sambian Kelod

DENPASAR

Sanur Beach
Sanur Kaja

Sindhu Bea

Bali Strait

Legian Beach
Legian

Dauh Puri Kauh
Panjer
Renon

Sanur

Kuta
Kuta Beach

Pedungan
Pemogan

Sanur Kauh
Sida Karya

Serangan

DENPASAR SELATAN

Tuban Beach

Sesetan

Ngurah Rai Bypass

Ngurah Rai International Airport

Tuban

Serangan Island

Kedonganan

Benoa Harbor
Tanjung Benoa

Jimbaran Beach

Benoa Bay

Jimbaran Bay
Jimbaran

Balangan Point
Pura Balangan

KAB. BADUNG

Ngurah Rai Bypass

Nusa Dua Beach

Dreamland Beach
Bingin Beach
Padang-padang Surfing
Suluban Surfing
Suluban Point
Suluban Beach

Pecatu Indah Resort

KUTA
Bukit

Garuda Wisnu Kencana Statue

Memedi Hill 151m

Ungasan Hill 203m

Benoa

Nusa Dua

Nusa Dua Beach
Gegar Point
Pura Geger

Pura Luhur Uluwatu
Pura Kulat

Pecatu

Ungasan

B u k

Payung Hill 103m

Mebulu Point
Nyang-nyang Surfing

Pura Masuka

Pura Batu Pageh

Pura Gunung Payung

Green Bowl Surfing Area

Soka Beach
Enjung Kebo Iwa
Enjung Menalo
Enjung Pamegalan
Enjung Bulung Dayo
Enjung Panggung
Enjung Boro'an

30°30'

08°40'

| 58 | 59 | 60 | 61 |
| 4 | 5 |

115°00' 115°10'

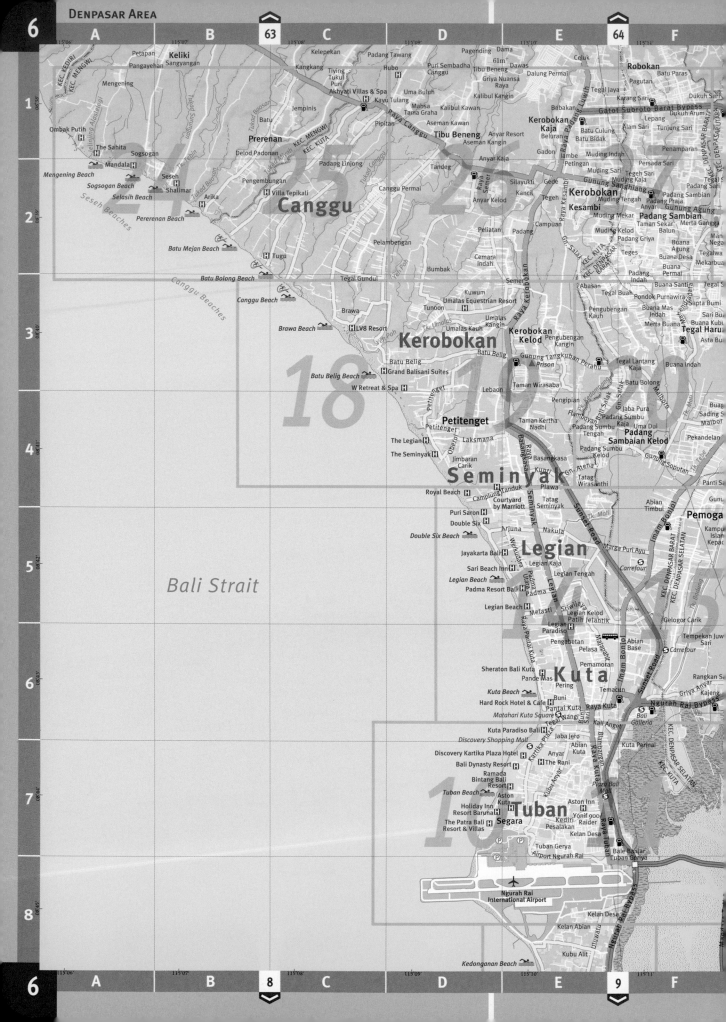

| A | B | C | **14** | D | E | F |

Mandiri

08°43'30"

1

Samudera ℝ
Sol Paradise
Segara Beach
Kuta Paradiso

Melasti Beach
Karthi Ⓗ
Benny's ℝ
Bali Garden Ⓗ Bui
Gu
Batan Waru ℝ

2

DISCOVERY SHOPPING MALL Ⓢ Ⓗ Home @36
Periplus Bookshop ★
Ifiori Waterb
ℝ Park
Ⓗ Adhi Jay:
Discovery Kartika Plaza Hotel Ⓗ Pusi
Ayu
Sun Island Ⓗ Ⓗ Bali Rani

Bali Strait

Thai ℝ Day
ℝ Express Beac
Golden Lotus ℝ **Green Garden**
Bali Dynasty Resort Ⓗ ▲ Bali Ratu Spa
Queens of ℝ
C-Line Ⓢ India ℝ
Ⓗ Febri's
The Eden Ⓗ *Taman Sari*
Santika Beach Ⓗ Kunyit Bali ℝ Ⓗ The Rani Hotel & S

08°44'00"

3

Ramada Bintang Bali Resort Ⓗ Bintang Ⓗ Mini
Kuta **Tuban**
Pantri ℝ Ⓗ Bali Bagus
Tuban Beach ⌇ Ma Joly ℝ ▲ PT. Ivo
Ⓗ Palm *Samudra* Ⓗ The Vira
The Sandi Phala Ⓗ
Zero Six ℝ Bakung's Ⓗ *Kuta Icon*
Beach ▲
Rama Beach Ⓗ

4

Green Garden Beach Resort and Spa Ⓗ Risata Bali Resort The Tusita
Ⓗ Aston Kuta Ⓗ
Tea Tree Spa ▲ *Warna Segara* Ⓗ J. Boutique *Wantilan*
SA Cafe Ⓗ ▲
Holiday Inn Resort Baruna Ⓗ Maesa Ⓗ
Lotus ℝ Pujasari ℝ Ⓗ Sekar *Kedi*
Tavern *Kimia Farma* Sari
▲
Segara *SMPN 1 Kuta* ▲ Ⓗ Wantilan

5

The Patra Bali Resort & Villas Ⓗ Ayu Nadi
Bali Segara Ⓗ Gg. Puri Gerenceng
Curug Tiga Palapa ℝ Bugils Bali
Jerman Beach ⌇ Bali Prani Ⓗ Anom Village
Pura Ksatria Dalem 🎋 Al ikhlas ☾ Harris
Tuban

08°44'30"

Pertamina
Tank Yard ▲
Ⓟ *Warung*
Ⓟ *Madiun* ℝ

6

International
Terminal
Fukutaro
Airport Ⓟ *Periplus Bookshop* Ⓢ
Ⓟ *Angkasa Pura I* ▲

Domestic Terminal

08°45'00"

7

60

✈ **NGURAH RAI INTERNATIONAL AIRPORT**

8

Kelan Beach ⌇

115°12'00"
115°12'30"
115°13'00"

1

Mangrove
Information
Center ▲

Pura Prapat
Nunggal

2

3

Pelabuhan

DESA PEDUNGAN
DESA KUTA

4

Mandara Toll Road

11

Dermaga

5

Benoa Harbor

Wahana Tirta ★

Jangkar Mas
Ikan Tuna 3 [H] Mandiri [B]

B e n o a

[H] Bounty Cruises
[H] Waka Louka Cruises
[H] Sea Safari Cruises
[R] Bali Marina

Dermaga 2

Karaoke Bali Beer [R]

Benoa Harbor

Ikan Tuna Raya Timur

Ikan Tuna Raya Barat

Ikan Tuna 2
[B] BNI 46

Bali Hai Cruises
Bemo Terminal
Dermaga 1

Benoa Harbor

6

Benoa Harbor

PT Gilontas ▲
Indonesia

PT Bali ▲
Mina Utama
Ikan Tuna 1

[R] ☪ † [P] [H] Quick Silver
Container Park

[P]
Container Park

Benoa Bay

Benoa Harbor

Mabua Express to Lembar (Lombok) 2–2.5 hours

7

Mandara Toll Road

8

Pan
Bhinne

G   H   J   K   L   M

115°13'30"   115°14'00"   115°14'30"

Tempat Pembuangan
Sampah Akhir (TPA)
Suwung

Algatech Kyowa
Aquaculture Laboratory

Koyac Bali
Yacht Club

Tepi Pantai
Pojok

Dolphin Lodge

Serangan
Kaja

Blue Water
Express

Serangan
Tengah

Serangan

Turtle Center

Serangan Pojok

Serangan
Peken

Kelurahan
Serangan

Serangan
Kawan

SMPN 11
Denpasar

Turtle Water Park

Pura Dalem
Kahyangan

BALI MANGROVE PARK

Inyah Point

Pura Sakenan

Tukad Sanekan

Tukad Guming

Penataran

Pantai Serangan

Tukad Ngenjung

Tukad Guming

Bugis

1

Tukad Pekaseh

Tukad Loloan

Pantai Serangan

Serangan
Dukuh

Tukad Punggawa

2

Pura Dalem
Susunan
Wadon

Pantai Serangan

Cafes

Benoa Bay

Pasar Desa
Serangan

3

Pura Dalem Cemara

Pantai Serangan

Serangan Island

4

Pantai Serangan

LAND UNDER RECLAMATION

5

Pantai Serangan

Pura Tunggak Tiying

6

LAND UNDER RECLAMATION

7

Badung Strait

sh
rket

Klenteng
Tanjung
Benoa

Benoa Cape

Mujahidin

Purwa Santi

8

Tanjung
Benoa Tengah

Segara
Lor

SDN 1 Tanjung
Benoa

Mabua Express to Lembar (Lombok) 2-2,5 hours

A   B   C   D   E   F

1

2

3

4

15

5

6

7

8

Pura Gajah Sesetan
Kenanga
Tegal Wangi
DESA PANJER
DESA SESETAN
Tukad Pule
Tukad Pakerisan
Sekolah Tinggi Ilmu Komputer Indonesia
Hardys Retailindo
SDN 5 Panjer
Tukad Citarum
Tukad Badung 14
Anggrek Bulan
Bali Holidays Tour
Melon
BRI
Kelapa
Apel
Gaduh
SDN 7 Sesetan
Puri Naga Mas
Tukad Badung 12 C
Tukad Badung 16
Hardy's Supermarket
Mangga Sari
Klapa Brezee
Conato's Bakery
Tukad Badung 18
Veterinary Medicine, Udayana University
Putra I Made Market
Nirwana Suites
Br. Bekul's Cemetery
Gelatik
Punglor
Tukad Badung 20
Taman Sari
Mandala Wangi
Bekul
DESA PANJER
Tukad Badung
Dukuh Pesirahan
Pulau Roti
DUKUH SARI
Warung Nikmat
Mandala Wangi Asri
Yeh Ning
Tukad Petanu
DESA SIDAKARYA
Gr City
DESA RENO
Pulau Moyo
Batas Dukuh Sari
Lantang Bejuh
Gumuk Sari
Indoraya Computer
Cafe Tahu
Dewata Indah
Rahmat
Cendrawasih
Bangau
DESA SIDAKAR
Betet
Curik
Jalak Bali
Indonesia Australia Language Foundation
Cenigan Sari
Cenigan Sari 1
Tegal Wangi 2
Undiknas
Dewata
Kerta Sari
Merpati
Rajawali
SDN 18 Sesetan
Cenigan Sari 3
Dewata 2
Dewata 4
Moyo Permai
P.M.2
3 W.D.
SDN 11 Sesetan
Beo
Cenigan Sari 7
Sari
Dewata 1
Mars City
Kerta Dalem 14
P.M.4
Beo
Blue Bird Taxi Group
Cenigan Sari
Kembar Asri
Raya Kerta Dalem
P.M.8
Garuda
Dukuh Sari
Hindu Cemetery
Tengah
K.D.3
P.M.10
P.M.7
Merak
Pegadaian
Sidakarya
Sidakarya
Sidakarya
K.D.2
Dharma Wiweka School
Punglor
Sesetan
Pegok
Taman Suci
Dukuh Merta Jati
Sekar Kangin
SDN 4 Sesetan
K.D.1
K.W.1A
Suwung Kangin
SMP Ganesa Denpasar
Piranha 1
Pegok
G.4
SMPN 6 Denpasar
STSI
Gurita 4
Palapa 1
Palapa 2
Palapa 1
Palapa 2
Pendidikan 1
Kerta Winangun 1
SDN 9 Sesetan
Plasahosting
Piranha
Kecamatan Denpasar Selatan
Gurita 3
Delod Tukad
Palapa 3
Palapa 4
Kerta Winangun 2
Gurita 1
Gurita 1
PT Djarum
Palapa 6
P.5
SMKN 2
Gagak
Graha Wisata
Kerta Usada
Puskesmas
Taman Sari
Palapa 7
Palapa 8
Palapa 9
SMAN 5
Kerta Raharja
Gurita
SDN 2,5,8 Sesetan
Palapa 9
Palapa 10
Palapa 11
Sanitasi
Kebudayaan
Bali International
Merta Sari
Kerta Bedulu 3
Wira Satu
Jadi Pesona
Pulau Moyo
Green Kori 3
PGSD
Palapa 10
P.11
Palapa 12
Palapa 13
Palapa 14
Graha Kerti
Akademi Sanitasi Pramuwisata
Pendidikan
Merta Sari
Kerta Bedulu 2
Kerta Petasikan
Taman Suc
Ikan Karper
Griya Dana
Baja
Monica Bali Villa
Kerta Bedulu 1
Kertha Lestari
Tirta Sari
Karya Dharma
Kresek
Prima Rasa Pangan
Bugis Cemetery
Puri Yuma
Villa Pondok Bambu
Lumba Lumba
Ikan Tongkol
Balai Karantina Hewan
Lumba Lumba
SDN 13 Sesetan
Mahabarata
Mutiara
SMP PGRI 4 Denpasar
Suwung Batan Kendal
Ikan Tuna
Damai
Ambengan
Raya Sesetan
Lam-gabe
Suwung Batan Kendal
Merta Sari
Pasar Suwung Batan Kendal
Rumah Potong Hewan (Abatoir)
Istana Regency
TNI AL
Suwung Permai
Ngurah Rai Bypass
KM16
Pesanggrahan
Panto Sari
Coconut Beach Resort Office
Panorama Leisure
Muslim Cemetery
Lintas Dimensi
Pesanggaran
Pesanggaran
SDN 5 Pedungan
Lotte Mart
Bugis Suwung
Pemelisan
Buntu Sari
Tempekan Pesanggaran
Ulam Kencana
Warung Arema
KM17
PT Paris Bali
Bali Surya Utama
M Tour
Pulau Serangan
DESA SIDAKARYA
Angkkosa Cargo Santika Wijaya
Koperasi Jasa Angkutan Taxi
PT Bali Foam Nusa Megah
Soto Ayam Surabaya
Pertamina
Coca-Cola
Indonesia Power (Pesanggrahan Power Station)
Suzuki
Yani
KM18
Halo Bali
Algatech Kyc Aquacult Labora
Depo Pertamina
Koyac Bali Yacht Club
PT Lir Antar N
Pasar Serangan
Serangan Kaja
Pura Dalem Penataran
Serangan Tengah
Serangan Pojok
Turtle Cer
TPA Suwung
Tempat Pembuangan Sampah Akhir (TPA) Suwung
SMPN 11 Denpasar
Kelurahan Serangan
Serangan Peken
Turtle Water Park
Serangan Kawan
Pelabuhan
Inyah Point
Pura Sakenan
Tukad Punggan
Tukad Guming
Tukad Ngenjung
Tukad Guming
Bugis
Bali Mangrove Park
Pulau Serangan
Penataran
Tukad Pekaseh
Tukad Lofoan
Penataran

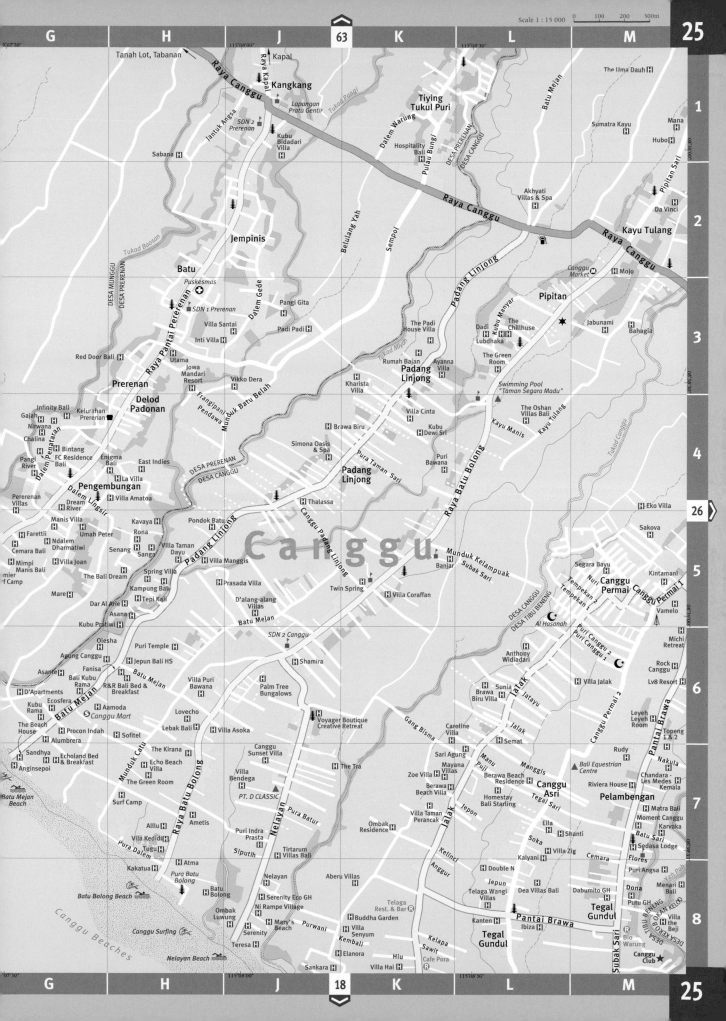

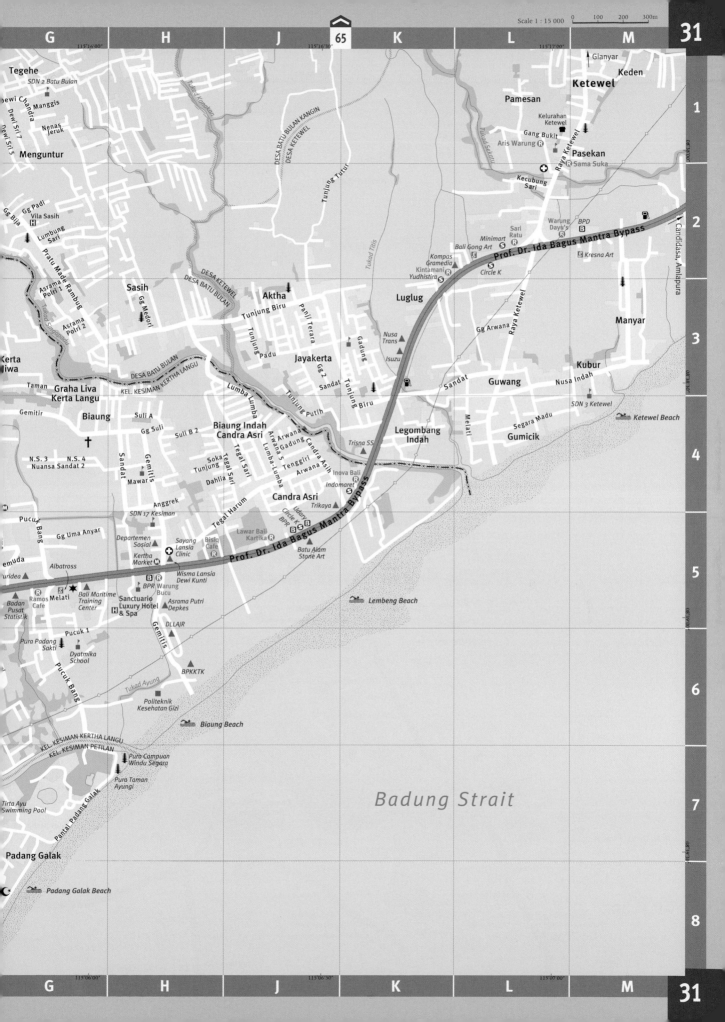

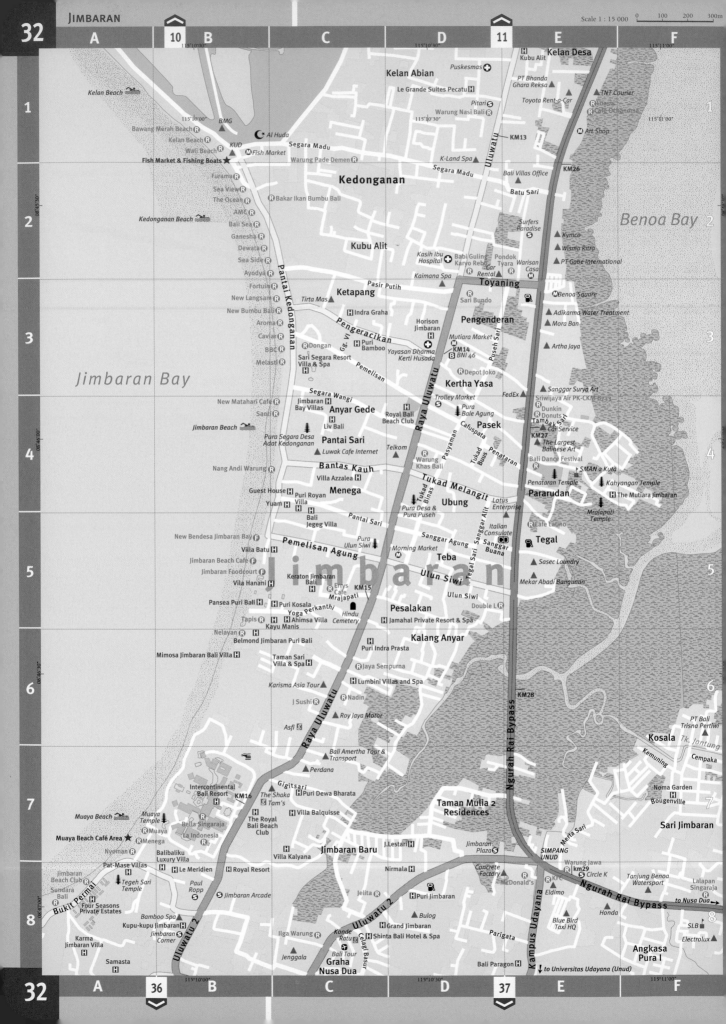

	A	B	C	D	E	F

Bali Strait

Cape Balangan

Balangan Beach

Flowerbud Bungalows

Balanga Sea View Bungalow

Jumeirah Bali (U/C)

Klapa New Kuta Beach

Dreamland Beach

Meritus

New Kuta Beach

Wuku Resort

Tukad Songkung

El Kabron Spanish Restaurant

The Calyx Villa

Chokcy's Place

Mick's Place

Duke's

The Bingin Beach House

Pondok Indah

The Retreat

Leggie

Dream View Villa

Bingin Beach

Suara Ombak

Sundaram's

Jabeki

Laguna Wailele

Romeo

Impossible Beach

Bingin Garden

The Temple Lodge

Suara Ombak

Alamanda Villas

Kembang Kuning

MU

Mario

Exclusive Bali Bungalows

Kesuma Sari

Villa Impossible

Villa Bayuh Sabbha

Merta Sari

Pantai Bingin

Anantara Uluwatu

Impossibles Beach

C. 151 Smart Villas

Wika's

Tukad Bingin

Pantai Bingin

Bingin Family Bungalow

Buana Sari

Villa Pemutih

Tanjung Simah

Pemutih

Bingin Inn

Buana Sari

Padang Padang Beach

Guna Mandala Inn

Lullaby Bungalows

Cempaka Indah Inn

Bangket

Blue Heaven View

Padang Padang Inn

54m

Imposible Surf Camp

Medori Putih Homestay

Blue Heaven

Padang Padang Sari

Kenanga Inn

Kongsi Inn

Deng Sari

Melasti Labuansait

Ayu Guna Inn

Bingin

Manggo Tree Cafe

Villa Capung

Pink Coco Bali

Castello Mataspi Villas

57m

Melasti Labuansait

62m

Labuan Sait Indah Inn

Labuan Sait

Yeye's

Umpeng

SDN 2 Pecatu

Belong Bunter Homestay

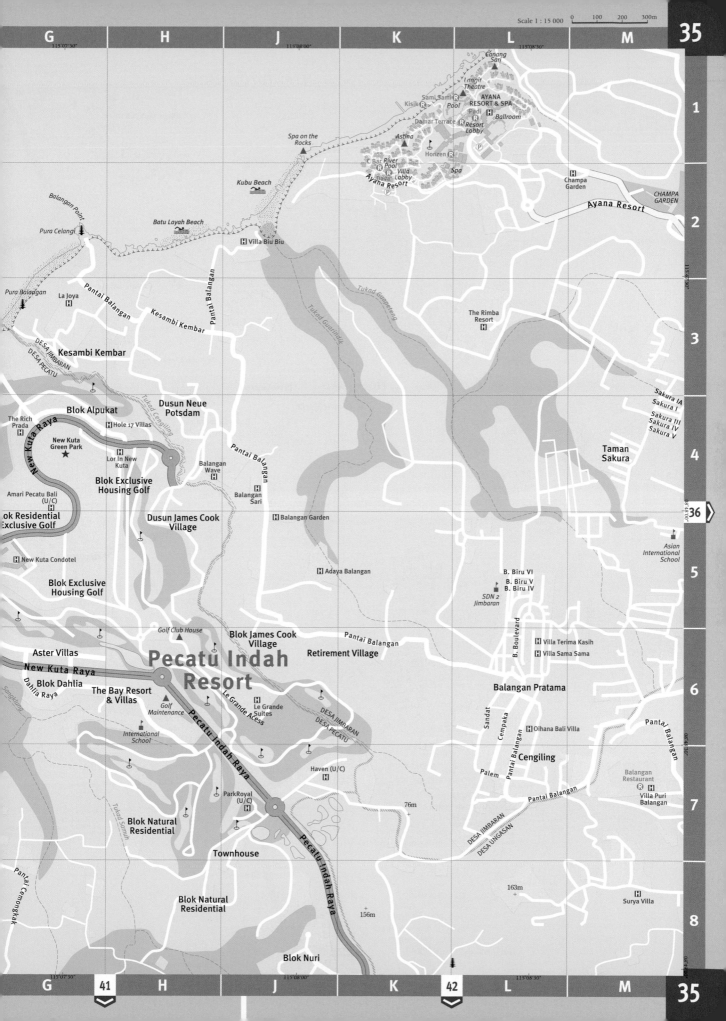

Canang
Sari

Langit
Theatre

Sami Sami   AYANA
Kisik   RESORT & SPA
Pool   Padi
Damar Terrace   Ballroom
Astina   Resort
Lobby
Honzen
C Bar River   Spa
Pool
Dava   Villa
Ayana Resort   Lobby

Spa on the
Rocks

Champa
Garden   CHAMPA
GARDEN

Ayana Resort

Kubu Beach

Batu Layah Beach

Balangan Point

Pura Celangi

Villa Biu Biu

Pura Balangan   Pantai Balangan

La Joya   Kesambi Kembar   The Rimba
Resort

DESA JIMBARAN   Pantai Balangan

DESA PECATU   Kesambi Kembar

Tukad Guanindik   Tukad Guanindik

Tukad Guapeteang

Sakura IA
Sakura I
Sakura III
Sakura IV
Sakura V

Blok Alpukat   Dusun Neue
Potsdam

The Rich
Prada   Hole 17 Villas

New Kuta
Green Park

Lor In New
Kuta

Blok Exclusive
Housing Golf

Pantai Balangan

Balangan
Wave

Balangan
Sari

Taman
Sakura

Amari Pecatu Bali
(U/C)

ok Residential
Exclusive Golf

Dusun James Cook
Village

Balangan Garden

Adaya Balangan

B. Biru VI
B. Biru V
B. Biru IV

Asian
International
School

New Kuta Condotel

SDN 2
Jimbaran

Blok Exclusive
Housing Golf

Golf Club House

Blok James Cook
Village

Pantai Balangan

Retirement Village

Villa Terima Kasih

Villa Sama Sama

Aster Villas

New Kuta Raya

Blok Dahlia

The Bay Resort
& Villas

Golf
Maintenance

International
School

Pecatu Indah
Resort

Le Grande Acess

Le Grande
Suites

DESA JIMBARAN

DESA PECATU

B. Boulevard

Balangan Pratama

Oihana Bali Villa

Sandat

Cempaka

Pantai Balangan

Cengiling

Palem

Pantai Balangan

Balangan
Restaurant

Villa Puri
Balangan

Blok Natural
Residential

ParkRoyal
(U/C)

Haven (U/C)

76m

Townhouse

Pecatu Indah Raya

Pecatu Indah Raya

Blok Natural
Residential

163m

Surya Villa

156m

Blok Nuri

Dahlia Raya

Songklung

Tukad Samuh

Pantai Cemongkak

DESA JIMBARAN

DESA UNGASAN

Benoa Bay

Mandara Toll Road

A B C D E F

1

Pet Shop
Wave Spa
Sekar Sejagat
SDN 9 Jimbaran
Taman Jimbaran
Mumbul
Polo Ralph Lauren
Coco Mart
Ithon Mart
Taman Werdi
Taman Bali
Indomaret
Pop!
Minimart
LPIA
Oakley
Minimart
Bulakan Sari
Mekar Sari
Mahanthika
Java Pillar Furniture
Circle K
Prodia

Indomaret
Avani
Oaks
Veteran Monument
Nusa Dua Circle
Chinese Cemetery
Taman Siswa
Kemuning
Christian Cemetery
KM31
Waterworld Watersport Shop
Wahyu Spa
dh Spa
Ellie's
Angsa Putih
Sonni Puteri
Adhi
Seven Angels
Moon Villa
Tee Spa
Sama Sama
Ngurah Rai Bypass
Gedong Sari
Spasion
Prodia
Circle K
Prudential
KM32
Adi Spa
Indomaret
BCA

Puri Mumbul Permai

Taman Jati
Taman Lawang
Tanadewa Luxury Villas & Spa
Taman Ria
SMK 1 Kuta Selatan
Villa Diamond Star Hill Resort & Spa
Yamaha
Redikon

2

Griya Mandiri
Kemuning 1
Taman Giri
DESA JIMBARAN
DESA BENOA
Giri Puspa
Paradise Loft Villas
Bayview Villa Residences
Tjendana Villas
Taman Mumbul
Taman Kebo Iwa
Amarossa
Taman Kerowa
Lila Nita
BPD
BNI 46
Mandiri

Kemuning
Sekar Jepun
Taman Sari Royal Heritage Spa
SMKN 1 Kuta
Puri Nusa Dua
Toya Spa
Villas S & Ren

3

Samantha Residences
Kemuning
Taman Griya
Permata Giri Estate
Real Estate Taman Mumbul
Royal Garden Residence
Taman Sari
Taman Nusa Indah
Dalem
Gang Olala
Pesona Bali Hill
Swiss Belhotel Bay View
The Bali Bay View Suites & Villas
Puri Nusa Dua
Lava East
Hardy's Nusa Dua
KM33
Villa Scena

4

Giri Hill Terrace
DESA JIMBARAN
DESA BENOA
Giri Hill Terrace
Beranda 2
Beranda Raya
Mumbul Garden
Palm Raya
Taman Mumbul Indah
Gang GM Taman Sari
Gang GM Pulasari
Gang Wrija
Taman Kebo Iwa
Goodway (Putra Bali Hill Village)
Global Village
Majestic Point Villas
Alsis S and K
PUJA MANDALA
Ibnu Batutah Mosque 1
Maria Bunda Segala Bangsa Catholic Church 2
Vihara Buddha Guna 3
Bukit Doa Christian Church 4
Pura Jagatnatha 5

Tk. Pemutih

37

Putra Bali Hill
Bougenville
Nusa Indah
Wisma Nusa Permai
Agranusa Signature Villas
Nusa Du Hill Resor

5

Giri Hill Terrace
Kampial Residence 2
Ancak
Puri Kampial
Kampial Indah
Kampial Market
Aqua
Darma Wangsa
Wisma Nusa Permai
Ithon Mart
Setra Gede
Bualan Kampial
Pura Dalem Kampial
Garden Land Residence
Bisma
Siligita
Permat Nusa D

6

Tk. Munden
Yamaha
Indomaret
Gang Kendal
Pura Dalem Penataran
Kampial Market
Tukad Beririt

Benoa
La Stella Bali
Melanting
Kel. Benoa
Menesa

7

Desa Jimbaran
Desa Benoa
Bellevue Heritage Villa
Darma Wangsa
Langon Bali Resort and Spa
Melari
Kampial Permai
Tukad Gagar

8

Sekolah Tinggi Pariwisata Bali
Cancer Mart
Park View Height Villas
Park View Height Private Estate
Raja Warung
Ocean Blue Hotel Bali
118m
Uppala Hills (U/C)
Ocean Blue
55m

Hardys Nusa Dua Hills Resort

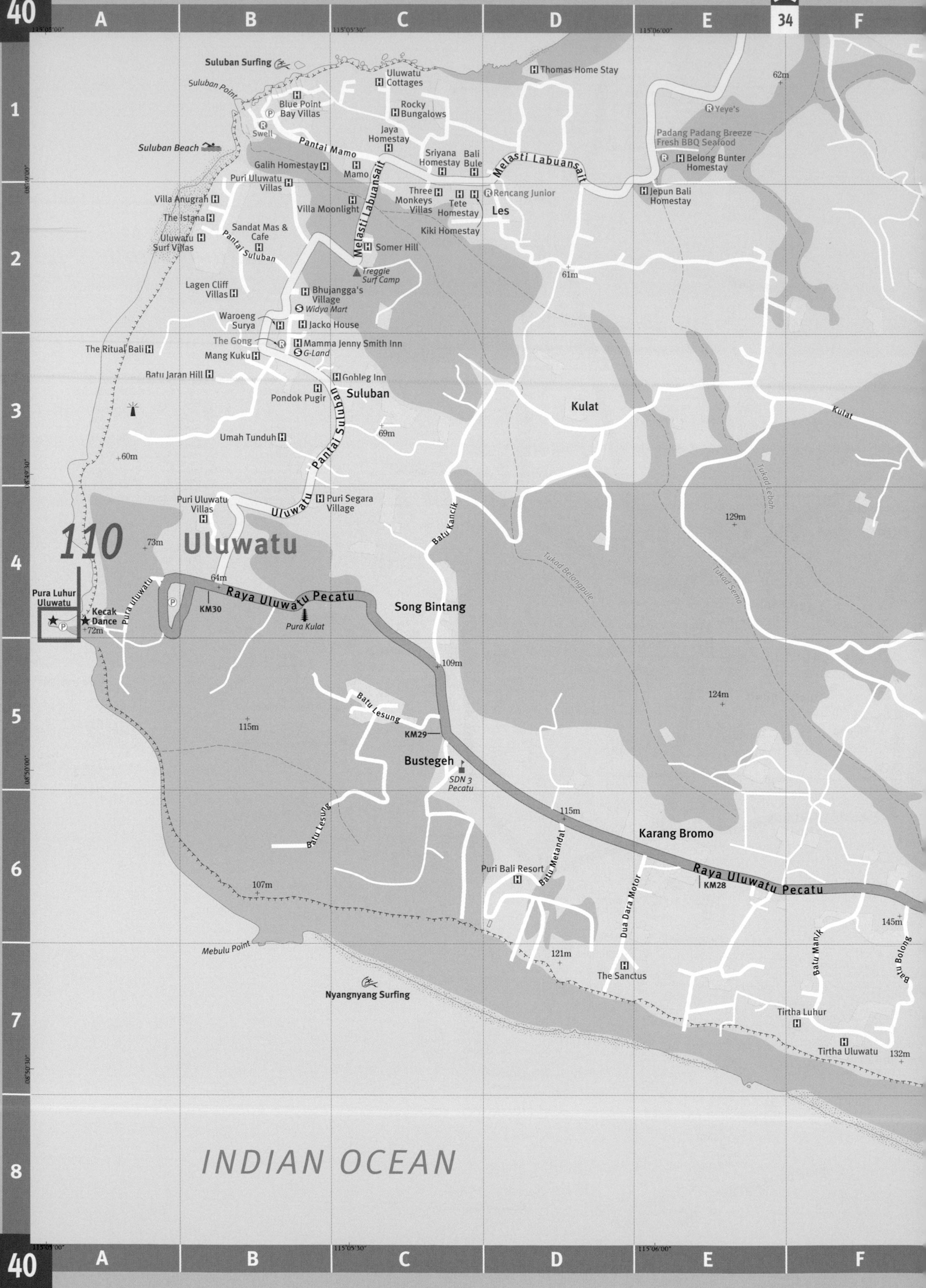

A B C D E F

1

Suluban Surfing
Uluwatu Cottages
Thomas Home Stay
62m
Suluban Point
Blue Point Bay Villas
Rocky Bungalows
Yeye's
Swell
Jaya Homestay
Padang Padang Breeze Fresh BBQ Seafood
Suluban Beach
Pantai Mamo
Sriyana Homestay Bali Bule
Belong Bunter Homestay
Galih Homestay
Mamo
Three Monkeys Villas Tete Homestay
Rencang Junior
Jepun Bali Homestay
Puri Uluwatu Villas
Villa Moonlight
Kiki Homestay
Les
Villa Anugrah
The Istana

2

Uluwatu Surf Villas
Sandat Mas & Cafe
Somer Hill
61m
Lagen Cliff Villas
Bhujangga's Village
Treggie Surf Camp
Waroeng Surya
Widya Mart
The Gong
Jacko House
Mamma Jenny Smith Inn
The Ritual Bali
Mang Kuku
G-Land
Kulat
Kulat
Batu Jaran Hill
Gobleg Inn
60m
Pondok Pugir
Suluban
69m
Umah Tunduh

3

Batu Kancik
129m
Tukad Lebah
Puri Uluwatu Villas
Puri Segara Village
Tukad Belongpule
Tukad Sema

4

110 73m **Uluwatu**
64m
Raya Uluwatu Pecatu
Song Bintang
Pura Luhur Uluwatu
KM30
Kecak Dance
Pura Kulat
+72m
109m
124m

5

115m
Batu Lesung
KM29
Batu Lesung
Bustegeh
SDN 3 Pecatu
115m
Karang Bromo
Raya Uluwatu Pecatu
107m
Puri Bali Resort
Dua Dara Motor
KM28
145m
Mebulu Point
121m
Batu Manik
Batu Bolong

6

7

Nyangnyang Surfing
The Sanctus
Tirtha Luhur
Tirtha Uluwatu 132m

8

INDIAN OCEAN

Ayu Guna Inn
Labuan Sait Indah Inn
Labuan Sait
Bingin
Pantai Bingin
57m
Melasti Labuansait
Tukad Belantong
SDN 2 Pecatu
Buana Sari
Rambo Homestay
Umpeng
3D Warung & Homestay
Gg. Jepun 1
Sari Sekapa
Sari Sekapa 1
Kamafari Hostel
167m
Canang Sari Villas
Pantai Cemongkak
Pantai Cemongkak
Villa Capung
Midnight
Green Mango
The Eyes
Castelo
Matasapi Villas
Top Hill Villas
Green Mango
+158m
Tukad Songkiung
152m
166m
Blok Natural Residential
142m
Puncak Wisesa
Tukad Uwi
Puncak Wisesa
69 Homestay & Mart
Indah Manis Private Villa
Temu Dewi
SDN 5 Pecatu
Temu Dewi
Pagpagan
Peratu Ruken
173m
Peratu Ruken
Dauh Puseh
Peratu Rukeh
Pecatu Kauh
Raya Uluwatu Pecatu
KM24
Kelurahan Pecatu
Pecatu
Peratu Rukeh
Bambang Kembar
Puskesmas
Peratu Keting
LPD
SDN 4 Pecatu
Pecatu Kangin
Baler Setra
Pura Cuplatan
SDN 6 Pecatu
Giri Sari
Selonding
KM25
213m
Batu Nunggalan
KM27
KM26
164m+
Raya Uluwatu Pecatu
Pura Selonding
Goa Lempeh
Gang Fiduk
Bangbang Kembar
lukpuluk
Batu Nunggalan
Pura Selonding
Villa Plenilunio
160m
Khayangan Estate
Sangkar
Il Ristorante
The Spa
Bulgari Hotels & Resorts
Goa Lempeh
Goa Lempeh
165m
Outrigger Panorama Bali Resort & Spa
The Edge

Blok Nuri

Blok Orange Village

Griya Alam Pecatu

Palapa Mosque

Retirement Village

Dreamland Luxury Villa & Spa

Ungasan Hill 203m

Villa Sami Sami

Balangan

Bali She Villa

Le Nixun Villa & Spa

Nirma Water

Taman Paradise

KM21

152m

Mahagiri Villa & Spa

Kahuripan

Koperasi Giri Mitra

Pepito

Griya Alam Pecatu

Blok Arjuna

Koramil Kuta Selatan

Raya Uluwatu

Bakung Sari

Blok Sahadewa

KM22

Gg. 2

Samantha Residence

Pura Masuka

Hindu Cemetery

198m

Toya Ning II

Wana Giri

Temu Dewi

Indah Manis Private Villa

Nabor

Dreamland Surfcamp

Pura Masuka

164m

KM23

Bendesa

Pura Masuka

Sari Kaya

Pecatu Kauh

Temudewi

Semut

Aisis Luxury Villas & Spa

Bayuh

KM24

Raya Uluwatu Pecatu

SDN 5 Pecatu

+209m

Blimang Sari

+ 210m

Tunjung

Kertha Lestari

144m

Pura Masuka

Tk. Kubongbukai

Baler Setra

Tukad Pangpang

Kumba Boutique Villas & Spa

140m

Anggrek

Langui Kangin

Banjar Wijc Kusuma

Ratna

Bangbang Kembar

213m

Blimbing Sari 1

DESA UNGASAN

DESA PECATU

Taman Nusa

153m

Chateau de Bali

Wijaya Kusumah

Belimbing Sari I

Blimbing Sari 1

Uluwatu Peak

155m

Tk. Belongkeng

Alila Villas

Belimbing Sari I

Tembiyak

Pantai Selatan Gau

Karma Kandara

159m

Alila Villas Uluwatu

110m

Semara Luxury Villa

Karma Kandara

Di Mare

Pura Masuka

Karma Spa

Beranda Bukit

DESA JIMBARAN
DESA KUTUH

DESA JIMBARAN
DESA BENOA

Puri Dharwangsa Villa

123m

Hardys Nusa Dua Hills Resort Ⓗ

Ocean Blue Ⓗ

Ocean Blue Ⓗ

Raya Kampial

Puri Bunga Residences

Gubuk Sari

139m

DESA BENOA
DESA KUTUH

142m

Darma Wangsa

SDN 2 Kutuh

Kutuh

Perumahan Praja Prahita

DESA BENOA
DESA KUTUH

Tukad Gunungpayung

Petangan

Banjar Kaja Jati

SDN 3 Kutuh

Bali International Advisory Services

Ⓗ Villa Emanjo

SDN 6 Kutuh

Balai Banjar Petangan

Ⓗ Manuh's Guest House

Ⓗ Villa Bukit Pesona

Gunung Payung

Payung Hill 103m

Panthi Giri

121m

Nusa Dua Selatan

Gunung Payung

Jaba Pura

122m

Nusa Dua Retreat &Spa Ⓗ

Melasti II

Tukad Mejan

116m

Pantai Pandawa

78m

Pura Gur Payur

118m

Kutuh Water View Villas Ⓗ

Tukad Babi

71m

Pantai Pandawa

Celagimantis

106m

Gapura Vista Ⓗ

Timbis Paragliding

Villa Bidadari Ⓗ

102m

Villa Latitude Bali Ⓗ

Bali Paintball ★ Ⓗ
Villa Karang Putih

Villa Karang Ⓗ

Nagasutra Villa Ⓗ

Pandawa Beach

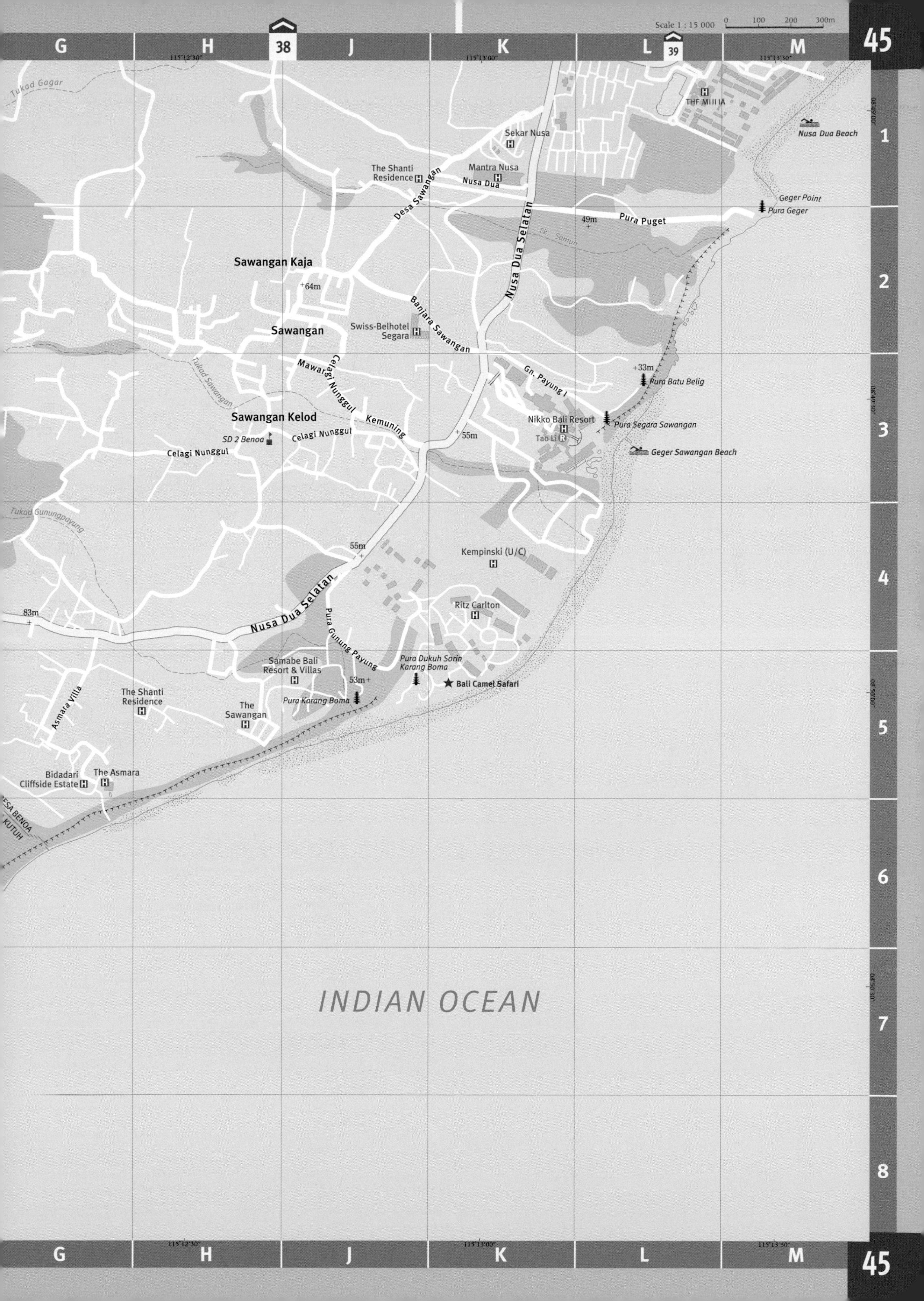

Scale 1 : 15 000
0 100 200 300m
G
H
38
J
K
L
39
M
115°12'30"
115°13'00"
115°13'30"
08°49'00"
08°49'30"
08°50'00"
08°50'30"
1
2
3
4
5
6
7
8
Tukad Gagar
THE MULIA
Nusa Dua Beach
Sekar Nusa
The Shanti Residence
Mantra Nusa Dua
Desa Sawangan
Geger Point
Pura Geger
49m
Pura Puget
Tk. Samuh
Nusa Dua Selatan
Sawangan Kaja
64m
Banjara Sawangan
Swiss-Belhotel Segara
Sawangan
Mawargi
Celagi Nunggul
Gn. Payung I
33m
Pura Batu Belig
Tukad Sawangan
Kemuning
Nikko Bali Resort
Pura Segara Sawangan
Sawangan Kelod
SD 2 Benoa
Celagi Nunggul
55m
Tao Li
Geger Sawangan Beach
Celagi Nunggul
Tukad Gunungpayung
55m
Kempinski (U/C)
Ritz Carlton
83m
Nusa Dua Selatan
Pura Gunung Payung
Samabe Bali Resort & Villas
Pura Dukuh Sorin Karang Boma
53m
Bali Camel Safari
Asmara Villa
The Shanti Residence
Pura Karang Boma
The Sawangan
Bidadari Cliffside Estate
The Asmara
DESA BENOA
KUTUH
INDIAN OCEAN
G
H
J
K
L
M

A   B   C   D   E   F

Gunung
Batu Sari
Teba Rejo
Lapangan Berburu
Tabah
Pongkung Tabah
Pegongan

Hindu Cemetery
Kelurahan Taman

Taman
Batu Bayan
Chinese Cemetery
Raketan

Pasar Delod

Pasar Delod

Teguan

Hindu Cemetery

Tangga Yuda
Teguan
Pangembunga Sari

Bongkasa
Kelurahan Bongkasa

Teguan

Pangembungan

Kambang

Warung Kodok

Tegal Kuning

Tegal Kuning

Tegal Kuning

Finish Rafting

Biyukukung Suites & Spa

Sobek Rafting

Suargan Temple

Villa Puricamas

Taman Bebek
Sayan Terrace

Four Seasons Resort Bali at Sayan
Ayung Terrace
Villa Dhyan
View

Cafe Sayan
Kutuh

Indochine Dine & Lounge
Villa Nirwana
Sayan Dewata
The Mansion Resort Hotel & Spa

Kutuh

Baung
Kayumanis Ubud Private Villa & Spa
Bambu Indah Villa
Kelurahan Sayan
White Lotus Lodge

Djagra's Inn
Sayan

Samaya Ubud
Pende
Mas

Baung

Sindu Jiwa

Kuta Raga

Furamaxclusive Villas & Spa Ubud Bali

Tohpati
Hindu Cemetery

Semana

Pengiasan

Mambal

Pengiasan

Silang Karang
Raya Semana

Tengah
Buduk

Semana Resort

Ambengan

Tewel

Tewel

Tebongkang

Ayodya
Astina
Kelurahan Singekerta
Purna Sari

Lobong

Cafe Sanbo
Tunjung
Singekerta
Villa Arya
The Westin Ubud Resort & Spa
Artha Sari

Ketik Lantang

Raya Singekerta

Dangin Labak
Villa Wanakerta

Dauh Labak

Hindu Cemetery

Denpasar, Bali Bird Park

Puri Bunga
Payangan, Chedi, Bagawan Giri
Cahaya Dewata
Plumerta
Villa Saraswati
Payogan

White Water Rafting
View

Villa Indah
Blind Masseur
Villa Melati

Lungsiakan
Villa Santa Mandala
Rsi Markandya 2

Villa Imogiri

Chapung Se Bali Resort

Hindu Cemetery

Nasi Ayam Kedewatan
Citra Minang
Titi

Empu Tantular
Celeng
Kumaratih
Kuluk
Gunorta
SDN 2 Kedewatan

Bangkiansidem
Banjar Sari

Kedewatan
Kadewatan Anyar
Amandari Villa

Kenanga
Palm
Fly
Anom
Ulun Ubud Resort Hotel

Abi
Bliss Spa
Adi Asri
Toto
Sunari

Antonius Kho
Palava
Kusia

Kafe Karsa

Pondok Kecil
Kubudi Sakti
Sari Wang
Waka Di Ume Reso

Tropical Bale
Tropical Bale
Sunny Blow
Villa Jepun
Naughty Nuri's
Ozigo

FedEX Courier
Beji Ubud Resort
Villa Bukit Ubud
Uma Ubud
Neka Art Museum

Klub Kokos
Sunset Hill Villa
Bintang Peso
Bintang Pari Cotta
Villa Binta

Orgone Gallery
Nacho Mama
Kori Ubud Resort
Design Unit
Mozaic
Bali Video

Sanggingan
Anom Cottage
Tama
Ray Sandy

Ananda Cottages
Bukit Asri

Pita Maha Resort
Anhera
Indus
Villa Bhagawan
Danamon
I. M. Yang

Sari Organic
Bodag Maliah

Balo Galu
Sembahan Treatmer
Lila Gri
Samdadad Villag
Agris Homesta

Warung Pulau Kelapa
Campuan College
Anini Raka Resort & Spa
Warung Sanjii

Taman Indrakila
Wisata Cottages
Tankis
Sika

Ubud Sari Health Resort

Sembaha

Gaya Fusion of Senses
Sayan Ayu
Gaya

Rumah Cahaya
Pura Ulun Danu
Tourism College

Ubud

Threads of Life

Rumah Roda
Lenuk

Penestanan Kaja
Villa Dhyan
View

Gaya
Leke Leke
Cafe Vespa

Pondok Iman Villas
Taman Rahasia
Yellow Flower Cafe
Indo French Villa
Symon Studio

SMSR Art High School
Warwick Ibah Luxury Villas & Spa
Pura Gunung Lebah
Tjampuhan
Abangan

Sekar Ayu
Ubud Kaja
Puri Saraswati

Lady Bamboo
Puri Taman
Ubu

Campuan
Baligen
Santra Putra
Siddharthas
Made Bawa Bungalows

Lala & lili
Penestanan Bungalows
Dewa Bharata

Nandini Bali Resort & Spa Ubud
Pura Dalem Ubud

Campuan Ridge Walk
Pringga

Puri Agung

Penestanan
Penestanan Young Artists
Marajig

Ketut Soki
dOmah
The Sungu
De Munut Balinese Resort
Sri Ratih Cottages

Spies House
Beggar's Bush
Blanco Renaissance Museum
Ubud Kelod

Roof Garden
Miros
Samita DS
Tinnaa

Oka Wati
Pension

Raya Ubud
Ubud Market

Penestanan Kelod
Penestanan Kelod

Anna Sari
Wayan Toni
Whitney
Dirga Rahayu

Uma Sari Cottage

Bucu View Bungalow

Pondok Krishna
Jati
Honeymoon
Cempaka
Dewi Sita

Ubud

Public Market
Nick's Pension
Biah Biah
Wahyu

Pertiwi Bisma

Komaneka at Bisma

Nicks Hidden Cottages

Pondok Pundi Village Inn

Kafe Havana
Adi's Pertiwi Villa
Pondok Pekak
Loka House
Bumbu Bali
Komaneka at Bisma

Komaneka Art Gallery
Lumbungsari
Mandia
The Yulia Village
Warsa's Garden

Cafe Api Api

Nefatari Exclusive Villas

Sinteg Bungalow

Villa Mandi

Sacred Monkey Forest Sanctuary Cottage

Royal Kamuela
Ubud Inn
Fibra Inn
Barong Resort & S
Padangtegal Ke

Seraphim Art
Bali Pesto
Pura Dalem Agung
Lakeleke Hotel & Restaurant

Monkey Forest

Waka Namya
Padi Prada
Suite & Spa
Coffee

Dewi
Puri Jatem
Pondok Bamboo
Camplung Sari
Garden View
Tegal Sari

Dewi Sr
Villa Semana
Padangtegal Kelod

Alam Indah
Saren Indra
Chili Cafe
Swasti

Greenfield Bungalows

Indian Delites
Copper

Gemala Jewelry
Taco Casa & Grill
Putri Dewata

Ratu
Villa
Arma

Alam Shanti
Swasti Homestay
Villa Sonia

Panorama Raka
Pondok Impian
The Sunti
Bali Breeze

Ar

Kertiyasa Bungalow
Swasti Eco Cottages
Pizza Bagus
Bali Breeze

Pengosekan Kaja

Bamboo Foundation
Alam Jiwa

The Ubud Village Resort & Spa
Nyuhkuning
Widya Kusuma Wood Carvings Museum

Casa Ganesha
Bhoja

Michi Retreat
Villa Beji Indah

Hindu Cemetery

Pengosekan Kaja

Bali Spirit Hotel & Spa
Bali Tourist Service

Mumi Art Studio

Nyuhkuning

Batik Workshop

Harmony Villas
Bumi Ubud Resort

Guci GH
Kebun Indah

Pengosekan Kelod

Desa Sanctuary

Abian Semal

Silungan, Singapadu

A   B   C   D   E   F

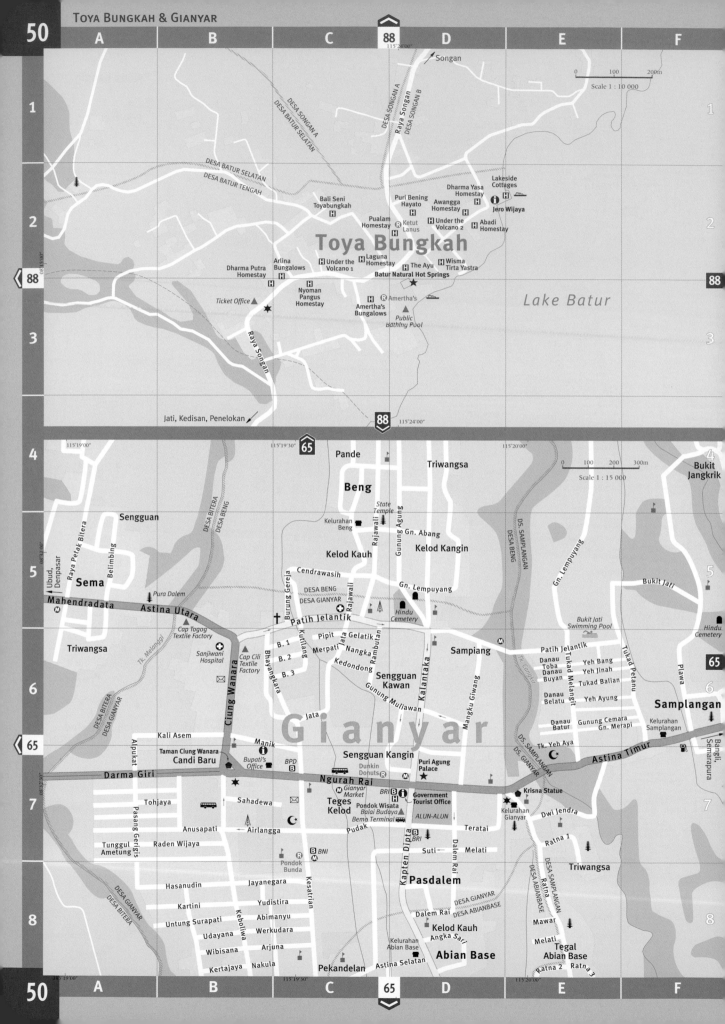

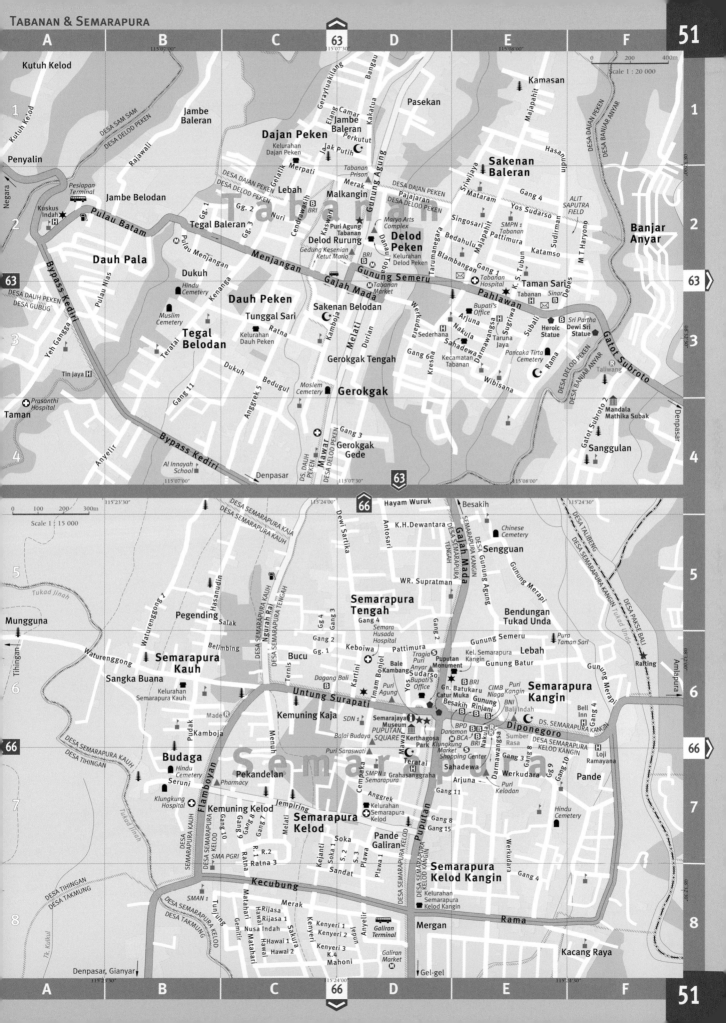

Tabanan & Semarapura Map

Map 1: Tabanan (Scale 1 : 20 000)

Grid columns A–F, rows 1–4. Route marker 63.

Kutuh Kelod, Penyalin, Negara, Desa Sam Sam, Desa Delod Peken, Jambe Baleran, Rajawali, Dajan Peken, Kelurahan Dajan Peken, Gerayutuakilang, Elang, Camar, Jambe Baleran, Perkutut, Kakatua, Bangau, Pasekan, Kamasan, Majapahit, Hasanudin, Desa Dajan Peken, Desa Banjar Anyar

Pesiapan Terminal, Kuskus Indah, Pulau Batam, Dauh Pala, Jambe Belodan, Tegal Baleran, Gg. 1, Gg. 2, Gg. 3, Nuri, Cendrawasih, Merak, Malkangin, Jak Putih, Gunung Agung, Tabanan Prison, Pajajaran, Desa Delod Peken, Sriwijaya, Mataram, Sakenan Baleran, Singosari, Yos Sudarso, SMPN 1 Tabanan, Gang 4, Alit Saputra Field, Banjar Anyar

Bypass Kediri, Desa Dauh Peken, Desa Gubug, Pulau Nias, Pulau Menjangan, Dukuh, Menjangan, Kenanga, Hindu Cemetery, Muslim Cemetery, Dauh Peken, Kelurahan Dauh Peken, Tunggal Sari, Ratna, Sakenan Belodan, Kamboja, Melati, Durian, Gajah Mada, Gunung Semeru, Puri Agung Tabanan, Gedung Kesenian Ketut Mario, Delod Rurung, Danau Tabah, BRI, Tabanan Market, Werkudara, Kelurahan Delod Peken, Delod Peken, Blambangan, Tarumanegara, Bedahulu, Pattimura, Gang 1, Tabanan Hospital, Bupati's Office, Arjuna, Nakula, Sederhana, Sadewa, Darmawangsa, Taruna Jaya, Sugriwa, Subali, Pancaka Tirta Cemetery, Rama, Pahlawan, Tabanan, Sinar, Debes, Heroic Statue, Dewi Sri Statue, Sri Partha, Taman Sari, K. S. Tubun, Sudirman, M T Haryono, Katamso

Yeh Gangsa, Tegal Belodan, Teratai, Muslim Cemetery, Tin jaya, Prasanthi Hospital, Taman, Anyelir, Dukuh, Gang 11, Bedugul, Anggrek 5, Al Innayah School, Bypass Kediri, Moslem Cemetery, Gerokgak, Mawar, Gerokgak Gede, Gang 3, DS. Dauh Peken, DESA Delod Peken, Gerokgak Tengah, Gang 6, Gang 5, Kresna, Wibisana, Kecamatan Tabanan, Gatot Subroto, Gatot Subroto 2, Taliwang, Mandala Mathika Subak, Sanggulan, Denpasar, Desa Banjar Anyar, Desa Delod Peken

Map 2: Semarapura (Scale 1 : 15 000)

Grid columns A–F, rows 5–8. Route marker 66.

Munguna, Tukad Jinah, Tihingan, Waturenggong 1, Waturenggong, Pegending, Salak, Hasanudin, Belimbing, Desa Semarapura Kaja, Desa Semarapura Kauh, Ngurah Rai, Desa Semarapura Tengah, Hayam Wuruk, Besakih, Antosari, Dewi Sartika, K.H.Dewantara, Chinese Cemetery, Gajah Mada, Desa Semarapura Kangin, Semarapura Tengah, Sengguan, WR. Supratman, Gunung Agung, Gunung Merapi, Bendungan Tukad Unda, Desa Talibeng, Desa Semarapura Kangin, Desa Pakse Bali

Semarapura Kauh, Sangka Buana, Kelurahan Semarapura Kauh, Bucu, Gg. 1, Gang 2, Gang 3, Gang 4, Keboiwa, Semara Husada Hospital, Kartini, Gunung Semeru, Kel. Semarapura Kangin, Lebah, Gunung Batur, Pura Taman Sari, Gunung Merapi, Rafting, Amlapura, Ternis, Dagang Bali, Made, Untung Surapati, Imam Bonjol, Puri Agung, Pattimura, Tragia Puri Anyar, Sudarso, Bupati's Office, Puputan Monument, Catur Muka, Gunung Rinjani, Gn. Batukaru, Besakih, BNI, BRI, CIMB Niaga, Puri Kangin, Bali Indah, Semarapura Kangin, DS. Semarapura Kangin

Kamboja, Pudak, Kemuning Kaja, SDN 1, Semarajaya Museum, PUPUTAN SQUARE, Balai Budaya, Puri Saraswati, Kerthagosa Park, BPD, Danamon, BCA, Sumber Rasa, Diponegoro, Loji Ramayana, Bell Inn, Pande, Budaga, Hindu Cemetery, Seruni, Flamboyan, Menuh, Pekandelan, Pharmacy, Klungkung Hospital, Kemuning Kelod, Jempiring, Melati, Gang 10, Gang 9, Gang 8, Gang 7, SMPN 1 Semarapura, Grahasanggraha, Kelurahan Semarapura Kelod, Semarapura Kelod, Anggrek, Cempaka, Mawar, Teratai, Klungkung Market Shopping Center, Sahadewa, Arjuna, Darmawangsa, Gang 3, Gang 9, Gang 10, Werkudara, Puri Kelodan, Hindu Cemetery

Desa Semarapura Kauh, Desa Tihingan, Desa Takmung, SMA PGRI, R.1, R.2, Ratna, Ratna 3, Kecubung, SMAN 1, Tunjung, Genitir, Matahari, Nusa Indah, Hawai 1, Hawai 2, Merak, Rijasa, Rijasa 1, Sakura, Kenyeri 1, Kenyeri 2, Kenyeri 3, K.4, Mahoni, Jepun, Anyelir, Galiran Terminal, Galiran Market, Kejanti, Soka 1, S.2, S.3, Plawa, Sandat, Pande Galiran, Gang 8, Gang 15, Puputan, Semarapura Kelod Kangin, Kelurahan Semarapura Kelod Kangin, Mergan, Rama, Werkudara, Gang 4, Kacang Raya, Gel-gel, Denpasar, Gianyar, Tk. Kulkul

Bali Sea

Buluh Bay

Labuhan Aji Bay

Enjung Sangiang

Dive Centres
1. Spice Dive
2. Malibu Dive Center
3. Sunrise Dive Center
4. Raja Dive Center
5. Permai Dive Center

Restaurants
1. Poco Lounge
2. Akar
3. Zigis Studio One
4. Lumbung Bar
5. Jasmine Kitchen
6. Seyu
7. Bali Apik
8. Bali Bintang
9. Kakatua
10. Warung Kopi Bali
11. Warung Jepun Bali
12. Warung Gula
13. Kenyir Manir

Hotels
1. Zen Resort
2. Nirwana Seaside Cottages
3. Pondok Elsa
4. Angsoka
5. Harris Homestay
6. Padang Lovina
7. Puri Manik Sari
8. Chonos
9. Rattan Resto (Amadeus)

Padmasari
Mega Ayu Homestay
Tanjung Alam
Nugraha Lovina
Samudra Beach Cottages
Villa Elsa
Pantai Mas
Agus Homestay
Mini Holiday
Tekumas Village
Bingin Banjah
Asah

Lesehan Ikan Bakar
Wahyu Dana
Dolphin Beach
Adirama Beach
Billibo
Lilin Lovina Beach
Karina Beach
Clinic. Lovina
Pura Segara Tigawasa
Bali Aga Karaoke
Puri Bunga
Enjung Sangiang
Adjani
Massage
Bali Dewata
Chata Bali
Lian
Warung Betutu
Money Changer
Bike Rental
Spice Dive
Adirama
Singa Pizza
Lovina Pool & Spa
Kelurahan Kali Asem
Penimaan
Bunut Panggang
Kali Asem

Aditya Beach Resort
Made's Warung
Lovina Villa Property
Tropis Living
Spice Beach Water Sport
Puri Tasik Madu
Mutiara
Lovina Cafe
Octopus Garden
Money Changer
Superman
Bali Lovina Beach Cottages
Lovina Beach
Purnama
Kaliwang
Sunrise Dive Ctr
Kantin 21
Lovina Grand Bar
Acyas Cafe
Diving School

Sea Breeze Cabins
Biyu Nasak
Pura Segara
Binaria Bea
Aneka Lovina
Spice Dive
Villa Teman
Pura Dalem
Dolphin Statue
Bayu Kartika
Astina
Tropis Club
Tepe Villa Lux
Taman Lily's
Oyee
Boruna
Dupa
Padi Dive Center
Malibu
Car Rental
Money Chang

Raya Singaraja (Raya Lovina)

LOVINA

98

98

76

Saputra Bungalows
Karang Anyar

Candi

Pura Pusa
Artha
Subagan
Sengkidu
Raya Sengkidu
Bayside Bungalows
Geringsing Homestay
Bayshore Villas
Sedap Malam
Candi Beach
Bali Stingray Dive Center
Dwi Utama
Laris Manis
Pondok Wisata
Candi Beach
Nusa Indah Bungalows
Bintang
Villa Anjani
Mendira
Anom Beach

Taman Semadi Para Atma Temple (Pura Dalem)
Candi Permai
Simpang Pasedahan
Dasawana Villa Resort
Oke
BPD
Kelapa Mas Homestay
Lotus Bungalows
Bali Samudera Arrirang
Suputra Pondok Wisata
Warung Sinartha
Sri Artha Homestay
Ari Homestay
Garden Gardens
The Water
Bambu Gar
Raya Candidasa
Pondok Pisang
Rama Candidasa Resort
Sari Jaya
Bayu Paneeda
Flamboyant
Bali Santi Candidasa
Terrace
Bali Palms Resort
Catra Apartments
Rumah Nancy
Toké Cafe
Lotus Seaview
Nirwana Cottages
Mendira Beach

Amuk Bay

Bali Sea

Agung Bay

Banyualit Beach

Enjung Buntekan

Kalibukbuk

Frangipani Beach
Lovina Beach Resort
Taman Bali
Juni Artha

Villa Taman Ganesha
Bali Paradise
Puri Bali
Lovina Beach Houses V
Aquatropic Dive
Starlight
Gino Feruci Villa
Sartya
Ray

Banyualit

Warung Dolphin
Bias
Banyualit
Suma
Perama
Melamun
Saraswati
Yoga Homestay

Lilacita
Celuk Agung Beach

Celuk Agung

Bali Grand
Sunsets Resort
Gede Homestay
Bungalows
Warung Rasta
Warung Putu
Mandara Chico Bungalows
Bayu Mantra
Puspa Rama
Puri Mandhara

Sri Homestay
Villa Agung Beach Inn
Bamboo
Permai Dive Resort
Bali Taman Beach Resort

Xhotel Trade
Warung Bintang Karaoke
RM Sitha

Anturan

Mandiri Homestay
Munduk
Mumbul GH

Volcano Discotheque
Suci Homestay
Satya

Bali Vanila

Bali Vanilla Factory
Lovina Health Center

Dharma Jadra

Anita
Telkom
Villa Kelapa
Ayodya
RRI Singaraja
Sunset Ayu
Sunset Ayu Bungalow
Marina
Gossip
Indra Pura
Maydinie

Raya Singaraja (Raya Lovina)

Pura Dalem
Anturan

Khi Khi
Angsoka
Wr. Anda
Wr. Kae
Puri Ayodya Museum
Oasis
Aramirth Spa
Lovina Spa
Ga Madre
Kraton
Nusbog
Pasar Ratu
Cempaka
Pasar Kalisari
Sakuntala Massage
Malibu Dive Center
Lotus House of Art
Adi
Wisnu Dive Center
Prima Tours

Kelurahan Anturan
Anyar

Lebak

Kiki Watersport
Wr. Watersport
Pulestis Beach
Raya Kalibukbuk
Lupa Lupa Cottages
Kalibukbuk 4
Pura Wengi
Cendrawasih

Celuk Buluh

Celuk buluh

Pasar

Beach

Scale 1 : 17 500
0   200   400m

115°01'30"
115°02'00"
08°08'30"
115°02'30"
115°03'00"
08°30'00"
08°30'30"

Candidasa

Samuh

Hindu Cemetery

Samuh Kelod

Puri Bagus

Gloria
Bicycle Rental

dasa

ngan Hill 226m

Tukad Samuh

Pandan Harum Stage
Candidasa
Dewa Bharata
Sasrabahu
Agung Homestay
Baruna Water Sport
Rama Ocean View
Cantiloka
Toko Family
Toko Gemino
Pura Candidasa
Bali Ceramics

Villa Sasoon
Villarossa
Puri Tina
Pantai Indah

Sekar Orchid
Puri Pudak
Asoka Beach
Ida Beach Village
Puri Bagus

The Rishi Resort
Pondok Bambu Seaside
D'Tunjung Resort
Candidasa Lagoon
Le 48 Zen & Happy Rezort
Pandawa
Rama Shinta

Tirafella Beach
Resort Prima
Arco Iris Resort
B House
Mutiara Bali
Gengsong
Bali Shangrila Beach Club

Segara Wangi Homestay
Geringsing
Ashyana Candidasa
Villa Pantai Bali
Candidasa Sunrise
side Cottages
Wiratha's Bungalows
Puri Bali Homestay
Homestay Ayodya
Fajar Candidasa
Ary Home Stay
Puri Pandan
Homestay Lilaberata
The Natia
Villa Rama
The Rama
Beachfront Villa Jukung
Niwana Resort
Gedong Gandhi Ashram
Kelapa Mas
Ida's Homestay
Sindhu Brata Inn
Aquaria
Alam Asmara Dive Resort
Discovery Candidasa
Puri Oka Beach
Pantai Indah

Marine Reserve

Candidasa Beach

Amuk Bay

Scale 1 : 10 000
0   100   200m

115°34'30"
08°09'30"
115°34'00"
08°31'00"
115°34'30"

Scale 1 : 15 000

0 100 200 300m

A B C 74 D E F

1

Sulahan

Dukuh

Dukuh

Penelokan

Brahmana Bukit

Kelurahan Cempaga

Puri Bukit

Sriwijaya

Pura Kehen

Dewi Sri Cafe

balinese temple

Sidem Bunut

Kediri

Mataram

Blam

bangan

Pekuwon

Sasana Budaya Art Center

Sriwijaya

2

Penglumbaran

Raya Susut

Lebah

Pura Manik Tirtha

Airlangga

Cempaga

Pura Dalem Slaungan

Gunaksa

Tembuku, Bangbang

Pande

Bisma

Salya

Baladewa

Kresna

Kap. Anom Mudeta

Rama

Dastarata

Laksmana

Sugriwa

DESA SUSUT

DESA CEMPAGA

3

DESA SUSUT
DESA DEMULIH

Demulih

Pura Dalem Purwa

Demulih

Tirta Buana Swimming Pool

Gang 10

Pura Kanginan

Gang 7

Cendrawasih

Wibisana

Pura Panataran Cempagno

Sadewa

Arjuna

Brahmana Pande

Bima

Pura Puseh

Yudistira

DESA CEMPAGA
DESA KAWAN

Bangli

Nuri

Pura Nataran Agung

Losmen Dharmaputra

Waturenggong

Pura Rajan

Waturenggong

4

73

Asylum Hospital

Kusuma Yudha

Lettu Anom

Harmoni Cafe

Artha Sastra Inn

BPD

Kutai

BangIi Inn

Majapahit

Nyalian

74

RSUD

Kawan

Pura Agung

Kelurahan Kawan

Satria Mahottama Statue

Bemo Terminal

Nangka

Blimbing

butan

Ram

Geria

Hindu Cemetery

Pura Dalem Cungkub

5

Puri Dencarik

Tegal Lalang

6

Brigjen Ngurah Rai

Merdeka

Pule

Lettu Konten

Lettu Sobat

Bupati's Office

Lettu Lila

Catur Adnyana

Bebalang

Putra Bali

Hindu Cemetery

Tk. Melangit

7

DESA KAWAN
DESA BEBALANG

Kecamatan Bangli

Sri Partha

Honda

RTN

Hindu Cemetery

Suzuki

Pura Dalem Penunggekan

Lagaan

Tegal

DESA IEHEM

DESA KAWAN

Taman Kelod

Pura Dalem

8

Pulung

Sedit

Sudamala

Sdm 2

Sdm 1

Raya Bangli

Kelurahan Bebalang

Bebalang

Sidan, Gianyar

A B C 74 D E F

Scale 1 : 15 000

0 100 200 300m

A **B** **76** **C** **D** **E** **F**

115°36'00" 115°36'30" 115°37'00"

Gelumpang

Hindu Cemetery

Batan Nyuh Kelod

Bale Punduk Kelod

1

Raya Gelumpang

Tukad Jonga

Juwuk Manis

Susuau

Gelumpang

Serma Natih

R.A. Kartini

Belong

Serma Gejer

Tegal Linggah

2

Tukad Peladung

DESA KARANG ASEM

DESA PADANG KERTA

Tukad Mahapi

Taman

RSUD (Amlapura Hospital)

Ngurah Rai

Sultan Agung

Pendem

DESA KARANG ASEM

DESA TEGAL LINGGAH

Raya Tegal Linggah

Tk. Nyuling

3

Moslem Cemetery

Hindu Cemetery

Jaya Tirtha

Bupati's Office

Ngurah Rai

Lettu Arti

Karang Cermen

Tulamben, Amed, Singaraja

Dukuh

Sedap Malam

Pekundelan

Lettu Bajra

Puri Agung Palace

Teuku Umar

4

Untung Surapati

DESA PADANG KERTA

DESA SUBAGAN

Bintang Kejora Pastoran Katolik

Yamaha

Ampel

Puri Gede & Puri Kertasura Palaces

Sport Center

Lettu Sintha

Villa Amlapura

H

Sumbar Rasa

76

76

Serma Anom

Jelantik

Tampuagan

Celuk Negara

Betanha

Rumah Makan Segar

DESA TEGAL LINGGAH

5

Tk. Sampe

Galiran Kaler

Hasa Pudin

Lumayan

Jend. Gatot Subroto

Lahar Mas Homestay

Clock Tower

Teuku Umar

Nazamudin

Tohpati

Lettu Alit

Pasar Hewan

Kap. Gebun

BPD B

Gajah Mada

Kedok Darsana

BRI

DESA TUMBU

A m l a p u r a

Tk. Pati

Bemo Stop for Tirta Gangga/ East Coast

Honda

Pondok Rasa

Diponegoro

Banggras

Karang Langko

Permata B

Bemo & Bus Terminal

Kesatria

BRI

Karang Asem

Ujung Water Palace, Amed

6

Sri Partha

Jend. Sudirman

Honda Kecamatan Karang Asem

Subagan

Pesagi

Dangin Sema

Bhayangkara

Kelurahan Karang Asem

DESA KARANG ASEM

Bhayangkara

DESA TUMBU

DESA KARANG ASEM

Karang Sekong

Gunung Agung

GKPB

DESA KARANG ASEM

DESA SUBAGAN

7

Clock Tower

K.H. Saman Hudi

Genteng

Kelurahan Subagan

Segara Katon

SDN 10 Karang Asem

Ujung Beach

Tukad Jonga

Pesagi

Bangli, Kintamani, Klungkung

Gede

Jeruk

Salak

Ahmad Yani

Tukad Krukuk

Tukad Bangka

8

Tengah

Galiran Kelod

Candidasa, Manggis, Klungkung

115°36'00" 115°36'30" 115°37'00"

A **B** **76** **C** **D** **E** **F**

Scale 1 : 15 000

A map of Negara showing streets and place names including: Kali Akah, Desa Kalikakh, Desa Baler Bale Agung, Kelurahan Baler Bale Agung, Nusa Indah Raya, Tanjung, Blok C, Kebon, Bougenville, Melati, Anggrek, Kerta Sari, Kerta Sari 2, Nangka, Kerta Sari 1, Plawa, Plawa 6, Plawa 4, Plawa 1, Plawa 5, Jempiring, Banjar Pendem, Rajawali, Cendrawasih, Pendem, Gang 5, Komplek TNI, Gelatik, Gelatik 2, Gelatik 1, Gang 1, Merak, Desa Pendem, Desa Dauh Waru, Baler Bale Agung, Soka, Satria, Kutilang, Gang 4, Rajawali, Gang 2, Hindu Cemetery, Udayana, Desa Baler Bale Agung, Tinyeb, Bimasena, Buana Karya, Desa Banjar Tengah, RSU Negara, Wijaya Kusuma, Ratna, Gang 2, Gang 1, Gang 2, Gang 2, Cendrawasih, Kelurahan Pendem, Sri Hamerta Boga, Mendaya Rambut Siwi, Gilimanuk, Nakula, Mahadewa, Yudistira, Arjuna Gang 2, Arjuna Gang 3, BRI, A. G. 1, Clinic Darmausada, Ahmad Yani, Taman Sari, Taman Sari, Minang, Sudirman, Segara Mandala, Madri, Kap. Saestu Hadi, Kelurahan Banjar Tengah, Banjar Tengah, Dr. Sutomo, Yos Sudarso, Ijo Gading, Tour & Travel, Sri Partha, Honda, Nugraha Utara, Supratman, Gang Aliyah, Gang 2, Wibisana, Negara, Pahlawan, Supratman 2, Prima Agung, Prima Agung, SMAN 1, Salya, Surya Asri, Gang 1, Gatot Subroto, Tis, Ana, Wira Pada, Wira Pada, Banamon, Ngurah Rai, Surya, Honda, Kecamatan Negara, Pulau Nias, Gang 5, Gang 6, Gang 7, Arjuna, Gang 1, Pertukangan, Gang 1, Gunung Rinjani 1, Gunung Semeru 2, Gunung Semeru 3, Gunung Semeru 4, Gn. Semeru, Ketutug, Pulau Buton, Pulau Lembongan, Pulau Singkep, Danau Beratan, Ketapang, Traditional Market, Danau Tondano, Gang 2, Danau Buyan, Gang 2, Danau Kelimutu, Gn. Batukaru, Gunung Semeru, Gang 6, Gunung Agung, Danau Beratan, Buffalo Races, Kelurahan Lelateng, Kepundung, Gunung Batur, Lelateng, Danau Mindanau, Desa Lelateng, Desa Loloan Barat, Durian, Kerobokan, Desa Loloan Timur, Kelurahan Loloan Timur, Desa Batu Agung, Danau Tamblingan, Lateng Terusan, Danau Poso, Nangka, Durian, Kedondong, Loloan Timur, Gunung Merapi, Desa Loloan Timur, Danau Segara, Kenari, Kelurahan Loloan Barat, Gn. Tangkuban Perahu, Pulau Jawa, Terusan, Raya Tegal Bandeng, Loloan Barat, Muslim Cemetery, Merta sari, Gunung Raung, Muslim Cemetery, Gunung Krakatau, Awen Merta Sari, Kenari, Muslim Cemetery, Desa Loloan Timur, Desa Tegal Badeng Timur, Desa Lelateng, Desa Batu Agung, Desa Budeng

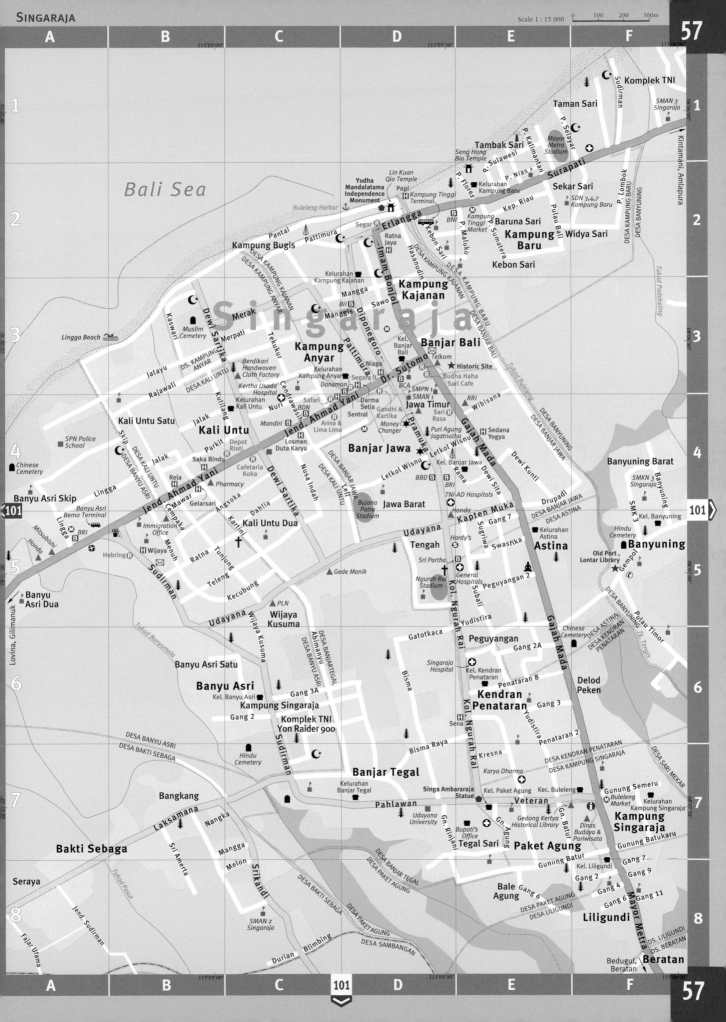

Bali Sea

Komplek TNI

Taman Sari

SMAN 3 Singaraja

Tambak Sari

Seng Hong Bio Temple

Mayor Metra Stadium

Surapati

Sekar Sari

Kelurahan Kampung Baru

SDN 3,4,7 Kampung Baru

Kampung Baru

Baruna Sari

Widya Sari

Kebon Sari

DESA BANYUNING

Yudha Mandalatama Independence Monument

Lin Kuan Qio Temple

Kampung Tinggi Terminal

Pop!

Kampung Tinggi Market

Buleleng Harbor

Erlangga

BNI

Segar

Ratna Jaya

Kampung Bugis

Pantai

Pattimura

Kampung Kajanan

Kelurahan Kampung Kajanan

Mangga

Merak

Manggis

Sawo

Banjar Bali

Kel. Banjar Bali

Telkom

Historic Site

Muslim Cemetery

Lingga Beach

Kampung Anyar

Kelurahan Kampung Anyar

Niaga

Segara II

Dr. Sutomo

BCA

Budha Haha Sari Cafe

Berdikari Handwoven Cloth Factory

Kertha Usada Hospital

Kelurahan Kali Untu

Safari

Danamon

Darma Setia

SMPN 1

SMAN 1

RRI

Wibisana

Kali Untu

Mandiri

Nuri

Gandhi & Kartika

Jawa Timur

Sari Rasa

Sedana Yogya

SPN Police School

Arina & Lima Lima

Money Changer

Puri Agung Jagatnatha

Banjar Jawa

Chinese Cemetery

Banyu Asri Skip

Losmen Duta Karya

Saka Bindu

Letkol Wisnu

Kel. Banjar Jawa

Rama

Dewi Sita

Dewi Kunti

Banyuning Barat

SMKN 3 Singaraja

Banyuning

SMK 3

Kel. Banyuning

Rela

Cafetaria Koka

BBD

BRI

Jawa Barat

TNI-AD Hospitals

Honda

Kapten Muka

Drupadi

Kelurahan Astina

Hindu Cemetery

Old Port Lontar Library

Banyuning

Gempol

Banyu Asri Bemo Terminal

Immigration Office

Wijaya

Kali Untu Dua

Bujana Patra Stadium

Hardy's

Tengah

Udayana

Sugriwa

Swastika

Astina

Banyu Asri Dua

Hebring

Sri Partha

General Hospitals

Ngurah Rai Stadium

Peguyangan 2

Subali

Peguyangan

Yudistira

Pulau Timor

Wijaya Kusuma

Gede Manik

Gatotkaca

Peguyangan

Chinese Cemetery

PLN

Bisma

Singaraja Hospital

Kel. Kendran Penataran

Penataran 8

Kendran Penataran

Delod Peken

Banyu Asri Satu

Banyu Asri

Kel. Banyu Asri

Kampung Singaraja

Gang 3A

Gang 2

Komplek TNI Yon Raider 900

Sena

Bisma Raya

Kresna

Karya Dharma

Kec. Buleleng

Gunung Semeru

Buleleng Market

Kelurahan Kampung Singaraja

Bangkang

Laksamana

Nangka

Mangga

Melon

Srikandi

Hindu Cemetery

Banjar Tegal

Kelurahan Banjar Tegal

Pahlawan

Udayana University

Singa Ambararaja Statue

Kel. Paket Agung

Bupati's Office

Gedong Kertya Historical Library

Dinas Budaya & Pariwisata

Veteran

Kampung Singaraja

Bakti Sebaga

Seraya

Tegal Sari

Paket Agung

Bale Agung

Kel. Liligundi

Liligundi

Beratan

Bedugul, Beratan

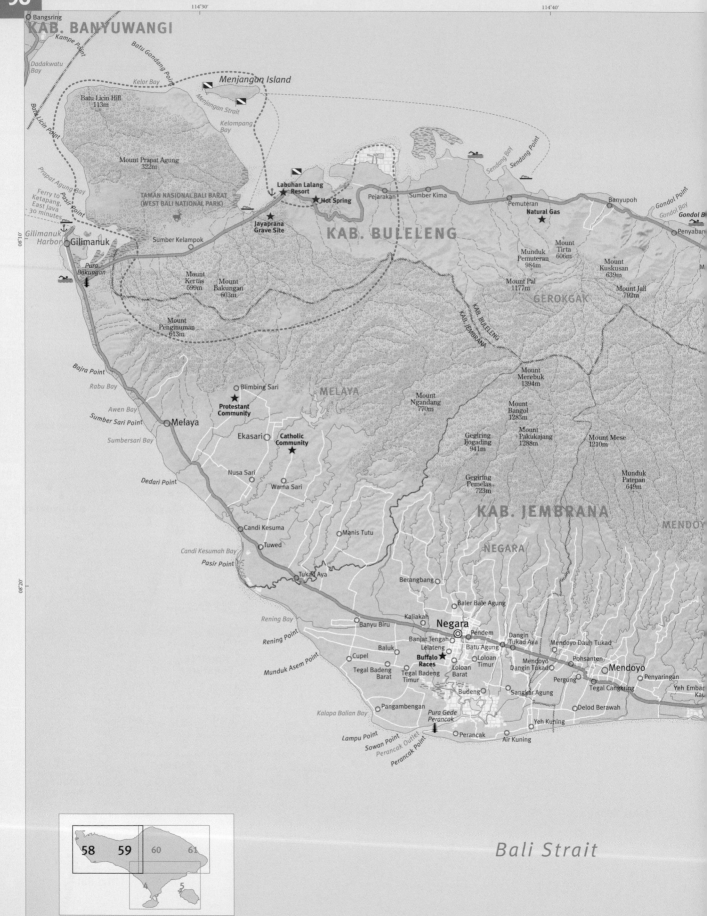

KAB. BANYUWANGI

Bangsring
Kampe Point
Dadakwatu Bay
Batu Gondang Point
Kelor Bay
Menjangan Island
Menjangan Strait
Batu Licin Hill 113m
Batu Licin Point
Kelompang Bay
Mount Prapat Agung 322m
Prapat Agung Bay
Labuhan Lalang Resort
Hot Spring
TAMAN NASIONAL BALI BARAT (WEST BALI NATIONAL PARK)
Pejarakan
Sumber Kima
Sendang Bay
Sendang Point
Pemuteran
Natural Gas
Banyupoh
Gondol Point
Gondol Bay
Gondol Bay
Penyaban

KAB. BULELENG

Ferry to Ketapang, East Java 30 minutes
Pasir Point
Gilimanuk Harbor
Gilimanuk
Jayaprana Grave Site
Sumber Kelampok
Munduk Pemuteran 984m
Mount Tirta 606m
Mount Kuskusan 639m
Mount Jah 792m

Pura Bakungan
Mount Kertas 599m
Mount Bakungan 603m
Mount Pal 1177m
GEROKGAK

Mount Penginuman 613m

Bajra Point
Rabu Bay
Awen Bay
Sumber Sari Point
Sumbersari Bay
Dedari Point

Blimbing Sari
Protestant Community
MELAYA
Mount Ngandang 770m
Mount Merebuk 1394m
Mount Bangol 1283m
Mount Pakukajang 1288m
Mount Mese 1210m

Ekasari
Catholic Community
Gegiring Ijogading 941m

Nusa Sari
Warna Sari
Munduk Patepan 649m

Melaya
Gegiring Pemelas 723m
KAB. JEMBRANA

Candi Kesuma
Manis Tutu
MENDOYO

Candi Kesumah Bay
Tuwed
NEGARA

Pasir Point
Tukad Aya
Berangbang

Rening Bay
Baler Bale Agung
Rening Point
Banyu Biru
Kaliakah
Negara
Pendem

Munduk Asem Point
Cupel
Baluk
Banjar Tengah
Lelateng
Batu Agung
Dangin Tukad Aya
Mendoyo Dauh Tukad

Tegal Badeng Barat
Buffalo Races
Tegal Badeng Timur
Loloan Timur
Loloan Barat
Mendoyo
Dangin Tukad
Pohsanten
Mendoyo

Pangambengan
Budeng
Sangkar Agung
Perung
Tegal Cangkring
Penyaringan

Kalapa Balian Bay
Pura Gede Perancak
Yeh Kuning
Delod Berawah
Yeh Embar Kau

Lampu Point
Sowan Point
Perancak Outlet
Perancak Point
Perancak
Air Kuning

Bali Strait

| 58 | 59 | 60 | 61 |
| 4 | 5 |

NORTHWESTERN BALI

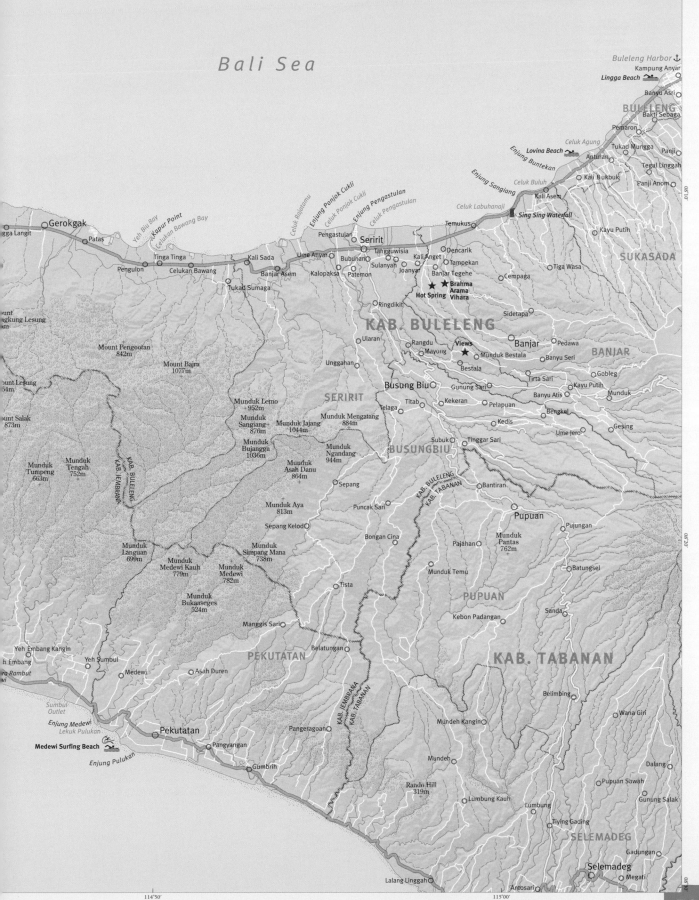

Scale 1 : 200 000

0   2   4   6km

Bali Sea

Buleleng Harbor ⚓
Kampung Anyar
Lingga Beach ∿
Banyu Asri
BULELENG
Bakti Sebaga
Pemaron
Celuk Agung
Tukad Mungga
Panji
Lovina Beach ∿
Anturan
Enjung Buntekan
Tegal Linggah
Kali Bukbuk
Panji Anom
Celuk Buluh
Enjung Sangiang
Kali Asem
Celuk Labuhanaji
Sing Sing Waterfall ⚑
Temukus
Kayu Putih
SUKASADA

Gerokgak
ga Langit
Patas
Pengulon
Tinga Tinga
Kali Sada
Celukan Bawang
Banjar Asem
Kalopaksa
Patemon
Tukad Sumaga
Celuk Rojagomu
Enjung Ponjok Cukli
Celuk Ponjok Cukli
Enjung Pengastulan
Celuk Pengastulan
Pengastulan
Ume Anyar
Bubunan
Seririt
Tangguwisia
Sulanyah
Joanyar
Kali Anget
Dencarik
Tampekan
Banjar Tegehe
Tiga Wasa
Cempaga
Ringdikit
★ **Hot Spring** ★ **Brahma Arama Vihara**
Sidetapa

Yeh Biu Bay
Kapur Point
Celukan Bawang Bay

KAB. BULELENG

Mount Pengootan 842m
Mount Bajra 1077m
Ularan
Rangdu
Mayong
Views ★
Munduk Bestala
Bestala
Banjar
Pedawa
Banyu Seri
BANJAR
Goblek
Kayu Putih
Munduk
Unggahan
Tirta Sari
Banyu Atis

ount Lesung
54m
ount Salak
873m
Munduk Lemo +952m
Munduk Sangiang+ 876m
Munduk Jajang 1044m
Munduk Mengatang 884m
SERIRIT
Busung Biu
Telaga
Titab
Kekeran
Gunung Sari
Pelapuan
Kedis
Bengkel
Ume Jero
Gesing

Munduk Bujangga 1036m
Munduk Asah Danu 864m +
Munduk Ngandang 944m
BUSUNGBIU
Subuk
Tinggar Sari

Munduk Tumpeng 663m
Munduk Tengah 752m
KAB. IEMBRANA / KAB. BULELENG
Sepang
Munduk Aya 813m
Puncak Sari
KAB. BULELENG / KAB. TABANAN
Bantiran
Pupuan
Pujungan

Munduk Languan 699m
Sepang Kelod
Munduk Medewi Kauh 779m
Munduk Medewi 782m
Munduk Simpang Mana 738m
Bongan Cina
Pajahan
Munduk Pantas 762m
Batungsel

Munduk Bukaaseges 524m
Tista
Munduk Temu
PUPUAN
Kebon Padangan
Sanda

Manggis Sari
Yeh Embang Kangin
h Embang
ra Rambut
vi
Yeh Sumbul
Medewi
Asah Duren
Belatungan
PEKUTATAN
KAB. TABANAN

Sumbul Outlet
Enjung Medewi
Lekuk Pulukan
Medewi Surfing Beach 🏄
Enjung Pulukan
Pekutatan
Pangyangan
Gumbrih
Pangeragoan
KAB. IEMBRANA / KAB. TABANAN
Mundeh Kangin
Mundeh
Belimbing
Wana Giri

Rando Hill 319m
Lumbung Kauh
Lumbung
Tiyling Gading
Dalang
Pupuan Sawah
Gunung Salak

Lalang Linggah
Antosari
SELEMADEG
Selemadeg
Megati
Gadungan

Bungkulan Point

Penarukan Point

Pura Beji
Sangsit
Yudha Mandalatama Independence Monument
Buleleng Harbor
Kampung Baru
Kampung Anyar
Lingga Beach
Banyu Asri
Banjar Jawa
Astina
Banyuning
SINGARAJA
Bakti Sebaga
Lili Gundi
Beratan
Pemaron
Sari Mekar
Kampung Singaraja
Penglatan
Pohbergong
Petandakan
Tukad Mungga
Sukasada
Nagasepaha
Alas Angker
Panji
Sambangan
Pegadungan
Panji Anom
Padang Bulia
Tegal Linggah
Ambengan
Silang Jana
Pegayaman
Gitgit Waterfall
Gitgit

Kubu Tambahan
Bungkulan
Kerobokan
Penarukan
Jineng Dalem
Jaga Raga
Pura Dalem
Bengkala
Menyali
Sinabun
Suwug
Sudaji
Sawan
Bila
Tamblang
Bebetin
Bukit Bebetin 443m
Sekumpul
Bontihing
Pakisan
Galungan
Lemukih

Bukti
Pura Pojok Batu
Pacung
Julah
Bondalem
Les
Penuktuk
Depeha
Tunjung
Sembiran
Tejakula
Satra
Madenan
Tajun
Dausa
KAB. BULELENG
KAB. BANGLI
Kutuh
Subaya
Mendah Hill 688m
Yeh Mempeh Waterfall
Siakin

Mount Tengayang 1117m
Mount Mengandang 1363m
Mount Langlang 1501m
Tambakan
Pura Tegeh Kuripan
Bantang
Suka Wana
Pangejaran
Selulung
Mt. Penulisan 1746m
Pingga
Catur
Belantih
Daup
Serahi
Mount Ba 1412m

Wana Giri
Lake Buyan
Panca Sari
Mount Penggilingan 2153m
Mount Catu 1865m
KAB. BULELENG
KAB. BADUNG
Bali Handara Kosaido Country Club
Candi Kuning
Lake Beraton
Mount Mangu 2020m
Kintamani
Batur Selatan
Pura Batur
Batur Utara
Lake Tamblingan
Mount Tapak 1909m
Botanical Garden (Kebun Raya)
Pura Luhur Beratan
Bukit Mungsu Indah
Pura Gubug Tamblingan
Mount Lesung 1865m
Lubang Nagaloka
Mount Pucuk 1629m
KAB. BULELENG
KAB. TABANAN
Pura Ulun Danu Bratan
Mount Pohen 2063m
Mountain View
Kedisa
Buah
Batur Tengah
Belok Sidan
Batu Kaang
Gunung Bau
Binyan
Uliah
Manik Liyu
Belancan
Mengani
Pelaga
Lembean
Bayung Cerik
Banyung Gede
Bunutin
Mangguh
Katung
Bonyoh
Sekar Dadi
Mount Sengayang 2087m
Mount Adeng 1826m
Mount Batukaru 2271m
Batunya
Antapan
Langgahan
Sekaan
Abuan
Pengotan
Batu Riti
Bangli
Kerta

Persiapan Sulangai
Pupuan
Penglumbaran
Tiga
Pura Luhur Batu Karu
Jati Luwih
Senganan
Angseri
Apuan
Mekar Sari
Taro
Kayu Bihi
Wongaya Gede
Babahan
Buahan
Puhu
Holy Spring
KAB. GIANYAR
KAB. BANGLI
Traditional Village
Yang
Candi Kuning
Luwus
Bukian
Sebatu
Pura Sakenan
Wana Giri
Tengkudak
Tua
Petang
Persiapan Pangsan
Manukaya
Tirta Empul
Sulahan
Kubu
Penebel
Mengesta
Biaung
Perean
KAB. TABANAN
KAB. BADUNG
KAB. GIANYAR
KAB. BADUNG
Kedisah
Gunung Kawi
Pitra
Payangan
Pura Yeh Gangga
Petiga
Perean Tengah
Payangan (Melinggih)
Kelusa
Tampak Siring
Susut
Tembu
Penatahan
Melinggih Kelod
Rice Terraces
Cempaga
Pura Kehen
Dalang
Jegu
Hot Spring
Kenderan
Petak Kaja
Carang Sari
Tegal Lalang
Keliki
Topeng Dance
Demulih
Bangli
Gunung Salak
Rejasa
Buruan
I Gusti Ngurah Rai Memorial
Kedewatan
Sanding
Abuan
Kawan
Pejeng Kaja
Petak
Apuan
Bebalang
Tohpati
Kesiut
Tunjuk
Marga
Sembung
Caubelayu
Pura Telaga Waja
Petulu
Pejeng Kangin
Suwat
Pura Krobokan
Bungbun
Timpag
Butterfly Park
Wana Sari
Selan Bawak
Reptile Park
Monkey Forest & Pura Bukit Sari
Sangeh
Taman
White Water Rafting
Sayan Ridge
Ubud Village
KAB. BANGLI
KAB. KLUNGKUNG
Gadungan
Megati
Riang Gede
Buahan
Tegal Jadi
Kuwum
Sobangan
Werdi Bhuana
Punggul
Selisih
Nyalian

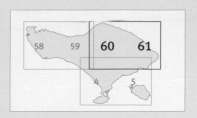

Bali Sea

mbi Renteng

Tembok

Ngis Point

KAB. BULELENG
KAB. KARANGASEM

Tianyar Barat

Tianyar Tengah

Tianyar   ★ **Salt Panning**

Belandingan

induk
andang
397m

Songan A

an B

Sukadana

Sukadana Point

Ban

Batu Ringgit

Lake Batur

Trunyan
★ **Bali Aga Village,
Gede Pancering,
Jagat Temple**

spring, Volcanic

Kubu   ★ **Salt Panning**

Diving-WW II "The Liberty" Wreck

Mount Abang
2151m

Dukuh

Tulamben   ★ **Tulamben Marine Reserve**

ter

g Tudinding
ang Songan

Batu Niti Point

Tapis Hill
1608m

Laba Sari

Amed   ★ **Salt Panning**

Mount Agung
2567m

Datah

Purwa Kerthi

Bunutan

Culik

Keresek Hill
238m

Kerta Mandala

Pura Besakih
★
Besakih

★ *Pura Pasaran
Agung*

Tista

Pidpid

*Pura
Lempuyang*

Mount Bisbis
1065m

Mount Nampu
729m

Abang   ★ **Rice
Terraces**

*Gili
Selang*

Mount Seraya
1238m

Pempatan

Ababi

Tiying Tali

Seraya Timur

Menanga

Sebudi

Tirtha Gangga ★

injoan

Rendang

Bukit

Budakeling

Padang Kerta

Tegal Linggah

Seraya

Muncan

Duda Utara

Jungutan

Bebandem

Selat

Duda

Bungaya
Kangin

Amlapura
◎

Seraya
Barat

Ngoek Hill
512m

Sibetan

Tumbu

san

Nongan

Duda Timur

Karang Asem

Bungaya

Subagan

Sidemen

Ngis

Selumbung

Tenganan

Pertima

★ **Puri Taman Ujung
(Floating Palace)**

★ **Salt Panning**

Pesaban

nglan

Bugbug

≋ *Ujung Beach*

egak

Tangkup

Manggis

Lombok Strait

Gegelang

Ulakan

Nyuh Tebel

★ **Marine
Reserve**

Candidasa

★ **Marine
Reserve**

Mulu Point

Kuan Island

**Marine
Reserve** ★

Iti Point

115°30'   115°40'

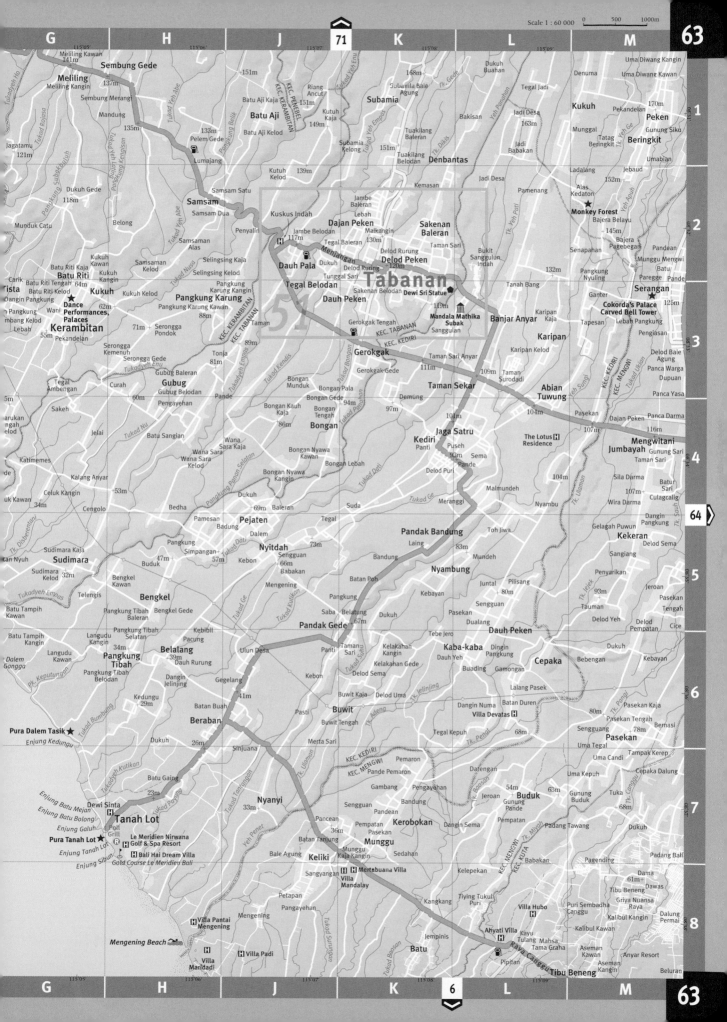

A · B · C · D · E · F

63

A B C D E F

Pangkung Languan
51m
Yeh Satang
Pangkung Selepa
Medewi
Pulukan
+137m
169m
245m
316m
322m
Pangkung Pangi

Sablong
51m
Delod Setra
Temukus
Asah Duren
+274m
272m
258m

Yeh Sumbul
Salepa
41m
Ledok
101m
Arca
83m
Pangkung Sepit
Pangkung Plah
Pangkung Pusuh
Pangkung Kenang
181m
162m

Resinggahan
Loloan
+40m
Pulukan
57m
Sagah
276m

KEC. MENDOYO
KEC. PEKUTATAN
Krisnarendra Baru [H]
Ledok
34m
71m
Yeh Lebah Pangyangan Kauh
Tukad Kuteh

Tinjaya [H]
16m
Pulukan [R]
26m
Pekutatan
37m
55m
Rukun

Medewi Bay Resort [H]
Tinggi
Loji
Pasar
Dangin Pangkung
+24m
Swastika
31m
Tukad Pangyangan

Enjung Medewi
West Bali Coast
Medewi Estuary
Pulukan Estuary
Lekuk Pulukan
Puri Dajuma Beach Resort
Dauh Pangkung
Yeh Kuning
Medewi Bay Resort [H]
Pangyangan
Tengah
Rukun

Medewi Surfing Beach
[H][R]
Enjung Pulukan
[H] Villa Galuh
Cepaka
Sengguan
Pasar
Gumbrih

Yeh Lebah Estuary
4m
7m
7m
26m

Bali Strait

114°54'   114°55'   114°56'   114°57'   114°58'   114°59'

Yuwuk Manis Kelod

537m

Mangenu Anyar

Munduk Gawang

Yeh Aya

Tk. Bongsah

626m   Sandingan

Panjahan
+539m   645m

1

Pengyyangan

389m

433m

527m

Antap Gawang

568m   +540m

Yeh Sibuh

351m

Bangal

592m

Yeh Lebah

417m

311m

291m   Bading Kayu

KEC. PEKUTATAN
KEC. PUPUAN

476m

426m

KEC. PUPUAN
KEC. SELEMADEG

+561m
Auman
Dajan Semu

+544m

Pangedan Kaja

429m   455m

489m

2

Tukad Serangsong

183m

433m   Kadewatan

432m
449m+

408m
402m

Penataran

Auman
Delod Semu

507m   Pangedan Kelod

Tukad Bengkala

+467m
Nyuh Gading

3

jung   Sari

Tukad Gumbrih

376m

313m

344m

328m

Padewatan Hill
398 m

481m

Puncak Sari   Dukuh

+505m

Tukad Balang

407m

432m

Pura Dalem
Nyuhgading

Mundeh
+407m

Beji

Pangeragoan
Dauh Tukad

Pangkung Balu   Tukad Cengkelung   Yeh Leh

Yeh Leh

554m+

+571m

Bangkiang
Jaran

Rando Hill
319m

438m

418m+

424m   Pura Dayang Sari

Pancoran

Pura Puseh
418m +

Dauh Siong

4

Batu Bara

KEC. PEKUTATAN
KEC. SELEMADEG

165m   358m

Tukad Pesuangan

Tukad Bakung

Yeh Kayu

Tegal Kontang
Lumbung Kauh
407m

70

Pangeragoan
Dangin Tukad

Pengeragoan

Selabih Pangkong
Kuning

Pk. Sinongkau

Pangkung Jembul

Pendaan Hill
433m

389m +   349m+

5

Santai
Segar

Selabih
Tengah

Selabih Wana
Sari

+41m

Pangkung Kuning

Tukad Selabih

Bukit Tumpeng

Tukad Meceh

302m

Yeh Silah

Delod
Ceking

363m

Yeh Bakung

Bagelen Yogya

Mekayu

Tk. Mekayu

120m

74m
76m
64m

Beja

123m

179m

Tukad Silah

236m

Pajeng Hill
310m

152m

6

Desa Anyar

Daren   165m

Kukuh

Tk. Petengahan

Suraberata

Tukad Balian

Villa Zolima [H]

Lalang Linggah
Kangin

7

Gajah Mina Beach Resort [H]

Enjung Ngejer

Balian Beach

Balian Estuary

**Lalang
Linggah**

Villa Belanda [H]

Tukad Pedungan

Tk. Tireman

Pengererengan
Kelod
52m

39m
Bunian

Tukad Klecung

Bali Strait

Pedungan Estuary

Suwan Galuh Beach

Enjung Borosan

Tireman Estuary

8

Ibus Estuary

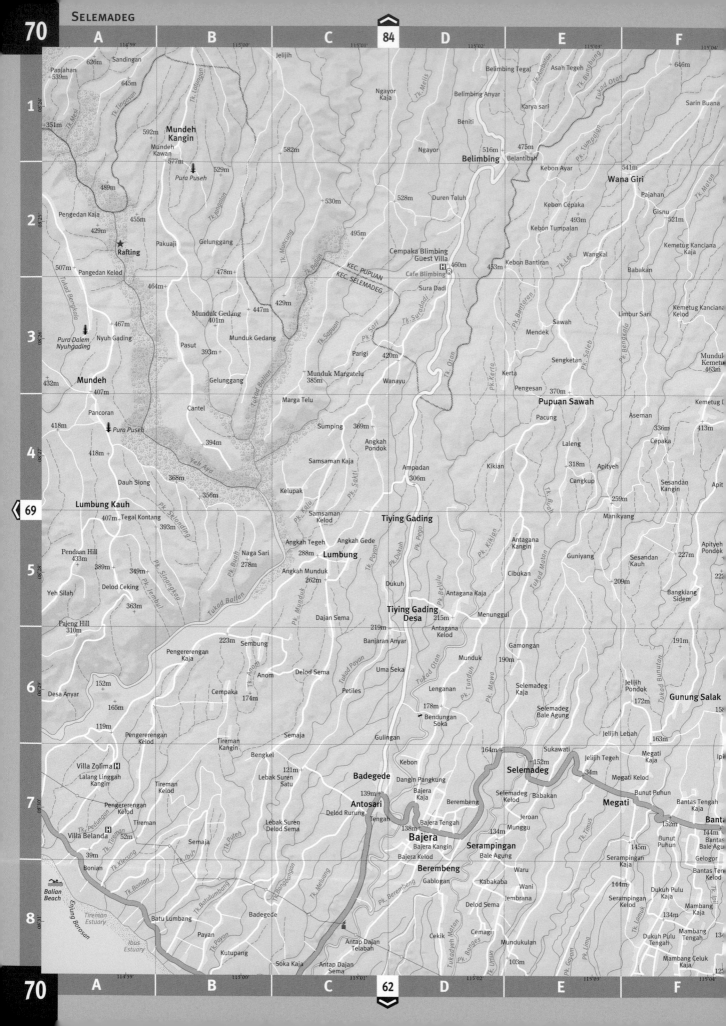

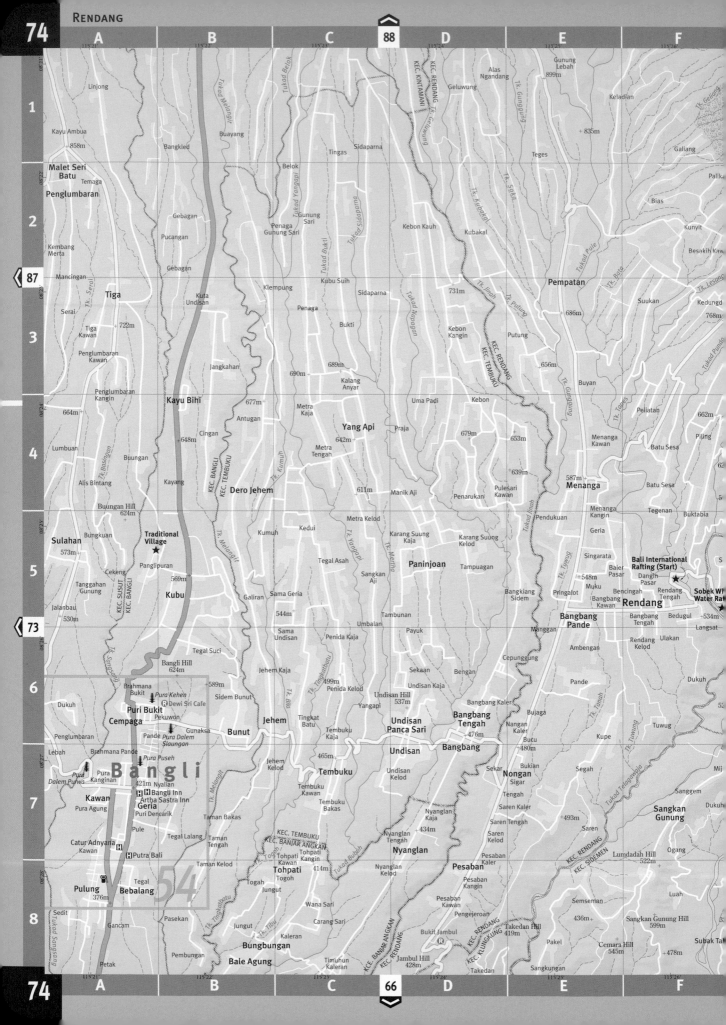

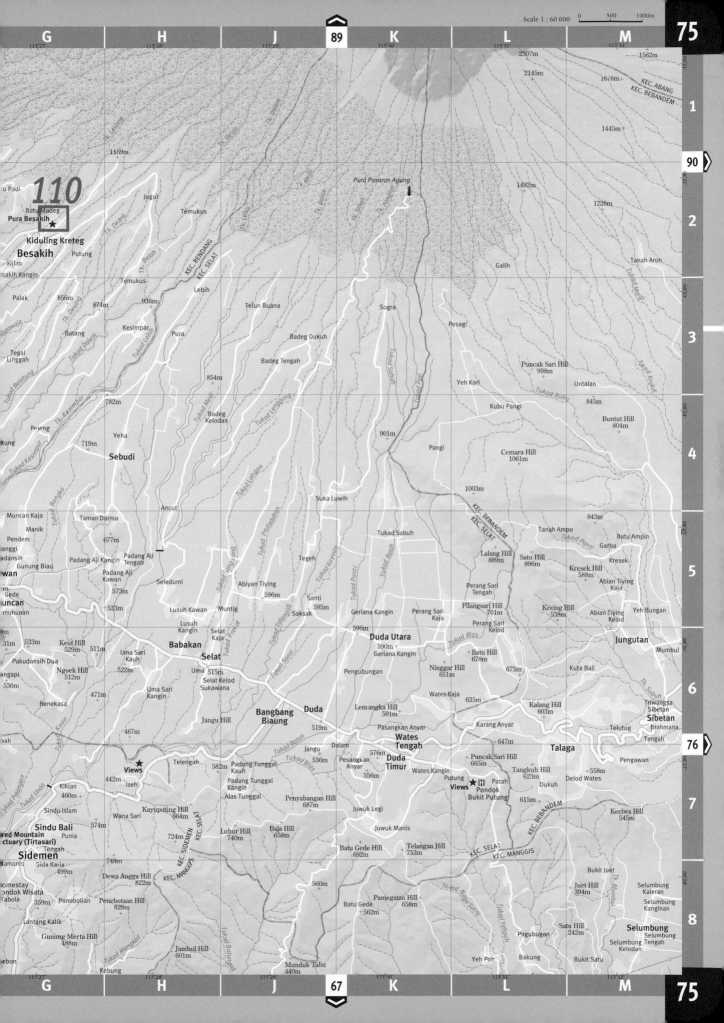

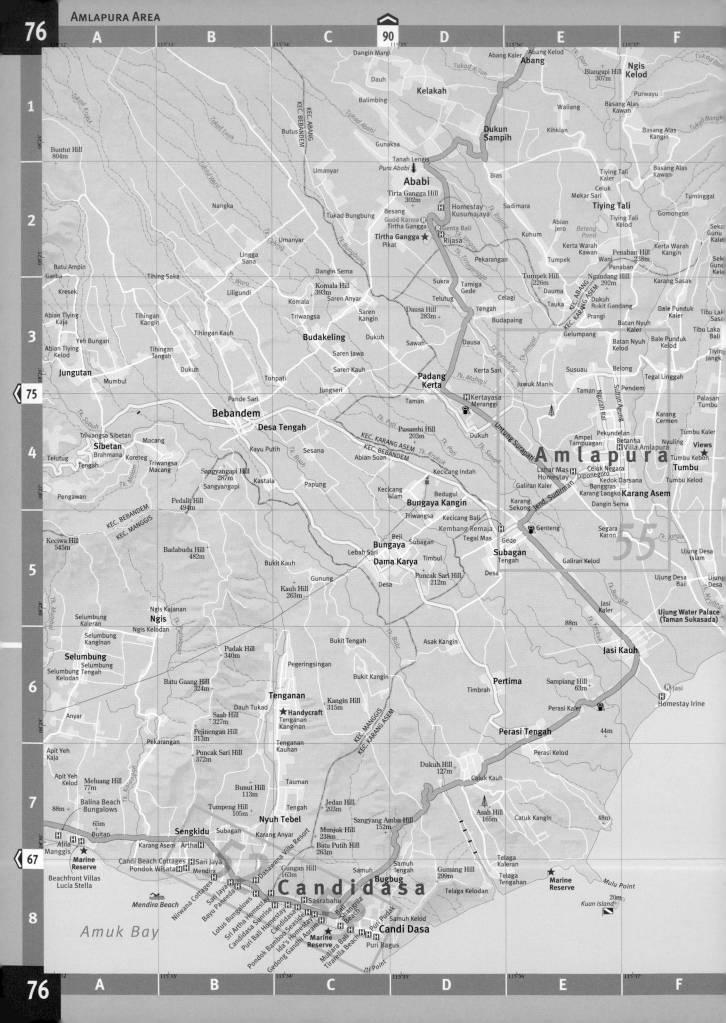

Amuk Bay

1

2

3

4

5

6

7

8

Mount Ambyar Sari 308m

Mount Nyangkrut 349m

Pk. Klatakan

Pk. Awen

Tk. Nyangkrut

Tk. Sumbersori

252m

253m

96m

Blimbing Sar

Ambyar Sari

Protestant Commun

Pura Tirta Segara Rupek

Bajra Point

Klatakan

Rabu Bay

Awen Bay

Sumber Sari

Tk. Sumber Sari

Pangkung Tanah Kauh

Melaya Tengah Krajan

Pangkung Tanah Kangin

Sumber Sori Point

Melaya Tengah Kaja

Melaya Krajan

Karang Sari

Sumber Sari Bay

Melaya Tengah Kelod

Pk. Melaya Pantai

Tk. Melaya

Nusa Sari

Melaya Krajan

Pasar

Melaya

Melaya Pantai

Pangkung Dedari

20m

Anyar Sari Kangin

15m

Dedari Point

Tk. Melaya

Anyar Sari

Nusa S Ke

Tetelan

Tk. Sangiang Gede

4m

Bali Strait

Candi Kusuma

Candi Kusuma Bay

Tukad Aya Estuary

Pasir Point

Tk. Apo Bali

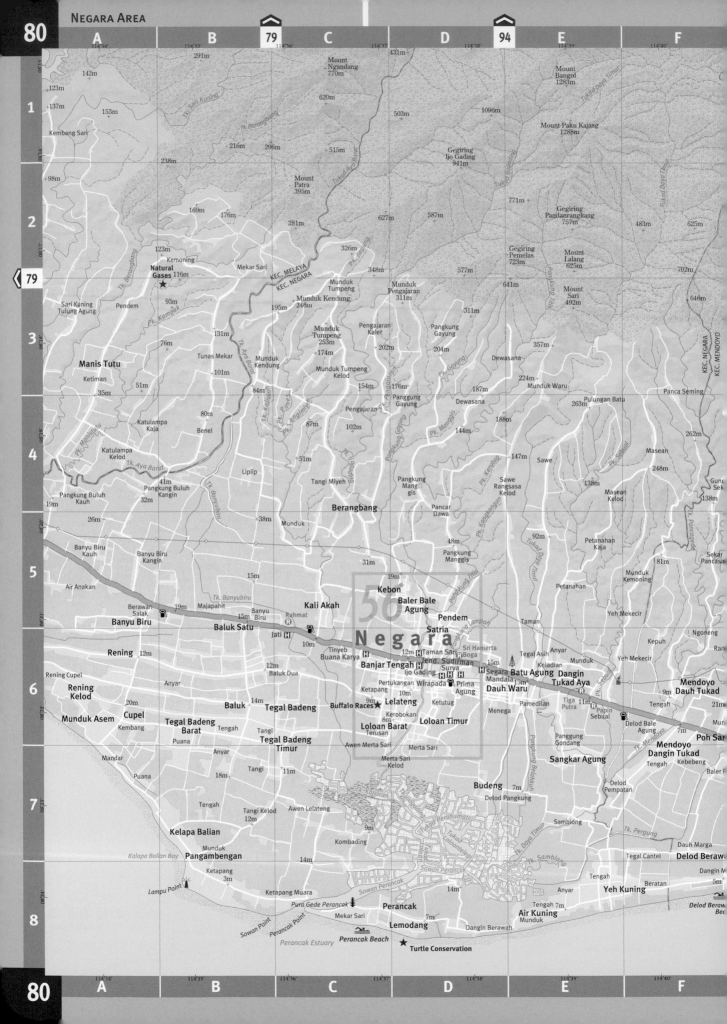

770m
1009m
1013m
Munduk Jajang 1044m
KEC. SERIRIT
KEC. BUSUNG BIU
Munduk Ngandang 944m
Munduk Bujangga 1036m
930m
Munduk Mengatang 884m
444m
452m+
470m
Batu Megaan
308m
Selokah
Kedis Kauh
Timbul
Tk. Dati
Tk. Jehe
569m
Pangkung Pelit
770m+
761m
642m
842m
Tk. Asas
Tk. Sieng
Tinggar Sari Kanginan
Tinggar Sari
Tinggar Sari Kauhan
Subuk
766m
818m
785m
640m+
661m *Tk. Kunyit*
544m
560m+
Asah
Pk. Pelit
Pk. Yehgiang
Belulang
Pucak Sari
613m
Tk. Titab
Pk. Tangianan
Pk. Bukbuk
Munduk Asahdanu 864m
KEC. BUSUNG BIU
KEC. PUPUAN
Sepang
Pertigaan
803m+
Tegal Asih
Kemoning
794m
721m
Seleksek
652m
Teja Bukit
Tk. Selui
Munduk Aya 813m
Pk. Yehapit
Gunung Sari
Apit Yeh
Tk. Melesung
Kembang Rejasa
Tk. Sakti
Munduk Temu Kaja 770m
Pk. Babak
Asah Badung
Sepang Kelod
Kerobokan
Pk. Yehdahan
667m
643m+
Ume Kaja
407m
Tk. Baas
Beteng
Bongan Cina
Bongan Cina Kaja
627m
Dauh Pangkung
Yeh Bau
657m+
Bujak
805m+
Dalem
Munduk Temu
Munduk Temu Kelod
Kelau
582m
676m
Gunung Merta
Pangkung Kunyit
632m
Tk. Ketemba
Panataran Bujak
503m
Puseh
633m
570m
652m
Tista
Dada Putih
644m
597m+
Angga Sari Kaja
Tk. Uintang
809m
Batu Kapal
554m
Penataran
Tk. Panayangan
Yeh Leh
537m
597m+
553m+
Tangis
Yeh Ha
528m
Munduk Tengah
Munduk Mengenu
Tk. Aya
Tk. Bunut
Tk. Bangsah
514m
Manggis Sari
Gunung Jawi
Munduk Ngandang
Lalang Gading
608m
723m
561m
+599m
Belatungan
582m
Apit Yeh
485m
644m
583m
Gali Ukir Kelod
573m+
515m
Pasut
Kebon Jero Kauh
Kebon Jero Kangin
Munduk Kebon Kudungan 599m
584m
KEC. BUSUNG BIU
KEC. PEKUTATAN
Yuwuk Manis Kaja
Dajan Ceking
549m
Tk. Bangsah
626m
Sandingan
54m
Yuwuk Manis Kelod
537m+
Mangenu Anyar
Munduk Gawang
Yeh Ayo
539m+
Panjahan
645m
Tk. Mesi
Tk. Tingasan
KEC. PEKUTATAN
KEC. PUPUAN
389m
433m
Antap Gawang
351m
KEC. PUPUAN
KEC. SELEMADEG
Bangal
592m
Mundeh Kawan
Tk. Merangsang
Yeh Leboh

1
2
3
4
5
6
7
8

114°54′ 114°55′ 114°56′ 114°57′ 114°58′ 114°59′

84

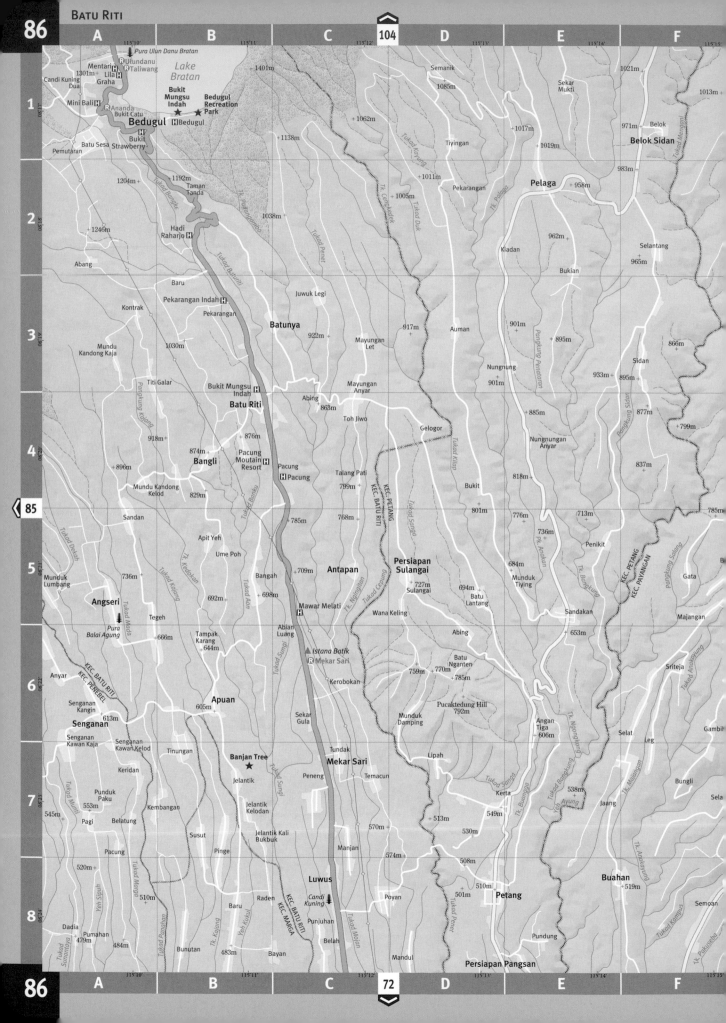

A B C D E F (column headers, top and bottom)

1 2 3 4 5 6 7 8 (row markers)

Lake Bratan

Pura Ulun Danu Bratan
Ulundanu
Mentari · Taliwang
Lila Graha
1301m
Candi Kuning Dua
Mini Bali
Bukit Catu
Ananda
Bedugul
Bukit Strawberry
Batu Sesa
Pemutaran
Bukit Mungsu Indah
Bedugul Recreation Park
+1401m
+1062m
Semanik
1085m
Sekar Mukti
1021m
1013m
+1138m
1017m
971m · Belok
Belok Sidan
+1011m
1019m
983m
Tiyingan
Pekarangan
Pelaga
+958m
1204m +
+1192m
Taman Tanda
1038m
+1005m
962m
Kiadan
Selantang
965m
Abang
Hadi Raharjo
+1246m
Baru
Juwuk Legi
917m
Auman
Bukian
Pekarangan Indah
Pekarangan
Batunya
922m
Mayungan Let
901m
+895m
Sidan
866m
Kontrak
Mundu Kandong Kaja
1030m
Nungnung
901m
933m +
895m
Titi Galar
Bukit Mungsu Indah
Batu Riti
Mayungan Anyar
Abing
863m
+885m
877m
918m +
876m +
Toh Jiwo
Gelogor
Nungnungan Anyar
+799m
Bangli
874m +
Pacung Mountain Resort
Pacung
837m
+896m
Mundu Kandong Kelod
829m
Pacung
Talang Pati
799m +
Bukit
818m +
Sandan
768m
801m
776m
713m
785m
Apit Yeh
785m
684m
736m
Ume Poh
Antapan
Persiapan Sulangai
Munduk Tiying
Penikit
736m
Bangah
709m
727m
694m
Penebel
Munduk Lumbang
692m +
698m
Sulangai
Batu Lantang
Sandakan
Angseri
Pura Balai Agung
Tampak Karang
644m
Mawar Melati
Wana Keling
653m
Abing
Majangan
Tegeh
666m
Abian Luang
Istana Batik
Mekar Sari
759m
Batu Nganten
770m
785m
Angan Tiga
606m
Sriteja
Anyar
Senganan Kangin
613m
Apuan
605m
Kerobokan
Munduk Damping
Pucaktedung Hill
792m
Selat
Leg
Gambih
Senganan
Senganan Kawan Kaja
Senganan Kawan Kelod
Tinungan
Banjan Tree
Sekar Gula
Tundak
Mekar Sari
Lipah
Kerta
538m
Jaang
Bungli
Sela
Keridan
Jelantik
Peneng
Temacun
549m
513m
530m
Punduk Paku
553m
Kembangan
Jelantik Kelodan
Manjan
570m
508m
501m
510m
Petang
Buahan
519m
Pagi
Belatung
Susut
Pinge
Jelantik Kali Bukbuk
574m
Pacung
520m
Raden
Luwus
Candi Kuning
Poyan
Dadia
479m
Pumahan
484m
510m
Baru
Bunutan
483m
Bayan
Punjuhan
Belah
Mandul
Semoan
Pundung
Persiapan Pangsan

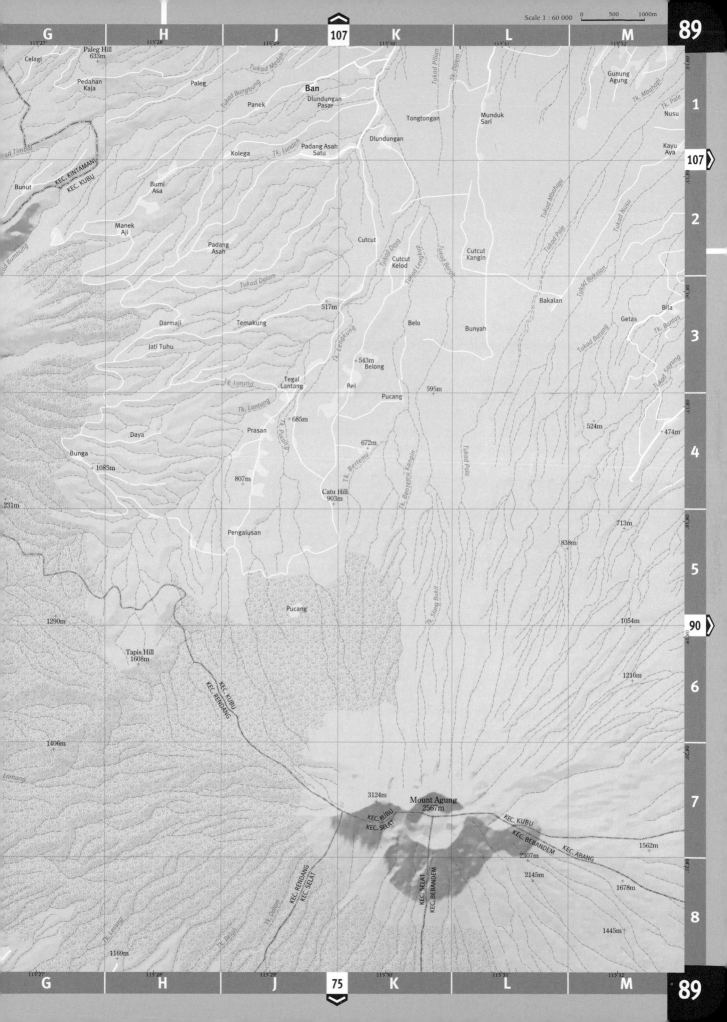

115°27'   115°28'   115°29'   115°30'   115°31'   115°32'

Celagi
Paleg Hill
633m
Pedahan
Kaja
Paleg
Ban
Dlundungan
Pasar
Tukad Medan
Tukad Bungbung
Panek
Tongtongan
Munduk
Sari
Gunung
Agung
Tk. Mbahapi
Tk. Pole
Nusu

1

Bunut
KEC. KINTAMANI
KEC. KUBU
Kolega
Tk. Lundeh
Padang Asah
Satu
Dlundungan
Kayu
Aya

107

Manek
Aji
Bumi
Asa
Padang
Asah
Cutcut
Tukad Daya
Cutcut
Kelod
Cutcut
Kangin
Tukad Mbahapi
Tukad Pale
Tukad Bakalan
Tukad Nusu

2

Tukad Dalam
517m
Belo
Bunyah
Bakalan
Getas
Bila
Tk. Bontos

Darmaji
Temakung
Belong
+543m
595m
524m
+474m
Tukad Batang

3

Jati Tuhu
Tk. Lurung
Tegal
Lantang
Bel
Pucang
Tk. Tengkung
Tk. Sayung

Daya
Tk. Lantang
+685m
Tk. Pucang
672m
Prasan
Tukad Pala

4

Bunga
+1085m
807m
+
Catu Hill
903m
+
Tk. Bertemu
Tk. Bertemu Kangin

231m

Pengalusan
713m
838m

5

1290m
Pucang
Tk. Siang Bukit
1054m

90

Tapis Hill
1608m
1216m

6

1406m
+
KEC. KUBU
KEC. RENDANG

Lantang
3124m
+
Mount Agung
2567m
KEC. KUBU
KEC. SELAT
KEC. KUBU
KEC. BEBANDEM
KEC. ABANG
1562m

7

KEC. RENDANG
KEC. SELAT
KEC. SELAT
KEC. BEBANDEM
2307m
2145m
1678m

8

1169m
1445m+

115°27'   115°28'   115°29'   115°30'   115°31'   115°32'

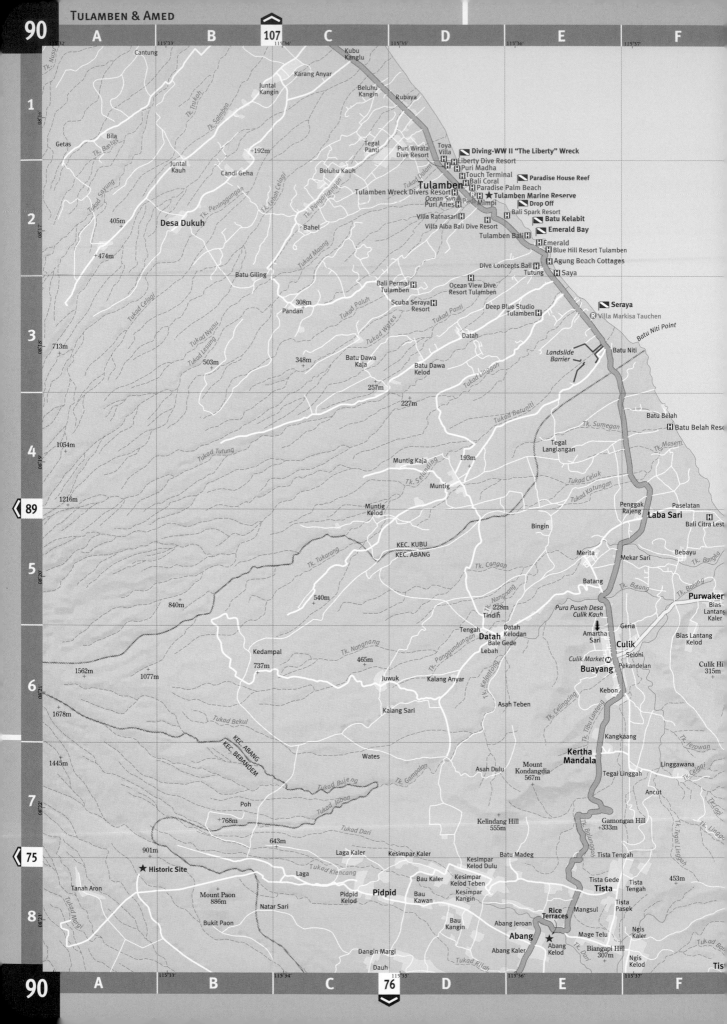

Scale 1 : 60 000

▲ Temple Point

Pura Gili
Mancana

◤ Bat Cave

Pos 2

Bali Sea

Kolaf Point

Tanjung Point

Burung Point

Rejasa Point

Pegametan Bay

Salt Pond

Menjangan

Penerusan Bay

Suntarpao Bay

Kaping Bay

Sumber Kima Bay

Pegametan

Naya Gawana
Resort & Pier

Gebang Bay

Banyu Wedang Bay

Mimpi Resort
Hotel

Banyu Wedang

Santi Sari

Bangsal Point

Letkol Wisnu Airfield

Menjangan Jungle &
Beach Resort

Bajul Bay

Villa Sari Bumi

Sumber Kima

Sumber
Kesambi Homestay
Nikmat

42m

Lovina Dive Center
Menjangan

Malibu Lovina

Pejarakan

Tegal Sari

Labuhan Lalang
Pier

Labuhan Lalang

Goris

Trima Bay

Hot Spring ★

36m

Palengkong

Goris Kelod

Sendang Luar

102m

**Jayaprana
Grave Site** ★

+79m

Munduk
Celangi
57m +

65m

63m

Munduk
Kemiri
160m +

105m

233m

Munduk
Lingker

Munduk Lingker
258m

90m

76m

Tk. Teluk Trima

259m

315m Pk. Ambyorsari

166m

146m

160m

152m

267m

423m

Tk. Sumber Batok

109m

Mount Banyu Wedang
363m

388m

401m

451m

108m

126m

**TAMAN NASIONAL BALI BARAT
(WEST BALI NATIONAL PARK)**

225m

Mount Hulu
Teluk Trima
236m

351m

371m

572m

227m

220m

213m

KEC. GEROKGAK

KEC. MELAYA

347m

338m

662m

222m

168m

Mount
Bangkrangjaran
334m

303m

321m

379m

734m

853m

−245m

+206m

182m

227m

271m

531m

726m

656m

165m

Mount
Jatukangsa
202m

318m

643m

+676m

176m

Mount Melaya
340m

Mount
Sangiang
1003m

906m

726m

+164m

256m

635m

165m

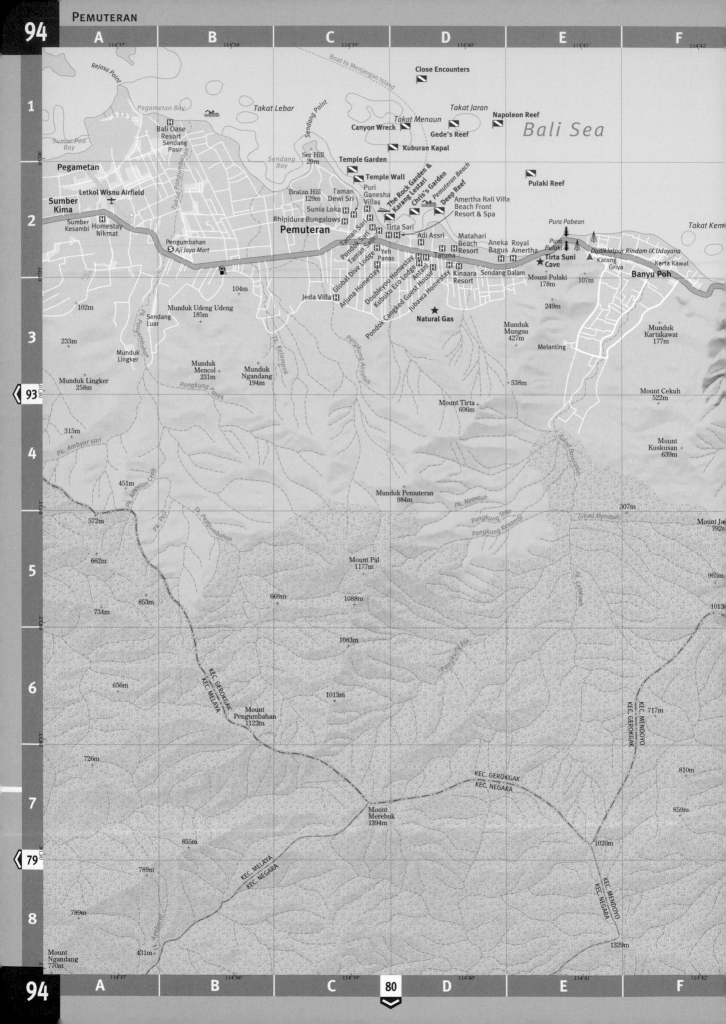

Scale 1 : 60 000   0   500   1000m

114°43'   114°44'   114°45'   114°46'   114°47'   114°48'

Bali Sea

Gondol Point

+47m

BBRPBL

Gondol   *Gondol Bay*

Taman

🏊 *Gondol Beach*

219m

Penyabangan

Menak

Ketapang Bay

Madan

Munduk Taruk 127m

Segara Mukti

Tegil Kiuh

Mount Kernong 231m

Musi

Bisri

Batu Agung

Sangga Langit

Gerokgak

Mount Perigi 231m

Tukad Pule

9m

Pk. Legod

Merta Sari 11m

281m

Mount Musi ~239m

Kayu Putih

Renon

Kedese

Patas

558m

116m   106m

Kayu Putih Kelod

26m

453m

188m   84m   Pal Besi

Merta Sari Kelod

Tegal Sari Kelod

43m

310m

180m

142m

889m   1154m

Munduk Batas 156m

Munduk Renon 175m

Munduk Kontrak 214m

Munduk Ngandang 269m

1165m

Munduk Gidal 368m

1113m

KEC. GEROKGAK

KEC. MENDOYO

Mount Pangkung Lesung 995m

229m

553m

1188m+

1216m

1233m+

1067m

1113m

609m

935m

777m+

1094m

1080m

850m

697m

1018m

1060m

114°43'   114°44'   114°45'   114°46'   114°47'   114°48'

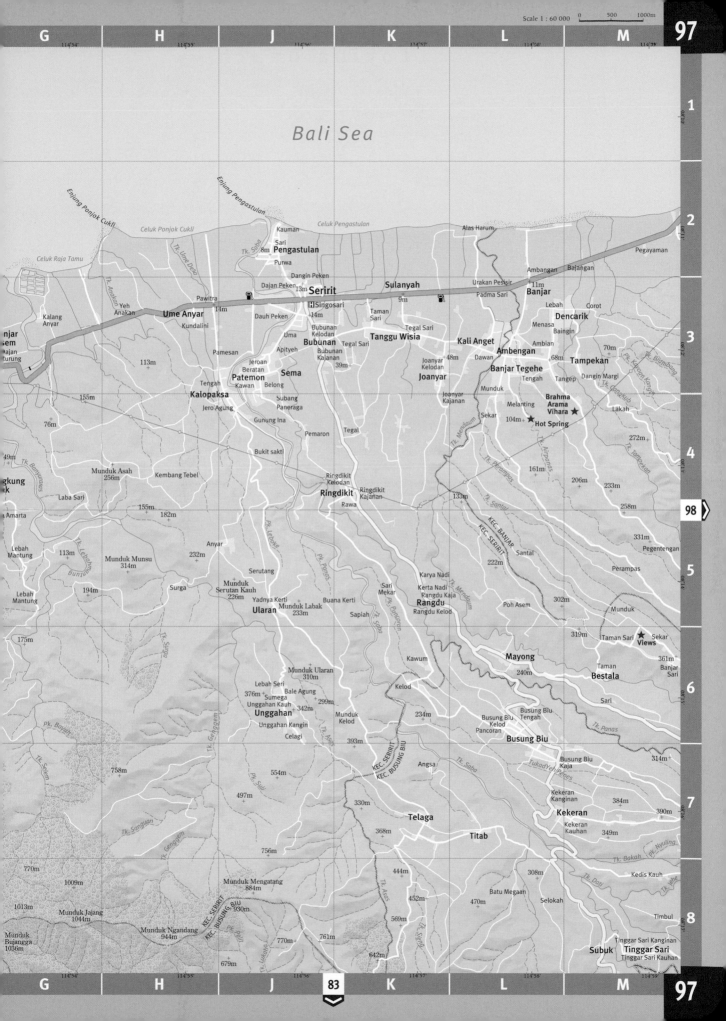

Bali Sea

Enjung Ponjok Cukli

Enjung Pengastulan

Celuk Ponjok Cukli

Celuk Pengastulan

Celuk Raja Tamu

Tk. Ume Desa

Tk. Anakan

Kauman

Sari

8m **Pengastulan**

Alas Harum

Pegayaman

Purwa

Dangin Peken

Ambangan   Bajangan

Kalang Anyar

Dajan Peken   13m **Seririit**

Sulanyah

Urakan Pesisir

11m

Pawitra

Ambangan

Padma Sari

Banjar

Yeh Anakan

14m

Dauh Peken

9m

Lebah

Corot

Ume Anyar

H**Singosari**

Taman Sari

Menasa

Baingin

Dencarik

Kundalini

14m

Uma

Bubunan Kelodan

Tanggu Wisia

Tegal Sari

Ambian

70m

Pamesan

Bubunan

Tegal Sari

Dawan

Ambengan

68m

Tampekan

113m

Apityeh

Bubunan Kajanan

39m

Joanyar Kelodan

48m

Banjar Tegehe

Tangep

Dangin Margi

Tk. Gongkub

Jeroan Beratan

Sema

Belong

Joanyar Kajanan

Joanyar

Tengah

Brahma Arama Vihara ★

Tk. Kayen Kangin

Tk. Brambang

Patemon

Kawan

Munduk

Melanting

Lakah

Tengah

Sekar

104m ★

Hot Spring

272m

Kalopaksa

Jero Agung

Subang Paneraga

Pemaron

Tegal

104m ★ Hot Spring

161m

206m

233m

155m

Gunung Ina

Bukit sakti

133m

Tk. Alpanas

258m

76m

Ringdikit Kelodan

Kembang Tebel

Ringdikit Kajanan

Tk. Santal

331m

49m

Munduk Asah 256m

Ringdikit

Rawa

222m

Santal

Pegentengan

113m

Laba Sari

155m

182m

Anyar

232m

KEC. BANJAR

KEC. SERIRIT

Perampas

Lebah Mantung

Munduk Munsu 314m

Serutang

Sari Mekar

Karya Nadi

Poh Asem

302m

Munduk

319m

194m

Surga

Munduk Serutan Kauh 226m

Yadnya Kerti

Buana Kerti

Kerta Nadi

Rangdu Kaja

Rangdu

Rangdu Kelod

Taman Sari

Views ★

Sekar

175m

Ularan

Munduk Labak 233m

Sapiah

361m

Bestala

Banjar Sari

Kawum

Mayong

240m

Taman Sari

Munduk Ularan 310m

Kelod

234m

Busung Biu Tengah

Sari

Lebah Seri

376m

Bale Agung

Munduk Kelod

Busung Biu Kelod Pancoran

Busung Biu Kaja

314m

Sumega 342m

299m

Unggahan Kauh

Unggahan

Unggahan Kangin

393m

Busung Biu

Tukad Yeh Panes

Celagi

Tk. Bayuh

Pk. Bayuh

554m

Angsa

Tk. Soba

Kekeran Kanginan

384m

Tk. Selem

497m

330m

Telaga

Kekeran Kauhan

Kekeran

390m

758m

368m

Titab

349m

Tk. Sanguan

756m

444m

308m

Kedis Kauh

770m

1009m

Munduk Mengatang 884m

452m

Batu Megaan

470m

Selokah

Tk. Dati

Timbul

1013m

Munduk Jajang 1044m

KEC. SERIRIT

KEC. BUSUNG BIU

930m

569m

Munduk Ngandang 944m

Pk. Beili

770m

761m

642m

Subuk

Tinggar Sari

Tinggar Sari Kauhan

Tinggar Sari Kanginan

Munduk Bujangga 1036m

679m

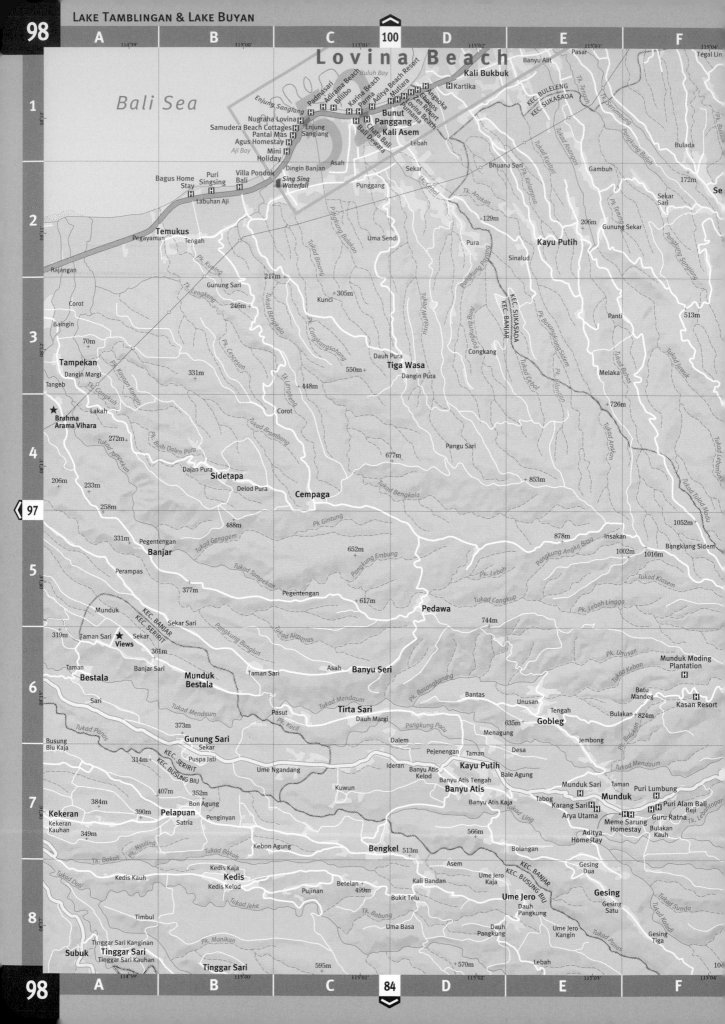

Bali Sea

Lovina Beach

A | B | C | 100 | D | E | F

Kali Bukbuk
Banyu Alit
Pasar
Tegal Lin

Enjung Sanglang
Padmasari
Adirama Beach
Billibo
Karina Beach
Parma
Aditya Beach Resort
Mutiara
Angsoka
Khaos
Kartika
KEC. BULELENG
KEC. SUKASADA
Bulada

Nugraha Lovina
Samudera Beach Cottages
Pantai Mas
Agus Homestay
Enjung
Sangiang
Chalé Bali
Bali Dewata
Kali Resort
Lovina Beach
Purnama
Bunut
Panggang
Kali Asem
Lebah
Sekar
Bhuana Sari
Sekar Sari
Gambuh
172m
Se

Aji Bay
Mini
Holiday

Bagus Home
Stay
Puri Singsing
Villa Pondok
Bali
Dingin Banjan
Asah
Punggang
Sing Sing
Waterfall
Uma Sendi
+129m
Pura
Sinalud
206m
Gunung Sekar
Kayu Putih

Labuhan Aji
Temukus
Pegayaman
Tengah
217m+
Gunung Sari
Kunci
+305m
Dauh Pura
Congkang
KEC. SUKASADA
KEC. BANJAR
Panti
513m

Rajangan
246m+
Tiga Wasa
Dangin Pura
Melaka

Corot
Baingin
70m
331m
550m+
+448m
+726m

Tampekan
Dangin Margi
Tangeb
Lakah
Corot
Pangu Sari
1052m+

★
**Brahma
Arama Vihara**
272m+
Puth Dalen Pura
Dajan Pura
Sidetapa
Delod Pura
677m
+853m
Insakan
1002m
1016m
Bangkiang Sidem

206m
233m
258m
Cempaga
878m

97

331m
Pegentengan
488m
Pk Gintung
652m+
+617m
1002m
Perampas
Banjar
744m

377m
Pegentengan
Pedawa
Pk. Lebah Lingga

Munduk
319m
Taman Sari
★
Views
Sekar Sari
Sekar
361m
Asah
Banyu Seri
Munduk Moding
Plantation

Taman
Banjar Sari
**Munduk
Bestala**
Taman Sari
Batu
Mandeg
Kasan Resort

Bestala
Sari
Pasut
Tirta Sari
Dauh Margi
Bantas
Unusan
Tengah
Bulakan +824m

Busung
Biu Kaja
373m
Pk. Kecil
Dalem
Menagung
635m
Gobleg
Jembong

Gunung Sari
Sekar
Puspa Jati
Dalem
Pejenengan
Taman
Desa
Munduk Sari
Taman
Puri Lumbung

314m+
KEC. SERIRIT
KEC. BUSUNG BIU
Ume Ngandang
Ideran
Banyu Atis
Kelod
Kayu Putih
Bale Agung
Tabog
Karang Sari
Munduk
Puri Alam Bali
Beji

Kekeran
384m
407m
352m
Bon Agung
Kuwun
Banyu Atis Tengah
Banyu Atis
Banyu Atis Kaja
Arya Utama
Meme Sarung
Homestay
Guru Ratna
Bulakan
Kauh

Kekeran
Kauhan
349m
390m
Pelapuan
Satria
Penginyan
Kebon Agung
566m
Aditya
Homestay
Bolangan

Busung
Biu Kaja
Kedis Kaja
Kedis
Kedis Kelod
Pujinan
Betelan+
499m
Bengkel 513m
Asem
Kali Bandan
Ume Jero
Kaja
KEC. BANJAR
KEC. BUSUNG BIU
Gesing
Dua
Gesing

Timbul
Bukit Telu
Uma Basa
Ume Jero
Dauh
Pangkung
Gesing
Satu
Gesing
Tiga

Subuk
Tinggar Sari
Tinggar Sari Kanginan
Tinggar Sari Kauhan
Tinggar Sari
595m+
+570m
Dauh
Pangkung
Ume Jero
Kangin
Lebah

Bali Sea

Galira

Puri Bagus Lovina [H]
Ranggon Bali [R] [R] Warung Bambe

Baruna Cottage [H]
Puri Bedahulu [H] Immigration Office
Permai Dive Resort   Jati Reef   Dangin Margi
Happy Beach Inn [H] [R] Bayu Gede   Pemaron
[H] [H] Trisna
Bali Rani Bungalow [H] [H] Dharma Kerti   Dauh Margi
Kubu Lalang Bungalow [H]   Happy Bungalow   Babal

Sri Homestay [H]   Batu Pulu

Agung Bay   Dharma Yasa   Tukad
Lilacita   [H] Dharma Jadra   Mungga
Lovina Beach   Munduk   Dharma Semedi
Gino Feruci Villa   Suci Homestay [H]
Maydinie   [H] Satya   Anturan
Marina   Anyar
Lovina [H]   Celuk Buluh   Pasar   Labak   Tega
Beach Resort   Lingg
Banyu Alit
Kali Bukbuk
Buluh Bay   Kali Bukbuk   KEC. BULELENG
Padmasari   Aditya Beach Resort   Kartika   KEC. SUKASADA
Adirama Beach   Mutiara   L o v i n a
Bilibo   Chandra   B e a c h
Karina Beach   Zen Resort
Parma   Lovina Beach
Nugraha Lovina [H]   Purnama
Samudera Beach Cottages [H]   Bali Dewata [H]   Chata   Lebah
Pantai Mas [H]   Enjung Sangiang   Bali   Bulada
Agus Homestay [H]   Kali Asem   Desa Selat
Mini Holiday [H]

104

Bali Sea

Alas Sari
Art 200
Puri Baru Ponjok Batu
Pura Pojok Batu
Alas Sari
Pacung
Kubu Anyar
Julah
Kawanan
Kelod Kuta Bondalem
Kelod Kauh
Bondalem
Susuk
Tegal Sari
Bondalem
Kelod Kangin
Celagi Bantar
Celagi
Kaja Kauh
Batur
Bondalem
Kaja Kangin
Suka Darma
Selombo
Tejakula
Kelodan
Suci
Tejakula
Tejakula
Kawanan
Kanginan
Tejakula
Sila Darma
Tengah
Tejakula
Anta Pura
Bayad
Sembiran
Kanginan
Sembiran
Sembiran
Kawanan
Nangka
396m

Tk. Ongos
Tukad Dalem
Tk. Pahut
Tk. Pontoh Batu
Tukad Kambing
Tukad Munggal
Tukad Glagah
Tk. Bengkeh
Tk. Pangpang
Tk. Puang
Tukad Candi
Tk. Bunghung
Tk. Desa
Tukad Veh Along
Tk. Songkutu
Tukad Titi
Tukad Loven
Tukad Desa
Tukad Bantes
Tk. Anyar
Tk. Koyehan Kangin
Tukad Buahan
Tukad Pelisan
Tukad Nangka
Tukad Munggal

Bukit Seni
803m
KEC. TEJAKULA
KEC. KUBU TAMBAHAN
Tk. Bongkah
Madenan
Kelodan
562m
727m
KEC. TAJAKULA
KEC. KINTAMANI
718m
789m
Panggung
Madenan
Kejanan
Tk. Melan
Keduran
Gentah
865m
820m
Madenan
826m
Mendaa Hill
688m
915m
796m
Kutuh
538m
Subaya
967m
KEC. TEJAKULA
KEC. KINTAMANI
1007m
Sangambu
Tukad Poljan
Tk. Sambongan
Tukad Samuh
Tukad Yehutang
Tukad Doya
Tukad Les
Bakungan
1053m
1074m
1086m
Tahab
Hembut
922m
Angan Sari
989m
1055m

1
2
3
4
5
6
106
7
8

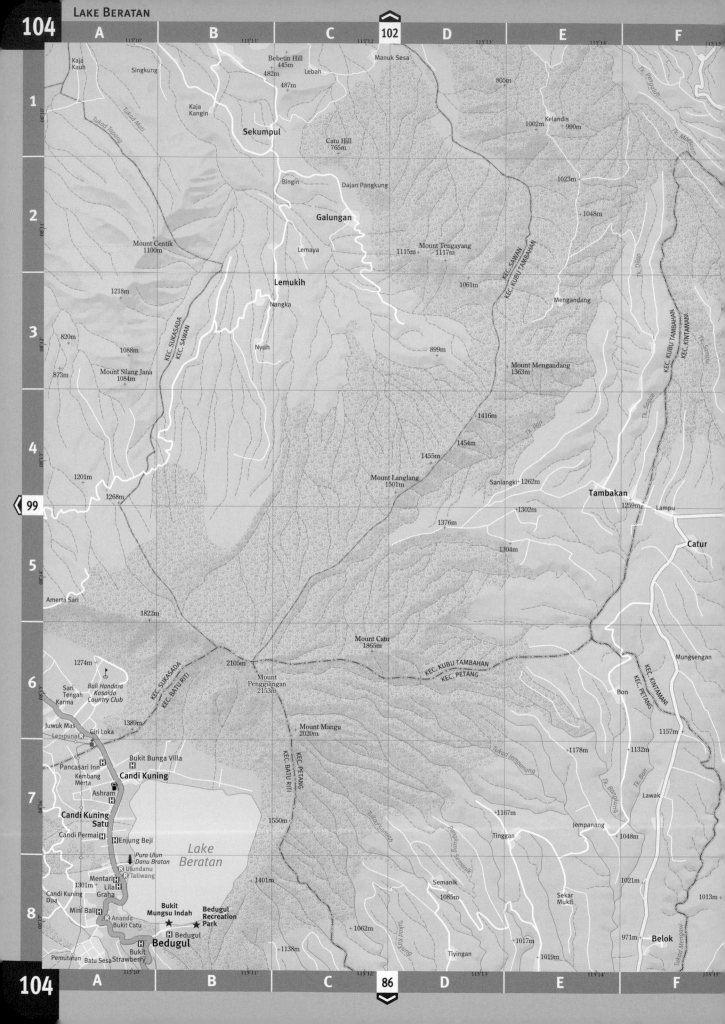

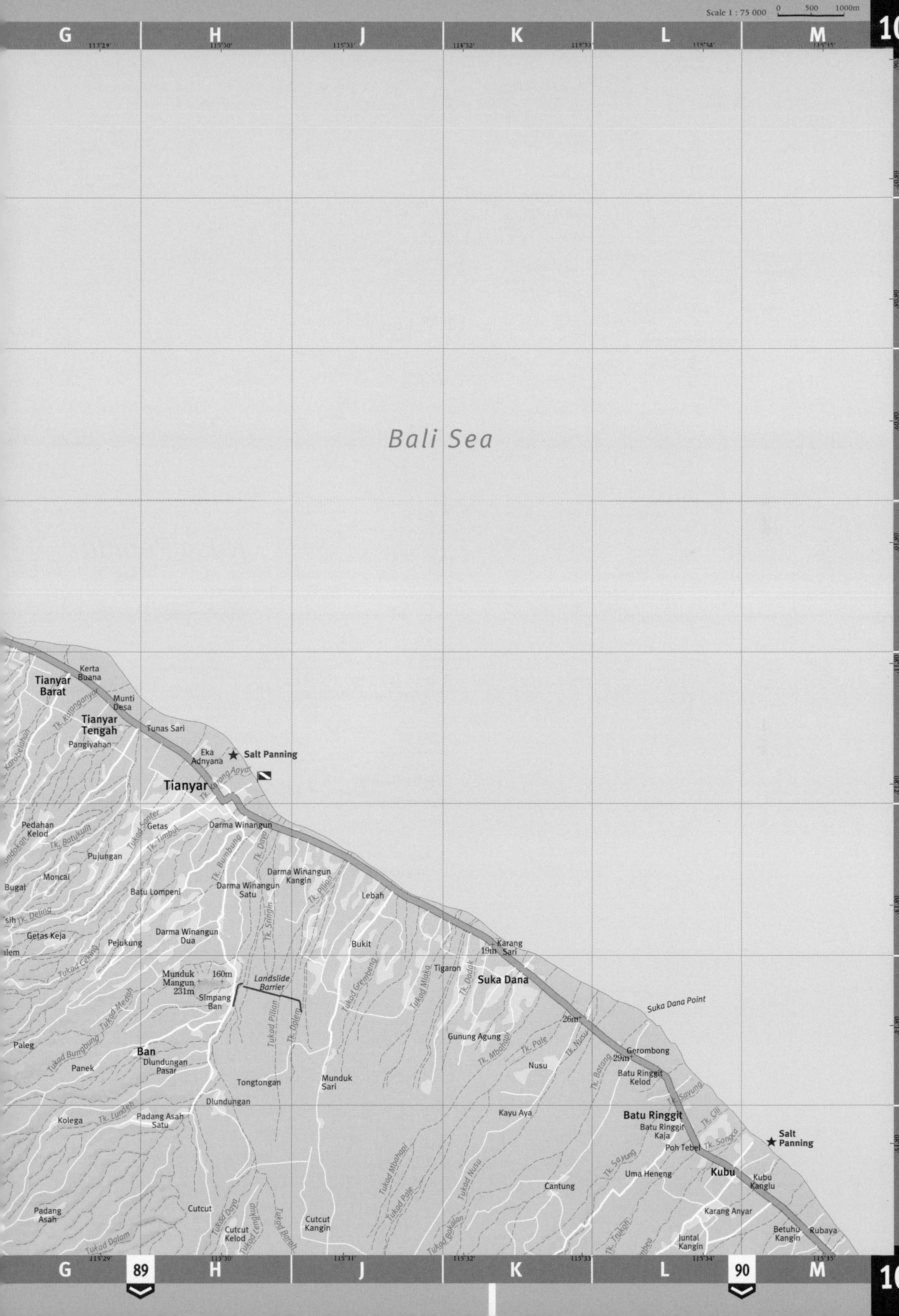
Scale 1 : 75 000
0
500
1000m
G
H
J
K
L
M
1
2
3
4
5
6
7
8
Bali Sea
Kerta Buana
Tianyar Barat
Munti Desa
Tianyar Tengah
Tk. Karanganyar
Tunas Sari
Pangiyahan
Eka Adnyana
Salt Panning
Tk. Karang Anyar
Tianyar
Pedahan Kelod
Tk. Batukulit
Tukad Santer
Getas
Tk. Timbul
Darma Winangun
Pujungan
Tk. Bumbung
Tk. Daya
Moncal
Bugal
Darma Winangun Kangin
Darma Winangun Satu
Tk. Pilian
Batu Lompeni
Lebah
Tk. Deling
Tk. Sringin
Getas Keja
Darma Winangun Dua
Pejukung
Bukit
Karang Sari
19m
Tukad Ceking
Munduk Mangun
231m
160m
Landslide Barrier
Simpang Ban
Tigaron
Suka Dana
Tukad Grembeng
Tukad Mlaka
Tk. Dadak
Tukad Meagh
Tukad Pilian
Tk. Dalem
Suka Dana Point
26m
Paleg
Tukad Bungbung
Gunung Agung
Tk. Mbahapi
Tk. Pale
Tk. Nusu
Ban
Panek
Dlundungan Pasar
Gerombong
29m
Nusu
Tk. Batang
Batu Ringgit Kelod
Tongtongan
Munduk Sari
Tk. Sayung
Dlundungan
Kolega
Tk. Lundeh
Padang Asah Satu
Kayu Aya
Batu Ringgit
Batu Ringgit Kaja
Tk. Cili
Salt Panning
Poh Tebel
Tk. Songca
Tukad Mbahapi
Tukad Nusu
Tk. Sajung
Uma Heneng
Kubu
Kubu Kanglu
Tukad Pale
Cantung
Padang Asah
Cutcut
Tukad Daya
Cutcut Kelod
Tukad Lengkup
Tukad Barah
Cutcut Kangin
Tukad Bakalan
Tk. Trukan
Karang Anyar
Juntal Kangin
Betuhu Kangin
Rubaya
Tukad Dalem
89
90

A   B   C   D   E   F

115°25'   115°26'   115°27'   115°28'   115°29'   115°30'   115°31'

Badung Strait

to Sanur, thr.

Shipwreck Surf Break
Blue Corner
Entai Cape
Puri Indah
Ta Chi Cottages
Kaja Satu
Lacerations Surf Break
Agung's Lembongan Lodge
Nusa Lembongan Bongalows
Ketut
Main Ski Inn & Restaurant
Nusa Indah
Jungut Batu
Bungalow Number 7
Baruna
Johnny's Losmen
MANGROVE FOREST
Sakenan Mangrove/ Jack Point
Pemaroan Cape
to Padangbai, 45-60 mins.
Biasmuntig Cape
SD
Ped
Tugu
Prapat
Tanah Bias
Pura Dalem Penataran Ped
Ped
FNPF
Pendem
Ring Sameton Inn

Playground Surf Break
Kaja Dua
Pangkung Hill 29m
Telaktak
Mutiara Bungalow
3m
Prapat Kelod

Nusa Lembongan

Sanghyang Cape
Windu
Mushroom Beach Bungalows
56m
Kangin Dua
Cheningan Channel
Kelod Dua
Gelumpang Cape
Toyo Pakeh
Losmen Terang
Tk. Prapat
Nyuh
Waka Nusa Resort
Dream Beach Huts
Kaja
Kawan
Lembongan
Kangin
Kelod
Cavehouse
Ceningan Cove
Ceningan Wall
Anyar
Tk. Benkaryo
Biaung
Bodong
Pendem Hill 206m
207m   196m
Uwung Bay
Pemalikan Point
Pemulikan Bay
Penguntolan Point
Penyuntalan Bay
Batu Talenan Point
Lebaoh Bay
Hanging Bridge
Ceningan Kangin
Jetty Resort
Ceningan Kangin
Gamat Bay
Tk. Lanjang
Sebunibus
Adegan Kawan   191m
Adegan Kangin
Serangeh
Ser

Batu Talen
Lebaoh Cape
Gua Betel Bay
Ceningan Reef Surf Break
Le Pirate
Batu Melang
Ceningan Kawan
Nusa Ceningan
Namaste Bungalow
115m+
Sakti
Senangka
Senengka
Tingjajang
Adegan
Tegeh Hill 227m
Sarang Burung Walet Cave
Twilight Bungalows
Jenny's Place
The Palms
Dafish
Secret Point Huts
Trevelly
Tatabunut Hill 66m
Lebuah Bay
Ketapan Point
Gua Lawah Cape
104m
Batu Mejinong I.
Crystal Bay
Tk. Sai
Spring +152m
Cemulik
Penaga
Cubang
Belebet
Metakih
Tk. Boyur
Tk. Palung

Batu Melawang Point
Luah Bay
Luah Point
Kuanji Bay
Kuaji Point
Cekungan Point
Pemalikan Point
Song Piling Point
Pandan Bay
Naup Point
Payung Bay
Payung Cape
Penina
116m
Penaga
176m
Mendak Sari Hill 222m
Pangkot
Tk. Ambu
Angas
Klumbu
Bale

Tegeh Point
Melajeng Cape
Gunung Cemeng Bay
Tk. Oyah
Sompang
171m
Pikad
Tukad Pandon
Pondok Kaha Kaja
Bucang
Tk. Penida
Nusa Penida
Pura Puncak Mundi
521m+

Seganing Cape
163m
Pondok Kaha Kelod
Lemba Hill 210m
Bunga Mekar
Jelijih Hill 267m
Pondok Kelod
Mendak Sari Hill 338m
Tk. Wani
Tukad Toban

Lebanah Point
Batu Melawang
Tukad Oyah Bay
Tk. Kaming
Tk. Wasu
Penangkidan
Tk. Kaming
Tukad Pikan
Batu Madeg Kelod
Penutuk
Dahan 338

Batu Belede Point
Panggang Hill 210m+
Karang Dawa
206m
Sebuluh
Tk. Sentulan
Batu Madeg Kaja
Gahang
Batu Madeg
Batu Madeg Kaja
Prembon
Tk. Temeleng
Tk. Maksan
Dehan Hill 313m
Dahan

Sari Point
111m
Blidung Hill 205m
Beme Hill 191m
Tegah Hill 290m
Klicung Hill +210m
Tk. Pusoh
Dehan

Blidung Point
Mlajeng Point
Nusa Batu Pahet
Dalem Hill 186m
Salak
Klicung Hill
Mawan
Tk. Cacah
Tk. Segaring
Spring
Salen
Pangkung Anyar

Gunung Cemeng Point
Pirerekan Hill +193m
Tk. Kircung
Cacah
Seganing Bay
Seganing Waterfall
Macang
Tk. Batuseho
Sukun

Banah Point
Semuputeh Hill 229m
Pangkung Gedu
Tk. Pangkung
Pangkung Hill 239m
257m
Antepan
Nusa Banah
Nusa Batu Melawang
Nusa Batu Meling
Old Manta Point   40m
Batu Meling
Batu Meling Point
Batu Meling Bay
252m+
Peguyangan

Pehikan Point

INDIAN OCEAN

Manta Point/ Batu Lumbung
23m+
Nusa Batu Jinengan
Mant

Toyo Pakeh Strait

115°25'   115°26'   115°27'   115°28'   115°29'   115°30'   115°31'

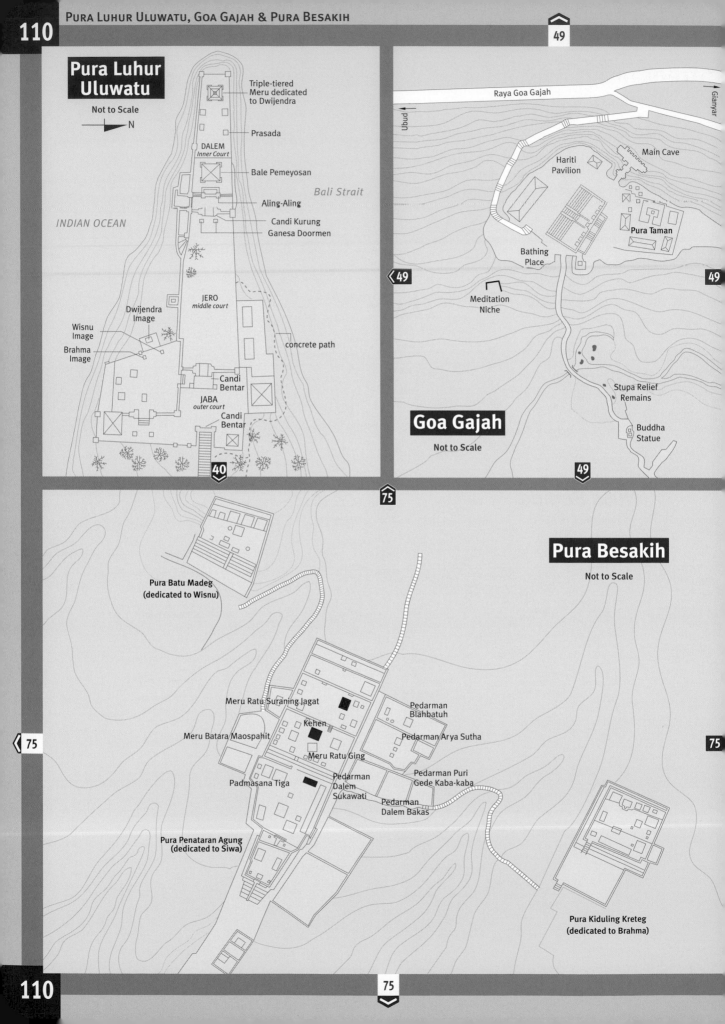

Pura Luhur Uluwatu

Not to Scale

N

- Triple-tiered Meru dedicated to Dwijendra
- Prasada
- DALEM *Inner Court*
- Bale Pemeyosan
- Aling-Aling
- Candi Kurung
- Ganesa Doormen

Bali Strait

INDIAN OCEAN

- Dwijendra Image
- Wisnu Image
- Brahma Image

JERO *middle court*

concrete path

- Candi Bentar
- JABA *outer court*
- Candi Bentar

Goa Gajah

Not to Scale

Raya Goa Gajah

Ubud

Gianyar

- Main Cave
- Hariti Pavilion
- Pura Taman
- Bathing Place
- Meditation Niche
- Stupa Relief Remains
- Buddha Statue

Pura Besakih

Not to Scale

- Pura Batu Madeg (dedicated to Wisnu)
- Meru Ratu Suraning Jagat
- Kehen
- Meru Batara Maospahit
- Meru Ratu Ging
- Padmasana Tiga
- Pedarman Dalem Sukawati
- Pedarman Dalem Bakas
- Pedarman Blahbatuh
- Pedarman Arya Sutha
- Pedarman Puri Gede Kaba-kaba
- Pura Penataran Agung (dedicated to Siwa)
- Pura Kiduling Kreteg (dedicated to Brahma)

Street Index

A

Abang, Gunung (Gianyar) 50 D5
Abasan Indah 20 B1
Abimanyu (Dangin Puri Kauh) 28 F6
Abimanyu (Gianyar) 50 B8
Abimanyu (Singaraja) 57 C6
Abimanyu (Tonja) 29 J3
Abun Subak 23 G2
Adelia 30 B7
Adhiaksa 21 L2
Adi Pura 20 E6
Adi, Pulau 21 H6
Agung, Gunung (Amlapura) 55 A7
Agung, Gunung (Gianyar) 50 D5
Agung, Gunung (Klungkung) 51 E5
Agung, Gunung (Negara) 56 D6
Agung, Gunung (Singaraja) 57 E7
Agung, Gunung (Tabanan) 51 D2
Agung, Kapten 29 G7
Ahmad Yani (Amlapura) 55 B8
Ahmad Yani (Denpasar) 28 E3
Ahmad Yani (Negara) 56 C4
Ahmad Yani, Jendral 57 B4
Air Mancur 20 F4
Airlangga (Bangli) 54 D2
Airlangga (Gianyar) 50 B7
Airport Ngurah Rai 11 G6
Akasia (Sumerta) 29 M7
Akasia (Tegal Harum) 20 E3
Akasia 1 .... 29 M7
Akasia 2 .... 29 M7
Akasia 3 .... 29 M7
Akasia 4 .... 29 M7
Akasia 5 .... 29 M7
Akasia 6 .... 29 M7
Akasia 7 .... 29 M7
Akasia 9 .... 30 A7
Akasia 10 .... 30 A7
Akasia 11 .... 30 A7
Akasia 13 .... 30 B7
Akasia 16 .... 30 A7
Akasia 16A 30 B8
Akuntansi 36 F6
Alamanda (Panjer) 22 B7
Alamanda (Tibu Beneng) 26 B4
Alas Arum, Tukad 21 M7
Alasari 27 H6
Alila Villas 42 C7
Alit, Lettu 55 D5
Aliyah, Gang 56 F5
Alor, Pulau 21 J5
Alpukat 50 A7
Amal 20 E2
Amanlane 20 B8
Amanusa 39 G8
Ambengan 48 B8
Ambon, Pulau 21 K3
Amphi 39 K5
Andong, Raya 47 J2
Angga Buana 20 D1
Anggada 19 L2
Anggraeni 22 E3
Anggrek (Kerobokan Kelod) 19 K4
Anggrek (Kesiman Kertha Langu) 31 H4
Anggrek (Kesiman) 30 B8
Anggrek (Klungkung) 51 D7
Anggrek (Negara) 56 C1
Anggrek (Sumerta Kaja) 29 K4
Anggrek (Ungasan) 42 F6
Anggrek 5 (Tabanan) 51 C4
Anggrek Bulan 28 C1
Anggrek Merah 21 M6
Anggur 25 K8
Angkara 29 J6
Angkasa Argo Permai 28 B1
Angkasari 50 D8
Angsa (Kemenuh) 49 J8
Angsa (Kerobokan) 26 D7
Angsa (Pemecutan Kaja) 28 D4
Angsoka 29 H6
Angsoka (Singaraja) 57 C4
Anisa 19 G3
Anom Mudeta, Kapten 54 D2
Anom, Lettu 54 C4
Anom, Serma 55 D4
Anoman 29 K1
Antariksa 21 J5
Antosari 51 D5
Anturan 53 M3
Anusapati 50 B7
Anyelir (Kerobokan Kaja) 27 H4
Anyelir (Klungkung) 51 D8
Anyelir (Seminyak) 19 L8
Anyelir (Sumerta) 29 M7
Anyelir (Tabanan) 51 B4
Anyer 10 .... 30 E1
Aora 43 .... 19 K6
Aora 44 .... 19 K6
Apel (Kesiman) 30 B8
Apel (Sesetan) 21 M8
Apolo 21 J5
Arema 28 B7
Arjuna - Ungasan 43 K4
Arjuna (Bangli) 54 D3
Arjuna (Dauh Puri Kaja) 28 F6
Arjuna (Gianyar) 50 B8

Arjuna (Kerobokan Kelod) 19 J3
Arjuna (Kerobokan) 26 D6
Arjuna (Klungkung) 51 E7
Arjuna (Negara) 56 C5
Arjuna (Sanur Kauh) 23 H7
Arjuna (Seminyak) 14 C2
Arjuna (Tabanan) 51 E3
Arjuna (Tonja) 29 J3
Arjuna (Ubud) 46 E3
Arjuna, Gang 1 .... 56 C4
Arjuna, Gang 2 .... 56 B4
Arjuna, Gang 3 .... 56 B4
Aroma 28 B7
Artha Buana 20 D2
Arti, Lettu 55 E4
Aru, Pulau 21 L4
Arwana 31 J4
Arwana 4 .... 31 J4
Arwana 5 .... 31 J4
Asahan, Tukad 22 B6
Asem 26 D8
Asem 1 .... 20 E2
Asem 2 .... 20 E2
Asem 3 .... 20 E2
Asem 6 .... 20 E2
Asem 7 .... 20 E2
Asem 9 .... 20 E2
Asem 12 .... 20 E2
Asem 13 .... 20 E1
Aseman Bagus 1 .... 26 D3
Asih 23 K7
Asmara Villa, The 45 G5
Asrama Polri 1 .... 31 G3
Asrama Polri 2 .... 31 G3
Astina (Kuta) 36 D6
Astina (Ubud) 48 C8
Astina Selatan 50 D8
Astina Timur 50 E7
Astina Utara 50 B5
Astinapura 39 G4
Atena 7, Gunung 20 B6
Awangga 39 H5
Aya 9, Yeh 22 F5
Aya 9C, Yeh 22 E5
Aya 9D, Yeh 22 E5
Aya 9E, Yeh 22 E6
Ayana Resort 35 M2
Ayodya 48 C8
Ayung, Yeh 50 E6

B

Babadan 24 F5
Bacan, Pulau 21 K5
Bacangan 36 C8
Badak (Benoa) 33 K8
Badak (Dalung) 27 H3
Badak 1 .... 22 D2
Badak 2 .... 22 D2
Badak 2A 22 D2
Badak 3 .... 22 D2
Badak Agung 22 C2
Badak Agung 1 .... 22 C2
Badak Agung 2 .... 22 C2
Badak Agung 3 .... 22 C2
Badak Agung 4 .... 22 C2
Badak Agung 6 .... 22 C1
Badak Agung 8 .... 22 C1
Badak Agung 10 .... 22 C2
Badak Agung 11 .... 22 C2
Badak Agung 12 .... 22 C1
Badak Agung 13 .... 22 C1
Badak Agung 14 .... 22 C1
Badak Agung 15 .... 29 K8
Badak Agung 15 .... 22 C1
Badak Agung 16 .... 29 K8
Badak Agung 17 .... 29 K8
Badak Agung 18 .... 29 K8
Badak Agung 19 .... 29 K8
Badak Agung 20 .... 29 K8
Badak Agung 22 .... 29 K8
Badak Agung 24 .... 29 K8
Badak Sari 1 .... 22 D1
Badak Sari 2 .... 22 D1
Badak Sari 3 .... 22 D1
Badak Sari 4 .... 22 D1
Badak Sari 5 .... 22 D1
Badik 21 M4
Badung 19 G3
Badung 1, Tukad 22 E5
Badung 2, Tukad 22 E5
Badung 3, Tukad 22 E5
Badung 4, Tukad 22 E6
Badung 5, Tukad 22 E5
Badung 6, Tukad 22 E5
Badung 7, Tukad 22 E6
Badung 8, Tukad 22 E6
Badung 9, Tukad 22 E6
Badung 10, Tukad 22 E6
Badung 11, Tukad 22 E7
Badung 11B, Tukad 22 E7
Badung 12, Tukad 22 E7
Badung 12C, Tukad 16 F1
Badung 13, Tukad 22 E7
Badung 13A, Tukad 22 E7
Badung 14, Tukad 22 E8
Badung 14A, Tukad 22 E7
Badung 15, Tukad 22 E7
Badung 16, Tukad 22 E8
Badung 17, Tukad 22 E7
Badung 18, Tukad 22 E8

Badung 19, Tukad 22 E8
Badung 19C, Tukad 22 F8
Badung 20, Tukad 16 F2
Badung 21, Tukad 22 E8
Badung 9A, Tukad 22 E6
Badung 9B, Tukad 22 E6
Badung Timur, Tukad 22 E8
Badung, Tukad (Denpasar Selatan) 22 E6
Baja 16 D4
Bajang Sari 23 J6
Bajra, Lettu 55 D4
Bakung 30 E2
Balada 19 M4
Baladewa 54 D3
Balangan Biru V 36 A6
Balangan Biru VI 36 A6
Balangan Boulevard 36 A6
Baler Setra 41 M6
Bali Cliff 43 J5
Bali Cliff, Raya 43 K7
Bali Deli 19 L7
Bali Griya 20 B6
Bali Jeep St. 20 C2
Bali, Pulau (Denpasar Barat) 21 K4
Bali, Pulau (Singaraja) 57 E2
Balian, Tukad (Gianyar) 50 E6
Baliku 1 .... 26 E7
Baliku 2 .... 26 D7
Bamboo 18 E2
Bambu (Kerobokan Kelod) 19 K1
Bambu (Ungasan) 43 3G
Banda, Pulau 21 K1
Bang, Yeh 50 E6
Bangau (Pemecutan Kaja) 28 D5
Bangau (Sidakarya) 16 E2
Bangau (Tabanan) 51 D1
Bangka, Pulau 21 H7
Bangli, Raya 54 C8
Banjar Bandang 26 E7
Banjar Pendem 56 E2
Banjar Sari 11 G1
Banjar Werdhi 21 H6
Banjara Sawangan 45 K2
Bantan 26 C3
Bantan Kangin 26 C2
Bantas Kauh 32 C4
Banteng 29 G5
Banteng 96 .... 21 H3
Banyu Poh, Tukad 21 M5
Banyu Sari 5, Tukad 21 M6
Banyu Sari, Tukad 21 L5
Banyuning 57 F4
Banyuning, Tukad 22 C5
Barara 26 D7
Barito 1, Tukad 22 B7
Barito 5, Tukad 22 D6
Barito, Tukad 22 D6
Baru, Tukad 21 G8
Basangkasa, Raya 19 K7
Basuki Rahmat 22 D3
Batako (Pemecutan Kelod) 20 F6
Batako (Sesetan) 22 B8
Batam 1, Pulau 21 K2
Batam 2, Pulau 21 K2
Batam, Pulau 51 B2
Batan Kepel 20 F7
Batang Hari, Tukad 22 C6
Batanghari 1, Tukad 22 C5
Batanghari 1A, Tukad 22 C5
Batanghari 1B, Tukad 22 C5
Batanghari 3, Tukad 22 C5
Batanghari 4, Tukad 22 C5
Batanghari 4B, Tukad 22 C5
Batanghari 4C, Tukad 22 C5
Batanghari 5A, Tukad 22 B6
Batanghari 6A, Tukad 22 C6
Batanghari 6B, Tukad 22 C5
Batanghari 6C, Tukad 22 C5
Batanghari 7, Tukad 22 D6
Batanghari 8, Tukad 22 C6
Batanghari 9, Tukad 22 C6
Batanghari 10, Tukad 22 C6
Batanghari 10A, Tukad 22 C6
Batanghari 11, Tukad 22 D6
Batanghari 11A, Tukad 22 C7
Batanghari 12, Tukad 22 C6
Batanghari 14, Tukad 22 C7
Batanta, Pulau 20 F7
Batas 21 G8
Batas Dukuh Sari 16 A2
Batu Agung 1, Tukad 22 B7
Batu Agung, Tukad 22 B7
Batu Bayan 48 A2
Batu Belig 19 H3
Batu Bolong, Raya 25 H7
Batu Kancik 40 C4
Batu Karu 19 J2
Batu Lesung 40 B6
Batu Manik 40 F7
Batu Mejan 25 J5
Batu Metandal 40 D6
Batu Nunggalan 41 G7
Batu Sari (Tibu Beneng) 25 M7
Batu Sari (Tuban) 32 E2
Batukaru Beji 28 C8
Batukaru, Gunung (Klungkung) 51 E6
Batukaru, Gunung (Negara) 56 E6
Batukaru, Gunung (Singaraja) 57 F7
Batur (Padang Sambian Kelod) 20 C2

Batur (Sanur Kauh) 23 H7
Batur 1, Danau (Jimbaran) 37 K3
Batur 2, Danau (Jimbaran) 37 K3
Batur 4, Danau (Jimbaran) 37 K3
Batur Sari (Panjer, Denpasar Selatan) 22 B5
Batur Sari (Sanur Kauh) 23 J7
Batur, Danau (Gianyar) 50 E6
Batur, Gunung 15 J1
Batur, Gunung (Klungkung) 51 E6
Batur, Gunung (Negara) 56 E6
Batur, Gunung (Singaraja) 57 E8
Baung 48 C6
Bawean, Pulau 21 J5
Bayangkara 11 H1
Bedahulu (Denpasar) 29 G1
Bedahulu (Tabanan) 51 E2
Bedahulu 1 .... 28 F2
Bedahulu 2 .... 29 G2
Bedahulu 3 .... 28 F2
Bedahulu 4 .... 29 G2
Bedahulu 5 .... 28 F2
Bedahulu 6 .... 29 G2
Bedahulu 7 .... 28 F1
Bedahulu 9 .... 28 F1
Bedahulu 10 .... 28 F1
Bedahulu 11 .... 28 F1
Bedahulu 12 .... 29 G1
Bedahulu 14 .... 29 G1
Bedahulu 15 .... 29 G1
Bedahulu 16 .... 29 G1
Bedahulu 17 .... 28 F1
Bedahulu 18 .... 29 G1
Bedahulu 19 .... 28 F1
Bedahulu 20 .... 29 G1
Bedahulu 22 .... 29 G1
Bedugul (Kerobokan) 26 E3
Bedugul (Sesetan) 16 D2
Bedugul (Tabanan) 51 C3
Beji Ayu 14 E2
Bekangdam 15 L6
Bckisar 22 D8
Bekul Umanadi 20 B8
Belatu, Danau 50 E6
Belibis (Sesetan) 21 L6
Belibis (Tonja) 29 H1
Belimbing (Denpasar) 29 H6
Belimbing (Gianyar) 50 A5
Belimbing (Klungkung) 51 C6
Beliton 28 F7
Belulang Yah 25 K2
Beluran 27 G3
Bendesa 42 C4
Benesari 14 D6
Bengkel 26 F4
Beo (Denpasar) 16 B2
Beo (Kerobokan) 26 D8
Beo (Sesetan Kaja, Sesetan) 21 L6
Beraban 19 J5
Beranda 2 .... 38 C4
Beranda Raya 38 C4
Beratan, Danau (Denpasar Selatan) ... 23 J5
Beratan, Danau (Negara) 56 C6
Berlian (Dauh Puri Kelod) 21 L5
Berlian (Kerobokan Kelod) 19 L4
Besakih (Klungkung) 51 E6
Besakih (Kuta) 15 K6
Bet Ngandang 1 .... 17 K3
Bet Ngandang 2 .... 17 L4
Betet 16 B2
Bhayangkara (Amlapura) 55 E6
Bhayangkara (Gianyar) 50 B6
Bhayangkara 1 .... 50 C6
Bhayangkara 2 .... 50 C6
Bhayangkara 3 .... 50 C6
Bhinneka Jatijaya 11 H4
Bhuana Shanti 4 .... 26 F1
Biak, Pulau 21 J2
Bidadari 19 L6
Bidadari 2A 19 L6
Bidadari 9 .... 19 L6
Bikini 20 C4
Bikini 1A 20 C3
Bikini 3 .... 20 C3
Billiard 19 M8
Bilok, Tukad 23 H6
Bima (Bangli) 54 D3
Bima (Kerobokan Kelod) 19 L1
Bima (Kerobokan) 26 D5
Bima (Renon) 22 E6
Bima (Tibu Beneng) 26 B6
Bimasena 56 A4
Bina 19 L8
Binas, Tukad 32 D4
Bingin Sari 37 G5
Bintan 5 .... 26 C3
Bintang Buana 20 D1
Bisma (Bangli) 54 D2
Bisma (Benoa) 38 E5
Bisma (Dangin Puri Kauh) 28 F5
Bisma (Singaraja) 57 D6
Bisma (Ubud) 46 D3
Bisma Raya (Singaraja) 57 D7
Biu, Yeh 21 L6
Blambangan (Bangli) 54 D2
Blambangan (Kuta) 14 E8
Blambangan (Tabanan) 51 E2
Blimang Sari 42 B5
Blimbing (Denpasar) 29 G6
Blimbing (Bangli) 54 D5

Blimbing (Singaraja) 57 C8
Blimbing Sari 1 .... 42 F6
Blok C 56 C1
Blong Bidadari 36 C6
Blubuh Sari 1 .... 26 F1
Blubuh Sari 2 .... 26 F1
Blubuh Sari 3 .... 26 F1
Blubuh Sari 4 .... 26 F1
Blubuh Sari 5 .... 26 F1
Blubuh Sari 6 .... 26 F1
Blubuh Sari 7 .... 26 F1
Blubuh Sari 8 .... 26 F1
Bonsai 20 E3
Boom Baba 19 K3
Bougenville (Jimbaran) 32 F7
Bougenville (Kuta) 38 D5
Bougenville (Negara) 56 C1
Braban 19 H6
Bratan Gang 22, Danau 23 K3
Brumahanyar 49 J1
Buaji 29 M4
Buaji Agung 1 .... 23 G1
Buaji Agung 2 .... 23 G1
Buaji Agung 3 .... 23 G1
Buaji, Tukad 21 M7
Bualu Indah (Bualu) 39 G5
Buana Alit 20 D2
Buana Asri 20 D1
Buana Ayu 20 D1
Buana Dwipa 20 D2
Buana Giri 20 D1
Buana Kubu 20 E2
Buana Lestari 20 D1
Buana Mekar 20 D1
Buana Merta 20 D1
Buana Putra 20 D1
Buana Putri 20 D1
Buana Raya 20 D2
Buana Sari 34 E8
Buana Tori 20 D1
Buaya 22 F7
Bucu 26 D5
Buduk, Raya 48 C7
Bugis 19 J6
Bukit Damai 36 E4
Bukit Hijau 36 D4
Bukit Jati 50 F5
Bukit Lestari 36 E4
Bukit Permai 32 A8
Bukit Tunggal 28 E8
Bulakan Sari 38 C1
Bulan Bali 19 J3
Buluh Indah 28 A5
Buluh Indah 1 .... 28 B6
Buluh Indah 3 .... 28 B5
Buluh Indah 4 .... 28 B5
Buluh Indah 5A 28 B5
Buluh Indah 6 .... 28 B5
Buluh Indah 7 .... 28 B5
Buluh Indah, Raya 28 A5
Bumbak 26 B6
Bumbak Dauh 26 B8
Bumbak Daun 26 B7
Bumbak Kauh 18 F1
Bumi Ayu (Denpasar) 28 B6
Bumi Ayu 3 .... 23 L8
Bumi Ayu B 28 B6
Bumi Ayu E 28 B6
Bumi Ayu F 28 B7
Bumi Ayu G 28 B6
Bumi Ayu H 28 B7
Bumi Ayu I 28 B6
Bumi Ayu J 28 B7
Bumi Jimbaran Asri 36 F5
Bumiayu (Sanur) 23 L8
Bumiayu 1 (Sanur) 23 L8
Bumiayu 2 (Sanur) 23 L8
Bumiayu 3 (Sanur) 23 L8
Bumiayu 4 (Sanur) 23 L8
Bung Tomo 28 C3
Bung Tomo 8 .... 28 C4
Bunga Ungu 19 G4
Bungin 1 .... 21 H6
Bungin, Pulau 21 J7
Buni 29 J1
Buni Sari 14 E8
Buntu (Panjer) 21 M4
Buntu (Seminyak) 19 L7
Buntu (Tegal Kerta) 28 A7
Buntut 19 J3
Burung Gereja 50 C5
Buton, Pulau (Denpasar Barat) .. 21 K5
Buton, Pulau (Negara) 56 F6
Buus, Tukad 32 D4
Buyan 1, Danau (Denpasar) .. 23 J6
Buyan 2, Danau (Denpasar) .. 23 J5
Buyan 3, Danau (Denpasar) .. 23 J6
Buyan 4, Danau (Denpasar) .. 23 K5
Buyan 5, Danau (Denpasar) .. 23 K6
Buyan Barat, Danau (Kuta) ... 37 K3
Buyan, Danau (Denpasar) 23 J6
Buyan, Danau (Gianyar) 50 E6
Buyan, Danau (Kuta) 37 K3
Buyan, Danau (Negara) 56 C7
Bypass (Gianyar) 50 A7

C

Cafuspata 32 D4
Calonarang 39 H5
Camar (Denpasar Selatan) 21 L6

Camar (Tabanan) 51 D1
Camplung Tanduk/ Dhyana Pura .. 19 K8
Campuan 5 .... 48 D7
Campuan Ridge Walk 46 C1
Campuan, Raya 46 B1
Candi Beach 52 B7
Candidasa 53 L5
Candidasa, Raya 52 E7
Candra Asih 31 J4
Candra Metu 30 F1
Canggu 26 E8
Canggu Padang Linjong 25 J5
Canggu Permai 1 .... 25 M5
Canggu Permai 2 .... 25 M6
Canggu, Raya (Canggu) 25 L2
Canggu, Raya (Kerobokan) ... 26 E4
Cargo 19 J6
Cargo Indah 28 B1
Cargo Indah 2 .... 28 B1
Cargo Indah 4 .... 28 A1
Cargo Permai 28 B2
Carik 26 C7
Carik 1 .... 28 C7
Carik 2 .... 28 B7
Carik 3 .... 28 B7
Catur 2A 28 A2
Cava, Tukad 22 C5
Celagi Basur 32 C8
Celagi Nunggul 45 J3
Celepuk 23 G5
Celuk 2 .... 23 J7
Celuk 3 .... 23 J8
Celuk 4 .... 23 J8
Celukbuluh 53 J4
Celuring 30 C8
Cemara (Kerobokan Kelod) ... 26 D8
Cemara (Kesiman) 30 C7
Cemara (Pedungan) 21 K7
Cemara (Sanur) 17 K5
Cemara (Tibu Beneng) 25 M7
Cemara 1, Gunung (Denpasar Barat) .. 20 F2
Cemara, Gunung (Denpasar Barat) .. 20 F2
Cemara, Gunung (Gianyar) ... 50 E6
Cempaka (Denpasar Barat) ... 21 K2
Cempaka (Gelogor Carik) 15 H3
Cempaka (Jimbaran) 32 F7
Cempaka (Kerobokan Kelod) .. 19 G5
Cempaka (Kesiman Petilan) .. 30 B5
Cempaka (Klungkung) 51 D7
Cempaka (Renon) 23 G4
Cempaka (Sanur) 23 K8
Cempaka (Sekuta) 17 K1
Cempaka (Sesetan) 21 M7
Cempaka (Singaraja) 57 B5
Cempaka (Sumerta Kaja) 29 J4
Cempaka (Ubung) 28 D2
Cempaka Biru Selatan 2 .... 28 A3
Cempaka Gading 36 D7
Cempaka Putih 30 D1
Cendrawasih (Bangli) 54 C4
Cendrawasih (Dangin Puri Kaja) .. 29 H3
Cendrawasih (Dauh Puri Kelod) .. 21 K3
Cendrawasih (Gianyar) 50 C5
Cendrawasih (Kali Bukbuk) ... 53 J4
Cendrawasih (Kerobokan Kelod) .. 19 G4
Cendrawasih (Negara) 56 F2
Cendrawasih (Sidakarya) 16 E2
Cendrawasih (Singaraja) 57 C4
Cendrawasih (Tabanan) 51 C2
Cengan Sari 4 .... 22 F1
Cengan Sari 5 .... 22 F1
Cengan Sari 6 .... 22 F1
Cengan Sari 9 .... 23 G1
Cengan Sari 7 .... 16 C2
Cening Sari 16 C3
Cening Sari 3 .... 16 C3
Cening Sari 4 .... 16 C3
Ceningan, Pulau 21 J4
Ceroring (Dangin Puri Kauh) .. 29 H6
Ceroring (Kerobokan Kelod) .. 19 J1
Ceroring (Seminyak) 19 L7
Cilincing, Tukad 22 D6
Ciliwung 2, Tukad 22 D6
Ciliwung, Tukad 22 D6
Citarum 1, Tukad 22 D5
Citarum 3, Tukad 22 D5
Citarum 5, Tukad 22 D5
Citarum F1, Tukad 22 D6
Citarum M, Tukad 22 D7
Citarum O, Tukad 22 D7
Citarum P, Tukad 22 D7
Citarum, Tukad 22 D7
Ciung Wanara (Denpasar Timur) .. 22 D4
Ciung Wanara (Gianyar) 50 B6
Ciung Wanara 1 .... 22 D4
Ciung Wanara 2 .... 22 D4
Ciung Wanara 4 .... 22 D4
Ciung Wanara 5 .... 22 D4
Ciung Wanara 6 .... 22 D4
Cokorda Agung Tresna 22 C2
Cokorda Putra Selatan 47 G4
Cuculan 15 H3
Curik (Kerobokan Kelod) 19 H1
Curik (Pedungan) 16 A2
Curug Tiga 10 E5
Cut Nyak Dien 22 C3

D

D.I. Panjaitan 22 C3
Daha 28 E2

Dahlia (Dangin Puri Kangin) .. 29 J4
Dahlia (Dauh Puri, Denpasar Utara) .. 21 K2
Dahlia (Kesiman Kertha Langu) .. 31 H4
Dahlia (Kesiman) 30 C6
Dahlia (Padang Sambian Kelod) .. 20 C4
Dahlia (Pemecutan Kaja) 28 A4
Dahlia (Singaraja) 57 C4
Daksina 26 E6
Dalem 38 D3
Dalem Gede 25 J3
Dalem Lingsir 25 G4
Dalem Penataran 25 G4
Dalem Rai 50 D7
Dalem Warung 25 K1
Dam T. Badung 20 F6
Damai (Kerobokan Kaja) 26 E2
Damai (Panjer) 22 A7
Damai 1 .... 26 E2
Damai 5 .... 26 E2
Damar 21 H8
Danau Batur (Sanur Kaja) 23 K5
Danau Batur (Tibu Beneng) .. 26 C2
Danau Batur 1 .... 26 D2
Danau Buyan 17 M3
Danau Poso 17 J4
Danau Tamblingan 17 L3
Danau Tempe 17 G4
Danau Tempe 1 .... 17 H3
Danau Tondano 4 .... 17 K1
Danau Tondano 5 .... 23 J6
Dangin Utama 15 K3
Dapdap 21 G7
Darma 19 H2
Darma Wangsa 38 E5
Darmajaya 22 B7
Dastarata 54 E2
Daton 23 K7
Dawas 26 E1
Dawas, Raya 26 E1
Debes (Kerobokan) 29 G8
Debes (Tabanan) 51 F3
Dedari Villa 37 G6
Delapan 17 K2
Delima (Kesiman) 30 B8
Delima (Padang Sambian) 28 A8
Delod Peken 23 H6
Demulih 54 A4
Dermaga 12 D5
Dermaga 1 .... 12 E6
Dermaga 2 .... 12 E5
Desa Sawangan 45 J1
Dewa, Gang 21 H4
Dewata (Seminyak) 19 K7
Dewata (Sidakarya) 16 D2
Dewata 1 .... 16 D3
Dewata 2 .... 16 E2
Dewata 4 .... 16 E2
Dewata Indah 16 E2
Dewi Chandra 30 F1
Dewi Kunti 29 M8
Dewi Kunti (Singaraja) 57 E4
Dewi Madri 29 L8
Dewi Madri 1 .... 22 E2
Dewi Madri 2 .... 22 E2
Dewi Madri 3 .... 22 E2
Dewi Madri 4 .... 22 E1
Dewi Madri 5 .... 22 E1
Dewi Madri 9 .... 22 E1
Dewi Saraswati 19 J2
Dewi Saraswati 2 .... 19 M6
Dewi Saraswati 3 .... 19 M7
Dewi Sartika (Denpasar Barat) .. 21 L3
Dewi Sartika (Klungkung) 51 D5
Dewi Sartika (Kuta) 10 F5
Dewi Sartika (Singaraja) 57 C4
Dewi Sita (Seminyak) 19 M8
Dewi Sita (Singaraja) 57 E4
Dewi Sri (Pemogan) 15 H3
Dewi Sri (Renon) 22 F8
Dewi Sri (Seminyak) 14 E4
Dewi Sri 1 .... 14 E3
Dewi Sri 4 .... 14 E3
Dewi Sri 5 .... 31 G1
Dewi Sri 7 .... 31 G1
Dewi Supraba 29 J3
Dewi Uma (Renon) 22 F8
Dewi Uma (Sumerta Kelod) .. 29 L8
Dewisita 46 E4
Dharma Wangsa (Kutuh) 44 B3
Dharmawangsa (Benoa) 38 A7
Dharmawangsa (Klungkung) .. 51 E7
Dharmawangsa (Tabanan) 51 E3
Dieng 6 .... 20 C2
Dieng 7 .... 20 C2
Dieng 9 .... 20 C2
Dieng 10 .... 20 C2
Diponegoro (Amlapura) 55 D5
Diponegoro (Denpasar) 21 L1
Diponegoro (Klungkung) 51 E6
Diponegoro (Singaraja) 57 D3
Dipta, Kapten 50 D7
Dona 25 M8
Drona 19 J7
Drupadi (Seminyak) 19 J8
Drupadi (Singaraja) 57 E4
Drupadi (Sumerta Kelod) 29 K8
Drupadi 1.(Seminyak) 19 K7
Drupadi 1 (Denpasar Timur) .. 22 D2
Drupadi 3 .... 19 J8

Drupadi 2 .... 22 D2
Drupadi 3 .... 22 D2
Drupadi 4 .... 22 D2
Drupadi 5 .... 22 D1
Drupadi 6 .... 22 D1
Drupadi 7 .... 29 K8
Drupadi 10 .... 22 D1
Drupadi 11 .... 29 L8
Drupadi 12 .... 29 K8
Drupadi 13 .... 22 D1
Drupadi 13 .... 22 D1
Drupadi 14 .... 29 L8
Drupadi 15 .... 29 L8
Drupadi 16 .... 29 K8
Drupadi 17 .... 29 L8
Dua Dara Motor 40 D6
Dugdugan, Lettu 55 D1
Dukuh (Bangli) 54 A1
Dukuh (Tabanan) 51 C3
Dukuh (Ubud) 47 M5
Dukuh Anyar 20 D7
Dukuh Indah 19 K1
Dukuh Sari 23 G6
Durian (Dangin Puri Kauh) ... 29 G6
Durian (Negara) 56 C7
Durian (Padang Sambian) 28 A8
Durian (Singaraja) 57 C8
Durian (Tabanan) 51 D3
Duyung 18 D1
Dwarawati (Benoa, Kuta) 39 H5
Dwarawati (Jimbaran, Kuta) .. 32 F8
Dwi Indah 22 F8
Dwi Jendra 50 E7

E

Elang (Kuta) 36 C6
Elang (Padang Sambian Kelod) .. 20 C1
Elang (Tabanan) 51 C1
Elang (Tuban) 11 G6
Empel, Tukad 22 B8
Empu Gandring 28 E1
Empu Tantular 48 D1
Erlangga 57 D2
Esa 20 A2
Esna 19 H7
Ester 19 K4

F

Fajar Utama 57 A8
Family 21 .... 22 A7
Flamboyan (Klungkung) 51 B7
Flamboyan (Denpasar Timur) .. 22 E3
Flamboyan (Panjer) 22 B7
Flamboyan (Pemogan) 15 H3
Flores (Canggu) 25 M7
Flores, Pulau (Denpasar Barat) .. 21 J4
Flores, Pulau (Singaraja) 57 E2
Foxy 30 C6
Frangipani 25 H4
Futsal 15 H2

G

Gada 21 M4
Gadon 1 .... 26 F4
Gadon 2 .... 26 F4
Gadung (Batu Bulan) 31 K3
Gadung (Dangin Puri Kangin) .. 29 J6
Gadung (Kesiman Kertha Langu) .. 31 J4
Gadung (Pedungan) 21 K7
Gadung (Sesetan) 21 M7
Gadung (Sumerta Kauh) 29 K6
Gagak 16 E4
Gajah Mada (Amlapura) 55 E5
Gajah Mada (Denpasar) 28 F7
Gajah Mada (Klungkung) 51 E5
Gajah Mada (Singaraja) 57 E6
Gajah Mada (Tabanan) 51 D3
Galang 1, Gunung 15 J1
Galang 1, Pulau 20 F8
Galang, Pulau 20 C6
Galeria 23 J5
Galung 28 E6
Gambuh 36 E4
Ganag Buanasari 36 E4
Ganda Pura 30 D4
Ganda Pura 1 .... 30 D4
Ganda Pura 1G 30 D4
Ganda Pura 2 .... 30 D4
Ganda Pura 3 .... 30 D4
Ganda Pura 3G 30 D4
Ganesha 43 G3
Ganetri 1 .... 29 K3
Ganetri 3 .... 29 L3
Gang 1 (Dauh Puri Kaja) 28 F4
Gang 1 (Tonja) 29 K2
Gang 2 (Dauh Puri Kaja) 28 F4
Gang 2 (Tonja) 29 K2
Gang 3 (Dauh Puri Kaja) 28 F4
Gang 3 (Kerobokan Kelod) 19 G2
Gang 4 (Kesiman Petilan) 30 A4
Gang 4 (Tibu Beneng) 26 B3
Gang 5 .... 29 G4
Gang 6 .... 19 G2
Gang 7 (Kerobokan Kelod) 19 G2
Gang 8 .... 27 H8
Gang 9 (Dangin Puri Kaja) 29 G4
Gang 9 (Kerobokan Kelod) 19 G2
Gang 10 (Dangin Puri Kaja) .. 29 G4
Gang 10 (Kerobokan Kelod) .. 19 G2

Street Index

Gang 11.....28 F4
Gang 12.....29 G4
Gang 15.....19 H2
Gang 16 (Kerobokan Kelod).....19 G2
Gang 17.....19 G2
Gang 18.....19 H3
Gang 21.....19 H3
Gang 28.....29 M2
Gang 385.....19 M5
Gang Arwana.....31 L3
Gang Balai (BPPT).....15 M6
Gang Batu Merah.....26 B8
Gang Bija.....31 G2
Gang Bisma.....25 K6
Gang Bukit.....31 L1
Gang Bungin.....15 L1
Gang Citra.....17 H4
Gang Drona.....27 G4
Gang Gadon.....26 F3
Gang I. L..... 29 L2
Gang Jepun 1.....41 J2
Gang Mawar.....26 B5
Gang Medori.....31 H3
Gang Padi.....31 G2
Gang Palapa.....10 F5
Gang Suli.....31 H4
Gang Triti.....29 H2
Gang Tukad Balian.....17 G4
Gang Uma Anyar.....31 G5
Gang VI.....32 C3
Gang Wrja.....38 D5
Gangga (Dauh Puri Kauh).....21 K2
Gangga (Pemecutan Kaja).....28 C6
Gangga 1.....28 C6
Gangga 2.....28 C6
Gangga 3.....28 C6
Gangga 4.....28 C6
Gangga 4, Tukad.....22 B4
Gangga, Yeh.....51 A3
Gangsian.....26 E6
Garuda (Dangin Puri Kelod).....22 A2
Garuda (Dauh Puri Kelod).....21 K3
Garuda (Kuta).....36 C6
Garuda (Panjer).....22 D8
Garuda (Renon).....22 F7
Garuda (Sesetan).....16 B3
Garuda (Ubung).....28 D3
Garuda Wisnu Kencana.....36 E6
Gatot Subroto (Dauh Puri Kaja).....28 F2
Gatot Subroto (Negara).....56 D5
Gatot Subroto (Tabanan).....51 F3
Gatot Subroto (Tonja).....29 J2
Gatot Subroto 1.....29 G1
Gatot Subroto 1-1.....29 G2
Gatot Subroto 1-10.....29 H1
Gatot Subroto 1-11.....29 G1
Gatot Subroto 1-12.....29 H1
Gatot Subroto 1-13.....29 G1
Gatot Subroto 1-14.....29 G1
Gatot Subroto 1-15.....29 G1
Gatot Subroto 1-16.....29 G1
Gatot Subroto 1-17.....29 G1
Gatot Subroto 1-18.....29 H1
Gatot Subroto 1-19.....29 G1
Gatot Subroto 1-2.....29 H2
Gatot Subroto 1-3.....29 H1
Gatot Subroto 1-4.....29 H1
Gatot Subroto 1-5.....29 G2
Gatot Subroto 1-6.....29 H1
Gatot Subroto 1-7.....29 G2
Gatot Subroto 1-8.....29 G1
Gatot Subroto 1-9.....29 G1
Gatot Subroto 1/23.....29 G2
Gatot Subroto 2.....29 G2
Gatot Subroto 2 (Tabanan).....51 F4
Gatot Subroto 4.....29 G2
Gatot Subroto 4-11.....29 G3
Gatot Subroto 4-K.....29 G3
Gatot Subroto 6.....28 F3
Gatot Subroto 6-A.....28 F2
Gatot Subroto 6-B.....28 F2
Gatot Subroto 6-C.....28 F2
Gatot Subroto 6-D.....28 F2
Gatot Subroto 6-E.....28 F2
Gatot Subroto 6-F.....28 F2
Gatot Subroto 6-G.....29 G3
Gatot Subroto 6-H.....28 F3
Gatot Subroto 6-I.....28 F3
Gatot Subroto 6-J.....28 F3
Gatot Subroto 6-L.....28 F3
Gatot Subroto 6-M.....29 G3
Gatot Subroto 6-N.....28 F3
Gatot Subroto 6-O.....28 F3
Gatot Subroto 6-P.....28 F3
Gatot Subroto 6-Q.....28 F3
Gatot Subroto 6-R.....28 F3
Gatot Subroto 6-S.....28 F3
Gatot Subroto 6-T.....28 F3
Gatot Subroto Barat Bypass.....28 B2
Gatot Subroto Timur Bypass.....30 C2
Gatot Subroto, Jendral (Amlapura).....55 D5
Gatotkaca (Denpasar).....28 F6
Gatotkaca (Singaraja).....57 D6
Gebun, Kapten.....55 E5
Gede 1, Gunung.....20 E1
Gede, Serma.....21 L3
Gedong Sari (Benoa).....38 D1
Gedong Sari (Kerobokan Kelod).....19 K3
Gejer, Serma.....55 E2
Gelatik (Gianyar).....50 C6

Gelatik (Jimbaran).....36 C6
Gelatik (Kerobokan Kelod).....19 G3
Gelatik (Negara).....56 E3
Gelatik (Pemecutan Kaja).....28 D3
Gelatik (Pemecutan Kelod).....20 E7
Gelatik (Sidakarya).....16 E1
Gelatik (Tabanan).....51 C2
Gelatik 1 (Negara).....56 E3
Gelatik 2 (Negara).....56 E3
Gelogor Asri.....15 H3
Gelogor Carik.....15 G7
Gelogor Indah.....15 H4
Gelora.....21 H2
Gelumpang.....55 D1
Gelumpang, Raya.....55 B1
Gemitir.....30 F3
Gemitir (Klungkung).....51 C8
Gemitis.....31 H4
Gempol.....57 F5
Genata.....30 C8
Genetri.....29 K2
Gentong, Raya.....49 H1
Geraytuakilang.....51 C1
Gerinding, Tukad.....21 M5
Gigitsari.....32 C7
Gili Tepekung.....21 K4
Gilibiaha 1.....21 K4
Giri Kencana.....36 F5
Gita Kencana.....36 D3
GM Pulasari, Gang.....38 D4
GM Taman Sari, Gang.....38 D4
Goa Gajah 1.....49 J7
Goa Gajah, Raya.....49 J7
Goa Gong (Jimbaran).....37 H6
Goa Gong (Ungasan).....43 L1
Goa Lempeh.....41 L8
Godel.....19 M3
Gopal.....23 G1
Goris, DR.....21 M3
Goutama.....46 F4
Goutama Selatan.....46 F4
Graha Wisata.....16 E4
Green Kori 3.....16 A5
Greya Giri.....22 A8
Gria Muding Sari.....27 H4
Griya Anyar.....15 G7
Grudugan, Tukad.....22 B8
Grya Indah.....28 A5
Gubuk Sari.....44 B2
Guming, Tukad.....13 K2
Gumuk Sari.....16 C2
Gunung Abang.....28 B8
Gunung Agung.....28 A6
Gunung Arjuna.....20 B4
Gunung Atena.....19 M6
Gunung Batukaru.....28 C8
Gunung Batukaru 6.....28 D8
Gunung Batur.....28 C7
Gunung Bromo.....28 B8
Gunung Catur 2.....28 A2
Gunung Catur 4.....28 A2
Gunung Dorolonda.....20 D4
Gunung Fujiyama.....28 B4
Gunung Fujiyama 1.....28 B4
Gunung Fujiyama 1 B.....28 B4
Gunung Fujiyama 1 C.....28 B4
Gunung Fujiyama 1A.....28 B4
Gunung Fujiyama 2.....28 B4
Gunung Fujiyama 3.....28 B4
Gunung Indian.....20 C3
Gunung Indrakila.....28 A4
Gunung Indrakila 1.....28 B8
Gunung Kapur.....28 B8
Gunung Karang 3.....21 G1
Gunung Kawi.....28 E7
Gunung Kelimutu 7.....21 G3
Gunung Kelimutu 9.....21 G3
Gunung Kelimutu 10.....20 F3
Gunung Kelimutu 19.....21 G3
Gunung Kerinci.....28 E8
Gunung Krakatau.....28 D8
Gunung Lebah.....20 E2
Gunung Lebah 1.....20 F2
Gunung Lumur.....20 C4
Gunung Lumut 1.....20 D5
Gunung Mangu.....20 G1
Gunung Mas.....20 C1
Gunung Merapi.....28 D7
Gunung Merbuk.....28 A8
Gunung Muliawan.....28 B8
Gunung Patas.....27 H8
Gunung Payung.....11 H1
Gunung Payung 1.....20 B6
Gunung Payung I.....45 K3
Gunung Penulisan.....28 E8
Gunung Resimuka.....28 B8
Gunung Resimuka Barat.....28 A8
Gunung Resimuka Barat 1.....28 A8
Gunung Ringin 1.....20 F2
Gunung Ringin 2.....20 F2
Gunung Salak.....27 G7
Gunung Sanghiang.....27 H5
Gunung Sari.....47 J4
Gunung Sari 4.....20 F3
Gunung Sewu.....20 C3
Gunung Slamet.....20 B5
Gunung Soputan.....20 B5
Gunung Soputan 1.....20 E7
Gunung Talang.....20 D4
Gunung Talang 8.....20 D4

Gunung Talang Selatan.....20 D4
Gunung Tambora.....28 E8
Gunung Tangkuban Perahu.....19 L3
Gunung Ungaran.....28 D8
Gunung Welirang.....28 D8
Gunung Wilis.....20 C2
Gurita.....16 B4
Gurita 1.....16 B4
Gurita 3.....16 B4
Gurita 4.....16 B3

H

H.O.S Cokroaminoto.....28 C1
Halmahera, Pulau.....21 L4
Handayani.....22 B8
Hang Tuah.....23 J4
Hanoman (Kerobokan Kelod).....19 L2
Hanoman (Ubud).....46 F5
Harum.....23 G6
Hasanudin (Amlapura).....55 C5
Hasanudin (Denpasar).....28 F8
Hasanudin (Gianyar).....50 B8
Hasanudin (Klungkung).....51 B5
Hasanudin (Singaraja).....57 D2
Hasanudin (Tabanan).....51 E1
Hawai.....51 C8
Hawai 1.....51 C8
Hawai 2.....51 C8
Hayam Wuruk (Babakan Sari).....22 F2
Hayam Wuruk (Klungkung).....51 D4
Hayam Wuruk (Sumerta Kelod).....29 L7
Himalaya.....28 B4
Hiu.....25 K8
Hubdam.....15 K6
Hubdam 1.....15 L6
Hubdam 2.....15 L5
Hubdam 3.....15 L5
Hubdam 4.....15 L5
Hubdam 5.....15 K5
Hubdam 6.....15 K5

I

I Gusti Gede Sunandi.....11 G5
Ida Bagus Manik (Sukma).....47 G6
Ida Bagus Mantra, Prof. Dr., Bypass (Kesiman).....31 J5
Ida Bagus Mantra, Prof Dr., Bypass (Klungkung).....66 D7
Ida Bagus Oka, Dr.....21 M4
Ijo Gading, Tukad.....22 B5
Ikan Karper.....16 C4
Ikan Tongkol.....16 D5
Ikan Tuna (Sesetan).....16 C5
Ikan Tuna 1 (Benoa Harbor).....12 D6
Ikan Tuna 2 (Benoa Harbor).....12 D6
Ikan Tuna 3 (Benoa Harbor).....12 D5
Ikan Tuna Raya Barat.....12 D6
Ikan Tuna Raya Timur.....12 E5
Imam Bonjol (Denpasar Barat).....21 J2
Imam Bonjol (Klungkung).....51 D6
Imam Bonjol (Pemecutan Kelod).....15 G4
Imam Bonjol (Pemecutan).....28 E8
Imam Bonjol (Singaraja).....57 D2
Imbora.....21 H2
Impossible Beach.....34 E6
Indah, Pulau.....21 G5
Indra.....19 L1
Indrakila.....30 B2
Indrakila Ujung 1.....28 A8
Indrakila Ujung 2.....28 A8
Indraprasta.....36 D7
Indus.....28 B5
Inna Grand Bali Beach.....23 L5
Intan.....26 D8
Intan LC-2.....29 H1
Intan LC-2/4.....29 H2
Intan LC-2/6.....29 H1
Intan Permai.....19 L4
Intan Sari.....19 L4
Intaran.....23 H6
Inti Kulit.....19 J6
IPLT.....15 M6
Irian.....36 C5
Irrawadi, Tukad.....21 M6

J

Jago.....19 M5
Jakarta.....36 C5
Jala Suci.....29 G2
Jalak (Kuta).....36 C6
Jalak (Singaraja).....57 B4
Jalak (Tegal Kerta).....28 B7
Jalak (Tibu Beneng).....25 K7
Jalak Bali.....16 B2
Jalak Putih.....51 C1
Jalan 157.....21 M8
Jambu.....27 H5
Jantuk Angsa.....25 H1
Japa, Kapten.....29 H8
Jata.....50 C6
Jatayu (Dangin Puri Kangin).....29 H4
Jatayu (Seminyak).....19 K7
Jatayu (Singaraja).....57 B3
Jatayu (Tibu Beneng).....25 L6
Jatayu (Tonja).....29 H1
Jatayu (Ubud).....46 F6
Jatayu (Ubung).....28 D2
Jatayu 1.....28 E2
Jatayu 2.....28 E2

Jati Indah.....19 M5
Jawa, Pulau.....56 F7
Jaya Giri.....29 J8
Jaya Giri 1.....22 B2
Jaya Giri 2.....22 C2
Jaya Giri 3.....22 B2
Jaya Giri 4.....22 C2
Jaya Giri 5.....22 B2
Jaya Giri 7.....22 B1
Jaya Giri 8.....22 C2
Jaya Giri 10.....22 C1
Jaya Giri 11.....22 B1
Jaya Giri 12.....22 C1
Jaya Giri 13.....22 B1
Jaya Giri 14.....22 C1
Jaya Giri 15.....29 J8
Jaya Giri 16.....29 J8
Jaya Giri 17.....29 J8
Jaya Giri 18.....29 J8
Jaya Giri 19.....29 J8
Jaya Giri 20.....29 J8
Jaya Giri 21.....29 J8
Jaya Giri 22.....29 J8
Jaya Giri 23.....29 J8
Jaya Tirtha.....55 D3
Jaya, Letda.....29 H7
Jayakarta.....28 E2
Jayakarta 1.....28 F2
Jayakarta 2.....28 F2
Jayakarta 3.....28 F2
Jayakarta 4.....28 F2
Jayakarta 5.....28 F2
Jayanegara.....50 B8
Jelantik.....55 D4
Jembawan.....46 F5
Jempiring (Dangin Puri Kangin).....29 H6
Jempiring (Klungkung).....51 C7
Jempiring (Negara).....56 D3
Jempiring (Seminyak).....20 A8
Jempiring (Ubud).....28 C1
Jenggala.....15 K5
Jepon.....25 L7
Jepun (Dangin Puri Kangin).....29 J6
Jepun (Jimbaran).....36 C4
Jepun (Kerobokan Kelod).....19 J2
Jepun (Klungkung).....51 D8
Jepun (Padang Sambian Kelod).....20 A1
Jepun (Sanur Kaja).....23 H3
Jepun (Sanur).....23 K8
Jepun (Seminyak).....19 K7
Jepun (Sesetan).....21 L7
Jepun (Tibu Beneng).....25 L8
Jepun (Ubung).....28 D2
Jepun Dadu.....30 C2
Jepun Kuning.....30 D2
Jepun Pipil.....30 D2
Jepun Pipil 2.....30 D2
Jepun Pipil 3.....30 D2
Jepun Pipil 5.....30 D2
Jepun Putih.....30 D2
Jero Gedung.....47 H3
Jeruk.....55 A7
Jeruk (Batu Bulan).....31 G1
Jeruk (Kesiman).....30 C8
Jeruk (Tonja).....29 J1
Jerutis.....30 B8
Jimbaran IX, Tukad.....37 L1
Jimbaran VII, Tukad.....37 L1
Jimbaran X, Tukad.....37 L1
Jimbaran XI, Tukad.....37 L1
Jimbaran XIV, Tukad.....37 L1
Jinah 1, Tukad.....22 B4
Jinah 3, Tukad.....22 B4
Jinah 5, Tukad.....22 B4
Jinah, Tukad.....22 B4
Jinah, Yeh.....50 E6
Jodog, Serma.....21 L3
Jogja.....36 C5
Juanda Karta Wijaya.....22 D3
Jukut Paku.....48 D8
Juwet Sari.....15 J4

K

K.H. Saman Hudi.....55 A7
K.S. Tubun.....51 E2
Kadal, Gang.....21 K4
Kae, Pulau.....21 K5
Kahuripan.....42 E2
Kahyangan.....19 H7
Kajeng.....46 E2
Kajeng, Letda.....22 B2
Kakatua (Sesetan).....21 L5
Kakatua (Tabanan).....51 D1
Kakatua (Ubung).....28 E2
Kalantaka.....50 D6
Kali akah.....56 A1
Kali Asem (Gianyar).....50 B6
Kalianget.....11 H1
Kaliasem.....29 G7
Kalibukbuk 4.....53 H4
Kalibukbuk, Raya.....53 H4
Kalimantan, Pulau.....57 L1
Kalpataru 1.....36 A7
Kamboja (Dangin Puri Kangin).....29 H6
Kamboja (Kerobokan Kelod).....19 H2
Kamboja (Kerobokan).....27 H6
Kamboja (Klungkung).....51 B6
Kamboja (Kuta).....11 H2

Street Index

Kamboja (Padang Sambian) 28 A4
Kamboja (Pedungan) 21 K7
Kamboja (Tabanan) 51 C3
Kamboja 3 .... 28 A4
Kamboja 5 .... 28 A4
Kamboja 10 .... 28 A5
Kampus Udayana 37 H4
Kanita 29 H5
Kanna 19 G6
Kapal, Raya 25 J1
Karang 1, Gunung 21 H2
Karang 2, Gunung 21 H1
Karang Mas Sejahtera 36 C3
Karang Putih 43 M6
Karang Sari (Denpasar Barat) 20 B3
Karang Sari (Sanur) 17 L3
Karang, Gunung 21 H2
Karma Kandara 42 F7
Karna (Dangin Puri Kauh) 28 F6
Karna (Ubud) 46 E4
Kartika (Dauh Puri) 29 G8
Kartika (Denpasar Selatan) 21 J6
Kartika (Kerobokan) 26 D8
Kartika (Kuta) 14 D8
Kartika 1 .... 29 G8
Kartika 2 .... 29 G8
Kartini (Denpasar) 28 F5
Kartini (Gianyar) 50 B8
Kartini (Klungkung) 51 D6
Kartini (Singaraja) 57 C5
Kartini, R.A. (Amlapura) 55 D2
Karya 27 H5
Kasna 29 J5
Kasuari (Sanglah, Denpasar) 21 L5
Kaswari (Dangin Puri Kaja, Denpasar) 29 H3
Kaswari (Singaraja) 57 B3
Kaswari (Tabanan) 51 C2
Katalia 29 H3
Katalia Pasek 21 M7
Katamso 51 E2
Katos, Serma 21 L3
Katrangan 29 L6
Kawasan Nusa Dua Resort 39 K5
Kawe 1, Pulau 21 J5
Kawe 2, Pulau 21 J5
Kawe, Pulau 21 J5
Kayu Aya/ Laksmana 19 H6
Kayu Cempaka 26 E5
Kayu Cendana 19 H6
Kayu Ceruring 26 E5
Kayu Jati 19 H6
Kayu Jati 1 .... 19 G6
Kayu Manis 25 L4
Kayu Meranti 26 F5
Kayu Nangka 26 F5
Kayu Tasak 26 F5
Kayu Tulang 25 L4
Kebak Sari 20 E7
Keboiwa (Klungkung) 51 D6
Keboliwa 50 B8
Kebon Sari (Negara) 56 D2
Kebon Sari (Singaraja) 57 D2
Kebudayaan 16 E4
Kecak 29 J2
Kecapi 19 H5
Kecubung (Denpasar) 29 K6
Kecubung (Klungkung) 51 C8
Kecubung (Singaraja) 57 C5
Kecubung Sari 31 L2
Kedawatan 48 B3
Kedewatan 1 .... 48 D3
Kedewatan 2 .... 48 D4
Kediri (Bangli) 54 D2
Kediri (Tuban) 11 F4
Kediri, Raya (Tuban) 11 G4
Kedondong (Denpasar) 29 G6
Kedondong (Gianyar) 50 C6
Kedondong (Negara) 56 C7
Kejanti (Denpasar) 30 D4
Kejanti (Klungkung) 51 C7
Kelaci 22 E1
Kelapa (Sesetan) 21 M8
Kelapa (Tibu Beneng) 25 K8
Kelimutu 1, Gunung 21 G2
Kelimutu 2, Gunung 21 G3
Kelimutu 3, Gunung 21 G2
Kelimutu 5, Gunung 21 G3
Kelimutu, Danau 56 C6
Kelimutu, Gunung 21 G2
Kelinci 25 K7
Kelinci, Gang 21 K3
Kelingkung 23 H6
Kelor 21 G7
Kembali 25 K8
Kembang Jepang 23 G1
Kembang Kertas 29 J2
Kembang Matahari 29 M6
Kembang Soka 20 E2
Kembar Asri 16 C3
Kemuning (Jimbaran) 32 F7
Kemuning (Kuta) 38 A3
Kemuning (Sawangan) 45 J3
Kemuning (Ubung) 28 D1
Kemuning 1 .... 38 A2
Kemuningan 29 H7
Ken Dedes 28 C1
Kenanga (Dangin Puri Kauh) 29 H6
Kenanga (Denpasar Selatan) 21 M7
Kenanga (Kerobokan Kelod) 19 L3
Kenanga (Tabanan) 51 B3

Kenari (Dangin Puri Kaja) 29 G3
Kenari (Lelateng, Negara) 56 B8
Kenari (Loloan Barat, Negara) 56 C7
Kenari (Denpasar Barat) 20 C4
Kenari (Denpasar Selatan) 23 G4
Kenari (Tegal Kerta) 28 B7
Kenari 1 .... 29 H3
Kenari 12A 29 G3
Kenari 2A 29 G3
Kenari 3 .... 29 G3
Kenari 4 .... 29 G3
Kenari 5 .... 29 G3
Kenari 6 .... 29 G3
Kenari 8 .... 29 G3
Kencana (Jimbaran) 36 D3
Kencana (Sumerta) 29 L5
Kendal, Gang 38 C6
Kendedes 43 J3
Kenyeri (Kerobokan Kelod) 19 J1
Kenyeri (Klungkung) 51 C8
Kenyeri (Tonja) 29 K3
Kenyeri 1 (Klungkung) 51 C8
Kenyeri 2 .... 29 K2
Kenyeri 2 (Klungkung) 51 C8
Kenyeri 3 .... 29 K2
Kenyeri 3 (Klungkung) 51 C8
Kenyeri 4 (Klungkung) 51 C8
Kepaon 21 G8
Kepaon Indah 15 L5
Kepulauan Riau 57 E2
Kepundung (Denpasar) 29 G6
Kepundung (Negara) 56 C6
Kerinci, Danau 23 J4
Keris 21 M4
Kerobokan, Raya (Kerobokan Kelod) 19 K4
Kerobokan, Raya (Kerobokan) 26 F6
Kerta Bedulu 1 .... 16 E5
Kerta Bedulu 2 .... 16 E5
Kerta Bedulu 3 .... 16 E4
Kerta Bedulu 4 .... 16 F5
Kerta Dalam 1 .... 16 F3
Kerta Dalam 2 .... 16 F3
Kerta Dalam 3 .... 16 F3
Kerta Dalem 16 F3
Kerta Dalem 14 .... 16 F3
Kerta Husada Raharja 16 F4
Kerta Petasikan 16 F5
Kerta Pura 2 .... 30 D5
Kerta Pura 4 .... 30 D5
Kerta Pura 5 .... 30 D5
Kerta Rahayu 16 F4
Kerta Sari (Denpasar) 29 G4
Kerta Sari (Negara) 56 C2
Kerta Sari 1 (Negara) 56 D2
Kerta Sari 2 (Negara) 56 D2
Kerta Winangun 1 .... 16 F3
Kerta Winangun 1A 16 F3
Kerta Winangun 2 .... 16 F4
Kertajaya 50 B8
Kertanegara 28 E2
Kertapura (Denpasar Barat) 20 E6
Kertapura I (Denpasar Barat) 20 F6
Kertapura II (Denpasar Barat) 20 F6
Kertapura III (Denpasar Barat) 20 E6
Kertapura IV (Denpasar Barat) 20 E6
Kertapura VI 20 E6
Kertapura VII (Denpasar Barat) 20 E6
Kertapura VIII (Denpasar Barat) 20 F6
Kesambi 30 F5
Kesambi Indah 27 G7
Kesambi Kembar 35 H3
Kesambi, Raya 27 G6
Kesari 17 L3
Kesari 2 .... 17 L2
Kesatria 2 .... 11 G4
Kesatria 55 E5
Kesatria 1 .... 11 G4
Kesatria 4 .... 11 G4
Kesatrian 50 C8
Ketewel, Raya 31 L1
Ketut Bal 27 H2
Ketut Lestari 17 J3
Ki Hajar Dewantara (Denpasar Timur) 22 D2
Ki Hajar Dewantara (Klungkung) 51 D5
Kidul 20 C1
Kidul, Gang 20 B6
Kidul, Gunung (Dauh Puri Kauh) 21 J1
Kidul, Gunung (Padang Sambian Kelod) 20 C1
Kintamani 49 H1
Kiwi 28 A8
Koala 15 H3
Komodo 22 F7
Komodo, Pulau 21 K5
Konten, Lettu 54 C6
Kori Nuansa 37 K5
Kori Selatan 37 J5
Krakatau 1, Gunung (Denpasar) 21 J1
Krakatau, Gunung (Negara) 56 D8
Kresek 16 D5
Kresna (Bangli) 54 D3
Kresna (Dauh Puri Kaja) 28 F7
Kresna (Legian) 14 D3
Kresna (Singaraja) 57 E7
Kresna (Tabanan) 51 D3
Kresna (Tibu Beneng) 26 E1
Krishna 19 H3
Krisna 19 L5
Kroya 29 M5
Kuba Asri 23 J7
Kubang Batu 37 L2

Kubu Alit 19 K4
Kubu Anyar 14 E8
Kubu Anyar 1 .... 11 G3
Kubu Dauh 19 K6
Kubu Gunung 27 H1
Kubu Kresna 19 L3
Kubu Lebak 19 J4
Kubu Manyar 25 L3
Kubu Anyar 19 J4
Kulat 41 H5
Kumbakarna 28 E6
Kunti 26 D7
Kunti 1 .... 19 L7
Kunti 2 .... 19 M7
Kuntul (Dauh Puri Kelod) 21 L5
Kuntul (Panjer) 22 D8
Kuru Setia 43 H8
Kurukseta 39 H4
Kusuma Atmaja, Dr 22 D3
Kusuma Bangsa 28 C4
Kusuma Bangsa 1 .... 28 D3
Kusuma Bangsa 2 .... 28 D4
Kusuma Bangsa 3 .... 28 D4
Kusuma Bangsa 4 .... 28 D4
Kusuma Bangsa 5 .... 28 D4
Kusuma Bangsa 6 .... 28 D4
Kusuma Bangsa 7 .... 28 D4
Kusuma Dewa 1 .... 28 C3
Kusuma Dewa 2 .... 28 C3
Kusuma Dewa 3 .... 28 C3
Kusuma Sari 17 L4
Kusuma Yudha 54 C4
Kuta, Raya 14 E8
Kutai 54 D4
Kuteh 26 D8
Kutilang (Gianyar) 50 C6
Kutilang (Kerobokan Kelod) 26 D8
Kutilang (Negara) 56 E4
Kutilang (Sanur Kaja) 23 J3
Kutilang (Singaraja) 57 B4
Kutuh 48 C4
Kutuh Kelod 51 A1
Kuwum 26 D8
Kuwum 1 .... 26 D8

L

Lagaan 54 C8
Lagun 39 H2
Laksamana (Singaraja) 57 B7
Laksmana (Bangli) 54 E3
Laksmana (Denpasar Timur) 22 F2
Laksmana 1 (Denpasar Timur) 22 F2
Laksmana 2 (Denpasar Timur) 22 F2
Laksmana 3 (Denpasar Timur) 22 F2
Laksmana 4 (Denpasar Timur) 22 F2
Laksmana 5 (Denpasar Timur) 22 F2
Laksmana 6 (Denpasar Timur) 22 F2
Laksmana 7 (Denpasar Timur) 22 F2
Laksmana 8 (Denpasar Timur) 22 F3
Laksmana 9 (Denpasar Timur) 22 F3
Laksmana 10 (Denpasar Timur) 22 F3
Laksmana 11 (Denpasar Timur) 22 F3
Laksmana 12 (Denpasar Timur) 22 F3
Laksmana 14 (Denpasar Timur) 22 F3
Laksmana 15 (Denpasar Timur) 22 K7
Lalang Buana 23 K7
Lalangtemu 36 E3
Lange 20 B8
Languan, Tukad 22 A6
Langui Kangin 42 E4
Langui Kauh 43 G3
Langui T Ning 43 H2
Lantang Hidung 17 K2
Lanyahan 49 H2
Lapangan Berburu 48 A1
Laplapan, Raya 47 L1
Laskar 30 B7
Lasmana 19 J6
Lasmana Oberoy 19 G6
Lateng Terusan 56 B7
Laviana 52 F3
Lawu, Gunung 21 J1
LC Gatsu Barat 27 H3
LC. 9 .... 28 A3
Le Grande Acess 35 J6
Lebah (Bedulu) 49 K7
Lebah (Kerobokan Kelod) 19 J6
Lebah 3, Gunung 20 F2
Lebah 4, Gunung 20 F3
Lebak 53 M4
Lebak Sari 19 H4
Leci (Kesiman) 30 B8
Leci (Padang Sambian) 28 A7
Legian 14 D5
Leli (Negara) 56 B1
Leli (Singaraja) 57 D4
Lely (Dangin Puri Kangin) 29 H7
Lely (Sanur) 23 J6
Lembongan, Pulau 56 F6
Lempuyang, Gunung (Denpasar Barat) 20 F2
Lempuyang, Gunung (Gianyar) 50 D5
Lestari (Kerobokan Kelod) 19 H2
Lestari (Panjer) 22 C7
Lila, Lettu 54 C6
Lilacita 29 M5
Lilip 26 F3
Lima Dua 19 L5
Limanam 19 L5
Lingga 57 A4
Lingga, Pulau 21 G7

Listra 21 H8
Loloan, Tukad 13 L1
Lombok, Pulau 57 F2
Loviana 53 J3
Lulu 19 J2
Lumba Lumba (Batu Bulan) 31 J3
Lumba Lumba (Sesetan) 16 C5
Lumba-Lumba (Tanjung Benoa) 33 G2
Lumbung Sari 31 G2
Lumut 19 J7
Lumut 2, Gunung 20 D5
Lumut 3, Gunung 20 C5
Lumut 4, Gunung 20 C5
Lumut, Gunung 20 C5
Lungsiakan, Raya 48 D1

M

M.H Thamrin 28 E7
M.T. Haryono (Denpasar Utara) 21 L1
M.T. Haryono (Tabanan) 51 F2
M.T. Haryono 1 .... 29 G8
Made 19 K7
Made Kawi, Serma 21 L3
Made Lebah 49 G7
Made Pil, Serma 21 L4
Made Putra, Letda 29 G8
Made Rambug, Pratu 31 G2
Madhu Sari 19 K3
Madri 56 B5
Madura, Pulau 21 L1
Mahabarata 16 D5
Mahadewa 56 A5
Mahantika 38 D1
Maharaja 19 J5
Mahasari 19 J5
Mahendradata (Denpasar Barat) 20 E2
Mahendradata (Gianyar) 50 A5
Mahkota 21 H3
Mahoni (Semarapura) 51 D8
Mahoni (Tuban) 11 H5
Majapahit (Bangli) 54 D4
Majapahit (Kuta) 14 F6
Majapahit (Tabanan) 51 E2
Mak Jo 36 E5
Malboro 1 .... 20 F6
Malboro 4 .... 20 F5
Malboro 5 .... 20 F5
Malboro 6 .... 20 F5
Malboro 7 .... 20 F5
Malboro 10 .... 20 F5
Malboro 11 .... 20 F5
Malboro 12 .... 20 F5
Malboro 13 .... 20 F5
Malboro 15 .... 20 F5
Malboro 17 .... 20 F5
Malboro 19 .... 20 F5
Malboro 21 .... 20 F5
Maluku (Ekasila) 21 K2
Maluku, Pulau (Singaraja) 57 E2
Mandala 22 F8
Mandala Sari 21 M4
Mandala Wangi (Sesetan) 21 M8
Mandala Wangi, Gunung (Tegal Langon) .. 21 J4
Mandara Toll Road 28 F1
Mandau 21 M4
Mandiri 11 G5
Mandiri, Raya 37 L3
Mangga (Kampung Kajanan, Singaraja) 57 D3
Mangga (Kerobokan) 26 D8
Mangga (Kesiman) 30 B8
Mangga (Seminyak) 19 L7
Mangga (Singaraja) 57 C7
Mangga (Tegal Kerta) 28 A7
Mangga Sari 21 M8
Manggis (Batu Bulan) 31 G1
Manggis (Kerobokan Kaja) 27 H6
Manggis (Singaraja) 57 C3
Manggis (Tibu Beneng) 25 L7
Mangku Giwang 50 D6
Mangku Rangkit 26 F5
Mango 18 F2
Manik 19 J5
Manik 50 B6
Manik Mas 36 D5
Maninjau, Danau 23 K4
Manu 25 L7
Manuk Rawa 29 H1
Marga Agung 15 G2
Marga Ayu 14 F3
Markisa 30 B8
Maruti (Dauh Puri Kelod) 21 K2
Maruti (Pemecutan Kaja) 28 E4
Mas (Bedulu) 49 M7
Mas (Sayan) 48 C4
Mas, Gunung 20 C2
Mas, Raya 49 G8
Mas, Tukad 22 B4
Matahari (Klungkung) 51 C8
Matahari (Padang Sambian) 28 A5
Matahari (Tonja) 29 H1
Matahari 1A 28 A4
Matahari 2B 28 A4
Matahari 3 .... 28 A4
Mataram (Bangli) 54 D2
Mataram (Kuta) 14 E6
Mataram (Tabanan) 51 E2
Mati 21 K7
Mawa, Tukad 22 C6
Mawar (Bangli) 54 D2
Mawar (Dangin Puri Kangin) 29 H6

Mawar (Denpasar Selatan) 21 K7
Mawar (Gianyar) 50 E8
Mawar (Kerobokan Kelod) 19 K5
Mawar (Kesiman Kertha Langu) 31 H4
Mawar (Klungkung) 51 D6
Mawar (Sanur Kaja) 23 J3
Mawar (Seminyak) 20 B8
Mawar (Singaraja) 57 B4
Mawar (Tabanan) 51 C4
Mawar (Ubung) 28 D2
Mawar 5 ....23 J3
Mawar 9 ....23 J3
Mawar 10 ....23 J3
Mawar 11 ....23 J3
Mayor Metra 57 F8
Mecutan 36 E6
Medan 36 C5
Medori 19 M8
Meduri (Kerobokan Kelod) 19 K5
Meduri (Sumerta Kaja) 29 K7
Meduri (Sumerta) 29 L5
Mega Buana 20 D1
Mekar Buaji 30 B8
Mekar Sari (Kerobokan Kelod) 19 L3
Mekar Sari (Kuta) 38 C1
Mekar Sari (Seminyak) 30 B6
Melang Kaja 43 M3
Melangit 1, Tukad 22 A5
Melangit 2, Tukad 22 A5
Melangit, Tukad (Gianyar) 50 E6
Melangit, Tukad (Jimbaran) 32 D4
Melangit, Tukad (Panjer) 22 B5
Melasti (Legian) 14 C5
Melasti (Ungasan) 43 J6
Melasti II 44 A5
Melasti Labuansait 41 K3
Melasti V 43 M4
Melati (Abian Base, Gianyar) 50 E8
Melati (Benoa, Kuta) 38 B7
Melati (Dangin Puri Kangin) 29 H6
Melati (Gianyar, Gianyar) 50 D7
Melati (Kerobokan Kelod) 19 H6
Melati (Kesiman Kertha Langu) 31 G5
Melati (Kesiman) 30 C6
Melati (Ketewel) 31 L4
Melati (Klungkung) 51 C7
Melati (Negara) 56 C2
Melati (Padang Sambian Kelod) 20 B1
Melati (Padang Sambian) 28 A5
Melati (Pemecutan Kelod, Denpasar Sel.) ...21 J2
Melati (Pemogan) 21 G8
Melati (Sanur) 23 J7
Melati (Seminyak) 19 K7
Melati (Sesetan, Denpasar Selatan) 21 L7
Melati (Tabanan) 51 D3
Melati (Tegal Kerta) 28 A7
Melati (Tibu Beneng) 26 D3
Melati (Tonja) 29 J4
Melati (Ubung) 28 D1
Melati 2 ....23 J7
Melati 4 ....28 A5
Melati Indah 21 M7
Melon (Padang Sambian) 20 E1
Melon (Sesetan) 21 L8
Melon (Singaraja) 57 C8
Mendra, Serma 21 L4
Menet Sari 28 C7
Menjangan 51 C2
Menjangan, Pulau (Denpasar Barat) 21 K5
Menjangan, Pulau (Tabanan) 51 B2
Menori 29 M5
Mentawai 26 C7
Menuh (Klungkung) 51 C6
Menuh (Singaraja) 57 B5
Menur (Dangin Puri Kauh) 29 H6
Menur (Tonja) 29 J4
Menur (Ubung) 28 C2
Menuri 30 D3
Menuri 1 ....30 D3
Menuri 2 ....30 D3
Menuri 3 ....30 D3
Menuri 4 ....30 D4
Menuri 5 ....30 D4
Merak - Ungasan 43 K2
Merak (Jimbaran, Kuta) 36 C6
Merak (Kesiman Kertha Langu) 30 E2
Merak (Klungkung) 51 C8
Merak (Negara) 56 F3
Merak (Seminyak) 19 K7
Merak (Sesetan) 16 B3
Merak (Singaraja) 57 C3
Merak (Sumerta Kaja) 29 J4
Merak (Tabanan) 51 D2
Merak (Tegal Kerta) 28 A7
Merak (Ubung) 28 C1
Merapi (Padang Sambian) 20 C2
Merapi, Gunung (Gianyar) 50 E6
Merapi, Gunung (Klungkung) 51 E5
Merapi, Gunung (Negara) 56 E7
Merbabu 28 D7
Merdeka (Bangli) 54 D6
Merdeka (Denpasar Timur) 22 E2
Merdeka 1 (Denpasar Timur) 22 E2
Merdeka 10 ....22 E2
Merdeka 2 (Denpasar Timur) 22 E2
Merdeka 3 (Denpasar Timur) 22 E2
Merdeka 4 ....22 E2
Merdeka 6 ....22 E2
Merdeka 8 ....22 E1
Merdeka 9 ....22 E2

Merdeka Raya 14 F6
Merpati (Dangin Puri Kaja) 29 H2
Merpati (Dauh Puri Kauh) 21 K3
Merpati (Dauh Puri Kelod) 22 A2
Merpati (Gianyar) 50 C6
Merpati (Jimbaran, Kuta) 36 C6
Merpati (Kerobokan Kelod) 26 E8
Merpati (Peguyangan) 28 E1
Merpati (Sanur Kaja) 23 K3
Merpati (Sesetan) 16 A2
Merpati (Singaraja) 57 C3
Merpati (Tabanan) 51 C2
Merpati (Tegal Kerta) 28 B8
Merpati 1 ....23 J3
Merpati 2 ....23 J3
Merpati 10 ....28 B7
Merta Agung 19 K3
Merta Ayu 19 M3
Merta Ayu 1 ....19 L4
Merta Nadi 19 K4
Merta Santi 15 K4
Merta Sari (Jimbaran) 32 E7
Merta Sari (Kerobokan Kelod) 19 J6
Merta Sari (Padang Sambian Kelod) 20 B2
Merta Sari (Sanur Kauh) 17 J5
Merta Sari (Seminyak) 19 K7
Merta Sari (Sidakarya) 16 D5
Merta Sari 1 ....16 E5
Merta Yasa 28 D6
Merta Yasa 1 ....28 D6
Mertajaya 28 C6
Meskipun 30 B8
MI 11 ....27 H3
Mick's Place 34 E6
Mila 19 K4
Milang 26 C7
Mindanau, Danau 56 B7
MIPA 36 F6
Mirah Delima 21 G3
Mirah Hati 21 G2
Mirah Pemecutan 1 ....21 H2
Mirah Pemecutan 2 ....21 H2
Mirah Pemecutan 3 ....21 H2
Misol 1, Pulau 21 H4
Misol 4, Pulau 21 H4
Misol 6, Pulau 21 H5
Misol 7, Pulau 21 H5
Misol 8, Pulau 21 H5
Misol 9, Pulau 21 H5
Misol 10, Pulau 21 H5
Misol 12, Pulau 21 G5
Misol 14, Pulau 21 H5
Misol 20, Pulau 21 H5
Misol, Pulau 21 H5
Monalisa 19 K3
Morabito Art Villa Road 18 D2
Morotai, Pulau 21 J5
Mrajapati 32 C5
Muding Asri 27 H5
Muding Batu Sangian 27 H4
Muding Batu Sangian 04 ....27 H4
Muding Batu Sangian 05 ....27 H3
Muding Batu Sangian 06 ....27 H3
Muding Batu Sangian 07 ....27 H3
Muding Batu Sangian 11 ....27 H2
Muding Kaja 27 H7
Muding Kelod 27 H7
Muding Mekar 27 H5
Muding Mudeh 27 H3
Muding Mudeh 2 ....27 H3
Muding Pertiwi 27 H4
Muding Sari 27 H4
Muding Tengah 27 H6
Mudita, Kapten 29 G8
Mudu Taki 27 H1
Muhammad Yamin, Prof 22 E3
Muhammad Yamin 1, Prof 22 E3
Muhammad Yamin 2, Prof 22 E3
Muhammad Yamin 3, Prof 22 E3
Muhammad Yamin 4, Prof 22 E3
Muhammad Yamin 5, Prof 22 E3
Muhammad Yamin 6, Prof 22 E3
Muhammad Yamin 7, Prof 22 E3
Muhammad Yamin 8, Prof 22 E3
Muhammad Yamin 9, Prof 22 E3
Muhammad Yamin 10, Prof 22 E3
Muhammad Yamin 11, Prof 22 E3
Muka, Kapten 57 E5
Mukti Sari 17 K3
Mulawarman 28 E2
Muliawan, Gunung 50 C6
Munduk Batu Belah 25 J4
Munduk Catu 25 H7
Munduk Kelampuak 25 L5
Munduk Sari 19 K1
Mungil 19 J4
Muntir 23 J8
Murai Batu 22 F7
Muria, Gunung 20 F1
Musi 1, Tukad 22 C4
Musi 2, Tukad 22 C4
Musi 3, Tukad 22 C4
Musi 4, Tukad 22 C4
Musi 5, Tukad 22 C4
Musi 6, Tukad 22 C4
Musi 7, Tukad 22 C4
Musi, Tukad 22 C4
Mutiara 26 E8
Muwardi 1, Dr 22 E3
Muwardi, Dr 22 E3

N
Nabor 42 A3
Naga 27 H7
Naga Sari 29 M8
Nagasari 3 ....30 A8
Nagasari 4 ....30 A8
Nagasari 5 ....30 B8
Nakula (Dangin Puri Kauh) 28 F6
Nakula (Denpasar Barat) 20 C5
Nakula (Gianyar) 50 B8
Nakula (Kerobokan) 26 D5
Nakula (Klungkung) 51 E6
Nakula (Negara) 56 A5
Nakula (Pemecutan Kelod) 14 F3
Nakula (Seminyak) 14 D2
Nakula (Tabanan) 51 E3
Nakula (Tibu Beneng) 25 M7
Nambi 28 F4
Nangka (Baler Bale Agung, Negara) 56 C2
Nangka (Bangli) 54 D4
Nangka (Dangin Puri Kaja) 29 G5
Nangka (Gianyar) 50 C6
Nangka (Kerobokan) 19 M2
Nangka (Loloan Barat, Negara) 56 C7
Nangka (Singaraja) 57 B7
Nangka (Sumerta Kaja) 29 K5
Nangka (Tonja) 29 H1
Narakusuma 29 L8
Narwastu 30 B8
Nata 26 E8
Natih, Serma 55 C2
Natuna, Pulau 21 L2
Nazamudin 55 D5
Nelayan 25 J7
Nenas (Batu Bulan Kangin) 31 G1
Nenas (Pemecutan Kelod) 21 G5
New Kuta Raya 34 F5
Ngenjung, Tukad 13 K2
Ngurah Rai (Amlapura) 55 D2
Ngurah Rai, Brigjen (Bangli) 54 C6
Ngurah Rai (Gianyar) 50 C7
Ngurah Rai (Klungkung) 51 C5
Ngurah Rai Bypass (Kesiman Petilan) 30 D6
Ngurah Rai Bypass (Kuta) 11 J2
Ngurah Rai Bypass (Mumbul to Siligita) ..38 D1
Ngurah Rai Bypass (Negara) 56 E5
Ngurah Rai Bypass (Sanur) 17 L2
Ngurah Rai Bypass (Sanur to Pantai Padang
  Galak) 23 K3
Ngurah Rai Bypass (Sesetan) 16 D5
Ngurah Rai Bypass (Siligita to Nusa Dua) ..39 H4
Ngurah Rai Bypass (Tuban) 32 E1
Ngurah Rai, Kolonel (Singaraja) 57 E5
Nias, Pulau (Denpasar Barat) 21 K4
Nias, Pulau (Negara) 56 F5
Nias, Pulau (Tabanan) 51 A3
Noja 29 L2
Noja 1 ....29 M4
Noja 2 ....29 M3
Noja Saraswati (Kesiman Petilan) 29 L2
Noja Saraswati (Tonja) 29 K1
Noja Sari 1 ....29 M3
Noja Sari 2 ....29 L2
Nuansa (Padang Sambian Kelod) 20 B7
Nuansa (Sanur Kaja) 23 J3
Nuansa Angkasa XVII 43 H4
Nuansa Raya 37 K6
Nuansa Sandet 2 ....31 G4
Nuansa Sandet 3 ....31 G4
Nuansa Sandet 4 ....31 G4
Nuansa Sari 29 H1
Nuansa Selatan 1-9 ....37 K5
Nuansa Timur 37 K6
Nuansa Udayana 1 ....37 K4
Nuansa Udayana 2 ....37 K4
Nuansa Udayana 3 ....37 K4
Nuansa Udayana 4 ....37 K4
Nuansa Udayana 5 ....37 K4
Nuansa Udayana 6 ....37 K4
Nuansa Udayana 8 ....37 K4
Nuansa Udayana 9 ....37 K4
Nuansa Utama 37 K6
Nuansa Utama 1 ....37 K4
Nuansa Utama 2 ....37 K4
Nuansa Utama 18 ....37 K5
Nuansa Utama 25 ....37 K5
Nuansa Utama 32 ....37 K5
Nuansa Utama Selatan 37 K5
Nuansa Utama Selatan V 37 K6
Nuri (Bangli) 54 C4
Nuri (Dangin Puri Kaja) 28 F4
Nuri (Jimbaran, Kuta) 36 C6
Nuri (Padang Sambian) 28 A4
Nuri (Renon) 22 F7
Nuri (Sanur) 23 K3
Nuri (Sesetan) 21 L6
Nuri (Singaraja) 57 C4
Nuri (Tabanan) 51 C2
Nuri (Tegal Kerta) 28 A7
Nuri (Tibu Beneng) 18 D1
Nuri 1 ....29 G4
Nuri 2 ....29 G4
Nuri 3 ....29 G4
Nuri 4 ....29 G4
Nusa Barung 21 J4
Nusa Dharma 38 E2
Nusa Dua 39 J4
Nusa Dua Selatan 43 L6

Nusa Indah (Dangin Puri Kelod) 22 B1
Nusa Indah (Ketewel) 31 M3
Nusa Indah (Klungkung) 51 C8
Nusa Indah (Kuta) 38 D5
Nusa Indah (Pemecutan Kaja) 28 A3
Nusa Indah (Singaraja) 57 C4
Nusa Indah (Sumerta) 29 L6
Nusa Indah (Ubung) 28 C1
Nusa Indah 1 ....28 A3
Nusa Indah 2 ....28 A3
Nusa Indah 3 ....28 A3
Nusa Indah 4 ....28 A3
Nusa Indah 5 ....28 A3
Nusa Indah 14 (Negara) 56 C1
Nusa Indah Raya (Negara) 56 C1
Nusa Indah Selatan 28 A3
Nusa Indah Selatan Utara 2 ....28 A2
Nusa Kambangan (Dauh Puri) 21 K1
Nusa Kambangan, Pulau (Dauh Puri Kauh) 21 J3
Nusa Penida 21 K5
Nusantara 11 H6
Nusantara (Bangli) 54 D3
Nyali, Tukad 23 H5
Nyanyang Sari 11 H3
Nyuh Bulan (Denpasar Barat) 21 G4
Nyuh Sawit 21 G4
Nyuhkuning (Mas) 46 C8
Nyuhkuning 1 ....48 E7

O
Obor 21 H8
Oka 21 J7
Olala, Gang 38 D3
Ombak 18 D1
Oos, Tukad 22 F6
Orchid (Kerobokan Kelod) 19 H4
Orchid (Sanur) 23 K7
Otan, Tukad 22 B6

P
Pacah 29 K3
Pacar (Dangin Puri Kangin) 29 J6
Pacar (Sanur Kaja) 23 L3
Padanan 26 E1
Padang Galak 30 F8
Padang Galak 23 K1
Padang Gallery 20 B5
Padang Indah 1 ....20 C1
Padang Indah 2 ....20 C1
Padang Kartika 27 H7
Padang Lalang 28 A7
Padang Linjong 25 H5
Padang Luwih, Raya 27 H2
Padang Satria 20 B5
Padang Teki 28 A7
Padi 22 B7
Padma 14 B3
Padma Utara 14 C4
Padonan, Raya 26 C3
Pahlawan (Negara) 56 D5
Pahlawan (Singaraja) 57 D7
Pahlawan (Tabanan) 51 E3
Pajajaran 51 D2
Pajang Sari 23 H6
Pakerisan, Tukad 22 B7
Pakis 30 C7
Pakis Aji 22 F1
Pakis Aji 3 ....22 F1
Pakis Aji 4 ....22 F1
Paksi Mas 29 G3
Paku Sari 21 M8
Palapa (Pemecutan Kelod) 21 H3
Palapa (Sesetan) 16 C4
Palapa 1 ....16 C3
Palapa 2 ....16 C3
Palapa 3 ....16 C3
Palapa 4 ....16 C3
Palapa 5 ....16 C3
Palapa 6 ....16 C4
Palapa 7 ....16 C3
Palapa 8 ....16 C4
Palapa 10 ....16 C4
Palapa 11 ....16 C4
Palapa 12 ....16 C4
Palapa 13 ....16 C4
Palapa 14 ....16 D4
Palem 36 A7
Palm Raya 38 C4
Palm Tree 19 H2
Paloma 19 K6
Panca Indah 28 A5
Pancoran 2, Tukad 22 C7
Pancoran, Tukad 22 C7
Panda (Batu Bulan) 30 F1
Panda (Pemogan) 15 H3
Pandan (Padang Sambian Kelod) 20 A1
Pandan (Pedungan) 21 K7
Pandan 1 ....20 A2
Pandan Harum 22 A8
Pandawa (Kerobokan Kelod) 19 J2
Pandawa (Renon) 22 F7
Pandawa (Tanjung Benoa) 33 J2
Pande (Nusa Dua) 39 G5
Pande (Renon) 22 F6
Pandu (Kerobokan Kelod) 19 G6
Pandu (Sumerta Kelod) 29 M8
Pandu 3 ....29 L8
Pandu 6 ....29 M8

Panestanan Kelod 46 A3
Panestanan, Raya 46 B3
Pangkung Sari 19 J5
Panji Terara 31 J3
Pantai 57 C2
Pantai Balangan 35 H3
Pantai Bingin 34 D8
Pantai Brawa 25 L8
Pantai Brawa, Raya 26 B4
Pantai Cemongkak 34 F6
Pantai Indah 53 L7
Pantai Karang 17 M2
Pantai Kedonganan 32 C3
Pantai Kuta 14 D8
Pantai Mamo 40 B1
Pantai Mengening 24 B3
Pantai Mengiat 39 J6
Pantai Mengiat 39 J6
Pantai Padang Galak 30 E7
Pantai Pandawa 44 A6
Pantai Peminge 39 H6
Pantai Pererenan, Raya 25 H3
Pantai Sanur 17 J5
Pantai Sari 32 C5
Pantai Selatan Gau 42 E7
Pantai Serangan 13 K2
Pantai Sindhu 23 L6
Pantai Suluban 40 B3
Panto Sari 16 B6
Parigata 32 D8
Parkit 57 B4
Pasang Gerigis 50 A7
Pasar Delod 48 A3
Pasar Hewan 55 D5
Pasek 36 B5
Pasir Putih 32 C3
Pasraman Unud 36 F3
Pasung 20 F8
Pasyaman 32 D4
Patih Jelantik (Kuta) 14 E5
Patih Jelantik (Denpasar) 21 L2
Patih Jelantik (Gianyar) 50 C5
Pattimura (Dangin Puri Kaja) 29 G5
Pattimura (Kampung Anyar, Singaraja) 57 D3
Pattimura (Kampung Kajanan, Singaraja). 51 C2
Pattimura (Klungkung) 51 D6
Pattimura (Kuta) 14 E5
Pattimura (Tabanan) 51 E2
Patuha, Gunung 21 G2
Payung, Gunung (Denpasar Barat) 20 C6
Payung, Gunung (Kuta) 44 C4
Pecatu Indah Raya 35 H6
Peguyangan 2 .... 57 E5
Pejeng Kaja - Tampak Siring 49 L2
Pejeng Kawan, Raya 49 J2
Pejeng Kelod 49 M7
Pejeng Kelod, Raya 49 L3
Pejeng, Raya 49 L4
Pekanbaru 11 H5
Pekandelan 26 E8
Pekaseh, Tukad 13 L1
Pelabuhan 16 A8
Pelangi 18 F4
Peldam 15 L5
Peldam 1 .... 15 L5
Peldam 2 .... 15 L5
Peldam 3 .... 15 L5
Peliatan (Kerobokan) 26 D7
Peliatan (Peliatan) 47 H5
Pelita 1 .... 21 L5
Pelita Sari 1 .... 21 K2
Pelita Sari 2 .... 21 K2
Pemamoran 23 K5
Pemaron, Tukad 22 B8
Pemelisan (Kedonganan) 32 C3
Pemelisan (Sesetan) 16 D6
Pemelisan Agung 32 C5
Pemogan 15 J2
Pemogan, Raya 15 J4
Pemuda (Kesiman Kertha Langu) 31 G5
Pemuda (Renon) 22 E4
Pemuda 1 (Renon) 22 E4
Pemuda 2 (Renon) 22 E4
Pemuda 3 (Renon) 22 E4
Pemuda 4 (Renon) 22 E4
Pemuda 5 (Renon) 22 E4
Pemuda 6 (Renon) 22 E4
Pemukiman 43 K1
Pemutih 34 D7
Penataran (Jimbaran) 32 D4
Penataran (Serangan, Denpasar Selatan) . 13 L1
Penataran 2 (Singaraja) 57 E6
Penataran 8 (Singaraja) 57 E6
Penataran Sari 20 F8
Pendawa 25 H4
Pendidikan (Benoa, Kuta) 33 K7
Pendidikan (Sesetan) 16 E4
Pendidikan 1 .... 16 D3
Peneta, Yeh 23 G4
Pengalasan 20 D3
Pengembak 17 J4
Pengembak 2 .... 17 H5
Pengeracikan 32 C3
Pengeubengan 19 L3
Pengiasan-Mambal 48 A8
Pengipian 19 M4
Pengosekan 49 G7
Pengosekan, Raya 46 F7
Pengubengan 19 M2
Pengubengan Kangin 27 G8

Pengubengan Kauh 19 L2
Pengulapan 36 E7
Penintaan 52 C3
Penyaringan 23 H8
Penyaringan 23 H7
Penyaringan 1 .... 23 G7
Penyaringan 3 .... 23 G7
Pepaya 19 J1
Peratu Keting 41 L5
Peratu Rukeh 41 L5
Peratu Ruken 41 K5
Perdamaian 19 H1
Perenan 26 B6
Perintis 21 J7
Perkutut (Dangin Puri Kaja) 29 H3
Perkutut (Dauh Puri Kauh) 21 J3
Perkutut (Jimbaran, Kuta) 36 C6
Perkutut (Seminyak) 19 K7
Perkutut (Tabanan) 51 D1
Permai 1 .... 26 F1
Permai 2 .... 26 F1
Permai 3 .... 26 F1
Permai 4 .... 26 F1
Persada 20 B4
Persawahan Asri 26 F2
Pertanian 36 F6
Pesagi 55 D6
Pesanggaran 16 B6
Pesanggrahan 16 A6
Pesiapan Bypass 51 B4
Pesona 2 .... 21 M7
Petak Bitera, Raya 50 A5
Petanahan Sari 37 L1
Petanu, Tukad 50 F6
Petingan 27 G4
Petitenget 19 G5
Petulu, Raya 49 H3
Pidada 1 .... 28 B2
Pidada 2 .... 28 C2
Pidada 3 .... 28 B2
Pidada 4 .... 28 B2
Pidada 5 .... 28 C2
Pidada 6 .... 28 C2
Pidada 7 .... 28 B2
Pidada 8 .... 28 C2
Pidada 9 .... 28 B2
Pidada 10 .... 28 C2
Pidada 11 .... 28 C2
Pidada 13 .... 28 C2
Pinang 21 M3
Pinang, Pulau 21 G6
Pipit (Denpasar) 28 B7
Pipit (Gianyar) 50 C6
Pipitan Sari 25 M2
Piranha 16 B4
Piranha 1 .... 16 B3
Pisang 26 D8
Piter 19 K7
Plawa (Gianyar) 50 F6
Plawa (Klungkung) 51 D7
Plawa (Negara) 56 D2
Plawa (Pemecutan Kelod) 21 G4
Plawa (Seminyak) 19 L8
Plawa (Sumerta Kauh) 29 J5
Plawa 1 (Klungkung) 51 D7
Plawa 1 (Negara) 56 D2
Plawa 4 (Negara) 56 D2
Plawa 5 (Negara) 56 D3
Plawa 6 (Negara) 56 C2
Poltek 36 F6
Pondok Asri 27 H2
Pondok Indah 28 B3
Pondok Indah 1 .... 28 B3
Pondok Indah 2 .... 28 B3
Pondok Indah 3 .... 28 B3
Pondok Indah 4 .... 28 B3
Pondok Indah Raya 2 .... 28 B3
Popies 1 .... 14 D7
Popies 2 .... 14 D6
Poso, Danau 56 B7
Prada 26 E8
Praiama 19 M4
Pralina 29 L4
Pramuka 57 D4
Pramuwisata 16 D4
Prana 19 G5
Pratama (Benoa) 33 L7
Pratama (Tibu Beneng) 26 B3
Pratama Clinic 33 K6
Pratama Raya 39 H2
Pucuk (Kesiman) 30 C7
Pucuk (Sumerta) 29 L5
Pucuk (Tegal Harum) 20 F3
Pucuk 1 .... 31 G6
Pucuk Bang 31 G5
Pudak (Dangin Puri Kangin) 29 J7
Pudak (Denpasar Selatan) 21 K7
Pudak (Gianyar) 50 C7
Pudak (Klungkung) 51 B6
Pudak (Sanur) 23 K7
Puji 25 L7
Pulau Adi Dalan 21 H5
Pulau Alor Permai 21 J5
Pulau Ambon 26 B6
Pulau Ayu 21 H6
Pulau Ayu 9 .... 21 H6
Pulau Ayu 11 .... 21 H6
Pulau Ayu 15 .... 21 H6
Pulau B. Sudirman 21 L4
Pulau B. Sudirman 2 .... 21 M2

Pulau B. Sudirman 3 .... 21 M2
Pulau Batam 3 .... 21 K2
Pulau Belitung 15 M1
Pulau Biak 1 .... 21 J2
Pulau Biak 2 .... 21 J2
Pulau Bintan 26 C6
Pulau Bungi 25 K1
Pulau Bungin 15 K1
Pulau Buru (Dauh Puri) 28 F8
Pulau Buru (Kerobokan) 26 C6
Pulau Buton 26 B7
Pulau Deli 26 B7
Pulau Dewata 1 .... 30 E7
Pulau Flores 26 B8
Pulau Flores 2 .... 21 J4
Pulau Flores 4 .... 21 J4
Pulau Flores 6 .... 21 J4
Pulau Galang 15 H2
Pulau Karimata 26 B8
Pulau Lingga 26 C6
Pulau Medang 26 C7
Pulau Misol 1 .... 21 H4
Pulau Misol 6 .... 21 H4
Pulau Misol 7A 21 H5
Pulau Misol 18 .... 21 G5
Pulau Moyo 15 M2
Pulau Moyo 2 .... 15 M2
Pulau Moyo 3 .... 15 M3
Pulau Moyo 4 .... 15 M3
Pulau Moyo 5 .... 15 M3
Pulau Moyo 6 .... 15 M3
Pulau Moyo 7 .... 15 M3
Pulau Moyo 8 .... 15 M3
Pulau Moyo 9 .... 15 M3
Pulau Moyo 10 .... 15 M3
Pulau Moyo 11 .... 15 M3
Pulau Moyo 12 .... 15 M3
Pulau Panjang 21 H6
Pulau Roti (Kerobokan) 26 B8
Pulau Roti (Pedungan) 15 M2
Pulau Saelus 21 G6
Pulau Saelus 2 .... 21 K7
Pulau Samosir 26 C6
Pulau Serangan 16 C6
Pulau Singkep (Kerobokan) 26 C6
Pulau Singkep (Pedungan) 15 M1
Pulau Sipora 26 C7
Pulau Yapen 21 J4
Pulau Yoni 15 K1
Pulau Yudistira 26 C7
Pule, Tukad (Raya Sesetan, Denpasar Sel) 21 L7
Pule, Tukad (Tegal Wangi, Denpasar Sel.) 21 M8
Pulet, Tukad 22 B7
Puncak Sari 20 B4
Puncak Wisesa 41 J4
Punggawa, Tukad (Panjer) 22 B8
Punggawa, Tukad (Serangan) 13 K2
Punglor 22 D8
Pungut Sari 23 L8
Pungutan 17 L1
Pungutan 1 .... 23 L7
Puputan (Klungkung) 51 D7
Puputan 1 .... 22 E3
Puputan 2 .... 22 E3
Puputan 3 .... 22 E3
Puputan Baru 28 A6
Puputan Baru D 28 A7
Puputan, Raya (Denpasar Timur) 22 B3
Pura (Bedulu) 49 L7
Pura (Pemogan) 21 G8
Pura Batur 25 J7
Pura Beten Kepur 26 B5
Pura Cupitan 41 H6
Pura Dalem (Anturan) 53 L3
Pura Dalem (Canggu) 25 H7
Pura Dalem (Renon) 22 F7
Pura Demak 20 E5
Pura Demak 1 .... 20 E5
Pura Demak 2 .... 20 E5
Pura Demak 4 .... 20 E5
Pura Demak Barat 20 E4
Pura Duwe 20 C4
Pura Gunung Payung 45 J4
Pura Kayu Putih 18 E3
Pura Masuka 42 E3
Pura Puget 45 L2
Pura Selonding 41 J7
Pura Taman 21 G8
Pura Taman Sari 25 K4
Pura Telaga Waja 19 G6
Pura Wates 26 B1
Pura Wates Canggu 26 B1
Pura Wengi 53 H4
Purba Indah 1 .... 28 A3
Purba Indah 2 .... 28 A3
Puri Aseman 26 B3
Puri Bagus 53 L6
Puri Bali 40 D6
Puri Canggu 25 M6
Puri Canggu 2 .... 25 M6
Puri Gading 36 B5
Puri Gading 1 .... 36 C6
Puri Gading 2 .... 36 C6
Puri Gading Timur 36 C6
Puri Gerenceng 10 F5
Puri Hasu 43 K2
Puri Kamboja 15 G3
Puri Kubu 19 K8
Puri Naga Mas 16 D1
Puri Nagamas 22 D8

Puri Nusa Dua 38 F3
Purnawarman 28 F2
Purwani 25 J8
Pusaka 11 G4
Puseh Sari 32 D3
Puspa 29 K5
Puspa Ayu 11 F2
Puspa Wresti 39 H5

R

Raden Wijaya 50 B7
Raharja 17 G5
Rahayu (Kerobokan Kaja) 27 G4
Rahayu (Kerobokan Kelod) 19 J4
Rahayu (Pemecutan Kelod, Denpasar Brt) 21 G4
Rahayu (Pemecutan Kelod) 21 H3
Rahayu 4 .... 21 H3
Rahmat 16 D2
Rajawali (Dauh Puri Kelod) 21 K3
Rajawali (Gianyar) 50 C6
Rajawali (Jimbaran, Kuta) 36 C6
Rajawali (Kaja, Sesetan, Denpasar Sel.) . 21 L6
Rajawali (Kerobokan) 26 D8
Rajawali (Negara) 56 D4
Rajawali (Pemecutan Kelod, Denpasar Brt) 20 D7
Rajawali (Renon, Denpasar Selatan) 22 F4
Rajawali (Renon) 22 F7
Rajawali (Sesetan) 16 D2
Rajawali (Singaraja) 57 B5
Rajawali (Tabanan) 51 B2
Raketan 48 B2
Rali Santi 19 L7
Rama (Bangli) 54 E2
Rama (Seminyak) 19 H7
Rama (Singaraja) 57 E4
Rama (Sumerta) 29 M6
Rama (Tabanan) 51 E3
Rama 4 .... 29 M7
Ramadewa 22 E6
Ramayana 8 .... 27 H7
Rambutan 29 G6
Rambutan (Bangli) 54 D6
Rambutan (Gianyar) 50 C6
Rampai 30 C8
Randu 29 M5
Ratna (Gianyar) 50 E8
Ratna (Kerobokan Kelod) 19 M8
Ratna (Kesiman) 30 B7
Ratna (Klungkung) 51 C7
Ratna (Negara) 56 D4
Ratna (Singaraja) 57 B5
Ratna (Tabanan) 51 C3
Ratna (Tibu Beneng) 26 D2
Ratna (Tonja) 29 J4
Ratna (Ubung) 28 D2
Ratna 1 (Gianyar) 50 E7
Ratna 1 (Klungkung) 51 C7
Ratna 2 (Gianyar) 50 E8
Ratna 2 (Klungkung) 51 C7
Ratna 3 (Gianyar) 50 E8
Ratna 3 (Klungkung) 51 C7
Ratna Gang 3 .... 29 J4
Ratna Sari 27 H4
Ratu 19 L7
Raung, Gunung 56 D8
Raya Sesetan (Pedungan) 21 L6
Raya Sesetan (Sesetan) 16 C4
Regong, Letda 29 G5
Rembulan 27 H6
Rembulan, Pulau (Bumi Sari) 21 J5
Rencong 21 M4
Resimuka Barat 28 A8
Resimuka Barat 3 .... 28 A7
Resimuka Barat 7 .... 28 A7
Reta, Letda 29 H8
Reta, Letda 22 A2
Rijasa 51 C8
Rijasa 1 .... 51 C8
Rinjani 21 G8
Rinjani 1, Gunung (Negara) 56 E5
Rinjani, Gunung (Denpasar Barat) 21 G1
Rinjani, Gunung (Klungkung) 51 E8
Rinjani, Gunung (Singaraja) 57 D7
Roon, Pulau 21 J3
Rotan 21 G8
RSI Markandya 1 .... 48 D1
RSI Markandya 2 .... 48 E1
RSI Markandya 3 .... 48 F2
RSUD 54 B5
RTN 54 D7
Rurung Dalem 26 F3

S

S. Parman 22 C3
Saba, Tukad 22 B6
Sabha, Gunung 15 H1
Sabha, Gunung 20 E7
Sada Sari 11 H2
Sada Sari Anyar 11 G5
Sadewa 54 D3
Saelus, Pulau 21 J6
Saestu Hadi, Kapten 56 C5
Sagamona 23 G4
Sahadewa (Dauh Puri Kaja) 28 F6
Sahadewa (Gianyar) 50 B7
Sahadewa (Kerobokan Kelod) 19 L2
Sahadewa (Klungkung) 51 E7
Sahadewa (Seminyak) 19 H7
Sahadewa (Tabanan) 51 E3

Sahadewa (Tibu Beneng) 26 C4
Sakaguru 15 K5
Sakuni 28 A6
Sakura (Dangin Puri Kangin) 29 H4
Sakura (Klungkung) 51 C8
Sakura (Ubung) 28 D1
Sakura I 36 B4
Sakura IA 36 B4
Sakura III 36 B4
Sakura IV 36 B4
Sakura V 36 B4
Salak (Amlapura) 55 A8
Salak (Klungkung) 51 C5
Salak (Sapta Bumi) 20 E1
Salak, Gunung (Tegal Lantang) 20 B3
Salia (Seminyak) 19 J8
Salya (Bangli) 54 D2
Salya (Denpasar) 28 F4
Salya (Negara) 56 B5
Salya 4 .... 28 F4
Samudra 10 E4
Sandal 26 C5
Sandat (Dangin Puri Kaja) 29 H3
Sandat (Kesiman Kertha Langu) 31 H4
Sandat (Kesiman) 30 B6
Sandat (Klungkung) 51 D8
Sandat (Negara) 56 B2
Sandat (Pemecutan Kelod) 20 E7
Sandat (Panjer) 22 C7
Sandat (Seminyak) 20 A8
Sandat (Ubud) 47 G2
Sandat 3 .... 29 H3
Sandat 4 .... 29 H4
Sanekan, Tukad 13 K1
Sang Hyang, Tukad 22 B6
Sangga Buana, Gang 28 C8
Sangga Langit 29 M2
Sanggar 29 J2
Sanggar Agung 32 D5
Sanggar Alit 32 D5
Sanggar Buana 32 D5
Sanggingan, Raya 48 E2
Sanitasi 16 D4
Santai 19 H4
Sanur Beach Street Walk 23 L4
Saraswati 29 J3
Saraswati (Denpasar Barat) 21 K3
Sari 29 H1
Sari 2, Gunung 15 H2
Sari Ayu 29 J2
Sari Bunga 29 G1
Sari Daging 23 G5
Sari Dewi (Padang Sambian Kelod) 20 B4
Sari Dewi (Seminyak) 19 H7
Sari Dewi (Tonja) 29 H1
Sari Gading 29 H2
Sari Kuning, Tukad 22 B6
Sari Sekapa 41 K2
Sari Sekapa 1 .... 41 J2
Sari, Gunung (Sanur Kauh) 23 H6
Sarinadi 19 K4
Sarinande 19 K8
Saritemuku 19 J7
Satelit 21 K5
Satiaki 28 F5
Satria (Benoa) 33 K6
Satria (Tuban) 11 H4
Satriya Buana 20 D1
Saturnus 21 K5
Sawa Gunung 49 M2
Sawira 26 E5
Sawit 25 K8
Sawo 57 D3
Sayang, Pulau 21 J5
Sebatik 21 K3
Sedap Malam (Amlapura) 55 B4
Sedap Malam (Kesiman) 29 M5
Sedap Malam (Nyuh Tebel) 52 A7
Sedap Malam (Sanur Kaja) 23 H3
Sedap Malam 2 .... 30 B6
Sedap Malam 3 .... 30 B6
Segara Ayu 23 M7
Segara Geni 23 L6
Segara Geni 33 J1
Segara Geni 33 K1
Segara Kulon 33 K2
Segara Lor (Serangan) 13 G8
Segara Lor (Tanjung Benoa) 33 J1
Segara Madu (Ketewel) 31 L4
Segara Madu (Tuban) 32 C1
Segara Merta 10 E5
Segara Perancak 18 C1
Segara Samuh 39 J2
Segara Wangi 32 C3
Segara, Danau 56 B7
Segina III B 20 E6
Segina VI 20 F6
Segina VI A 20 F6
Sejahtera 22 A7
Sekar 30 C7
Sekar 1 .... 31 G5
Sekar Jepun (Kuta) 38 D2
Sekar Jepun (Penatih Dangin Puri) 30 C2
Sekar Jepun 1 .... 30 C2
Sekar Jepun 2 .... 30 C2
Sekar Jepun 3 .... 30 C2
Sekar Jepun 4 .... 30 C2
Sekar Jepun 5 .... 30 B1
Sekar Jepun 6 .... 30 C1
Sekar Jepun 7 .... 30 C1

Sekar Jepun 8 .... 30 C1
Sekar Sari 30 E6
Sekar Tunjung 30 C2
Sekar Tunjung 1 .... 30 C2
Sekar Tunjung 2 .... 30 C2
Sekar Tunjung 3 .... 30 C2
Sekar Tunjung 4 .... 30 C2
Sekar Tunjung 5 .... 30 C2
Sekar Tunjung 6 .... 30 C2
Sekar Tunjung 7 .... 30 C3
Sekar Tunjung 8 .... 30 C2
Sekar Tunjung 9 .... 30 D3
Sekar Tunjung 10 .... 30 C3
Sekar Tunjung 11 .... 30 D3
Sekar Tunjung 12 .... 30 D3
Sekar Tunjung 16 .... 30 C3
Sekar Tunjung 17 .... 30 C3
Sekar Tunjung 18 .... 30 D3
Sekar Tunjung 19 .... 30 C3
Sekar Tunjung 20 .... 30 C3
Sekar Wangi 22 B8
Sekar Wangi 1 .... 31 G4
Sekar Wangi 2 .... 30 F4
Sekar Wangi 4 .... 30 F4
Sekar Waru 17 J4
Sekarsari 31 G6
Sekumpul 23 G6
Sekuta 23 K7
Selayar, Pulau (Denpasar Barat) 21 K3
Selayar, Pulau (Singaraja) 57 E1
Semana, Raya 48 B8
Semanggi 28 D1
Semarang 36 C5
Sembatu Bayam 48 B2
Semen 23 G7
Semer, Raya 26 E7
Semeru (Denpasar) 28 E7
Semeru 2, Gunung (Negara) 56 E5
Semeru 3, Gunung (Negara) 56 E6
Semeru 4, Gunung (Negara) 56 E6
Semeru, Gunung (Klungkung) 51 E6
Semeru, Gunung (Negara) 56 E6
Semeru, Gunung (Singaraja) 57 F7
Semeru, Gunung (Tabanan) 51 D2
Semila Sari Barat 28 B4
Seminyak 14 B2
Seminyak, Raya 19 L8
Sempati 11 G5
Sempol 25 K2
Semut 15 H3
Sengkidu, Raya 52 A6
Senuri 29 H5
Seram, Pulau 21 K3
Serangan, Pulau 21 K5
Serangan, Raya 13 J2
Seratus, Gang 21 H3
Seraya 1, Gunung 20 F1
Seraya, Gang 20 C1
Seraya, Gunung 20 F1
Seribu, Pulau 21 K4
Serma Made Oka 21 L4
Seroja (Sanur Kala) 23 K7
Seroja (Tonja) 29 J1
Seruni (Dangin Puri Kangin) 29 H5
Seruni (Kerobokan Kelod) 26 E8
Seruni (Klungkung) 51 B7
Sesar 21 K3
Seseh, Raya 24 E3
Sesetan Agung 21 L7
Sesetan, Raya 16 B2
Setiabudi (Kuta) 14 F7
Setiabudi (Pemecutan Kaja) 28 E6
Setra Dalem 21 L7
Setra Ganda Mayu 33 J4
Setra Ganda Mayu 2 .... 33 J4
Setra Ganda Mayu 3 .... 33 J4
Sidakarya 16 E3
Silang Karang 48 C6
Siligita 39 H5
Siligita 39 G4
Singaraja, Raya (Anturan) 53 K3
Singaraja, Raya (KaliAsem) 52 C3
Singekerta, Raya 48 D8
Singkep, Pulau (Denpasar) 21 J7
Singkep, Pulau (Negara) 56 F6
Singosari (Denpasar) 28 E2
Singosari (Tabanan) 51 E2
Singosari Utara 28 E1
Singosari-Kuta 14 E8
Sinta (Pemogan) 19 H8
Sinta (Seminyak) 14 A1
Sintha, Lettu 55 E4
Siputih 25 J7
Sita 26 C7
Siul 19 K6
Siulan 30 E1
Siulan 1 .... 30 E1
Skip 57 B4
Slamet 1, Gunung 20 F2
Slamet Riyadi 21 M2
Slamet Riyadi 1 .... 21 M2
Slamet Riyadi 2 .... 21 M2
SMK 3 .... 57 F5
Smu 3 .... 29 K6
Sobat, Lettu 54 C6
Sogsogan, Raya 24 D2
Soka (Kerobokan Kelod) 26 D8
Soka (Kerobokan) 27 H6
Soka (Kesiman Kertha Langu) 30 C4
Soka (Klungkung) 51 C7

Soka (Negara) 56 C3
Soka (Sanur) 23 K7
Soka (Sumerta Kaja) 29 K6
Soka (Tibu Beneng) 25 L7
Soka (Ubud) 47 G3
Soka 1 (Klungkung) 51 C7
Soka 2 (Klungkung) 51 D7
Soka 3 (Klungkung) 51 D7
Soka Sari 28 A3
Soka Sati 29 M5
Solo 36 C5
Solor 21 L4
Songan, Raya 50 D1
Soputan 1, Gunung 20 D7
Soputan Permai 20 D6
Soputan, Gunung 20 D7
Sri Amerta 57 B7
Sri Kahyangan 18 E2
Sri Rama (Legian) 14 D3
Sri Rama (Pemecutan Kaja) 28 E6
Sri Rama (Tonja) 29 K1
Srianggan, Danau 56 B5
Srikandi (Kuta) 39 H5
Srikandi (Padang Sambian Kelod) 20 B2
Srikandi (Singaraja) 57 C8
Srikarya 29 H5
Srikaya 28 A8
Sriwedari (Benoa) 46 F3
Sriwedari (Ubud) 49 G1
Sriwijaya (Bangli) 54 D1
Sriwijaya (Kuta) 14 E5
Sriwijaya (Tabanan) 51 E2
Sriwijaya (Ungasan) 43 J4
Stap 19 H4
STSI 29 K6
Suara Ombak 34 E6
Subak Buaji 30 B8
Subak Daksina 26 C1
Subak Sari 25 L5
Subak Sari 1 .... 18 E2
Subali (Kerobokan) 27 G5
Subali (Singaraja) 57 E5
Subali (Tabanan) 51 E3
Subita 29 K5
Subur 20 G2
Suci, Letda 29 G8
Sudamala (Bangli) 54 C8
Sudamala (Sanur) 17 K4
Sudamala 1 .... 54 C8
Sudamala 2 .... 54 C8
Sudirman (Banyu Asri, Singaraja) 57 B5
Sudirman (Banyuning, Singaraja) 57 F1
Sudirman (Negara) 56 E4
Sudirman (Tabanan) 51 E2
Sudirman 1, Panglima Besar (Denpasar) 21 M1
Sudirman Kartika 7 .... 21 M1
Sudirman RSAD 21 M1
Sudirman, Jendral (Amlapura) 55 B6
Sudirman, Jendral (Kuta) 57 A8
Sudirman, Panglima Besar (Denpasar) 21 M1
Sudu 21 M4
Sudut Indah 26 F6
Sugianyar 29 G7
Sugriwa (Bangli) 54 E3
Sugriwa (Singaraja) 57 E5
Sugriwa (Tabanan) 51 E3
Sugriwa ((Ubud) 46 F5
Suka Buana 30 B8
Suka Merta 17 H4
Sukun 19 M1
Sula, Pulau 21 K5
Sulatri 30 A3
Sulawesi (Denpasar) 28 F7
Sulawesi, Pulau (Singaraja) 57 E1
Suli (Dangin Puri Kangin) 29 H3
Suli (Kerobokan Kelod) 19 H2
Suli 1 .... 29 H5
Suli A 31 H4
Suli B2 .... 31 H4
Sultan Agung 55 E2
Sumatera (Denpasar) 28 F7
Sumatera, Pulau (Singaraja) 57 E2
Sumba, Pulau 21 K4
Sungi, Yeh 22 E5
Sunia Negara 15 K6
Sunrise 19 M3
Sunset Road (Kuta) 15 G6
Sunset Road (Pemecutan Kelod) 14 F3
Sunset Road (Seminyak) 19 L6
Supiori, Pulau 20 F7
Supratman 56 E5
Supratman 2 .... 56 E5
Surabaya 36 C5
Surabi 29 M4
Surapati (Denpasar) 29 H7
Surapati (Singaraja) 57 E2
Surya (Denpasar) 21 J6
Surya (Seminyak) 15 H2
Surya Buana 20 D2
Surya Buana 1 .... 27 G1
Susut, Raya 54 A3
Suti 50 D7
Sutomo (Denpasar) 28 E6
Sutomo 8 .... 28 E6
Sutomo, Dr (Negara) 56 C5
Sutomo, Dr (Singaraja) 57 D3
Sutoyo 28 F8
Suweta 49 G1
Suwung Batan Kendal 16 C5
Suwung Permai 16 C5

Swakarya Baru 21 M3
Swari 28 D5
Swastiastu 22 A8
Swastika 57 E5

T

Tabah 48 A1
Talang, Gunung 20 D3
Taman (Kerobokan Kelod) 18 F4
Taman (Kesiman Kertha Langu) 31 G3
Taman (Padang Sambian Kelod) 20 B4
Taman Asri 28 C7
Taman Bali 38 B1
Taman Ganesha 19 G5
Taman Giri 38 B2
Taman Griya (Jimbaran) 38 A3
Taman Griya (Pemecutan Kelod) 21 H3
Taman Jati 38 B1
Taman Jimbaran 38 A1
Taman Kebo Iwa 38 D2
Taman Kerowa 38 E2
Taman Lawang 38 B1
Taman Nusa 42 D6
Taman Nusa Indah 38 D3
Taman Pancing 15 H6
Taman Paradise 42 F1
Taman Peta 36 E4
Taman Pule 19 J7
Taman Ria 38 C2
Taman Sari (Benoa, Kuta) 38 D3
Taman Sari (Kuta) 11 F3
Taman Sari (Padang Sambian Kelod) 20 B3
Taman Sari (Sanur) 23 L8
Taman Sari (Sesetan) 21 L8
Taman Sari (Tanjung Benoa, Kuta) 33 K3
Taman Sari 1 .... 20 B3
Taman Sari Madu 19 M3
Taman Sari, Tukad (Denpasar Selatan) 22 B6
Taman Siswa 38 A1
Taman Suc 16 B5
Taman Werdi 38 B1
Tambak Sari 32 E4
Tambak Sari (Sanur) 17 J4
Tamblingan 1, Danau (Kuta) 37 K3
Tamblingan 2, Danau (Kuta) 37 K3
Tamblingan 3, Danau (Kuta) 37 K3
Tamblingan 4, Danau (Kuta) 37 K3
Tamblingan, Danau (Denpasar Selatan) 23 L7
Tamblingan, Danau (Kuta) 37 K3
Tamblingan, Danau (Negara) 56 A7
Tanah Kilap 15 G8
Tanah Sampi 26 F2
Tangga Yuda 48 C3
Tangkuban Perahu, Gunung (Denpasar) 20 B5
Tangkuban Perahu, Gunung (Negara) 56 D7
Tanimbar, Pulau 21 L4
Tanjung (Negara) 56 C1
Tanjung (Sanur) 17 H4
Tanjung Simah 34 D7
Tantri 28 D6
Tantular Barat 22 B3
Tantular, Letda 22 B2
Tapak Bela 29 H5
Tarakan, Pulau 21 J4
Tari Legong 29 J2
Tarumanegara 51 D2
Taruna 29 H1
Tasik Wulan 22 F7
Tatiapi 47 M3
Tatiapi Kaja 47 M3
Tatiapi Kangin 49 K5
Taulan Sari 19 K3
Tegal Abadi 20 B5
Tegal Arum 22 B8
Tegal Asri 20 B4
Tegal Bandeng, Raya 56 A7
Tegal Bingin 49 J8
Tegal Cupaek 26 D5
Tegal Cupaek 1 .... 26 D6
Tegal Cupaek 2 .... 26 D6
Tegal Dukuh 2B 28 A2
Tegal Harum (Kesiman Kertha Langu) 31 J4
Tegal Harum (Padang Sambian Kelod) 20 B4
Tegal Indah 20 B4
Tegal Jaya 22 B8
Tegal Kuning 48 B2
Tegal Linggah, Raya 55 F3
Tegal Permai 27 G1
Tegal Sari (Jimbaran) 32 D5
Tegal Sari (Kesiman Kertha Langu) 31 J4
Tegal Sari (Tibu Beneng) 25 L7
Tegal Sari (Ubud) 46 F2
Tegal Sari 3 .... 27 G1
Tegal Sari 10 .... 26 F1
Tegal Sari Raya 26 F1
Tegal Wangi (Denpasar Barat) 20 B4
Tegal Wangi (Jimbaran) 36 A1
Tegal Wangi (Kuta) 14 D8
Tegal Wangi (Sesetan) 16 C1
Tegal Wangi 2 .... 16 C2
Tegal Wangi, Tukad 21 M7
Tegeh Agung 23 K6
Tegeh Sari 14 F7
Teguan 48 B3
Tekukur 57 C3
Telaga Mas 23 J7
Telaga Waja 19 H5
Telaga Waja (Denpasar Selatan) 22 E4
Telaga Waja (Tanjung Benoa) 33 J5
Telagasari 43 H1

Buildings Index

Amanusa Golf 39 G7
Amanusa, Hotel 39 G8
Amari, Hotel 14 C3
Amaris, Hotel (Dewi Sri, Legian) 14 E4
Amaris, Hotel (Pratama, Nusa Dua) 39 J4
Amaris, Hotel (Sunset Road, Kuta) 15 G5
Amaris, Hotel (Teuku Umar, Denpasar) .. 21 H6
Amarossa, Hotel 38 D2
Amarta, Restaurant 33 K4
Amasya Villas, The 19 H6
AMC 32 B2
Amed Blue Star, Hotel 91 H5
Amed Bungalows 91 J7
Amed Scuba, Hotel 91 H6
Amel Home Stay, Hotel 46 F6
Amertha Bali Villa Beach Front Resort & Spa,
   Hotel 94 D2
Amertha's Bungalows 50 C3
Amertha's, Restaurant 50 D3
Ametis, Hotel 25 H7
Amino, Restaurant 14 D6
Amira, Hotel 14 D4
Amlapura, Villa 55 E4
Amor Bali Villas & Spa Resort 19 M6
Amore, Hotel 18 F1
Amori Villas 47 M6
Amori, Shopping 19 L7
Amour, Hotel 19 H3
Amphitheatre 36 F7
Amway 22 F3
Ana, Hotel 56 E5
Anacaraka Bali, Hotel 28 D7
Anahata, Hotel 49 J1
Ananda Cottages 48 D3
Ananda, Hotel 19 J7
Ananda, Hotel (Sanur) 23 L4
Ananda, Restaurant 104 A8
Anang 14 F8
Ananta, Hotel 14 B2
Anantara, Hotel 19 H8
Anantara, Hotel (Uluwatu) 34 C6
Anatara, Restaurant 14 E3
Anda Amed, Hotel 91 K6
Andalas, Restaurant 23 K6
Andaman, Hotel 26 D7
Andong, Hotel 47 J3
Andy's Surf Shack, Hotel 24 F6
Aneka Bagus, Hotel 94 D2
Aneka Data 29 H5
Aneka Lovina, Hotel 52 F2
Aneka Murah 21 G6
Aneka, Hotel 14 D7
Anemalou, Hotel 14 F4
Anfiona Art 19 M4
Angel, Restaurant 46 F5
Angel's Collection 19 M4
Anggrek 66, Hotel 14 C2
Anggrek, Hotel 14 D6
Anginsepoi, Hotel 25 G7
Angkasa Cargo 16 A6
Angsa Putih, Restaurant 38 C1
Angsoka, Hotel 52 F2
Angsoka, Shopping 53 G3
Anhera, Hotel 48 E3
Ani Ani, Hotel 19 G1
Anika Guest House 11 G6
Anini Raka Resort & Spa 48 D3
Anisa, Hotel 19 G3
Anita, Hotel 53 H3
ANK 28 E7
Anna Sari, Hotel 46 B3
Anni, Restaurant 29 G6
Annora Villas & Spa 14 B2
Anom 48 E2
Anom Beach, Hotel 52 B8
Anom Cottage 48 E3
Anom Village, Hotel 10 F5
Anom's Wood Carving 46 F5
Anomali, Restaurant 46 F4
Antani, Hotel 94 D2
Antar Daerah 28 E7
Antara Villas 14 E3
Antara, The, Hotel 26 E6
Anthony Widiadari, Hotel 25 L6
Antique, Hotel 19 J2
Antonius Kho 48 E2
Anyar Estate, Hotel 26 B7
ANZ Bank 21 K3
AP Denpasar 21 L1
Apa Kabar Village 91 J6
Apa Kabar, Restaurant 17 L4
Apache, Restaurant 14 E7
Apple, Hotel 26 D5
AQ-VA, Hotel 14 C3
Aqua Danone (Ungasan) 38 D5
Aqua Marine Diving 19 K3
Aqua, Hotel 18 F3
Aquablu, Hotel 53 K7
Aquaria, Hotel 14 E7
Aquarius Star, Hotel 14 E7
Aquaterrace Amed, Hotel 91 L7
Aquatropic Dive 53 H2
Ar Rahmat 14 D3
Arama Riverside Villas 14 D3
Arama, Hotel 14 D3
Araminth Spa 53 G3
Arana Suites, Hotel 14 E3

Arca 22 F2
Archipelago 17 K4
Arco Iris Resort 53 L7
Arena, Restaurant 19 K1
Arena, Restaurant (Nusa Dua) 33 L8
Arena, Restaurant (Sanur) 23 K6
Ari Homestay, Hotel 52 F7
Ari Putri, Hotel 17 K4
Ari, Restaurant 99 H7
Aria Villa 19 G4
Ariana, Hotel 26 B5
Arika, Hotel 24 F6
Arina & Lima Lima, Restaurant 57 J4
Aris Warung 31 L1
Ariski Ayu, Restaurant 19 H7
Arjuna 2, Hotel 46 E1
Arjuna Metapa Museum 49 K7
Arjuna, Hotel 14 D5
Arlina Bungalows 50 C2
Arma Resort 49 G7
Arma, Shopping 48 F7
Arman Villa 14 D2
Aroma 32 B3
Arsa Home Stay, Hotel 46 F6
Arsana, Hotel 49 G7
Arsip Daerah 22 C3
Art & Batik 14 F6
Art 200 .... 103 G4
Art Aruni 46 F6
Art Market (Bali Collection, Nusa Dua) .. 39 K5
Art Market (Jl. Danau Tamblingan, Sanur) . 23 L7
Art Market (Jl. Pratama, Tg Benoa) 33 K2
Art Market (Jl. Segara Samuh, Tg Benoa) .. 39 J2
Art of Body, The 19 K5
Art Shop 32 E1
Artemis, Hotel 19 K8
Artha Agung, Gallery 65 H3
Artha Graha Bank 21 L2
Artha Jaya 32 E3
Artha Sari 48 C7
Artha Sastra Inn, Hotel 54 D4
Artha, Hotel 52 B6
Artha, Hotel (Dauh Puri Kelod) 21 L3
Artini 3 Cottages & Spa 46 F8
Artini, Restaurant 46 F6
Artis, Hotel 19 G2
Arung Jeram 51 F6
Ary Home Stay, Hotel 53 H7
Ary Pudja, Gallery 65 G3
Arya Amed Beach Resort 91 J6
Arya Hiram 1, Hotel 18 F3
Arya Utama, Hotel 98 E7
Arya, Hotel 14 F6
Aryas Cafe 52 F3
As One, Restaurant 48 E1
Asa Paris, PT., Service Division 20 C7
Asabri 23 G4
Asana, Hotel 25 H5
Asante, Hotel 25 G6
Asasut Taqwa 11 J6
Asatu, Hotel 26 B2
Ascent Villa 36 D8
Asfi 32 C6
Ashling Villa 91 G5
Ashoka Canggu, Hotel 24 E5
Ashram, Hotel 99 M7
Ashyana Candidasa, Hotel 53 G7
Asialink 23 K8
Asian International School 36 B5
Asian Spice, Restaurant 14 D8
Asian's Trails, Restaurant 23 K6
Asih Usadha 29 G5
Askrido 22 D4
Asli, Hotel 18 E3
Asmara, Hotel 24 A3
Asmara, The, Hotel 45 G5
Asoka Beach, Hotel 53 M7
Asoma Talk 37 G5
Asrama Putri Depkes 31 H5
Asri, Restaurant 20 D7
Asta, Hotel 19 H3
Astagina, Hotel 14 C3
Astana Batubelig, Hotel 18 F3
Astana Kunti Suite Apartment 19 M6
Astana Kunti, Apartment & Villa 20 A7
Astana Kunti, Hotel 19 M7
Astana Lifestyle Club 19 L7
Astina Tours 22 E3
Astina, Hotel 52 F3
Astiti Shop 47 J1
Astiti, Hotel 47 G5
Aston Bali Resort and Spa 33 K5
Aston Denpasar, Hotel 28 D3
Aston Grand Kuta Residence, Hotel 14 E3
Aston Inn, Hotel 11 H4
Aston Kuta, Hotel 10 E4
Aston Legend Villas 17 L5
Aston Nandini Ubud Resort & Spa 72 F4
Aston, Hotel 36 D7
Astragraphia 27 H2
Asuna, Restaurant 33 K3
Asylum Hospital 54 C4
At Taqwa 29 J5
At Taufiq 30 E2
Atanaya, Hotel 14 F4
Athena Garden Villa, Hotel 20 A6
Atma, Restaurant 25 H8
Auditorium 37 H3
Australian Embassy 22 C3
Australian Int'l School 19 K4

Avalon, Hotel 18 E3
Avani 38 A1
Aven's 19 M5
Aviva, Hotel 19 J4
Awan Villas 19 G4
Awangga Homestay 50 D2
Awanti Villa 37 H7
Axmi Beauty Salon & Spa 46 E7
Aya's Rooms, Hotel 46 F4
Ayam Bakar Wong Solo 11 H2
Ayam Betutu 29 M8
Ayam Goreng Fatmawati 21 J3
Ayam Goreng Ibu Sunu, Restaurant 21 J5
Ayana Resort & Spa, Hotel 35 L1
Ayani Art Shop 49 H3
Ayanna Villa 25 K3
Ayen, Restaurant 21 G6
Ayodya Resort, The, Hotel (Nusa Dua) ... 39 K6
Ayodya, Hotel (Lovina Beach) 53 G3
Ayodya, Restaurant (Jimbaran) 32 B2
Ayodya, Restaurant (Sanur) 17 J4
Ayu Guna Inn, Hotel 34 C8
Ayu Minantri, Restaurant 22 A2
Ayu Nadi (Renon) 22 C5
Ayu Nadi (Tuban) 10 F5
Ayu Nadi Mini Market 20 E7
Ayu, The, Hotel 50 D2
Ayu's Kitchen, Restaurant 46 E3
Ayunda, Hotel 28 C2
Ayung Spa 72 F2
Ayung Terrace, Restaurant 48 C4

B
B House, Hotel 53 L7
b, Hotel 15 G4
Babar, Villa 62 D3
Babi Guling Karyo Rebo 32 D2
BaBiBu, Hotel 26 E5
Bacio, Restaurant 14 B2
Badan Kepegawaian Daerah 22 B2
Badan Kependudukan 22 C3
Badan Penanaman Modal & Perizinan ... 21 M3
Badan Pendidikan & Pelatihan Daerah ... 22 F2
Badan Pengawas Daerah 22 C2
Badan Pusat Statistik 31 G5
Badra Fine Art & Gallery 46 B1
Badri, Hotel 47 G5
Badung Market 28 E7
Badung Tourism 29 G7
Bag's City 39 L3
Bagelen Yogya, Restaurant 69 J6
Bagus Drug Store 17 L4
Bagus Home Stay 98 D2
Bagus, Café 33 K4
Bahagia, Hotel (Canggu) 25 M3
Bahagia, Hotel (Kerobokan) 19 H2
Bahiana, Restaurant 19 K8
Baik Baik Villas 14 D2
Baiturrahmat 28 F4
Bajaj 21 L7
Bajak Laut, Restaurant 22 B2
Bajra Santhi Monument 22 D3
Bakar Ikan Bumbu Bali, Restaurant 32 C2
Bakung Merdeka, Hotel 15 G6
Bakung Sari, Hotel 14 E8
Bakung's Beach, Hotel 10 E4
Bakwan Surabaya, Restaurant 21 J3
Bala Keselamatan 28 E4
Baladewa Empat, Hotel 19 G1
Baladewa Satu, Hotel 26 B8
Balai Arkeologi 21 L7
Balai Banjar 46 E4
Balai Banjar Geladag 21 J8
Balai Banjar Menesa 21 J7
Balai Budaya 51 D6
Balai Karantina Hewan 16 B5
Balai Latihan Kerja 15 G4
Balai Pemantapan Kawasan Hutan 22 B3
Balangan Garden, Hotel 35 J5
Balangan Sari, Hotel 35 J5
Balangan Sea View Bungalows 34 F3
Balangan Wave, Hotel 35 H4
Balboni, Restaurant 33 K3
Balcony, The, Restaurant 14 D5
Bale Kambang 51 D6
Bale Udang Mang Engking, Restaurant ... 14 F3
Bale, The, Hotel 39 H8
Baleka, Hotel 14 C3
Bali Adventure Tours 87 H8
Bali Aga Karaoke 52 C2
Bali Agung Village 19 J8
Bali Amed Fisherman's House, Hotel 91 H6
Bali Amertha Tour & Transport 32 C7
Bali Apik, Restaurant 52 E2
Bali Aroma Exclusive Villas 18 F4
Bali Asih, Hotel 26 D7
Bali Ayu, Hotel 19 H5
Bali Bagia, Restaurant 14 E8
Bali Bagus, Hotel 10 F3
Bali Bagus, Shop (Nusa Dua) 39 L4
Bali Bagus, Shopping (Sanur) 23 L7
Bali Bakery (Denpasar) 29 M8
Bali Bakery (Kuta) 14 F5
Bali Bali Estate, Hotel 19 J1
Bali Balo Motor, Hotel 26 B3
Bali Bay View Suites & Villas, The, Hotel .. 38 D3
Bali Beach Garden 102 E3
Bali Beach House, Hotel 91 H5
Bali Becik, Hotel 33 L7
Bali Beer, Karaoke 12 E5

Bali Bintang, Restaurant 52 E2
Bali Brasco 14 F3
Bali Breeze, Hotel 48 F7
Bali Breizh Divers 23 K3
Bali Buddha Cafe 47 G4
Bali Buddha, Restaurant 26 C5
Bali Bule, Hotel 40 C1
Bali Bunga, Hotel 19 H3
Bali Bungalo, Hotel 14 D6
Bali Camel Safari 45 K5
Bali Car Rental 14 D4
Bali Ceramics 53 K7
Bali Citra Lestari, Hotel 90 F5
Bali Clay Court, Hotel 19 G4
Bali Cliff, Hotel 43 K8
Bali Clinic 19 H6
Bali Coconut, Hotel 14 C3
Bali Collection and Entertainment Cplx .. 39 M3
Bali Computer Center 21 L2
Bali Corail, Hotel 27 J4
Bali Coral, Hotel 90 D2
Bali Cricket, Restaurant 17 K4
Bali Dance Festival 32 E4
Bali Deli, Restaurant 17 L3
Bali Deli, Shopping 19 L7
Bali Design 14 F5
Bali Dewata, Hotel 52 C3
Bali Dream House, Hotel 91 J5
Bali Dream Villa, The 19 M6
Bali Dream Villas 19 M7
Bali Dream, The, Hotel 25 G5
Bali Dwipa, Hotel 14 D6
Bali Dynasty Resort, Hotel 10 E3
Bali Easy, Hotel 26 C4
Bali Eco, Restaurant 22 F1
Bali Eka Beach Inn, Hotel 23 K4
Bali Electronic Center 21 H5
Bali Emerald Villas 17 L3
Bali Equestrian Centre 25 M7
Bali Ethnics 19 K6
Bali Galleria Mall 15 G8
Bali Garden, Hotel 10 F2
Bali Globe, Hotel 19 K8
Bali Golden Vila, Hotel 43 J6
Bali Golf & Country Club 39 J5
Bali Golf & Country Club 18 Holes 39 K7
Bali Gong Art 31 L2
Bali Gonzaga, Hotel 39 J3
Bali Gonzaga, Restaurant 39 J2
Bali Grand Sunsets Resort 53 M2
Bali Green Spa 14 F3
Bali Griya Shanti, Hotel 39 H6
Bali Hai Cruises, Hotel 12 E6
Bali Hai Dream Villa 24 A1
Bali Hai Dream Villa, Hotel 63 H7
Bali Hai Oke, Restaurant 23 L6
Bali Handara Kaisodo Country Club 17 J3
Bali Handara Kosaido Country Club 99 M6
Bali Happy Rent Car 11 H3
Bali Heaven, Hotel 26 D8
Bali Hoki, Hotel 23 K5
Bali Holidays Tour 21 M8
Bali House, The 20 D8
Bali Impian, Hotel 36 C8
Bali Indah, Restaurant (Sanur) 17 M2
Bali Indah, Restaurant (Klungkung) 51 E6
Bali International Advisory Services 44 B3
Bali International Convention Center 39 K3
Bali International School 23 K5
Bali International, Hotel 16 E4
Bali Island Villas & Spa 19 G5
Bali Jeep Adventure, Hotel 26 C3
Bali Jegeg Villa, Hotel 32 C5
Bali Kasih, Hotel 19 M7
Bali Kembali, Hotel 17 L3
Bali Khama Beach, Resort & Spa 33 K4
Bali Kita Motor 30 D2
Bali Kopi House 17 J4
Bali Koral Dive 33 K3
Bali Krisna 20 B5
Bali Kubu Rama, Hotel 25 G6
Bali Kuta Resort 14 E7
Bali Land Houses, Hotel 26 F6
Bali Land Office 19 K2
Bali Lovina Beach Cottages 52 E3
Bali Lovina, Hotel 100 D8
Bali Mandira, Hotel 14 C4
Bali Marina, Restaurant 12 E5
Bali Marine Sports 17 L4
Bali Maritime Training Center 31 G5
Bali Memorial 14 E6
Bali Mengening, Hotel 24 A2
Bali Merita, Hotel (Canggu) 24 E5
Bali Merita, Hotel (Kerobokan) 26 D7
Bali Mirah, Hotel 24 A3
Bali Mode 46 F5
Bali Mountain Retreat, Hotel 85 G7
Bali Mulia Villas 14 D3
Bali Mulia, Hotel 29 G4
Bali Museum 29 G7
Bali Mystique, Hotel 19 G5
Bali Nikmat, Restaurant 14 F4
Bali No. 1, Restaurant 17 L4
Bali Nusa Dua Clinic 39 J5
Bali Nusa Dua Convention Center, Hotel .. 39 J3
Bali Nyuh Gading, Hotel 19 H3
Bali Oase Resort 94 B1
Bali Oding 23 L7
Bali Okina 19 K3
Bali Oky 27 H3

Bali Olly, Villa 36 B7
Bali Paintball 44 B7
Bali Palms Resort 52 E8
Bali Paradise, Hotel 53 G2
Bali Paradise, Villa 36 B7
Bali Paragon, Hotel 32 D8
Bali Passion, Hotel 26 D6
Bali Pavilion, Restaurant 19 K5
Bali Permai Tulamben, Hotel 90 D3
Bali Pet Shop 26 C4
Bali Prani, Hotel (Denpasar) 28 D3
Bali Prani, Hotel (Tuban) 10 E5
Bali Prime, Hotel 19 J2
Bali Puri Ratu Villa 19 L7
Bali Rama, Hotel 27 M5
Bali Rama, The, Hotel 29 M8
Bali Rani Bungalow 100 E6
Bali Rani, Hotel 10 F2
Bali Ratu Spa 10 F3
Bali Reef, Resort 33 K3
Bali Relaxing Resort & Spa, Hotel 33 L7
Bali Reski Asih Cottage 19 H7
Bali Rich Luxury Villa 19 K5
Bali Rich Residence, Hotel 23 L3
Bali Royal Hospital 22 C3
Bali Royal International, Hotel 33 L7
Bali Royal, Hotel 33 I6
Bali Samudera Arrirang, Hotel 52 E7
Bali Sandy, Hotel 14 D6
Bali Sani, Hotel 14 C4
Bali Santi Candidasa, Hotel 52 E8
Bali Santika, Hotel 17 K2
Bali Sanur Beach Villas 23 M8
Bali Sari, Hotel 11 G4
Bali Sea Breeze, Hotel 19 K7
Bali Sea, Restaurant 32 B2
Bali Seaman's, Restaurant 23 L7
Bali Segara, Hotel 10 E5
Bali Seni Toyabungkah, Hotel 50 C2
Bali Senia, Hotel 17 K4
Bali Shangrila Beach Club, Hotel 53 L7
Bali She Villa 36 B8
Bali Shell Museum 15 G6
Bali Signature Villas 11 K7
Bali Siring, Hotel 47 G6
Bali Spark Resort 90 E2
Bali Spirit Hotel & Spa 48 E8
Bali Spirit, Shopping 46 F6
Bali Splat Mas 17 H4
Bali Stingray Dive Center 52 A8
Bali Subak, Hotel 14 C2
Bali Summer, Hotel 14 D7
Bali Sunshine Villa 19 H5
Bali Surf Outlet 14 F8
Bali Surya Utama 16 B6
Bali Sweet, Hotel 26 C4
Bali Swiss Villa 19 M7
Bali Taman Beach Resort 53 M3
Bali Taman Wana, Villas 79 H3
Bali Times, The 14 E2
Bali Tour 32 C8
Bali Tourism Office 22 C3
Bali Tourist Service 48 E8
Bali Tropic, Hotel 33 L8
Bali Tulip, Hotel 27 J2
Bali Unique 19 K2
Bali Usada 17 K1
Bali Van Rent-a-Car 11 J5
Bali Vanila, Hotel 53 K3
Bali Vanilla Factory 53 M3
Bali Video 48 E3
Bali Villa 49 L3
Bali Villa Ocean 24 D5
Bali Village, Hotel (Legian) 14 C3
Bali Village, Hotel (Tanjung Benoa) 33 K6
Bali Villas Office 32 E2
Bali Warma, Hotel 23 K6
Bali Wirasana, Hotel 23 L8
Bali Zen, Hotel 19 K3
Bali Zoo Park 65 G5
Bali-Palmira, Hotel 19 J1
Bali, Hotel 46 B4
Bali, Restaurant 11 J2
Balibaliku Luxury Villa, Hotel 32 B7
Baliberry, Restaurant 22 F1
Balicosy Villa 14 E3
Baligen, Hotel 46 A2
Baliku, Hotel 26 E8
Balilu Resort 91 K7
Balina Beach Bungalow, Hotel 67 M2
Balinda, Hotel 52 F3
Balindo Paradiso 20 F6
Baliwae 22 B1
Balok 48 F3
Balun, Hotel 28 E4
Bamboo Bali, Hotel 91 H5
Bamboo Foundation 48 E7
Bamboo Furniture 65 K3
Bamboo Spa 32 B8
Bamboo, Hotel 14 D6
Bamboo, Restaurant (Lovina) 53 M2
Bamboo, Restaurant (Ubud) 46 E4
Bambu Gardens, Hotel 52 F7
Bambu Indah Villa 48 D5
Bambu Villa 17 L2
Bambu, Restaurant 19 G5
Ban Homestay, Hotel 46 F1
Bandil 49 G8
Bangli Inn, Hotel 54 D4
Bangsal Mart 30 F7

Banjan Tree 86 B7
Banjan Anggarkasih 23 J4
Banjar Buruan 23 J5
Banjar Dangin Peken 23 H6
Banjar Kaja Panjer 22 A5
Banjar Kehen 30 B3
Banjar Langon 23 J5
Banjar Tatag Wirasanti CC 14 E1
Banjar Villa, The, Hotel 26 C6
Banjar, Café 22 E5
Banjar, Hotel 25 K5
Banjar, The, Hotel 26 D6
Bank Indonesia 22 B2
Banyan Tree, Hotel 43 H8
Banyu Asri Market 27 L8
Banyualit, Hotel 53 J2
Bapedalda 29 J7
Bappeda 22 E2
Baraka, Hotel 18 E3
Barakuda, Restaurant 52 F3
Baris, Gallery 65 G3
Barokah, Hotel 17 K3
Barong Bali, Hotel 14 D7
Barong Cafe Bungalow 91 K7
Barong Resort & Spa 46 E6
Barong, Hotel 46 E5
Baru Motor 30 C3
Baruna 47 J4
Baruna Beach Inn, Hotel 23 M6
Baruna Beach Market 23 L6
Baruna Cottage 100 F6
Baruna Dive 33 K2
Baruna Diving School 52 F3
Baruna Pavilion, Restaurant 23 M5
Baruna Water Sport 53 H7
Baruna, Hotel (Nusa Lembongan) 108 C1
Baruna, Hotel (Sanur) 23 L6
Baruna, Restaurant (Sunset Road) 15 G6
Baruna, Restaurant (Jl. Letda Tantular) 22 C3
Barunasari Villa 49 G2
Basket Convenience 33 K5
Basket Weaving 65 K3
Baskin Robbin, Restaurant 39 M3
Bata 28 D3
Batan Poh, Restaurant 17 L2
Batan Waru, Restaurant 10 F2
Batik & Tenun Ikat Lestari 23 J2
Batik Kartika Candra 30 D5
Batik Sekar Bali 46 F5
Batik Winotosastro 30 D5
Batik Workshop (Nyuh Kuning, Ubud) 48 F8
Batik Workshop (Raya Andong, Ubud) 47 J1
Batu Alam Stone Art 31 J5
Batu Belah Resort 90 F4
Batu Belig, The, Hotel 19 H3
Batu Bolong, Hotel 25 H8
Batu Bulan Bus Terminal 30 F1
Batu Bunga, Hotel 19 G3
Batu Jaran Hill, Hotel 40 B3
Batu Jimbar Private Estates 17 M2
Batu Jimbar, Restaurant 17 M2
Batu Kayu, Hotel 19 H3
Batur Sari, Restaurant 105 M8
Bawa 46 F3
Bawang Merah Beach 32 B1
Bayshore Villas 52 A7
Bayside Bungalows 52 A7
Bayu 52 F3
Bayu Buana Travel 15 G6
Bayu Cottages 91 K6
Bayu Gede, Restaurant 100 F6
Bayu Kartika, Hotel 52 F3
Bayu Mantra, Hotel 53 L2
Bayu Paneeda, Hotel 52 D8
Bayu Suta Hospital 33 K2
Bayuh Sabbha, Villa 34 D6
BBC 32 B3
BBD 57 D4
BBQ & Shabu-Shabu, Restaurant 14 F7
BBRPBL 95 G3
BCA (Gatot Subroto) 29 G2
BCA (Jalan Gunung Batur, Pemecutan) 28 F7
BCA (Jl. Diponegoro, Denpasar Utara) 21 L1
BCA (Jl. Imam Bonjol) 20 F6
BCA (Jl. P.B. Sudirman) 21 M4
BCA (Klungkung) 51 E6
BCA (Ngurah Rai Bypass, Nusa Dua) 39 G4
BCA (Ngurah Rai Bypass) 38 E2
BCA (Raya Sesetan) 21 L6
BCA (Singaraja) 57 D3
BCA (WR Supratman) 30 D3
BDB (Kuta) 14 F8
BDC (Sanur) 17 K4
BDN 57 C4
BDNI (Dauh Puri Kangin) 28 F8
Bea, Hotel 18 E1
Beach Fishmarket, Restaurant 17 M4
Beach House, The, Hotel 25 G6
Beachfront Villa Jukung 53 J8
Beachfront Villas Lucia Stella, Hotel 67 M3
Beachwalk Bali 14 C6
Beautiful Bali Villas 14 D4
Bebatu, Hotel 26 A7
Bebek Bengil 46 F7
Bedugul Recreation Park 104 B8
Bedugul, Hotel 104 B8
Bedulu Resort 91 H6
Begawan Market 21 G7
Beggar's Bush, Restaurant 46 B2
Beji Ubud Resort 48 E2

Belanda, Villa 69 M7
Bell Inn, Hotel 51 F6
Bella Kerobokan, Hotel 26 C8
Bella Singaraja 32 B7
Belle Bali, Hotel 26 C4
Bellevue Heritage Villa, Hotel 38 A7
Belmond Jimbaran Puri Bali, Hotel 32 B6
Belong Bunter Homestay, Hotel 34 A8
Belong Dua, Hotel 24 D4
Belos House, Hotel 47 G5
Beluga Restaurant & Watersport Cplx 33 K1
Bemo & Bus Terminal (Amlapura) 55 E5
Bemo Stop for Tirta Gangga/East Coast 55 B6
Bemo Terminal (Bangli) 54 D4
Bemo Terminal (Benoa Harbour) 12 E6
Bemo Terminal (Gianyar) 50 C7
Bemo Terminal (Singaraja) 57 A5
Bendega, Restaurant 22 C2
Bendesa, Hotel 14 D6
Bengawan Solo, Hotel 20 D8
Bengil, Hotel 46 F7
Benny's, Restaurant 10 F2
Benoa Harbour 12 D7
Benoa Quay Harbourside Villas 33 J2
Benoa Square 32 E3
Benoa, Café 33 K2
Berawa Beach Residence, Hotel 25 L7
Berawa Beach Villa 25 K7
Berdikari Cottage 101 L3
Berdikari Handwoven Cloth Factory 57 C3
Berdikari, Hotel 101 L3
Besakih Beach Resort 17 M1
Besakih Beach, Resort 23 M8
Best Western Kuta Beach, Hotel 14 C5
Best Western Premier, Hotel 14 F4
Best Western, Hotel 11 G3
Bestest, Restaurant 19 J8
Betty, Restaurant 28 F7
Beverly Hills Bali, The, Hotel 37 H7
Bhakti Rahayu (Jl. Danau Buyan) 23 J6
Bhakti Rahayu (Jl. Gatot Subroto 2) 29 G2
Bharata 48 F7
Bhavana Private Villas 19 J5
Bhima's Statue 39 J6
Bhujangga's Village 40 B2
Bhuwana, Hotel 48 F7
Bian Yue, Restaurant 19 H1
Biangs, Hotel 47 G5
Biarritz Handicraft Center 19 M8
Bias, Restaurant 53 J2
Bicycle Rental 53 M6
Bidadari Cliffside Estate, Hotel 45 G5
Bidadari Kerobokan, Hotel 26 E7
Bidadari Luxury, The, Hotel 26 B7
Big Bite, Restaurant 14 C7
Big Deal 19 K7
BII (Dauh Puri Kangin) 28 F7
BII (Jl. Diponegoro, Singaraja) 57 D3
BII (Jl. P.B. Sudirman, Denpasar Barat) 21 L4
BII (Ngurah Rai Bypass, Benoa) 39 G4
BII (Petulu) 47 H4
BII (Sanur) 23 L7
Bike Rental 52 D3
Bilyard Semat Sari 26 B5
Bima Cottages, Hotel 11 H3
Bima, Hotel 26 D5
BIMC, Hotel 15 G7
Bina Medika 29 H5
Bingin Beach House, The, Hotel 34 F6
Bingin Family Bungalow 34 E7
Bingin Garden, Hotel 34 E6
Bingin Inn, Hotel 34 D7
Bintang 48 E3
Bintang Bali Zepper 14 D3
Bintang Kejora Pastoran Katolik 55 B5
Bintang Kuta, Hotel 10 F3
Bintang Pari Cottage 48 F2
Bintang Pesona, Hotel (Denpasar) 29 L8
Bintang Pesona, Hotel (Ubud) 48 F2
Bintang Supermarket 14 C2
Bintang, Hotel (Canggu) 25 G4
Bintang, Hotel (Sanur) 23 K6
Bintang, Restaurant (Candidasa) 52 A8
Bintara 15 G7
Bio Warung 25 M8
Bird Market 29 G5
Biro Pusat Statistik (BPS) 23 G4
Bisiq Cafe 31 H5
Biskuat 27 H3
Bisnis Indonesia 29 H3
Bit of Bali.com 19 L2
Biv's, Hotel 19 K2
Biyu 52 F3
Biyu Kukung Suites & Spa, Hotel 48 C2
Biyu Kukung, Hotel 46 F7
Biyu Nasak, Restaurant 52 E3
BJB 21 J4
BJC Tours 17 G4
Black Pearl Villa 67 K5
Blackpepper 19 M8
Blacky's Bar 14 B3

Blanco Renaissance Museum 46 B3
Blimbing, Café 70 D2
Blind Masseur 48 C1
Bliss Spa 48 E2
Bliss Wayan, Hotel 14 E4
Bliss, Restaurant 39 H8
Bloo Lagoon, Hotel 67 M4
Blue Bird Taxi Group 16 B3
Blue Bird Taxi HQ 32 E8
Blue Duck, Hotel 18 E1
Blue Grove 39 L3
Blue Heaven, Hotel 34 B7
Blue Heaven, Restaurant 34 B7
Blue Hill Resort Tulamben 90 E2
Blue Moon Villas 91 K7
Blue Point Bay Villas 40 B1
Blue Water Express 13 M1
BMC (Kerobokan) 19 K4
BMG (Denpasar) 21 J4
BMG (Jimbaran) 32 E8
BMG (Jl. Raya Puputan, Denpasar Timur) ... 22 B3
BMG (Tuban) 11 J5
BMR Watersport 33 K2
BMW 15 G7
BNI (Jalan Legian) 14 D5
BNI (Jl. Diponegoro, Klungkung) 51 E6
BNI (Jl. Erlangga, Singaraja) 57 D2
BNI (Jl. Kesatrian, Gianyar) 50 C7
BNI (Jl. Ngurah Rai, Negara) 56 E5
BNI (Ngurah Rai Bypass) 23 K5
BNI (P.B. Sudirman) 21 J4
BNI (Raya Canggu) 26 C4
BNI 46 (Benoa Harbour) 12 D6
BNI 46 (Gajah Mada) 28 F7
BNI 46 (Gatot Subroto) 29 G2
BNI 46 (Jl. D. Tamblingan, Sanur) 23 L7
BNI 46 (Jl. Raya Puputan, Denpasar Tmr) ... 22 B3
BNI 46 (Ngurah Rai Bypass, Benoa) 38 E2
BNI 46 (Raya Uluwatu) 32 C3
BNI 46 (WR Supratman) 30 D3
BNP 47 G4
Bobbies, Restaurant 17 L5
Body & Soul 14 D2
Body & Soul (Bali Collection, Nusa Dua) 39 L3
Bolare 18 D2
Boneka, Restaurant 39 H7
Bonsai, Café 23 M7
Bora Bora Villas 19 H6
Borneo Antique Gallery 19 L7
Borneo, Restaurant 23 L6
Boshe Nite Club 11 J4
Botanical Garden (Kebun Raya Eka Karya) .. 99 L7
Bouganvile, Hotel 26 B8
Bounty Bali Tours 17 L2
Bounty Cruises, Hotel 12 E5
Bounty Ship 12 E5
Bounty, The, Hotel 14 D6
Bousen Villa 45 K1
Boutique 39 L3
Bow, Hotel 19 H3
BPC City, Hotel 20 B4
BPD (Amlapura) 55 E5
BPD (Bangli) 54 D4
BPD (Benoa) 38 E2
BPD (Candidasa) 52 D7
BPD (Dauh Puri Kaja) 28 F7
BPD (Dauh Puri Kauh) 21 G5
BPD (Gianyar) 50 C7
BPD (Ketewel) 31 M2
BPD (Klungkung) 51 E6
BPD (Ngurah Rai Bypass, Kuta) 14 F8
BPD (Renon) 22 F4
BPD (Singosari-Kuta, Kuta) 14 E8
BPD (Sumerta Kelod) 22 D3
BPD (Tuban) 11 G5
BPD (Ubud) 46 F4
BPK 22 C3
BPKD 22 C3
BPKKTK 31 H6
BPN (Jl. Kamboja, Denpasar) 29 J7
BPN (Jl. Cokorda Agung Tresna, Denpasar) . 22 C2
BPN (Petitenget) 19 L6
BPOM 22 C3
BPR 31 H5
BPR Hari Depan 31 J5
BPR Lestari (Denpasar) 21 J4
BPR Lestari (Sanur) 23 K5
BPR Picu Manunggal Sejahtera 11 J4
BPR Sari Sedana 21 L4
Brahma Arama Vihara 97 L3
Bramasa 49 G8
Brands Off 39 L4
Brasco Bags & Shoes 46 F8
Brata 1, Hotel 46 F6
Brata 2, Hotel 46 F6
Brawa Biru Villa 25 L6
Brawa Biru, Hotel 25 K4
Breadworks, Restaurant 48 D4
Breeze, Restaurant 14 C4
Breezes Bali Resort & Spa 19 J8
BRI (Cokorda Putra S.) 47 H4
BRI (Gajah Mada) 28 F7
BRI (Gatot Subroto Barat Bypass) 27 K2
BRI (Gatot Subroto) 29 H2
BRI (Hayam Wuruk) 29 M7
BRI (Imam Bonjol) 20 E8
BRI (Jl. Ahmad Yani, Negara) 56 C4
BRI (Jl. Cendrawasih, Tabanan) 51 C2
BRI (Jl. Danau Toba, Sanur) 23 K6

BRI (Jl. Dr. Kusuma Atmaja) 22 C3
BRI (Jl. Gajah Mada, Amlapura) 55 E5
BRI (Jl. Gn Batu Karu, Klungkung) 51 E6
BRI (Jl. Gunung Semeru, Tabanan) 51 D2
BRI (Jl. Jend. Ahmad Yani, Singaraja) 57 A5
BRI (Jl. Kapten Dipta, Gianyar) 50 D7
BRI (Jl. Kesatria, Amlapura) 55 E5
BRI (Jl. Nakula, Klungkung) 51 E6
BRI (Jl. Ngurah Rai, Gianyar) 50 D7
BRI (Jl. Pramuka, Singaraja) 57 D4
BRI (Jl. Teuku Umar, Pemecutan Kelod) ... 21 G5
BRI (Kamboja) 29 H6
BRI (Kedewatan 1) 48 D2
BRI (Peliatan) 47 H5
BRI (Raya Canggu) 26 B3
BRI (Raya Padang Luwih) 27 H1
BRI (Raya Sesetan) 21 L8
BRI (Raya Tohpati) 30 E3
BRI (Siligita, Nusa Dua) 39 G5
BRI (Jl. WR Supratman, Kesiman) 29 L5
BRI (Jl. WR Supratman, Kesiman Kerthalangu) 30 D3
Bridge, The, Restaurant 49 L1
Bridges Cafe 46 B2
BRIMOB 30 E2
Bruna, Hotel 14 C5
BTDC Office 39 J5
BTDC Staff Housing 39 J3
BTN (Denpasar) 29 G7
Buah Bali, The, Hotel 19 G5
Buana Karya, Hotel 56 A4
Bubba Gump, Restaurant 10 F2
Bubu Racok, Hotel 91 H5
Bubu, Restaurant 39 H7
Bucu View Bungalow 46 C4
Buddha Garden, Hotel 25 K8
Buddha Metta 19 K2
Buddha Seul 46 E6
Budha Haha, Restaurant 57 E3
Bue Surf 33 K4
Buffalo Races 56 B6
Buga, Restaurant 17 L1
Bugan, Hotel 19 H4
Bugils Bali, Restaurant 10 F5
Bujana Patra Stadium 57 D4
Buki Bali 19 K3
Bukit Asri, Hotel 48 E3
Bukit Bunga, Villa 99 M7
Bukit Doa, Christian Church 38 F4
Bukit Hideaway, Hotel 36 D8
Bukit Indah Homestay, Hotel 91 K7
Bukit Inn, Hotel 36 D7
Bukit Jambul, Restaurant 66 D1
Bukit Karang Villas 43 J6
Bukit Mungsu Indah, Hotel 86 B4
Bukit Mungsuindah 104 B8
Bukit Pesona, Villa 44 B3
Bukit Sari, Restaurant 39 J2
Bukit Strawberry, Hotel 104 A8
Bukopin (Jl. Kamboja) 29 H7
Bukopin Bank (Jl. Dewi Sartika) 21 L3
Buleleng Harbour 57 C2
Buleleng Market 57 F7
Bulgari, Hotel 41 J8
Bulih Beach, Hotel 91 J5
Bulog 32 D8
Bumas, Hotel 23 L8
Bumbu Bali, Restaurant (Jl. Pratama) 33 K5
Bumbu Bali, Restaurant (Jl. Suweta) 46 E3
Bumbu Desa, Restaurant 21 M3
Bumi Artha 21 M3
Bumi Asih Jaya 23 J4
Bumi Asih, Hotel 22 F4
Bumi Ayu Bungalows 17 L1
Bumi Ayu, Bungalows 23 L8
Bumi Putera 21 L2
Bumi Sakembang, Hotel 47 M8
Bumi Ubud Plaza 47 H4
Bumi Ubud Resort 48 F8
Bunga Desa, Hotel 18 E3
Bunga Permai, Hotel 47 G1
Bunga Permai, Hotel 72 F5
Bunga, Hotel 19 H3
Bungalow / Alang-alang Bambu, Hotel 66 C7
Bungalow Number 7, Hotel 108 C1
Bunutbolong 82 E7
Bupati's Office (Bangli) 54 C6
Bupati's Office (Buleleng) 57 E7
Bupati's Office (Gianyar) 50 B7
Bupati's Office (Karang Asem) 55 D3
Bupati's Office (Klungkung) 51 D6
Bupati's Office (Tabanan) 51 E3
Burnet Indonesia 17 L3
Bush Telegraph Pub, The 19 K8
Busted 30 F1
Busungsari, Restaurant 30 E7
Busy 47 H4
Butterfly Park 71 K6
Buyan Resort 99 L6
Bvilla, Hotel 19 J6
By Pass Ngurah Rai, Hotel 36 E7
By The Sea 19 J6

C

C-Line 10 E3
C151 Smart Villas 19 H7
C151 Smart Villas, Hotel (Dreamland) 34 D6
Cabe Rawit, Restaurant 19 L8
Cafe Api-Api 46 A5
Cafe Bamboo 17 M4

Cafe Bebek 14 E4
Cafe Cantik 17 K4
Cafe Club 29 L8
Cafe Da 47 J2
Cafe des Artistes 46 D3
Cafe Espresso 14 C5
Cafe Gayatri 46 E3
Cafe Havana 46 E4
Cafe Latino 32 E5
Cafe Lotus 46 E3
Cafe Lumut 17 L2
Cafe Me 21 J5
Cafe NGS 46 F6
Cafe Ochanoma 32 E1
Cafe Pora 25 K8
Cafe Sanbo 48 D7
Cafe Sayan 48 C4
Cafe Silfer 47 H5
Cafe Silik 36 D3
Cafe Tahu 16 D2
Cafe Vespa 48 D4
Cafe Warna 14 B3
Cafe, The 49 H8
Cafes 13 L2
Cafetaria Koka 57 C4
Cahaya Dewata, Hotel 48 C1
Cahaya Mulya 30 C2
Cahaya Tours 23 K7
Cahaya, The, Hotel 26 D7
Cahya Residence, Hotel 27 H3
Callego Beach Restaurant and Massage ... 18 F5
Camplung Mas, Hotel 14 C5
Campuan College 48 D3
Campuhan Sari Boutique 46 B2
Canang Sari Villa 41 K2
Canang Sari, Restaurant 23 K5
Canang Sari, Villa 41 K3
Canangsari Villa 41 K3
Cancer Mart 38 A8
Canderi, Restaurant 46 E3
Candi Beach, Hotel 52 B8
Candi Kuning 86 C8
Candi Permai 52 E7
Candi Permai, Hotel 99 M7
Candi Tebing Kalebutan 49 K5
Candidasa Sunrise, Hotel 53 G8
Candidasa, Hotel 53 H7
Candra Asri Bungalow 46 F6
Candra Healing 46 E4
Candra Rent Car 19 G4
Candraloka Amphitheatre 39 L5
Canggih, Restaurant 14 D4
Canggu Club 25 M8
Canggu Deli 18 E1
Canggu Market 25 M2
Canggu Mart 25 H6
Canggu Plaza 18 E1
Canggu Sunset Villa 25 J7
Canggu Surfing 18 B1
Canggu Tennis Court 18 E1
Canon 29 J2
Cantik Kerobokan, Hotel 19 J2
Cantik, Hotel 26 D7
Cantiloka, Restaurant 53 J7
Cap Cili Textile Factory 50 B6
Cap Togog Textile Factory 50 B6
Capung, Villa 34 C8
CAR 21 L3
Car Rental (Jimbaran) 32 D2
Car Rental (Jl. Pratama, Tanjung Benoa) ... 39 J2
Car Rental (Lovina Beach) 52 F3
Car Service 32 E4
Cardamon, Restaurant 33 K4
Carina 19 K3
Carlo 17 J4
Caroline Villa 25 K6
Carrefour (Imam Bonjol, Legian) 15 G3
Carrefour (Sunset Road, Kuta) 15 G6
Cas Cades 49 G3
Casa Artista, Hotel 19 J7
Casa D'Angel, Restaurant 20 B3
Casa Ganesha, Hotel 48 F7
Casa Grande 33 K7
Casa Indigo, Hotel 19 H4
Casa Mia, Restaurant 19 K4
Casa Minha, Hotel 14 E2
Casabela, Restaurant 33 K6
Casablanca Suite, Hotel 43 J5
Casablanca, Restaurant 17 L1
Casaluna, Restaurant 17 L3
Cascade Villa 19 L6
Cascade, Restaurant 49 J3
Cassanova 29 H2
Castello Mataspi, Villas 34 D8
Cat & Fiddle, Restaurant 17 K4
Catra Apartments, Hotel 52 E8
Cattle Market 64 B4
Catur Adi Putra, Hotel 28 E8
Catur Adnyana, Hotel 54 C6
Catur Muka Statue (Klungkung) 51 D6
Catur Mukha Statue (Denpasar) 29 G7
Cavehouse 108 B2
Caviar 32 B3
CDBS Radio 23 J3
Cekot, Restaurant 23 K3
Celagi, Restaurant 14 C4
Celeng 48 D1
Cellular-City 21 J3
Celuk Agung, Hotel 53 K3
Cemagi Beach, Hotel 24 B3

Cemagi Residence, Hotel 24 A3
Cemara Bali, Hotel 25 G5
Cemara Umalas, The, Hotel 19 J2
Cempaka Belimbing, Villas 84 E8
Cempaka Blimbing Guest Villa 70 D2
Cempaka Gading Villa 36 D6
Cempaka Kuta Guesthouse 14 F6
Cempaka, Hotel (Denpasar) 29 K7
Cempaka, Hotel (Lovina Beach) 53 G3
Ceningan Cove, Hotel 108 B2
Centara Grand Villas & Resort 39 J3
Centra Taum Resort 19 H4
Central City (U/C), Hotel 15 G6
Central Market (Jl. Siligita, Benoa) 39 G4
Central Parking 39 J5
Central Post Office 22 C3
Chalina, Hotel 25 G4
Champlung Sari, Hotel 46 E7
Chandara - Les Medes, Hotel 25 M7
Chandi, Restaurant 19 J6
Chandra Adi Graha, Hotel 29 G5
Chandra, Hotel 19 H3
Chapung SeBali Resort 48 F1
Charoen Pokphand Indonesia 29 L2
Chata Bali, Hotel 52 D3
Chateau de Bali, Hotel 42 D8
Chedi Sakala, The, Hotel 33 K2
Chedi Ubud, The, Hotel 49 J7
Chevrolet (Padang Sambian Kaja) 27 J2
Chevrolet (Ubung) 28 B2
Chez Gado Gado, Restaurant 19 H8
Chez Kin "1001 Nuits", Hotel 91 G5
Chez L'ami Yoan, Restaurant 19 K8
Chichi's Villa 19 H1
Chile Consulate 17 H4
Chili Cafe 46 C8
Chillhuse, The, Hotel 25 L3
Chillout, The, Restaurant 47 G3
Chinese Food, Restaurant 47 G3
Chokcy's Place 34 E6
Chong Gi-Wa, Restaurant 17 J4
Chonos, Hotel 52 F2
Christy Furniture 19 K5
Cianjur, Hotel 29 J5
Cianjur, Restaurant 22 E2
CIMB Niaga (Cokorda Putra S.) 47 G4
CIMB Niaga (Jl. Gatot Subroto, Karang) 29 G2
CIMB Niaga (Jl. Gatot Subroto, Tonja) 29 J2
CIMB Niaga (Jl. Gunung Batur, Pemecutan)28 E7
CIMB Niaga (Jl. Diponegoro, Klungkung) .. 51 E6
CIMB Niaga (Melati) 29 H6
CIMB Niaga (Ngurah Rai Bypass, Sanur) ... 23 K4
Cinnamon, Restaurant 23 L7
Cipaganti, Hotel 14 D4
Cipta Dharma School 29 K7
Citra Minang, Restaurant 48 D1
City Bank 21 H5
Clandys 22 C6
Clear, Restaurant 46 F4
Cleopatra, Hotel 102 C3
Clinic (Ngurah Rai Bypass, Benoa) 39 G4
Clinic (Ngurah Rai Bypass, Sanur) 23 K6
Clinic Lovina 52 D3
Clinik Darmausada 56 C4
Clink 30 E2
Clock Tower (Karang Asem) 55 D5
Clock Tower (Subagan) 55 A7
Club at The Legian, The, Hotel 19 H6
Club Bali Mirage, Hotel 33 K4
Club Mediterranee, Hotel 39 K2
Club Villas, The 19 K6
Coca Cola (Denpasar) 29 H1
Coca-Cola (Sesetan) 16 C6
Coco 39 K5
Coco Bistro, Café (Bali Collection) 39 M3
Coco Bistro, Restaurant (Ubud) 46 F3
Coco Mart (Jimbaran) 38 A1
Coco Supermarket (Petitenget) 19 J6
Coco Supermarket (Ubud) 46 F7
Cocobistro, Café (Jl. Pratama) 33 K5
Coconut Beach Resort Office 16 C6
Coconut Grove, Hotel 23 K6
Coconut, Restaurant (Tanjung Benoa) 33 K6
Coconuts, Restaurant (Ubud) 46 F2
Cocoon, Restaurant 14 B2
Cocos, Hotel 26 C7
Coffee Copper, Restaurant 46 D8
Cokorda's Palace Carved Bell Tower 63 M3
Colour me Asia 46 F4
Commonwealth (Legian) 14 E6
Commonwealth Bank (Jl. Teuku Umar) 21 K3
Como Shambala, Hotel 72 E4
Conato, Bakery 21 H5
Conato's Bakery 21 M8
Concrete Factory 32 D8
Conrad Bali, Resort 33 L7
Copasetic 47 G5
Coral Views Village 91 J6
Coral Villas 18 E2
Coriander, Restaurant 17 L2
Corner, Restaurant 47 G3
Cosa Nostra, Restaurant 19 K8
Costa Rica, Restaurant 23 L8
Costume 39 L3
Coto Makasar, Restaurant 11 J3
Courts 28 D4
Courtyard by Marriott, Hotel (Kerobokan) . 19 J8
Courtyard by Marriott, Hotel (Nusa Dua) .. 39 J6
Courtyard, Hotel 14 C3
Cozy GH 26 C8

Crazy Bule Bali 19 M7
Cristal Bali 11 J5
Crystal Marine Sports 17 M4
Culik Market 90 E6
Cuphorla, Hotel 14 F5
Custom 11 H5
CV. Kecak 30 D6
CV. Patra Bali 26 D4
Czech Consulate 17 J4

D

D Nini, Restaurant 19 H3
D'Alang Alang, Hotel 19 G3
D'alang-alang Villas 25 J5
D'Alma, Hotel 26 E6
D'Apartments, Hotel 25 G6
d'Djabu Villas 19 J5
D'sawah Umalas, Hotel 26 D6
D'Tunjung Resort 53 J7
D'Wina, Hotel 14 F4
D'Cost, Restaurant 22 B4
D'Goal Futsal 20 E8
D&G 39 L3
D&G Villas 14 E3
Da Vinci, Hotel 25 M2
Dabumito GH 25 M8
Dadi, Hotel 25 L3
Dafish 108 B3
Dagang Bali, Bank (Semarapura) 51 C6
Dah Arta, Hotel 91 J6
Daihatsu (Padang Sambian) 20 D6
Daihatsu (Sanur Kaja) 23 J3
Daivani, Hotel 27 J5
Daluman Villa 14 D2
Damai, Hotel 18 E1
Damar Terrace, Restaurant 35 K1
Dampati, Hotel 23 L6
Dana GH 26 E5
Danamon Bank (Cokorda Putra S.) 47 H4
Danamon Bank (Gatot Subroto) 29 G2
Danamon Bank (HOS Cokroaminoto) 28 D2
Danamon Bank (Jalan Gunung Agung) 28 D7
Danamon Bank (Jl. Diponegoro, Denpasar)21 L4
Danamon Bank (Jl. H. Wuruk, Denpasar) .. 22 F2
Danamon Bank (Jl. T. Umar, Denpasar) 21 J5
Danamon Bank (Klungkung) 51 E6
Danamon Bank (Negara) 56 E5
Danamon Bank (Raya Campuan) 48 E3
Danamon Bank (Raya Ubud) 46 F3
Danamon Bank (Singaraja) 57 C3
Danau Toba, Restaurant 21 J4
Dance Performances, Palaces 63 G3
Danger Art 46 B2
Danone Aqua (Kesiman Kerthalangu) 30 D2
Danone Aqua (Padang Sambian Kaja) 27 K3
Danoya, Hotel 19 G4
Dapur Alam, Restaurant 14 E5
Dapur Aroma, Restaurant 19 J3
Dapur Sunda, Restaurant 19 M8
Dar Al Arie, Hotel 25 G5
Dardi Asmat Art Papua 19 M5
Dari Bali 46 F4
Darma 28 E7
Darma Setia, Hotel 57 D4
Darma Wisata, Hotel 21 J2
Darma Wisata, Hotel 21 J2
Darmadi, Hotel (Denpasar) 28 E8
Darmadi, Hotel (Tuban) 11 H3
Darmana, Hotel 28 E4
Darwis Triadi 30 D5
Dasawana Villa Resort 52 E7
Dasico 30 E3
Dava Restaurant, Restaurant 35 K2
Dave & Pong's 47 G2
Dayu (Raya Mas) 49 G8
Dayu (Sugriwa) 46 F5
Dayu Beach, Hotel 10 F3
De Gun Riverside Villas 14 D4
De Lemon Gatsu, Hotel 29 G1
De Mellos, Hotel 26 D7
De Munut Balinese Resort 46 B3
De Vins Sky Villa 19 G4
De'Bharata, Hotel 14 D2
De'rich Villas 17 J5
De'Uma Lokha, Hotel 26 A8
Dea Villas Bali 25 L8
Dedari Graha, Hotel 21 L3
Deddy's Beach, Hotel 91 J7
Deep Blue Selang Resort 91 L7
Deep Blue Studio Tulamben, Hotel 90 E3
Deep, Restaurant 17 L4
Dejabu Villas 19 K7
Dekuta, Hotel 14 D7
Della Villas 43 3G
Delta (Dewi Sita) 46 F4
Delta (Raya Pengosekan) 46 F8
Delta Dewata 47 H3
Delta Wisata 46 D3
Den Bukit, Hotel 37 G3
Denim Denim 39 L3
Denpasar Junction 21 L3
Denpasar Tourism 29 G7
Departemen Hukum & HAM 22 B3
Departemen Kehutanan 22 C2
Departemen Sosial 31 H5
Departemen Tenaga Kerja 22 B3
Deperindag 22 B3
Depnakertrans 22 E3
Depo Bangunan (Padang Sambian Kelod) . 20 C4
Depo Pertamina (Sesetan) 16 B7

Building Index

Depot Joko 32 D3
Depot Rinti, Restaurant 57 C4
Dermawan, Hotel 29 G5
Desa Muda Village 19 L7
Desa Sanctuary, Hotel 48 F8
Desa Seni Resort 18 E2
Design Unit 48 E3
Desjoyaux Pools Bali 19 M8
Destiny, Hotel 19 J8
Destore, Villa 36 B7
Detri Bungalows 63 L6
Dewa Bharata, Hotel (Candidasa) 53 H7
Dewa Bharata, Hotel (Kuta) 14 E6
Dewa Bharata, Hotel (Ubud) 46 B3
Dewa Bungalow 46 F6
Dewa Ruci Statue 15 G7
Dewa, Hotel 46 F3
Dewangga, Hotel 46 E4
Dewani, Hotel (Kerobokan) 19 J2
Dewata Canggu, Hotel 18 D2
Dewata Gym 22 C4
Dewata Indah, Hotel 29 H2
Dewata TV 29 M7
Dewata, Restaurant 32 B2
Dewata, Shopping 30 E4
Dewi Art, Gallery 65 G4
Dewi Karya, Hotel 29 G3
Dewi Shinta, Hotel 29 H7
Dewi Sri Bungalows 46 F7
Dewi Sri Cafe 54 L1
Dewi Sri Statue 51 F3
Dewi Sri, Hotel 14 E7
Dewi, Restaurant 39 J6
Dewi Tirta, Hotel 19 K8
Dewi, Hotel 21 L1
DH, Spa 38 C1
Dharma Husada Hospital 21 L3
Dharma Praja School 28 F2
Dharma Putra Homestay 50 B2
Dharma Wiweka School 16 A3
Dharma Yadnya Hospital 30 D4
Dharma Yasa Homestay 50 D2
Dharmaputra, Losmen 54 D4
Dhea, Hotel 47 H4
DHL 23 K7
Dhyana Pura, Hotel 19 J8
Di Abing Villa 47 G5
Di Astana, Hotel 18 F4
Di Mare, Restaurant 42 F8
Di Uma, Hotel 19 J3
Diamond Star Hill, Resort & Spa 38 D2
Diana Villa's 19 K8
DIDU Furniture 14 F3
Dieba, Café 39 J2
Dijon, Restaurant 14 F7
Dillons Bungalows 91 G5
Dinas Budaya & Pariwisata 57 F7
Dinas Kebudayaan 22 E3
Dinas Kehutanan 22 B3
Dinas Kesejahteraan Sosial 22 B2
Dinas Kop & UKM 22 C3
Dinas Pendapatan 22 C2
Dinas Pendidikan (Jl. Kamboja) 29 H6
Dinas Pendidikan (Jl. Letda Tantular) ...22 A3
Dinas Perhubungan 29 K7
Dinas Perikanan & Kelautan 29 H5
Dinas Perindag (Jl. Kamboja) 29 J7
Dinas Perindag (Jl. DI Panjaitan) 22 C3
Dinas Perkebunan 22 C2
Dinas Pertambangan 22 C7
Dinas Pertanian & Tanaman Pangan 29 K5
Dinas Peternakan 29 H6
Dinas Sosial 29 J7
Dinas Tenaga Kerja 15 G4
Dinasti, Restaurant 23 L4
Dinda Rella, Hotel 26 B3
Dinda Rella, Shopping 19 L8
Dipan Resort, The 19 G5
Diponegoro, Hotel 21 L3
Diranie Art Shop 19 M5
Discovery Candidasa, Hotel 53 K7
Discovery Canggu Resort 18 D2
Discovery Kartika Plaza Hotel 10 F2
Discovery Shopping Mall 10 F2
Dispenda 22 A2
Divas, Restaurant 14 D7
Dive Center (Jl. Pratama, Tanjung Benoa)..39 H3
Dive Center (Ngurah Rai Bypass, Sanur) ...23 K7
Dive Concepts Bali, Hotel 90 D2
Dive Dive Bali 23 K7
Dive Masters 23 K7
Dive School 39 J2
Dive Today 17 L1
Diver Cafe Bungalow 91 H5
Diwangkara Beach, Hotel 23 L4
Diwangkara Holiday Villa 17 M2
DJ's, Café 21 M3
Djagra's Inn, Hotel 48 C5
Djaja, Hotel 28 F7
Djelita Handicraft Center 49 G8
dLima, Hotel 15 G5
DLLAJR 31 H5
DM Club, Restaurant 21 M3
Do-La-Re, Restaurant 11 J4
Dodiklatpur Rindam IX Udayana 94 E2
Doglas 14 F3
Dolphin Beach, Hotel 52 C2
Dolphin Lodge 13 M1
Dolphin Statue 52 F3
dOmah, Hotel 46 A3

Donald, Hotel 46 F4
Donald's, Restaurant 17 L5
Dong Dong Japanese, Restaurant 14 F5
Dongan, Restaurant 32 C3
Doremi Excellent School 22 E7
Double "S", Restaurant 23 L3
Double Dutch, Restaurant 17 L5
Double L, Restaurant 32 D5
Double M 28 F8
Double N, Hotel 25 L8
Double Six, Hotel 14 B2
Double You Homestay 94 C3
Downtown Villas 14 D2
DPC Ikapi Gianyar 47 G3
DPD-RI 22 D7
DPP Oraganda 29 J7
DPRD 22 D2
DPU (Denpasar) 22 C2
DPU (Jl. Danau Tamblingan, Sanur) 23 L8
DPU (Sanur) 23 M8
DPU (Ubung) 28 D2
Drancing Dragon Cottage 91 K6
Dream Beach Huts 108 B2
Dream River, Hotel 25 G4
Dream View Villa 34 E6
Dreamland Luxury Villa & Spa 42 D1
Dreamland Surfcamp 42 C3
Dreamland, Villa 36 C7
Drum Factory 46 E3
DS Mart 30 C3
Duke's, Hotel 34 F6
Dun'e, Restaurant 23 K3
Dunia Anak 21 L6
Dunkin Donuts
  (Gatot Subroto, Denpasar) 28 F2
Dunkin Donuts
  (Gunung Batur, Denpasar) 28 E8
Dunkin Donuts (Jimbaran) 32 E4
Dunkin Donuts
  (Jl. Hang Tuah, Sanur Kaja) 23 K4
Dunkin Donuts (Jl. Ngurah Rai, Gianyar) ...50 C7
Dunkin Donuts
  (Simpang Enam, Denpasar) 21 J4
Dunkin Donuts (Tuban) 11 H2
Dupa, Hotel 52 F3
Dura, Hotel 26 F5
Dusun, The, Hotel 19 H6
Duta Karya, Losmen 57 C4
Dutch Consulate 14 F6
Dutch Inn, Restaurant 14 E8
Duty Free Shop 14 F8
Dwi Santika, Hotel 27 M3
Dwi Utama, Restaurant 52 A8
Dyatmika School 31 G6

E

East Indies, Hotel 25 H4
Easta, Restaurant 14 C6
Eazy Suite, Hotel 14 E3
Ebony, Gallery 65 G4
Echo Beach Villa 25 H7
Echoland Bed & Breakfast, Hotel 25 G7
Eco Bag 46 F4
Eco Dive 91 H6
Economic Faculty (Udayana University) 37 G5
Ecosfera, Hotel 25 G6
Eddy's, Hotel 14 C2
Eden, Hotel 18 E3
Eden, The, Hotel (Tuban) 10 F3
Edenia Private Villas 43 J5
Edge Villas Bali, The, Hotel 41 L8
Edge, The, Hotel (Pecatu) 41 L8
Edward Forrer 21 G6
Egly, Villa 36 B7
Eiger (Teuku Umar) 21 J3
Eiger (Cokorda Putra S.) 47 H4
Eight Degrees South, Restaurant 33 L7
Eka Purnama Cottages 91 K7
Eka's Homestay, Hotel 47 G3
Ekasari 46 F6
Eko Villa 25 M4
Ekonomi (Jl. Pattimura) 29 H5
Ekonomi Bank (Jl. Teuku Umar) 21 K3
El Camedor, Restaurant 17 L2
El Pirata, Restaurant 39 H6
Elanora, Hotel 25 K8
Eldimo 32 E8
Electrolux 32 F8
Elephant Safari Park Lodge, Hotel 87 H7
Elite Havens Office 26 E7
Elizabeth Int'l 22 F3
Ella, Hotel 25 L7
Ellie's, Hotel 38 C1
Elysian Boutique, The, Hotel 19 H7
Emerald, Hotel 90 E2
Emergency Service 21 K4
Energy HS, Hotel 30 A8
Enigma Bali, Hotel 25 H4
Enjung Beji, Hotel 99 M7
Enzo, Hotel 18 E1
ER Tour 17 K3
Erlangga 21 K1
Erlangga 2 ....21 J3
Erom 14 D5
Errys Cafe 32 C5
Ethos Cafe 47 G3
Euro Café 36 F2
Euro Dive 91 G5
Eurodive and Amed Backpackers, Hotel ...91 L8
Ewa, Hotel 19 H4

Exclusive Bali Bungalows 34 E6
Exhibition Hall 36 F7
Exiles, Restaurant 49 G7
Extreme Toys (Bali Collection, Nusa Dua)..39 L3
Eyes, The, Hotel 41 H3

F

Fabulous, Hotel 26 C5
Facebar, Restaurant 19 K8
Faces, Restaurant 39 H8
Faculty of Animal Husbandry
  (Udayana University) 37 G5
Fair Trade Shop 46 D6
Fairway, Restaurant 46 F4
Fajar Candidasa Beach, Hotel 53 G8
Family Kitchen, Restaurant 14 F5
Family Spa 17 K5
Family, Hotel 47 H5
Fanisa, Hotel 25 G6
Fantasi Karaoke 23 K7
Farettii, Hotel 25 G5
Fashion 39 L3
Fashion One 20 F6
Fat Tuesday, Restaurant 17 M2
Fave, Hotel (Batu Belig, Petitenget) 19 J3
Fave, Hotel (Bypass Ngurah Rai, Tuban) ...11 H2
Fave, Hotel (C. Tanduk, Seminyak) 19 K8
Fave, Hotel (Dauh Puri Kauh, Denpasar) ...21 J5
Fave, Hotel (Pantai Kuta, Kuta) 14 D8
FC Residence Bali, Hotel 25 G4
Febri's, Hotel 10 F3
FedEx (Jimbaran) 32 E3
FedEx (Legian) 14 E4
FedEX Courier (Ubud) 48 E2
Fibra Inn, Hotel 46 E6
Fire Brigade (Nusa Dua) 39 J5
Fire Station (Jl. Imam Bonjol) 21 H4
Fire Station (Jl. Juanda Karta Wijaya) 22 E3
Fire Station (Seminyak) 20 A7
Fish Market 32 B1
Fish Market (Tanjung Benoa) 13 G8
Fita Art Shop 46 B1
Flamboyant, Hotel 52 E8
Flamboyant HS, Hotel 26 C3
Flat Polda Bali 29 H5
Flintstone 19 K3
Flora B, Hotel 11 H1
Flora Beach, Hotel 14 E8
Flores DMO 23 H7
Flowerbud Bungalows 34 F3
Fly, Restaurant 48 E2
Flying Elephants 46 F7
FNPF 108 F1
Fonta Dewata 21 H2
Fontana, Hotel 14 E4
Ford (Jl. Gatot Subroto, Denpasar) 29 J2
Ford (Jl. Teuku Umar, Denpasar) 21 J3
Formosa, Restaurant 14 F7
Fortuin 32 B3
Fortuna, Restaurant 14 F5
Four at Drupadi, Hotel 19 K6
Four Seasons Private Estates, Hotel 32 A8
Four Seasons Resort Bali at Sayan 48 C4
Fourteen Roses, Hotel 14 D6
Frangipani Beach, Hotel 53 G2
Frangipani, Restaurant 39 M3
Frank's Bar 14 B3
French Consulate 17 J5
Frestivo 19 K4
Freyja, The, Hotel 24 A3
Fruits Villa 17 K2
Fuji 28 E7
Fuji Image Plaza 14 F7
Fukutaro Airport, Restaurant 10 D6
Fukutaro, Restaurant (Legian) 14 D5
Fukutaro, Restaurant (Benoa) 39 H4
Furama 32 B2
Furama Villas & Spa Ubud Bali, Hotel......64 D3
Furamaxclusive Ocean Beach, Hotel 14 B3
Furamaxclusive Villas & Spa Ubud Bali 48 A7
Futsal Zone 23 J4

G

G-Land 14 E7
G-Land (Jl. Melasti, Suluban) 40 B3
G'ding 47 H4
Gadang Light, Restaurant 23 K6
Gajah Mina Beach Resort, Hotel 69 L7
Gajah Mina, Hotel 69 L7
Gajah, Hotel (Canggu) 25 G4
Gajah, Hotel (Legian) 14 D3
Galaxyan Atelier 46 F3
Galeri Esok Lusa 19 L6
Galih Homestay, Hotel 40 B1
Galiran Market 51 D8
Galiran Terminal 51 D8
Gallery Cafe 17 H4
Gallery Cofee, Restaurant 23 K6
Galuh, Hotel 48 F3
Gambelan, Restaurant 23 K3
Gamelan Maker 65 K4
Gamelan Smiths 66 C5
Gandhi & Kartika, Restaurant 57 D4
Gandhi Memorial School 22 F4
Ganesha 32 B2
Ganesha Art 28 F5
Ganesha Bookshop 19 G5
Gangga Sukta Handicraft 47 J2
Gangsa Villa, The 17 K3
Gangsa, The 17 K4

Ganidha Apartment 20 E6
Gapura Vista, Hotel 44 C7
Garden View Cottage 46 F6
Garden View, Hotel (Legian) 14 D4
Garden View, Hotel (Ubud) 46 D8
Garden Villa 19 M6
Garden, Restaurant (Nusa Dua) 39 J6
Garden, Restaurant (Ubud) 46 D3
Gardu Induk Pemecutan Kelod 20 E8
Garmen Indoraya Animale 14 F4
Garment Job Center 26 B3
Garuda Airlines (Cemara, Sanur) 17 K5
Garuda Airlines (Dangin Puri Kangin) 29 H5
Garuda Airlines (Dauh Puri Kangin) 29 H5
Garuda Airlines (Ngurah Rai Bypass, Sanur)
  ....23 K5
Garuda Airlines (Nusa Dua) 39 K4
Garuda Plaza 36 F7
Gate Inn, Hotel 19 M5
Gateway of India, Restaurant (Kuta).........14 F4
Gateway of India, Restaurant (Sanur) 17 L4
Gatotkaca Seraya Statue 11 J6
Gatra, The, Hotel 19 H3
Gatsu Indah, Hotel 28 E3
Gatsu Medika 28 F2
Gaya Fusion of Senses 48 D3
Gaya Villas 48 D3
Gaya, Restaurant 48 D4
Gazebo Bali 15 G5
Gazebo Beach, Hotel 23 M7
Gazebo Pattiserie, Restaurant 23 J7
Gecle, Restaurant 91 J6
Gede Homestay Bungalows 53 M2
Gede Manik 57 D5
Gede, Bar 23 H7
Gede, Restaurant 91 K6
Gedong Ayu, Hotel 30 F7
Gedong Gandhi Ashram, Hotel 53 J8
Gedong Kertya Historical Library 57 E7
Gedung Olah Raga & Kesenian 47 G7
Gedung Wanita Nari Graha 22 C3
Gelaeel 14 F8
Gelarsari, Hotel 57 B4
Gelora Perkasa 21 J3
Gema Kencana 30 D3
Gemala Jewelry 46 E8
Genah, Hotel 26 C2
Gending Kedis, Hotel 36 D3
General Hospitals (Singaraja) 57 E5
Generasi Motor 30 B2
Genesis, Restaurant 17 G4
Geneva Handicraft 19 K5
Genggong, Hotel 53 L7
Genta Bali, Restaurant 76 D2
Gentong Sari 49 H2
Geria Giri Santi, Hotel 91 H5
Geringsing Homestay, Hotel 52 A7
Geringsing, Hotel 53 G8
German Consulate 23 M8
Giant 14 F5
GIEB 29 H2
Gill's Cafe 46 F3
Ginger Moon, Restaurant 19 J6
Gino Feruci Villa 53 H2
Giordano 46 E5
Giri Putri Cave 109 J3
Git Git, Hotel 99 K1
GKN Building 22 C2
GKNI 22 D2
GKPB 55 B6
GKPBTirta Empul 26 E8
Glaze, Restaurant 33 K4
Global Dive Lodge, Hotel 94 C2
Global Extreme Net 19 K1
Global, Restaurant 62 B2
Globali Office, The 19 L4
Globetrotter, Restaurant 49 G3
Gloria, Restaurant 53 M6
Glory, Restaurant 14 D3
Glow Handicraft 47 J5
Goa Gajah Market 49 K7
Goa Gajah, Restaurant 49 K7
Goa Gong Temple 36 F5
Goa Jepang 66 B5
Goa, Restaurant 14 C2
Gobleg Inn, Hotel 40 C3
Gogo Bali 14 F5
Gold/Silver Smith 65 G6
Golden Buffalo 20 E6
Golden Kris Tours 23 K2
Golden Lotus, Restaurant 10 E3
Golden Tulip Essential, Hotel 27 M2
Golden Villas 17 L3
Golf Club House 35 F6
Golf Maintenance 35 H6
Gong Dewata, Restaurant 105 M7
Gong Futsal 20 E4
Gong Gede Music 65 G6
Gong, The 40 B3
Good Karma, Hotel 91 K6
Good Karma, Restaurant 76 D2
Goodway (Putra Bali Hill Village), Hotel ...38 D4
GOR Lina Bhuana 29 H5
GOR Yuwana Mandala 29 M1
Gorilla, Hotel 19 J4
Gosha, Restaurant 14 D5
Gossip, Restaurant 53 J3
Gourmand Deli, Restaurant 39 H7
Gourmet Cafe 19 H4
Government Tourist Office 50 D7

Governor's Office 22 D2
Gpib Ekklesia 11 J6
Graha Asih Hospital 11 J3
Graha Cakra Bali, Hotel 30 D3
Graha Cipta Hadiprana Bali 23 K3
Graha Mahkota 21 H5
Graha Paramitha, Hotel 23 K2
Graha Puspasari, Hotel 28 C2
Graha Sanggraha, Hotel 51 D7
Graha Ubud, Hotel 46 F5
Graha Usada 28 E4
Grahadi, Hotel 14 F8
Gramedia 28 F2
Granadha PWI Bali 28 E3
Grand Avenue Boutoque, Hotel ... 26 C6
Grand Bali Park, The, Hotel 29 G3
Grand Bali, The, Hotel 39 H6
Grand Balisani Suites, Hotel 18 E4
Grand Candra, Hotel 21 L1
Grand City Inn, Hotel 16 F2
Grand Hyatt Bali, Hotel 39 L5
Grand Inna Kuta, Hotel 14 D8
Grand Istana Rama, Hotel 14 D6
Grand Jimbaran, Hotel 32 D8
Grand Komodo 23 K4
Grand Mega, Hotel 15 G7
Grand Mirage Resort, Hotel 33 K4
Grand Puncak Sari, Restaurant 105 M7
Grand Santhi, Hotel 21 L2
Grand Sinar Indah, Hotel 14 C3
Grand Sunset, Hotel 14 F7
Grand Whiz, Hotel 39 J3
Grandmas, Hotel (Legian) 14 D5
Grandmas, Hotel (Seminyak) 19 J8
Grandmas, Hotel (Tuban) 11 H7
Grania Bali, Hotel 19 M7
Grapari 30 D2
Grasia Hospital 23 K3
Great Coffe, Restaurant 46 D3
Green Bowl Surfing Area 43 L8
Green Field, Hotel 46 E8
Green Garden Beach Resort & Spa, Hotel .. 10 E4
Green Garden, Hotel 10 F3
Green Manggo, Restaurant 41 K3
Green Mango, Hotel 41 J3
Green Room, The, Hotel (Seminyak) .. 19 K8
Green Room, The, Hotel (Canggu) .. 25 H7
Green Spa 33 L8
Green Zhurga, The, Hotel 19 M4
Greta, Hotel 19 G2
Griya Anom Sari, Hotel 28 D2
Griya Jamur, Hotel 19 G4
Griya Santrian Resort 23 M8
Griya Sanur, Hotel 18 F4
Griya Sanur, The, Hotel 17 K2
Griya Taman Mina (Mina Garden Palace), Hotel .. 72 C3
Grove Bumbak, The, Hotel 26 B6
GSM Indo 27 H3
Guardian Pharmacy 47 H4
Guci GH 48 F8
Gudang Garam 28 D4
Guest House Cardig Int'l, Hotel .. 10 F4
Guest House, Hotel 32 C4
Guling-Guling, Restaurant 47 J4
Guna Mandala Inn, Restaurant .. 34 C7
Gunung Agung 21 H4
Gunung Agung Bemo Terminal .. 28 D6
Gunung Kawi 73 K2
Gunung Merta, Hotel 47 J3
Gunung Sari, Restaurant 105 M8
Gurita Seafood 14 F4
Guru Ratna, Hotel 98 F7
Gusti HS, Hotel 26 E5
Gusti Kaler House, Hotel 47 G2
Gusti's, Hotel 46 E2
Gustis Garden Bungalows 46 F1

H

H&K, Villa 36 B7
Hadi Raharjo, Hotel 86 B2
Halcyon, Villas 36 D3
Hallo!, Restaurant 14 D2
Halo Bali 16 B7
Halo Bali Cafe 23 G5
Hamburg, Café 33 L6
Hanabi, Restaurant 39 M3
Hand Craft Bukandi 47 J5
Hanoman 46 F4
Hapel Semer, Hotel 26 E7
Happy Beach Inn, Hotel 100 E6
Happy Bungalow 100 F6
Happy Milenium Karaoke Restaurant .. 27 K2
Harapan Bunda 22 D4
Harapan Mulia School 20 F5
Harapan School 21 L6
Hard Rock Hotel & Cafe 14 C7
Hard Wood 49 H2
Hardi's 22 B6
Hardy's Supermarket
  (Jl. G. Subroto, Denpasar) 29 K2
Hardy's Supermarket (Sanur) ... 17 L2
Hardy's (Singaraja) 57 E5
Hardy's Nusa Dua 38 F3
Hardy's Supermarket (Sesetan) .. 21 L8
Hardys Nusa Dua Hills Resort 44 E1
Hardys Retailindo 16 D1
Harmoni Cafe 54 D4
Harmoni, Hotel 19 J8
Harmony Villas 48 F8

Harmony, Hotel (Kerobokan) 19 G3
Harmony, Hotel (Kuta) 14 D5
Harper, Hotel 14 D7
Harrad, Hotel 23 J8
Harris Homestay, Hotel 52 F2
Harris Resort 14 D6
Harris Sunset Road, Hotel 15 G5
Harris Tuban, Hotel 10 F5
Harris, Hotel (Drupadi, Seminyak) .. 19 J7
Harris, Hotel (Ngurah Rai Bypass, Kuta) .. 15 G7
Harris, Hotel (Raya Kuta, Tuban) .. 11 H2
Harris, Hotel (Raya Uluwatu, Jimbaran) .. 36 D8
Harum Sari Art 19 M4
Harvest Land Apartment 11 J2
Haven (U/C), Hotel 35 J7
Haven, The, Hotel 14 C2
Hawaii Bali 11 J3
Hayam Wuruk, Restaurant 29 M7
Heart Surrendering Sanctuary ... 23 J4
Hebring, Restaurant 57 B5
Hero 21 H5
Heroic Statue 51 E3
Hidden Paradise Cottages 91 K6
High Court 22 B3
Hindu Cemetery 53 J6
Hino 21 H3
Historic Site (Selemadeg) 71 G4
Historic Site (Singaraja) 57 E3
Hoka Hoka Bento, Restaurant ... 21 J3
Hole 17, Villas 35 H4
Holiday Inn Resort Baruna, Hotel .. 10 E4
Holiday Inn Resort, Hotel 33 L8
Holiday Inn, Hotel 14 F5
Holiday, Restaurant 14 E3
Home @36, Hotel 10 F2
Home Stay Asih, Hotel 92 B5
Homestay Ayodya, Hotel 53 G7
Homestay Bali Starling, Hotel ... 25 L7
Homestay Irine 76 F6
Homestay Lilaberata, Hotel 53 H7
Homestay Nikmat, Hotel 93 M4
Honeymoon GH 46 D3
Hongkong Garden, Restaurant ... 30 D6
Hongkong, Restaurant 28 E7
Honor 29 G5
Honzen, Restaurant 35 K1
Horison Jimbaran, Hotel 32 D3
Horison Sunset, Hotel 14 E2
Horison, Hotel 14 C2
Horse Stable 39 H5
Hospitality Bali, Hotel 25 K1
Hu'u Bar 19 G7
Hu'u, Hotel 19 G5
Hubo, Hotel 25 M1
Hurley, Restaurant 46 E3
Hurley, Shopping 19 L6
Husk, Restaurant 19 H8
Hutama Acomodation 47 G5
Hutama Karya 29 M8
Hyatt Regency, Hotel 17 M3
Hyundai 27 L2

I

I Gusti Art 47 G5
I Gusti Ngurah Rai Memorial 71 M5
I Gusti Ngurah Rai's Statue 11 H6
I Made Geriya 47 G8
I. M. Yang 48 E3
I.B. Sutarja, Gallery 65 G2
Ibis Styles, Hotel (Kuta) 15 G7
Ibis Styles, Hotel (Tanjung Benoa) .. 33 L8
Ibis, Hotel (Tuban) 11 H3
Ibiza 25 L8
Ibnu Batutah, Mosque 38 F4
Ibu Arsa Homestay & Rest., Hotel .. 47 H8
Ibu Daya, Restaurant 49 H8
Ibu Mangku, Restaurant 19 H6
Ibu Rai, Gallery 46 E4
Ibu Rai, Restaurant 46 E4
Ibumary, Gallery 65 H4
ICE 21 K3
Iconic, Hotel 19 H2
Ida Bagus Putra Cafe 49 H8
Ida Beach Village 53 M7
Ida Boutique 49 H3
Ida, Hotel 14 C2
Ida's Homestay, Hotel 53 J7
Ifiori, Restaurant 10 F2
Ijo Gading, Hotel 56 D5
Ijo Lumut, Restaurant 46 F4
Ikat Gallery 19 K4
Il Ristorante, Restaurant 41 J8
Ilga Warung 32 C8
Illam, Hotel 18 F3
Illy 17 J5
Imani, Hotel 26 B7
Immigration Office (Ngurah Rai Airport) .. 11 G6
Immigration Office (Singaraja) ... 57 B5
Immigration Office (Denpasar) ... 22 C3
Immigration Office (Pemaron, Lovina) .. 100 F6
Impian Manis, Villa 36 B7
Impossible Surf Camp, Hotel 34 D7
Ina Inn, Hotel 46 D3
Inada, Hotel 19 K8
Inaka, Restaurant 14 D2
Inata, Hotel 46 D6
Inchithai, Restaurant 33 K2
Indaco Warehouse 19 L2
Indah Manis Private, Villa 41 M4
Indah Manis, Hotel 26 E6

Indah Ragim, Hotel 24 F6
Indah Residence, Hotel 27 H2
Indi, Hotel 23 K6
Indian Delites, Restaurant 46 E7
Indian Dhaba, Restaurant 39 G4
Indian Embassy 22 B4
Indigo Tree, Restaurant 49 K4
Indigo, Hotel 14 B2
Indo French Villa 46 A1
Indochine Dine & Lounge, Restaurant .. 48 C4
Indochina Australia Language Foundation .. 16 B2
Indonesia Power
  (Pesanggrahan Power Station) .. 16 A6
Indonesia, Restaurant 15 G4
Indonesian Australian Language Foundation
  .... 29 G8
Indoraya Computer 16 D2
Indosat (Kerobokan) 27 M2
Indosat (Tuban) 11 J4
Indra Graha, Hotel 32 C3
Indra Inn, Hotel 29 H5
Indra Pura, Hotel 53 J3
Indraprastha Home Stay, Hotel .. 46 F5
Indus, Restaurant 48 E3
Infinity Bali, Hotel 25 G4
Inna Bali, Hotel 28 F7
Inna Grand Bali Beach, Hotel 23 L5
Inna Kuta, Hotel 11 G1
Inna Putri Bali, Hotel 39 K6
Inna Sindhu Beach, Hotel 23 M6
Inova Bali, Restaurant 31 K4
Intan Sari, Hotel 28 E7
Intaran Market 23 H6
Intercontinental Bali Resort, Hotel .. 32 B7
International Schools 35 H6
Inti Villa 25 H3
Ion Bali, Hotel 33 K4
Ipanema, Hotel 18 E3
Ipil Ipil, Café 23 H3
Irama Beach, Hotel 23 M7
ISI (Indonesian Institute of the Arts) .. 29 K6
Island Style 48 F8
Ismaya, The, Hotel 19 K1
Istana Batik 86 C6
Istana Bebek 49 J7
Istana Garden, Restaurant 23 L6
Istana Kuta Galleria 14 F5
Istana Semer 19 J1
Istana, The, Hotel 40 B2
Isuzu (Prof. Dr. Ida Bagus Mantra Bypass) .. 31 K3
Isuzu (Sunset Road) 15 G6
Isuzu/ Daihatsu (Jl. HOS Cokroaminoto) .. 28 E3
Italian Consulate 32 D5
Italian, The, Restaurant 39 G8
Ithon Mart (Ngurah Rai Bypass) .. 38 B1
Ithon Mart (Darma Wangsa) 38 E5
Ivasuki, Restaurant 15 G5
Ivory Resort 19 H4
Ixora Villas 19 G4
Ize Seminyak, Hotel 19 J7
Izy 47 H5

J

J House 19 J3
J Sushi 32 C6
J. Boutique, Hotel 10 F4
J.Co, Restaurant 23 K6
J.Lestari, Hotel 32 D7
J4 Legian, Hotel 14 E7
Jabeki, Hotel 34 F6
Jabunami, Hotel 25 M3
Jacko House, Hotel 40 B2
Jackresto, Restaurant 17 L2
Jade Villas 17 L4
Jagaditha, Hotel 24 A3
Jak Resto 15 G4
Jala Yasa Watersport 33 K3
Jalan-Jalan, Hotel 46 F8
Jalan, Hotel 47 G7
Jali, The, Restaurant 17 M2
Jamahal Private Resort & Spa, Hotel .. 32 D5
Jambu Luwuk, Hotel 19 G4
Jamkrindo 23 L4
Jamsostek 29 M8
Jamu 17 M1
Jamusara, Restaurant 46 F3
Jan's Tours 29 L6
Jangkar Mas, Hotel 12 D5
Janur Garden, Hotel 23 K7
Japanese Embassy 22 E4
JAS 11 G6
Jas Boutique Villas 14 D2
Jas Villas, The 19 J7
Jasa Raharja 29 M8
Jasmin Kerobokan, Hotel 27 G8
Jasmine Kitchen, Restaurant 52 E2
Jasmine, Hotel 18 E2
Jati Home Stay, Hotel 46 F5
Jati Manis, Hotel 26 B6
Jati Reef, Hotel 100 E6
Jati, Hotel 17 L3
Java Gallery, Hotel 19 J4
Java Pillar Furniture 38 C1
Javana Royal, Hotel 19 J4
Jawa Teras, Hotel 18 E2
Jawa Timur, Restaurant 49 H7
Jay's Villa 26 D6
Jaya 47 G4
Jaya Abadi 22 B7
Jaya Bungalow 46 F6

Jaya Dipa, Hotel 28 C2
Jaya Giri, Hotel 20 E8
Jaya Homestay, Hotel 40 C1
Jaya Printing 23 K6
Jaya Pub 14 D2
Jaya Sabha Governor Office 29 G7
Jaya Sempurna 32 C6
Jayakarta Bali, Hotel 14 B3
Jayaprana Grave Site 93 G4
Jazz Bar 23 K4
Jazz Cafe 47 G4
JB'r Point, Restaurant 36 D2
Je Je's, Restaurant 14 C4
JEC Garment 26 F4
Jeda Villa 94 C3
Jegeg Cafe 17 G5
Jelita 32 C8
Jembatan Budaya National Plus School .. 15 G4
Jendela House, Hotel 46 F3
Jenggala 32 C8
Jenny's Place, Hotel 108 B3
Jepun Bali Homestay, Hotel 40 E2
Jepun Bali HS, Hotel 25 H6
Jepun Bali, Restaurant 19 K8
Jepun, Restaurant 17 L4
Jero Wijaya 50 D1
Jetty Resort 108 C2
Jevy Kids 20 E7
Jimbaran Arcade 32 B8
Jimbaran Bay Villas, Hotel 32 C4
Jimbaran Beach 32 B4
Jimbaran Beach Cafe 32 B5
Jimbaran Beach Club 32 A8
Jimbaran Foodcourt 32 B5
Jimbaran High Land, Villa 36 E4
Jimbaran Hills Club, Hotel 43 K1
Jimbaran Plaza 32 D7
Jimmy Garment 15 G4
Jimmy Mart 33 L8
Jineng Tamansari, Hotel 14 F7
Jiwa Giri, Restaurant 99 L6
Jiwa Juice Cafe 34 B7
Jiwasraya (Jl. Diponegoro, Denpasar) .. 28 F8
Jiwasraya (Jl. Raya Puputan, Denpasar) .. 22 B3
Joe's Gone Diving 23 K7
Joehanda, Hotel 19 H4
Joger 11 H2
Johnny's Losmen, Hotel 108 B1
Josh Homestay, Hotel 91 H6
Joss, Hotel 19 G3
Jowa Mandari Resort 25 H3
JP's, Restaurant 19 K8
J1B 14 F5
Jubawa Homestay 94 D3
Jukung Bali Bungalows 91 H5
Jukung Dive 91 G5
Jukung, Restaurant (Nusa Dua) .. 39 K5
Junction, The, Restaurant 19 H6
Juni Artha, Hotel 53 H2
Junjungan Ubud Hotel and Spa .. 49 G1
Junno Boutique, The, Hotel 26 C1
Just Jeans 39 L3
Just Umbrella 14 F4

K

K Villas 19 J5
K-Land Spa 32 D1
K-Villas Jimbaran 36 D6
Kafe 46 F6
Kafe Karsa 48 F2
Kafu Kafu, Restaurant 36 F7
Kagemusha, Restaurant 48 F8
Kahyangan Temple 32 E4
Kaimana Spa 32 D2
Kaina, Hotel 19 K2
Kajane Mua Villas 46 D5
Kajane Yangloni, Hotel 49 H7
Kajeng Bungalow 46 E2
Kakatua, Hotel 25 H8
Kakatua, Restaurant 52 E2
Kalaspa Health Retreat 99 J5
Kaliuda 14 E7
Kaliwang, Restaurant 52 E3
Kalpatharu, Hotel 23 L7
Kalyan, Hotel 26 B8
Kalyani, Hotel 25 L7
Kamafari Hostel, Hotel 41 J2
Kamali, Hotel 26 E7
Kamandaki Resort & Spa 47 G3
Kamandalu Resort & Spa 49 H3
Kamaratih 48 E1
Kamasan Handicraft 47 H3
kaMaya Resort & Villas 17 H5
Kampial Market 38 D5
Kampoeng, Hotel 26 C5
Kampung Bali, Hotel 25 H5
Kampung Bali, Restaurant 14 F5
Kampung Tinggi Market 57 E2
Kampung Tinggi Terminal 57 D2
Kamuela, Hotel 17 L5
Kana, The, Hotel 14 F8
Kanaka, Hotel 26 B3
Kanishka Villas 19 L8
Kanten, Hotel 25 L8
Kantin 21, Restaurant 52 E3
Kantor Pajak Denpasar 22 B2
Kantor Pelayanan Pajak 22 A3
Kantor Perbekel 46 B1
Kaori Dupa 47 H2
Kapal Furniture 19 M5

Kapu Kapu, Restaurant 17 M1
Karana, Hotel 27 M8
Karang Mas 39 L3
Karang Sari Cave 109 J3
Karang Sari, Hotel 98 E7
Karina Beach, Hotel 52 D2
Karisma Asia Tour 32 C6
Karma 39 L4
Karma Jimbaran Villa 32 A8
Karma Kandara, Hotel 42 F8
Karma Seminyak, Hotel 19 K3
Karma Spa 42 F8
Karme Kome 46 E4
Karmila, Restaurant 39 G3
Karsuneka 29 H5
Karthi, Hotel 14 D8
Kartika Plaza 29 G8
Kartika, Hotel 53 G4
Kartika, Restaurant 15 G4
Kartini 46 D2
Karunia, Restaurant 27 M2
Karvaka, Hotel 25 M7
Karya Sari 21 L6
Karyadharma Hospital 57 E7
Kasa Bunga, Restaurant 22 E4
Kasan Resort, Hotel 98 F6
Kasih Ibu Hospital (Jimbaran).............. 32 D2
Kasih Ibu Hospital (Denpasar) 21 H5
Kasuma's, Restaurant 17 L4
Kasur Indah 15 G2
Katala Villas 17 L2
Katedral Roh Kudus 22 C4
Kavaya, Hotel 25 H5
Kavilla, Hotel 26 D8
Kawasaki 20 E6
Kawi Karma Bungalow 91 L7
Kawi, The, Hotel 19 J2
Kayan 47 H4
Kayana, The, Hotel 19 G5
Kayangan Dreams, The, Hotel 26 C5
Kayu Api, Restaurant 23 K5
Kayu Manis, Hotel 32 C5
Kayu Manis, Private Villa 39 J3
Kayu Manis, Restaurant 23 K6
Kayu Raja, Hotel 19 H5
Kayu Sujih Temple 36 E6
Kayumanis Inn, Hotel 29 H7
Kayumanis Ubud Private Villa & Spa ... 48 C5
Kayumas Inn, Hotel 21 L2
Kayun, Hotel 14 E5
Kayuputi, Restaurant 39 J7
Kazunoya, Restaurant 33 K6
KBPPP 22 F4
Kebayan, Restaurant 17 K4
Kebun Indah, Hotel 48 F8
Kecak, Restaurant 33 K4
Kecamatan Bangli 54 C7
Kecamatan Buleleng 57 E7
Kecamatan Denpasar Barat 27 M6
Kecamatan Denpasar Selatan 16 B4
Kecamatan Denpasar Timur 29 M5
Kecamatan Karang Asem 55 C6
Kecamatan Kuta 14 E1
Kecamatan Negara 56 F5
Kecamatan Tabanan 51 E3
Kecamatan Ubud 47 G4
Kedadi Nasi Uduk, Restaurant............. 14 E5
Kedai Bang Regar, Restaurant 14 F7
Kedaton, Restaurant 29 K7
Kedaung 21 G4
Kedonganan Beach 32 B2
Kei Villas 19 G5
Kejaksaan 22 C3
Kejaksaan Negeri 21 L2
Kejora Villas 23 L7
Kekailani, Hotel 24 A3
Kekailani, Villa 24 A3
Kelan Beach, Restaurant 32 B1
Kelapa Mas Homestay, Hotel 52 D7
Kelapa Mas, Hotel 53 J7
Kelapa, Hotel 26 B2
Kelurahan Abian Base 50 D8
Kelurahan Anturan 53 M4
Kelurahan Astina 57 E5
Kelurahan Baler Bale Agung 56 C1
Kelurahan Banjar Bali 57 D3
Kelurahan Banjar Jawa 57 E4
Kelurahan Banjar Tegal 57 D7
Kelurahan Banjar Tengah 56 C5
Kelurahan Banyu Asri 57 C6
Kelurahan Banyuning 57 F5
Kelurahan Bebalang 54 B8
Kelurahan Bedulu 49 L7
Kelurahan Beng 50 C5
Kelurahan Benoa 38 B6
Kelurahan Bongkasa 48 B4
Kelurahan Cempaga 54 D1
Kelurahan Dajan Peken 51 C1
Kelurahan Dauh Puri 28 F8
Kelurahan Dangin Puri Kaja 29 H2
Kelurahan Dangin Puri Kangin 29 H7
Kelurahan Dangin Puri Kauh 28 F5
Kelurahan Dangin Puri 29 H6
Kelurahan Dangin Puri Kelod 22 B2
Kelurahan Dauh Peken 51 C3
Kelurahan Dauh Puri Kaja 28 F6
Kelurahan Dauh Puri Kauh 21 J4
Kelurahan Dauh Puri Kelod 21 L4
Kelurahan Delod Peken 51 D2
Kelurahan Gianyar 50 E7

Kelurahan Kali Asem 52 D3
Kelurahan Kali Untu 57 C4
Kelurahan Kampung Anyar 57 C3
Kelurahan Kampung Baru 57 E2
Kelurahan Kampung Kajanan 57 D2
Kelurahan Kampung Singaraja 57 F7
Kelurahan Karang Asem 55 E6
Kelurahan Kawan 54 C5
Kelurahan Kendran Penataran 57 E6
Kelurahan Kerobokan 27 G5
Kelurahan Kerobokan Kaja 27 G2
Kelurahan Kerobokan Kelod 19 K4
Kelurahan Kesiman 29 M5
Kelurahan Kesiman Kertha Langu 30 F2
Kelurahan Kesiman Petilan 30 B4
Kelurahan Ketewel 31 L1
Kelurahan Kuta 14 E1
Kelurahan Legian 14 E4
Kelurahan Lelateng 56 C6
Kelurahan Liligundi 57 F8
Kelurahan Loloan Barat 56 C7
Kelurahan Loloan Timur 56 E7
Kelurahan Padang Sambian 27 K7
Kelurahan Padang Sambian Kelod 20 C5
Kelurahan Paket Agung 57 E7
Kelurahan Panjer 22 B6
Kelurahan Pecatu 41 L5
Kelurahan Pedungan 15 L1
Kelurahan Pejeng 49 L5
Kelurahan Pejeng Kaja 49 M1
Kelurahan Pejeng Kawan 49 J5
Kelurahan Pejeng Kelod 49 M6
Kelurahan Peliatan 47 H7
Kelurahan Pemecutan 28 D8
Kelurahan Pemecutan Kaja 28 E5
Kelurahan Pemecutan Kelod 21 G4
Kelurahan Pendem 56 E4
Kelurahan Petulu 49 H2
Kelurahan Prerenan 25 G4
Kelurahan Renon 22 F6
Kelurahan Samplangan 50 F6
Kelurahan Sanur 23 J6
Kelurahan Sanur Kaja 23 K5
Kelurahan Sanur Kauh 17 J2
Kelurahan Sayan 48 C5
Kelurahan Semarapura Kangin 51 E6
Kelurahan Semarapura Kelod Kangin ... 51 D8
Kelurahan Semarapura Kauh 51 B6
Kelurahan Semarapura Kelod 51 D7
Kelurahan Seminyak 19 M7
Kelurahan Serangan 16 F8
Kelurahan Sesetan 16 B3
Kelurahan Sidakarya 16 E4
Kelurahan Singekerta 48 C8
Kelurahan Subagan 55 B7
Kelurahan Sumerta 29 L5
Kelurahan Sumerta Kaja 29 J5
Kelurahan Sumerta Kauh 29 H7
Kelurahan Sumerta Kelod 29 K8
Kelurahan Taman 48 A1
Kelurahan Tanjung Benoa 33 J3
Kelurahan Tegal Harum 20 F2
Kelurahan Tegal Kerta 28 B8
Kelurahan Tibu Beneng 26 B3
Kelurahan Tonja 29 J1
Kelurahan Ubud 46 E3
Kelurahan Ubung 28 C1
Kelurahan Ungasan 43 J3

Khrisna Auto Car 30 D2
KIA Motor 27 K2
Kid Zone 11 J2
Kiki Homestay, Hotel 40 C2
Kiki Watersport 53 G4
Kikil Sapi, Restaurant 21 G6
Kimia Farma (Dauh Puri Kelod) 21 L3
Kimia Farma (Dewi Sartika) 10 F4
Kimia Farma (Ngurah Rai Bypass) 39 G4
Kimia Farma (Raya Kuta) 11 H3
Kinaara Resort 94 D2
Kind Villa Bintang Resort, Hotel 33 K5
Kintamani, Clinic 105 M7
Kintamani, Hotel 25 M5
Kintamani, Restaurant (Ketewel) 31 K2
Kintamani, Restaurant (Kintamani) 105 M9
Kipi, Hotel 18 F4
Kirana, The, Hotel 25 H7
Kisikisi, Restaurant 15 G6
Kiss Villas 19 H4
Kites 49 K6
Klapa Brezee, Hotel 21 M8
Klapa New Kuta Beach, Restaurant 34 F4
Klenteng Tanjung Benoa 33 K1
Klub Kokos, Hotel 48 F2
Klumpu Resort 17 L2
Klungkung Hospital 51 B7
Klungkung Market 51 D6
KMO Jewel 19 H6
Kocak, Restaurant 39 J7
Kodam IX Udayana (Dauh Puri) 21 L2
Kodam IX Udayana (Kesiman Petilan) ... 30 C5
Kodam Udaya (Titih Tengah) 28 F7
Koenokoeni, The, Hotel 19 H5
Koki Bali, Restaurant 39 J6
Koki, Restaurant 17 J4
KokoNut Suites, Hotel 19 J3
Kokoya, Restaurant 17 L3
Komala 47 J2
Komala Indah I, Hotel 14 C6
Komala Indah II, Hotel 14 C5
Komaneka Art Gallery 46 E5
Komaneka at Bisma, Hotel 46 C5
Komaneka Bisma, Hotel 46 D5
Komang Gallery Art 46 D3
Komea, Hotel 18 F2
Komersil 29 M5
Komilfo, Restaurant 17 M4
Komisi Pemilihan Umum 22 B2
Komisi Penyiaran 22 D2
Komodo Village 19 H2
Kompas Gramedia 31 K2
Konde Ratu 32 C8
Kongsi Inn, Hotel 24 B7
KONI 29 H6
Koperasi Jasa Angkutan Taxi 16 A6
Kopertis VIII 29 M1
Kopi Bali House, Restaurant 46 D7
Kopi Bali, Restaurant 17 L3
Kopi Luwak 47 G6
Kopi Made, Café 22 C4
Kopi Pot, The 14 D6
Korem 163 Wirasatya 21 M2
Kori Ubud Resort 48 D3
Kori, Restaurant 14 D6
Kost Joglo Model, Hotel 29 J3
Kota Jati 19 M3
Koyac Bali Yacht Club 16 F7
KPP 22 B3
KPU 22 D4
Krall, Hotel 26 B7
Kraton, Restaurant 53 G3
Kreneng 29 H7
Kreneng Bemo Terminal 29 H7
Kresna Art 31 M2
Kresna Karya, PT 22 F3
Krisna Art Gallery 21 L2
Krisna Bali Souvenirs 11 H5
Krisna Souvenir 14 F4
Krisna Statue 47 H4
Krisna Statue (Gianyar) 50 E7
Krisna Wisata Kuliner, Restaurant 11 J5
Krisna, Gallery 49 H8
Krisna, Shopping 21 J3
Krista Furniture 14 F3
Kriamaha Condotel, Hotel 14 F4
Kriyamaha Villa 14 E4
Kriya Spa 39 L5
Kt. Kuwaya, Hotel 46 F2
Ku De Ta, Restaurant 19 G7
Kubu Alit, Hotel 32 E1
Kubu Bidadari Villa 25 J1
Kubu d Kuwum, Hotel 26 C8
Kubu Dewi Sri, Hotel 25 K4
Kubu Diuma, Hotel 24 F5
Kubu Lalang Bungalow 100 E6
Kubu Pesisi Villas 14 B2
Kubu Pratiwi, Hotel 25 G5
Kubu Rama, Hotel 25 G6
Kubudi Sakti, Hotel 48 F2
Kubuku Eco Lodge 94 C3
Kubumanggala, Hotel 26 B8
KUD 32 B1
Kudus, Hotel 18 D2
Kue 47 G4
Kuluk 48 E1
Kumala Pantai, Hotel 14 B3
Kumala, Hotel 14 B3
Kumba Boutique Villas & Spa 42 D5
Kumba Ekabudi 49 G7

Kumbasari Market 28 E7
Kumbu 14 D3
Kune Bali Abadi 27 K3
Kuning, Hotel 26 B8
Kunja, The, Hotel 19 H4
Kunyit Bali, Restaurant 10 F3
Kupu-kupu Barong, Hotel (Ubud) 72 F6
Kupu-kupu Jimbaran, Hotel 32 A8
Kura-Kura Plaza (GWK) 36 F7
Kura-Kura, Restaurant (Nusa Dua) 39 L5
Kusia 48 E2
Kuskus Indah, Hotel 51 A2
Kusnadi, Hotel 14 C3
Kusuma Resort 14 C2
Kusuma Sakti, Hotel 49 G1
Kusumajaya Indah Bungalow 91 J5
Kusumajaya, Homestay 76 D2
Kuta Ardenia, Hotel 11 J3
Kuta Art Market 14 D8
Kuta Beach Club, Hotel 14 C4
Kuta Beach Heritage, The, Hotel 14 C7
Kuta Bungalow 14 D5
Kuta Center (Pertokoan) 11 G2
Kuta Central Park, Hotel 14 E5
Kuta Central Parking 14 F6
Kuta Icon 10 F4
Kuta Kitchen, Restaurant 11 J5
Kuta Lagoon, Hotel 14 D5
Kuta Market 14 E8
Kuta P. Seafood 14 E8
Kuta Paradiso, Hotel 14 D8
Kuta Playa, Hotel 14 C5
Kuta Puri, Hotel 14 D7
Kuta River View, Hotel 14 F7
Kuta Royal, Hotel 11 G3
Kuta Seaview, Hotel 14 C7
Kuta Timur Resort 11 J2
Kutuh Water View Villas 44 B6

L

L Hotel 19 H4
L'Assiette, Restaurant 19 K5
L'mawar Residence, Hotel 29 L8
La Bali HS 26 E6
La Cabana, Restaurant 14 C6
LA Fashion 15 G2
La Finca, Hotel 18 F3
La Indonesia 32 H4
La Lorraine, Restaurant 33 K4
La Lucciola, Restaurant 19 G6
La Monde, Restaurant 14 C4
La Pearl, Restaurant 14 E4
La Planca, Restaurant 14 A2
La Scala, Restaurant 33 K4
La Taverna, Hotel 23 L7
La Villa 25 H4
La Villa Bali 26 B4
La Villais 19 G2
Labake, Restaurant 14 F7
Labarracca, Restaurant 17 L2
Labha Villas 19 G2
Labha, Hotel 19 J2
Labuan Sait Indah Inn, Hotel 34 C8
Lady Bamboo Villa 46 E2
Laelia, Hotel 36 D3
Lagen Cliff Villas 40 B2
Laghawa Beach Inn, Hotel 23 M8
Lagoon, Café 39 K4
Laguna Garden Resto, Restaurant 33 K5
Laguna Homestay 50 C2
Laguna Spa 39 K4
Laguna Wailele, Hotel 34 E6
Laguna, Restaurant (Bali Collection) 39 M3
Laguna, Restaurant (Jl. Pantai Mengiat) ... 39 J6
Laguna, The, Resort & Spa 39 K4
Lahar Mas Homestay 55 C5
Lakaleke Hotel & Restaurant 46 D8
Lake Grace, Hotel 14 E4
Lakeside Cottages 50 D1
Lakra 19 K7
Lala & lili, Restaurant 46 A2
Lalapan Singaraja 32 H4
Lam-gabe, Restaurant 16 C5
Langit Biru, Restaurant 11 G6
Langon Bali Resort and Spa, Hotel 38 A7
Lapangan Puputan Margarana Renon ... 22 D3
Lapangan Tembak Perbakin 30 C4
Lapau, Restaurant 23 K7
Lara Bali, Hotel 26 B6
Largest Balinese Art, The 32 E4
Laris Manis, Restaurant 52 M3
Lautan Kupu - Kupu, Hotel 24 F5
Lava East 38 F3
Lavender, Hotel 14 F8
Law Faculty (Udayana University) 36 F5
Lawar Bali Kartika, Restaurant 31 J5
Lawar Bali, Restaurant 30 D7
Layar, The, Hotel 19 J5
Lazer, Restaurant 23 L7
Lazumba, Restaurant 19 K6
Le 48 Zen & Happy Rezort, Hotel 53 K7
Le Baron, Hotel 26 B2
Le Ga, Hotel 18 F4
Le Grande Suites Pecatu, Hotel 32 D1
Le Grande Suites, Hotel 35 J6
Le Jardien Boutique Villa 19 J8
Le Madre, Restaurant 53 G3
Le Mayeur Museum 23 L4
Le Meridien Nirwana Golf & Spa Resort ... 63 H7
Le Meridien, Hotel 32 B8

Le Pirate, Hotel.............................108 B2
Le Tebu, Restaurant 19 G6
Lean Village 91 K6
Lebak Bali, Hotel 25 H6
Lecuk Inn, Hotel 46 E1
Leggie, Hotel 34 F6
Leghawa, Restaurant 17 M1
Legian Beach, Hotel 14 C5
Legian Bungalow 14 D4
Legian Express, Hotel 14 E6
Legian Paradiso, Hotel 14 E5
Legian Village 14 D4
Legian, The, Hotel 19 G6
Legian Keraton Beach, Hotel............18 D2
Legong Keraton, Hotel 24 E5
Legong, Restaurant 17 L4
Leha Leha, Hotel 30 F6
Leke Leke, Restaurant 48 D4
Lela, Restaurant 21 G6
Lely Flower Shop 29 G4
Lembaga Penelitian 37 H5
Lembaga Penjamin Mutu Pendidikan ..22 B2
Lembah Spa 49 H3
Lembongan Island Beach, Hotel........28 E7
Lemon Chic 39 L4
Lemonade, Restaurant 46 E4
Lemongrass, Restaurant 19 K8
Lempuna, Restaurant 104 A6
Leo's Watersport 33 K2
Lesehan Ikan Bakar 52 C2
Lestari, Hotel 92 A6
Lestari, Restaurant 19 J8
Letkol Wisnu Airfield 93 M3
Letters Faculty (Udayana University) ..36 F5
Leyeh Leyeh Room, Hotel 25 M6
Lian, Restaurant 52 D3
Liberty Dive Resort 90 D2
Libi 21 J4
Library (Jl. Teuku Umar, Dauh Puri Kelod) ..21 K3
Library (Udayana University) 37 H5
Life Style, Hotel 21 K3
Likita, Hotel 28 B1
Lila Cita, Hotel (Lovina Beach)..........53 L2
Lila Cita, Hotel (Ubud) 48 F3
Lila Graha, Hotel 104 A8
Lilanita 38 E2
Lili Garden, Hotel 14 D6
Lili Grand, Hotel 99 M8
Lili House, Hotel 46 F8
Lilin Lovina Beach, Hotel 52 D2
Lily Jean 19 L8
Lily Kasoem Optical 21 J4
Lime Villas 18 F3
Lin Kuan Qio Temple 57 D2
Linen 19 K2
Lingga Beach 57 A3
Lingsar, Hotel 28 E7
Lintas Dimensi 16 D6
Lio 19 K6
Lio Collection 14 E3
Little India, Restaurant 17 L4
Liv Bali, Hotel 32 C4
Living Karma 19 J3
Living Room, The, Restaurant 19 G5
Liya Batik 47 J1
LLAJ Badung 30 E3
Loasis 32 E1
Lobi-lobi, Restaurant 23 M7
Locker 21 H5
Loco, Café 33 K7
Lodek, The, Hotel 19 K6
Loft, The, Hotel 26 E7
Loji 14 C4
Loji Ramayana, Hotel 51 F7
Loka House, Hotel 46 E4
Loka Sari, Hotel 49 H3
Lokha Umalas, The, Hotel 26 B7
Lokha, The, Hotel 14 D4
Lola Bali, Hotel 27 H5
Long Grain, Hotel 26 B2
Lor In New Kuta, Hotel 35 H4
Lor In, Hotel 65 K7
Lorraine, Hotel 19 L1
Losmen Taruna (YHI), Hotel 29 J6
Losmen Terang, Hotel 108 D2
Lotte Mart 16 C6
Lotus Bungalows 52 E7
Lotus Enterprise 32 E4
Lotus House of Art 53 H3
Lotus Mart 23 K4
Lotus Pond (GWK) 36 F7
Lotus Residence, The, Hotel 63 L4
Lotus Seaview, Restaurant 52 F8
Lotus Tavern, Restaurant 10 F4
Lotus Yoga Center 22 F2
Lotus, Hotel 29 M2
Lotus, Shopping 46 F7
Love Villa Bali 26 B6
Lovecho, Hotel 25 H6
Lovely Quiet garden Cafe' 46 D5
Lovina Beach 100 D7
Lovina Beach Houses V, Hotel 53 H2
Lovina Beach Resort 53 H2
Lovina Beach, Hotel 52 E3
Lovina Cafe 52 E3
Lovina Dive Center Menjangan 93 H3
Lovina Grand Bar 52 E4
Lovina Health Center 53 M3
Lovina Pool & Spa 52 D3
Lovina Spa 53 G3

Lovina Villa Property 52 D3
LP3I 21 L4
LPD (Pakraman) 46 E4
LPD (Pecatu) 41 L5
LPD Padang Tegal 46 F7
LPIA 38 C1
LPPP 37 H5
Lubang Nagaloka 99 J8
Lubdhaka, Hotel 25 L3
Lucky Paradise, Hotel 91 H6
Lucky, Restaurant 19 K8
Lucy's Batik 19 K6
Lukisan Sidik Jari Museum 22 F1
Lullaby Bungalows 34 B7
Lulu, Café 73 H3
Lumayan, Restaurant 55 C5
Lumbini Villas and Spa, Hotel 32 C6
Lumbung Bar 52 E2
Lumbung Indah 49 G7
Lumbung Mas, Gallery 65 H3
Lumbung Sari, Hotel (Legian) 14 D4
Lumbung Sari, Hotel (Ubud) 46 E5
Lumee Bali Shop 19 M5
Luna 2, Hotel 19 H8
Luna Bonita, Restaurant 33 K4
Lupa Lupa Cottages 53 H4
Lupin Music Studio 39 G3
Lusa, Restaurant 14 D5
Luthu, Restaurant 23 L6
Luwak Cafe Internet 32 C4
Luwak Ubud Villas 46 F2
Luxury Spa Villas 19 J6
Luxury Villa Onje 17 L3
LV8 Resort (Jalan Pantai Brawa) 26 A6
LV8 Resort (Morabito Art Villa Rd) 18 D2
Lynn Villa 27 K8

M

M Bali, Hotel 26 C6
M Tour. 16 C6
Ma Joly, Restaurant 10 E3
Mabhakti. 29 G5
Maccaroni, Restaurant 14 D7
Mackarenko, Hotel 26 B6
Made. 47 H4
Made Bawa Bungalows 48 D4
Made Budiasa 49 H7
Made Kertonegoro's Future Art 47 J2
Made Two, Restaurant 23 K4
Made, Hotel 21 L3
Made, Restaurant (Klungkung) 51 B6
Made's Warung (Lovina Beach) 52 D3
Made's Warung (Seninyak) 19 K8
Made's, Restaurant (Sanur) 23 L7
Madhya Villas 19 G5
Madiun, Restaurant 22 C2
Madra Homestay, Hotel 49 G7
Maesa, Hotel 10 E4
Magic Chocolate Bali. 23 J3
Magic Finger 46 F7
Magnolia, Hotel 26 C6
Mago, Restaurant 17 L5
Maguro, Restaurant 39 K3
Maha 46 D6
Mahagiri Villa & Spa 42 D1
Mahagiri, Hotel 23 L8
Mahajaya, Hotel 28 D2
Mahalaya, Spa 33 K4
Mahalini 4, Hotel 19 L7
Mahalini, Hotel 19 K6
Mahapala, Villa 23 L6
Maharaja, Restaurant 14 F8
Maharaja, Restaurant (Kintamani) 105 M7
Maharani 1, Hotel 14 C7
Maharani, Restaurant 14 E7
Maharta, Hotel 14 B3
Mahasaraswati School & University ...29 J6
Mahatma, Hotel 24 D4
Mahendra, Hotel 14 D7
Mahendradatta University 22 F3
Mahkota Furniture 21 H3
Mai Mai, Restaurant (Nusa Dua) 39 J6
Mai-Mai. 46 F7
Main Bar 14 D2
Main Ski Inn & Restaurant 108 C1
Majestic Point Villas, Hotel 38 F4
Malaathina, Hotel 26 C7
Malibu Dive Center (Dolphin Statue) ...52 D2
Malibu Dive Center (Raya Singaraja) ...53 H3
Malibu Lovina, Restaurant 93 H4
Malibu, Restaurant 52 F3
Malioboro, Restaurant 11 G5
Mall Bali (Ramayana) 21 L2
Mall Denpasar 21 L3
Mama & Leon 21 M3
Mama Rasa Sayang, Restaurant 21 G6
Mama Resto 22 E4
Mama's Warung 47 H5
Mama's, Restaurant 14 D5
Mamma Jenny Smith Inn, Hotel 40 B2
Mamo, Hotel 40 C1
Man & Woman Villas & Spa Resort ...19 M6
Man's, Restaurant 23 L6
Mana, Hotel 25 M1
Manah Liang Bungalow 99 G7
Manasa 29 H2
Mandala Mathika Subak Museum 51 F4
Mandala, Hotel (Canggu) 24 C4
Mandala, Hotel (Ubud) 47 G6
Mandhara Chico Bungalows 53 L2

Mandia, Hotel (Benoa Harbour) 46 E5
Mandiri Bank (Benoa Harbour) 12 E5
Mandiri Bank (Jl. Dr.Kusuma Atmaja) ...22 C3
Mandiri Bank
  (Jl. Gajah Mada, Pameregan) 28 E7
Mandiri Bank
  (Jl. Gajah Mada, Titih Tengah) 28 F7
Mandiri Bank (Jl. Pantai Kuta)...........14 D8
Mandiri Bank (Jl. Teuku Umar, Denpasar) ...21 K3
Mandiri Bank (Jl. Udayana) 29 G8
Mandiri Bank (Jl.Surapati) 29 G7
Mandiri Bank (Ngurah Rai Bypass, Benoa) ...38 F2
Mandiri Bank (Ngurah Rai Bypass) 23 K3
Mandiri Bank (Raya Kuta) 11 H3
Mandiri Bank (Simpang Enam, Denpasar) ...21 J5
Mandiri Bank (Singaraja) 57 C4
Mandiri Bank (Ungasan) 43 G1
Mandiri Homestay, Hotel 53 K2
Mandollow, Restaurant 33 K5
Mang Kuku, Hotel 40 B3
Mangga Madu, Restaurant 47 J4
Manggala, Hotel 26 B8
Manggo Tree Cafe 34 C8
Mango Sunset, Hotel 24 F6
Mango Tree Spa 72 F6
Mango, Restaurant 23 M6
Mangrove Information Center 15 J8
Manis Homestay, Hotel 91 G5
Manis Villa 25 G5
Manis, Gallery 65 H3
Manis, Restaurant 72 C3
Mano Surf Club 19 G6
Mansion Resort Hotel & Spa, The 48 D4
Mantra, Restaurant 19 G5
Manuaba Hospital 28 E4
Manuh's Guest House 44 B3
Marajig 48 D4
Marco Inn, Hotel 67 M4
Mardidadi, Villa 24 A3
Mare, Hotel 25 G5
Marga Mulya 21 H5
Margot Spa 30 F7
Marhean, Restaurant 28 F8
Mari's Gallery 19 K4
Maria Bunda Segala Bangsa, Catholic Church
  ....38 F4
Maridadi, Hotel 24 A3
Maridadi, Villa 63 H8
Marina, Hotel 53 J3
Marine Collections 19 L5
Marine Reserve 53 K7
Marine Reserve (Padangbai) 67 M3
Marinos Place, Hotel 14 D5
Marintur 17 L1
Mario Bldg 51 D2
Mario, Hotel 34 D6
Markisa, Hotel 26 D6
Marlee, Hotel 26 E6
Mars City, Hotel 16 F3
Martha Tilaar Spa 19 L7
Martina, Villa 67 M3
Mary's Beach, Hotel 25 J8
Marya Arts Complex 51 D2
Marzano, Restaurant 19 L7
Mas 48 F7
Masa Inn, Hotel 14 D7
Masimo, Restaurant 17 L4
Maso Christian, Hotel 26 B1
Maspion 29 H5
Massage 52 C3
Massari 49 H7
Massif Art 19 M4
Mastafa, Hotel 14 E6
Matahari Beach Resort, Hotel 94 D2
Matahari Bungalows 14 E6
Matahari Cottage 47 G4
Matahari Kuta Square 14 D8
Matahari Terbit, Hotel 33 K6
Matahari, Denpasar 21 L3
Matahari, Hotel 24 D4
Matra Bali, Hotel 25 M7
Mawar Homestay, Hotel 46 D3
Mawar Melati, Hotel 86 C5
Max, Hotel 26 D7
Maxi Boga, Restaurant 33 K6
Maxone, Hotel 36 D8
Maya 39 L3
Maya Loka, Restaurant 19 G4
Maya Ubud Resort & Spa 47 L5
Maya Ujol, Hotel 47 J4
Mayana Villas 25 K7
Mayang Sari, Restaurant 39 K4
Mayapada 28 E7
Mayasari Restaurant 47 L6
Maydinie, Hotel 53 H3
Mayor Metra Stadium 57 E1
Mayor's Office 28 F7
Mazda 30 D2
MB, Villa 36 B7
MBM 47 G3
McDonald's (Jl. PB Sudirman, Denpasar) ...21 M3
McDonald's (Sanur) 23 K6
McDonald's (Sunset Road) 14 E3
McDonald's (Uluwatu 2) 32 E8
Meads Boutique Villas, Hotel 33 K1
Meazza Futsal 20 C4
Medewi Bay Resort, Hotel 68 A2
Medewi Surfing Beach 68 B3
Meditasi Bungalow 91 L7
Mega 47 H4

Mega & Dive, Hotel 91 J5
Mega Art 28 F7
Mega Art Shop 30 E2
Mega Ayu Homestay, Hotel 52 C2
Mega Bank 21 G6
Mega Jaya 29 G2
Mega Kuring, Restaurant 22 E2
Megatritama 29 H8
Megumi 33 K7
Mekar Abadi Bangunan 32 E5
Mekar Sari Watersport 33 K1
Mekar Sari, Restaurant 86 C6
Mekong 19 L7
Melamun, Hotel 53 J3
Melanting 38 B6
Melanting Cottages 99 G7
Melasti 32 B3
Melasti Beach Resort 14 C4
Melasti Beach, Hotel 14 C8
Melasti, Restaurant 14 C4
Melati Cottages 46 A3
Melia Bali Villas & Spa Resort,Hotel ...39 K4
Melia Benoa, Hotel 39 J1
Melissa, Hotel 24 E5
Melka, Hotel 53 J3
Meme Sarung Homestay 98 E7
Meme, Restaurant 39 M3
Menari Bali, Hotel 25 M8
Menega 32 A7
Mengening, Villa 24 B4
Mengiat Fishing Boat Station 39 L7
Menjangan Jungle & Beach Resort, Hotel..93 H3
Mentari, Hotel (Bedugul) 104 A8
Mentari, Hotel (Sanur) 23 L3
Merah Putih, Restaurant 19 G4
Mercure Bali Nusa Dua, Hotel 39 H6
Mercure Resort sanur, Hotel 17 K5
Mercure, Hotel (Ngurah Rai Bypass) ..11 J2
Mercure, Hotel (Pantai Kuta) 14 D7
Meritus, Hotel 34 F4
Merpati Inn, Hotel 47 J1
Merry's House, Hotel 26 C3
Merta Nadi 14 D5
Merta Sari, Hotel (Hasanudin) 28 F7
Merta Sari, Hotel (Pantai Bingin) 34 E6
Merta, Hotel 46 E4
Mertabuana Villa, Hotel 63 K8
Mertha Yogya, Hotel 28 F8
Mesari Usada 29 H2
Messaluna Spa 47 G6
Metis, Restaurant 19 J3
Metro Renon Futsal 22 B3
Mexico 22 E4
Mexicola, Hotel 19 G6
MGM Club 23 J3
Michi Retreat Resort & Spa, Hotel 65 G2
Michi Retreat, Hotel (Canggu) 25 M6
Michi Retreat, Hotel (Ubud) 48 E7
Midnight, Hotel 41 J3
Mie 88 (Batu Belig) 19 J3
Mie 88 (Jl. Sumatra, Denpasar) 28 F7
Mie 88 (Patih Jelantik) 14 E5
Miki, Hotel. 14 E4
Miko Market 26 E7
Milano 46 E3
Mimosa Jimbaran Bali Villa, Hotel 32 B6
Mimpi Manis Bali, Hotel 25 G5
Mimpi Resort, Hotel 93 K3
Mimpi, Hotel 90 D2
Minang Permai, Restaurant 20 F6
Minang Saiyo Building 20 E2
Minang, Restaurant 56 E4
Mine, Restaurant 19 G5
Ming Garden, Restaurant 39 H6
Ming Le Resto 17 L4
Mini Bali, Hotel 99 M8
Mini Deli, Restaurant 19 H2
Mini Holiday, Hotel 52 A3
Mini, Restaurant (Tanjung Benoa) 33 K3
Mini, Restaurant (Tuban) 10 F3
Minimart (Jimbaran) 38 C1
Mira Cafe 14 C2
Mira, Hotel 29 G7
Mira, Restaurant 17 M2
Mirama Drug Store 23 K4
Miranda Homestay 105 L6
Mitra 10 ....27 L2
Mitsubishi 57 A5
MMN Hospital 22 F2
Mocca, Restaurant 19 L7
Modis, Spa 21 G5
Moena 30 D3
Moena Fresh 22 C6
Mojo Burritos, Restaurant 47 H4
Mojo, Hotel 25 M2
Moment Canggu, Hotel 25 M7
Momoya, Restaurant 46 F2
Monang Maning 28 C8
Moncol Pool & Spa 23 K8
Monica Bali Villa 16 E4
Monica Furniture 19 K1
Monik 19 L8
Monique Unique 23 L8
Moon Tee, Spa 38 C1
Moon Villas 19 G2
Moonshine Bungalows 91 J7
Mora Ban 32 E3
Morning Market 32 D5
Morodadi Prima 20 E5
Mount Agung View 39 M5

Mozaic, Restaurant 46 F8
Mozzarella's, Restaurant 14 D4
Mrajapati Temple 32 E5
MSA Cargo (Denpasar) 22 E1
MSA Cargo (Ubud) 49 H3
MU, Hotel 34 D6
Muaya Beach 32 A7
Muaya Temple 32 A7
Muaya, Restaurant 32 A7
Mudita Inn, Hotel 47 H7
Muhammadiyah School 28 E8
Mujahidin Mosque 13 G8
Mulia, The, Hotel 39 H8
Mumbul GH 53 L3
Munching Inn, Restaurant 14 D6
Munduk Moding Plantation, Hotel .. 98 F6
Munduk Sari Garden Villa 99 G7
Munduk Sari Nature Villa 99 G7
Munduk Sari, Hotel 98 E7
Murdana's Villa 46 A1
Murni Art Studio 48 F8
Murni's Warung 46 C2
Museum Gedong Arca
    (Archaeological Museum) 49 L6
Museum Kartun Indonesia Bali 15 G6
Mushashi, Restaurant 39 J7
Mushroom Beach Bungalows, Hotel .. 108 B2
Musium Manusia Purba 92 B5
Mutiara Bali Boutique, Hotel 19 H6
Mutiara Bali, Hotel (Candidasa) ... 53 L7
Mutiara Bali, Hotel (Petitenget) ... 19 H6
Mutiara Bank 21 J5
Mutiara Bungalow 108 D1
Mutiara Jimbaran, The, Hotel 32 F4
Mutiara Market 32 D3
Mutiara, Café 105 M8
Mutiara, Hotel (Lovina Beach) 52 E3
Mutiara, Hotel (Sesetan) 16 D5
Mutiara, The, Hotel 36 D3

N

Na'Uli Villa 49 H1
Nacho Mama 48 E3
Nadhi 20 E3
Nadia Art 19 L8
Nadin 32 C6
Nadya, Hotel 19 H3
Nafatari Exclusive Villas 46 A5
Naga Persada 20 A4
Naga Puspa, Restaurant 85 K7
Naga Sari, Hotel 14 D8
Naga Sutra Villa 43 M8
Naga Taksaka, Villa 36 B7
Nakula Familiar Inn, Hotel 28 F6
Nakula Villa, The 14 D3
Namaste Bungalow 108 D3
Namaste, Shopping 46 F7
Nana Homestay, Hotel 91 G5
Nanda, Hotel 20 E4
Nandia Art Studio 48 F7
Nandini Bali Jungle Resort & Spa, Hotel .. 72 F2
Nandini Bali Resort & Spa Ubud .. 46 B2
Nandya Health Center 22 E2
Nang Andi Warung 32 B4
Nani Gallery 46 E4
Naputo 46 E4
Narmada 20 E7
Nasi Ayam Kedewatan 48 D1
Nasi Tempong, Restaurant 21 H5
Nasi Timbel, Restaurant 11 J3
Natah Bale, Restaurant 17 K4
Natalie, Hotel 24 F5
Natia, The, Hotel 53 H7
National Park Headquarters 92 B6
National Search and Rescue Agency
    (Basarnas) 36 E3
Natrabu, Restaurant (Nusa Dua) .. 39 H4
Natrabu, Restaurant (Sanur) 23 K7
Natura Resort & Spa 49 L4
Nature Villa Resort & Spa 47 L1
Naughty Nuri's, Restaurant 48 E2
Naya Gawana Resort & Pier, Hotel .. 93 J3
Ndalem Dharmatiwi, Hotel 25 G5
Ne Keren 47 H4
Nefatari Exclusive Villas 48 D6
Negara Gallery 46 E5
Neka Art Museum 47 G3
Neka Art Museum 48 E2
Nelayan, Hotel 25 J8
Nelayan, Restaurant (Jimbaran) .. 32 B6
Nelayan, Restaurant (Tanjung Benoa) .. 33 K4
Neo Gatot Subroto Bali, Hotel 27 M2
Nero, Restaurant 14 D5
Nest Condotel, The, Hotel 39 J2
Nest, The, Restaurant 46 F1
Neuviz, Hotel 26 E7
Neva's, Hotel 19 J5
New 1001, Restaurant 17 K4
New Arena, Hotel 14 D7
New Bendesa Jimbaran Bay 32 B5
New Bumbu Bali 32 B3
New Dewata, Restaurant 20 E7
New Kuta Condotel, Hotel 35 G5
New Kuta Green Park, Hotel 35 G4
New Langsam 32 B3
New Matahari Cafe 32 B4
Ngiring Ngewedang, Restaurant .. 99 G7
Ngurah Rai School 26 F5
Ngurah Rai Stadium 57 D5
Ngurah Rai Statue 11 K6

Ni Luh Djelantik 19 K6
Ni Nyoman Warini, Hotel 46 F6
Ni Rampe Village 25 J8
Niaga, Hotel 57 D3
Nick's Pension, Hotel 46 D3
Nicks Hidden Cottages 46 C5
Night Market (Blambangan, Kuta) .. 14 F8
Night Market (Jl. P. Madura) 21 L1
Night Market (Jl. Raya Sesetan) .. 21 L4
Night Market (Raya Ubud, Ubud) .. 46 F3
Nikaya, Hotel 14 E3
Nike Villas 23 L8
Nikki, Hotel 29 G3
Nikko Bali, Resort 45 K3
Niksoma, Hotel 14 B3
Nina, Restaurant 33 K3
Nindya Karya 29 M7
Ning, Hotel 46 F3
Nirmala (Jl. Raya Uluwatu, Ungasan) .. 43 G1
Nirmala Sari, Hotel 47 J1
Nirmala, Hotel (Mahendra Datta) .. 27 M8
Nirmala, Hotel (Uluwatu 2) 32 D8
Nirvana 46 F4
Nirwa Home Stay, Hotel 46 D2
Nirwana Bali, Golf Course 63 H7
Nirwana Cottages 52 C8
Nirwana Resort 53 J7
Nirwana Seaside Cottages 52 F1
Nirwana Suites, Hotel 16 D1
Nirwana, Hotel 25 G4
Nismara, Hotel 19 G3
NISP 29 H5
Nissan 29 H2
Njana Tilen, Gallery 65 G3
NKR 19 M5
Nogo Ikat Center 23 M8
Noma Garden, Hotel 32 F7
Nomad, Restaurant 46 F3
Nona, Restaurant 23 L4
Nook Cafe 19 J3
Norbert's Villa 27 L8
Nosea Garden, Restaurant 33 K4
Nova 23 K4
Novotel Benoa, Hotel 33 K3
Novotel Nusa Dua, Hotel 39 J7
Novus Bali, Hotel 26 F6
Nuansa Indah, Hotel 29 H3
Nugraha Lovina, Hotel 52 B2
Nugraha Utara, Hotel 56 E5
Nugras Gallery 33 K5
Numero 39 L3
Nunung Primitive Art 19 M5
Nuriani, Restaurant 46 E8
Nurul Huda 11 J6
Nusa Bali 29 M8
Nusa Dua Beach, Hotel 39 K3
Nusa Dua Circle 38 A1
Nusa Dua Clinic 33 K6
Nusa Dua Gallery 39 K5
Nusa Dua Hill, Resort 38 F5
Nusa Dua Retreat & Spa, Hotel .. 43 M5
Nusa Dua, Hotel 39 J3
Nusa Garden Bungalow 109 H1
Nusa Gong Art 39 J6
Nusa Indah Bungalows 52 B8
Nusa Indah, Hotel (Kuta) 14 D8
Nusa Indah, Hotel (Nusa Lembongan) .. 108 C1
Nusa Indah, Restaurant 14 D7
Nusa Lembongan Bongalows, Hotel .. 108 C1
Nusa Trans (Padang Sambian) 20 D5
Nusa Trans (Gatot Subroto Timur Bypass) 30 E4
Nusa Trans
    (Prof. Dr. Ida Bagus Mantra Bypass) .. 31 K3
Nusbog, Restaurant 53 H3
Nya. Sugaia 49 G7
Nyaman, Hotel 19 H7
Nyima Budget Inn, Hotel 19 L6
Nyoman Ada 49 G3
Nyoman Astanas Inn, Hotel 49 G7
Nyoman Badri, Hotel 47 H5
Nyoman Gunarsa Museum 66 C6
Nyoman Jami 49 H2
Nyoman Made 46 D6
Nyoman Pangus Homestay 50 C3
Nyoman Sumerta Art 49 H7
Nyoman Togog 49 G8
Nyoman Warta, Hotel 47 H5
Nyoman, Restaurant (Bukit Permai) .. 32 A7
Nyoman, Restaurant (Merta Sari) .. 17 J5
Nyomans Beergarden, Restaurant .. 39 J6

O

O'India, Restaurant 14 E3
Oakley 38 C1
Oaks 38 A1
Oasis Lagoon, The, Restaurant ... 17 L2
Oasis, Hotel (Lovina Beach) 53 G3
Oasis, The, Hotel (Jalan Singosari – Kuta) . 14 D8
Oasis, The, Hotel (Jl. Pratama, Nusa Dua) . 33 K5
Oasis, The, Hotel (Kesari 2) 17 L2
Oazia, Hotel 26 C5
Oberoi Bali, The, Hotel 19 H8
Oberoi, The, Hotel 26 D6
Obonk, Restaurant 21 K3
Ocean Blue Bali, Hotel 38 B8
Ocean Blue, Hotel 44 F1
Ocean Sun 90 D2
Ocean Terrace Beach Front Dining . 39 K4
Ocean Terrace, Restaurant 39 L4
Ocean Valley Village 43 J6

Ocean View Dive Resort Tulamben .. 90 D3
Ocean, The 32 B2
Oceanea Biru Bali Tours & Travel .. 17 K3
Octopus Garden, Restaurant 52 E3
Oeat 46 F7
Ogah-Ogah Bar 47 J1
Ohana, Hotel 11 G3
Oihana Bali Villa 36 A7
OJ Villa 17 J5
Oka Kartini Bungalow & Galeri 47 H4
Oka Sari Spa 47 G4
Oka Wati, Hotel 46 E4
Oke, Restaurant 52 E7
Old Port, Lontar Library 57 F5
Olesha, Restaurant 25 G6
Olivia Inn, Hotel 15 G3
Oma Thia's Kitchen, Restaurant .. 19 L2
Omah Eyang, Hotel 27 G5
Omahqu, Hotel 27 G3
Omatha Village 29 M6
Ombak Laut, Hotel 24 A2
Ombak Luwung, Hotel 25 J8
Ombak Putih Bungalow 33 K3
Ombak Putih, Hotel 24 B3
Ombak Residence, Hotel 25 K7
Omsi, Hotel 23 M8
One Boutique, The, Hotel 18 F4
Only You, Hotel 91 J6
Oops, Restaurant 46 F3
Optik Melawai 39 L4
Orange, Hotel 26 B8
Orange, The, Restaurant 21 J3
Oranje, Hotel 22 F3
Oranje, Restaurant 23 L6
Oranjje, Hotel 14 D5
Orchid Villa 17 M2
Orchid, Hotel 19 H4
Orgone Gallery 48 E3
Origin Tours 23 K2
Ornamental Plant Market 23 G3
Ornamental Plants 30 E4
Osala, Hotel 28 C2
Oshan Villas Bali, The 25 L4
Osteria, Restaurant 19 G6
Ours, Restaurant 14 C5
Oyee, Restaurant 52 F3
Ozigo, Restaurant 48 E2

P

Paasha, Hotel 19 J6
Pacific Express Cargo 23 G4
Pacific Marina 33 K5
Pacific World Nusantara 17 K4
Pacto Tour 17 K2
Pacung 86 C4
Pacung Hotel & Restaurant 86 B4
Padang Lovina, Hotel 52 F2
Padang Padang Inn, Hotel 34 C7
Padang Padang Sari, Hotel 34 J7
Padang Raya, Restaurant 39 H4
Padang Sari, Restaurant 30 F7
Padangbai Beach, Hotel 67 L4
Paddy, Restaurant 85 K7
Padi Bali, Hotel 24 B3
Padi Bali, Restaurant 19 G7
Padi Collection 46 E3
Padi Dive Center (Lovina Beach) .. 52 F3
Padi Dive Center (Sanur) 23 K7
Padi GH 26 B6
Padi House Villa, The 25 K3
Padi Karo, Hotel 24 B2
Padi Padi, Hotel 25 J3
Padi Padi, Restaurant 15 G5
Padi Prada Suite & Spa, Hotel 46 E7
Padi, Restaurant (Sanur) 23 K7
Padi, Restaurant (Tulamben) 90 D2
Padi, Restaurant (Ungasan) 35 L1
Padi, Villa 24 B3
Padma Bahtera 22 E1
Padma Hastaa Spa 2 .... 46 C5
Padma Resort Bali 14 C4
Padma, Restaurant 33 K4
Padmasari, Hotel 52 B2
Padmastana 22 B4
Paduzzi, Restaurant 17 L4
Pager Bungalows 46 C2
Painting, Gold & Silver Smiths 66 E5
Pak Ada, Restaurant 23 K3
Pak Wuk, Restaurant 49 H2
Pakis Merah, Hotel 18 D1
Pala, Restaurant 17 J4
Palava 48 E2
Palay, Restaurant 17 M2
Palloma, Hotel 14 E3
Palm 48 D2
Palm Bali Villa 19 M7
Palm Garden, Hotel 17 L4
Palm River, Hotel 24 F5
Palm Suite Villa & Spa, The 17 G4
Palm Suite, Hotel (Petitenget) 19 J4
Palm Suite, Hotel (Tambak Sari) .. 17 J3
Palm Tree Bungalows 25 J6
Palm, Hotel 10 E4
Palma, Hotel 18 E2
Palms, The, Hotel 108 B3
Palmyra Cottages 26 D8
Panasonic 28 B2
Panca Sari Dive 33 K3
Panca Sari, Hotel 99 L6

Panca Yoga, Restaurant 105 M8
Pancasari Inn, Hotel 99 M7
Pandan Harum Stage 53 H7
Pandawa Mini Market 46 E4
Pandawa, Hotel 53 K7
Pandawa, Restaurant 46 E4
Pande Home Stay, Hotel 46 F6
Pande Permai Bungalows 46 D6
Pandora 46 E4
Pangi Gita, Hotel 25 J3
Pangi River, Hotel 25 G4
Pangsit Mie Ayam 29 G6
Panili Vanilla, Restaurant 48 F7
Panin (Imam Bonjol) 20 E8
Panjer Market 22 B6
Panorama 47 J1
Panorama Cottage I 14 E4
Panorama Cottage II 14 E5
Panorama Hill Apartment 36 D7
Panorama Leisure, Hotel 16 C6
Pansea Puri Bali, Hotel 32 K3
Pantai Indah, Hotel 24 F6
Pantai Mas, Hotel 52 A3
Pantai Mengening, Villa 24 A2
Pantekosta Church (Denpasar) 21 K3
Pantekosta Church (Sanur) 23 H5
Pantheon, Gallery 65 G4
Pantri, Restaurant 10 E3
Paon, Restaurant 39 M3
Paon, The, Restaurant 46 E2
Papa's Cafe 14 C5
Paparons, Pizza 21 G5
Papaya 14 F5
Papillon Garden, Hotel 26 B7
Paradise Bali Tour 11 J5
Paradise Loft Villas 37 M3
Paradise Palm Beach, Hotel 90 D2
Paradiso Inn, Hotel 14 D7
Parasol, Restaurant 14 C4
Parigata Resort 17 J4
Parigata Villas Resort 17 M4
Parigata, Hotel 17 M2
Park Regis, Hotel 14 F5
Park Royal (U/C), Hotel 35 J7
Park View Height Villas 37 M8
Parmi 49 G8
Pasar Anyar 11 J2
Pasar Desa Serangan 13 K3
Pasar Kalisari 53 G3
Pasar Kangkung 15 H2
Pasar Malam, Restaurant 33 K5
Pasar Oleh Oleh 11 H3
Pasar Pagi (Denpasar) 20 F7
Pasar Pagi (Legian) 14 D5
Pasar Patnadi 28 D4
Pasar Ratu 53 G3
Pasar Raya Kuta 11 J4
Pasar Senggol 27 J8
Pasar Serangan 16 F8
Pasar Suwung Batan Kendal 16 D5
Pasar Windhu Bhoga 15 K6
Pasifika Museum 39 K4
Pasir Ukir, Restaurant 23 K2
Pasundan, Restaurant 22 C2
Pat-Mase Villas, Hotel 32 A8
Pat-Mase, Villa 36 D3
Patra Bali Resort & Villas, The, Hotel .. 10 D5
Patricia, Hotel 23 K3
Paul Ropp 32 B8
Paul Smith 39 L3
Pavilion, Restaurant 19 H3
Pavilion, The, Hotel 23 L7
Pawon Sunda, Restaurant 11 H4
Payan Bedih, Bungalow 62 B2
Payogan Villa Resort & Spa, The, Hotel .. 72 F6
PDAM Nusa Dua 39 G4
Pedungan Market 21 J6
Peek a boo 23 K5
Pegadaian (Ngurah Rai Bypass) ... 39 G3
Pegadaian (Peliatan) 47 H6
Pegadaian (Pudak) 29 J7
Pegadaian (Raya Puputan) 22 B3
Pegadaian (Raya Sesetan) 16 C3
Pejeng, Hotel 49 K6
Pekarangan Indah, Hotel 86 B3
Pekik, Restaurant 23 L6
Pelangi Bali Bistro 14 E4
Pelangi Bali, Hotel (Jalan Pidada 5) .. 28 B2
Pelangi Bali, Hotel (Jalan Seminyak) .. 14 B2
Pelasa, Hotel 14 E5
Pelita Bangsa School 20 E4
PELNI 11 H3
Pemutih, Villa 34 C7
Penataran Temple 32 E4
Pendawa, Hotel 28 F7
Pendopo Antique 19 M8
Peneeda View, Hotel 17 M3
Penestanan Bungalows 46 A2
Pengadilan Hubungan Industrial .. 29 H6
Pengadilan Negeri 21 L2
Pengadilan Tinggi Tata Usaha Negara .. 22 B2
Penginapan Pondok Indah, Hotel .. 27 L8
Pengubengan Kangin Market 19 L3
Penguin FM Radio 28 B3
Pengukur Ukuran 49 M4
Penida Medica 20 E5
Penjor Bali 22 E4
Penta Medica 20 E5

Pepito (Raya Kediri) 11 G4
Pepito (Raya Kerobokan) 19 K4
Pepito Expres 37 L2
Pepito, Restaurant 42 F1
Peppers Sentosa Villa and Spa 19 H5
Perada Bali, Hotel 30 F7
Perahu 89, Hotel 19 M5
Perama Tour & Travel 46 F8
Perama, Hotel 53 J3
Perdana 32 C7
Pererenan Villas 25 G4
Pergola, Restaurant 23 K6
Pering 49 H7
Peringatan Serangan Umum
    Kota Denpasar 29 H2
Periplus Bookshop (Bali Collection) 39 K5
Periplus Bookshop (Bali Deli, Seminyak) .. 19 L7
Periplus Bookshop
    (Discovery Shopping Mall) 10 F2
Periplus Bookshop (Hardy's, Sanur) 17 L2
Periplus Bookshop
    (Ngurah Rai Int'l Airport) 10 E6
Periplus Bookshop (Seminyak Square) 19 H6
Periplus Bookshop (Ubud) 46 E4
Permai Dive Center 52 D2
Permai Dive Resort
    (Dharma Jadra, Lovina) 53 M2
Permai Dive Resort
    (Dharmakerti, Lovina) 100 F6
Permata Hati 20 D4
Permata Bank (Amlapura) 55 E5
Permata Bank (Denpasar) 21 L3
Permata, Bank (Gatot Subroto) 29 H2
Permata, Bank (Jalan Danau Tamblingan) . 17 M2
Permata, Bank (Raya Ubud) 46 E3
Pertamina (Jalan Udayana) 29 G7
Pertamina (Ngurah Rai Bypass) 16 B6
Pertamina Elpiji 30 B2
Pertamina Tank Yard 10 E5
Pertani 29 K7
Pertiwi 1, Restaurant 46 C6
Pertiwi 2, Restaurant 46 K8
Pertiwi Bisma, Hotel 46 C4
Pertiwi Resort & Spa 46 E5
Pertokoan Br. Semer 26 E8
Perusahaan Perdagangan Indonesia 29 L7
Pesiapan Terminal 51 A2
Pesona Bali Hill, Hotel 38 D3
Pesona Beach Inn, Hotel 14 D7
Pesraman, Hotel 17 K4
Pet Shop 38 A1
Petani, Restaurant 46 F7
Petanu, Restaurant 49 J7
Pete's Place, Hotel 19 G6
Petulu-Heron Village 49 H2
Petulu, Restaurant 49 G3
PGSD 16 B4
Phalam Batik 30 D2
Phalosa, Hotel 18 E4
Piaggio 15 G2
Piasan, Restaurant 39 J3
Pica 46 E3
Picola, Hotel 17 K4
Piliau Residence, Hotel 27 H5
Pioneer Service Center 30 C4
Pita Loka, Restaurant 105 M8
Pita Maha Resort 48 E3
Pitari 32 D1
Pizza Bagus 48 F7
Pizza Hut (Gatot Subroto) 29 G2
Pizza Hut (Jl. Adhiaksa, Dauh Puri) 21 L3
Pizza Hut (Jl. Diponegoro) 21 L2
Pizza Hut (Jl. Teuku Umar) 21 J5
Pizza Hut (Ngurah Rai Bypass) 23 K6
Pizza Ria 17 M3
Planet Hollywood, Restaurant 14 F8
Planet Surf 19 M3
Plantation, Restaurant 72 F5
Plasa Sunset Road 14 E2
Plasahosting 16 A4
Plataran Canggu, Hotel 26 E6
Plaza Bali Mall 11 J4
Plaza Telcom 47 H4
Plengkung 11 H2
PLN (Jl. Gunung Mandala Wangi) 21 K1
PLN (Jl. Letda Tantular, Denpasar) 22 A3
PLN (Jl. M.T. Haryono, Denpasar Utara) ... 21 L1
PLN (Jl. Udayana, Singaraja) 57 C5
PLN (Ngurah Rai Bypass) 14 F8
PLN (Sunset Road) 15 G6
PLN Padang Sambian 20 D2
Plumerta, Restaurant 48 D1
Poch, The, Restaurant 23 L8
Poco Loco, Restaurant 39 J6
Poco Lounge, Restaurant 52 E1
Police Headquarters 29 J5
Polisi Militer 21 M3
Polisi PP 22 C3
Politeknik Kesehatan 22 A3
Politeknik Kesehatan Gizi 31 H6
Politeknik Negeri Bali 36 E5
Polo (Bali Collection, Nusa Dua) 39 L4
Polo (Camplung Tanduk) 19 K8
Polo (Raya Ubud) 46 F3
Polo (Wenara Wana) 46 E4
Polo Ralph Lauren (Ngurah Rai Bypass) .. 38 A1
Polo Ralph Lauren (Waribang) 30 D6
Poltabes Denpasar 27 J5
Poltekom Bali 22 B2
Pond, The, Restaurant 46 E7

Pondok Agung, Hotel 33 J2
Pondok Alit, Hotel 19 H3
Pondok Ayu, Hotel 23 K7
Pondok Bali, Villa 98 B2
Pondok Bamboo Music Shop 46 E7
Pondok Bambu Seaside, Hotel 53 J7
Pondok Bambu, Hotel 46 F1
Pondok Batu, Hotel 25 H5
Pondok Bulan Mas, Hotel 49 G3
Pondok Bunda, Restaurant 50 C8
Pondok Cangked Guest House 94 D3
Pondok Dukuh, Hotel 18 F4
Pondok Elsa, Hotel 52 F1
Pondok Ganesha HS, Hotel 26 E5
Pondok Iman Villas 46 A1
Pondok Impian, Hotel 48 F7
Pondok Indah, Hotel 34 D6
Pondok Kecil 2, Hotel 48 F2
Pondok Kesuma Wisata, Hotel 99 G6
Pondok Kori, Hotel 27 L3
Pondok Krishna, Hotel 46 D3
Pondok Kuring, Restaurant 22 A4
Pondok Mas, Gallery 65 H3
Pondok Nipuri, Hotel 18 F4
Pondok Nyoman Resort 24 F6
Pondok Pisang, Hotel 52 D8
Pondok Pugir, Hotel 40 B3
Pondok Pundi Village Inn 46 D5
Pondok Rasa, Restaurant 55 D5
Pondok Sakti, Hotel 49 G2
Pondok Sara, Hotel (Seminyak) 14 C2
Pondok Sara, Hotel (Umalas 1) 19 J2
Pondok Sari, Hotel (Tibubeneng) 18 E2
Pondok Sari, Hotel (Pemuteran) 94 C2
Pondok Tempo Doeloe, Restaurant 15 G7
Pondok Tyara 32 E2
Pondok Wisata Bagus 71 K5
Pondok Wisata Gili Kembang, Hotel 92 B5
Pondok Wisata Kesuma, Hotel 99 H7
Pondok Wisata Marta 71 K7
Pondok Wisata, Homestay 67 G1
Pondok Wisata, Hotel (Candidasa) 52 R8
Pondok Wisata, Hotel (Denpasar) 30 D6
Pondok Wisata, Hotel (Gianyar) 50 C7
Pool Grill, Restaurant 63 H7
Pop!, Hotel (Erlangga) 57 D2
Pop!, Hotel (Legian) 14 D5
Pop!, Hotel (Ngurah Rai Bypass) 38 B1
Pop!, Hotel (Teuku Umar) 21 H5
Popiler II 30 E2
Poppies Cottage 14 E7
Poppies Cottage II 14 D7
Poppies, Restaurant 14 E7
Porch, The, Restaurant 17 L1
Pos TNI-AL 109 K3
Potato Head Beach Club 18 F5
Pourquoi Pas 19 L6
PP 22 F2
Prada, Restaurant 39 M3
Pradha Villas 19 H6
Pradhaana Boutique, Hotel 19 K8
Praety, Hotel 47 H5
Prama Sanur Beach, Hotel 17 K5
Prambanan, Restaurant 47 J4
Prani Legian, Hotel 14 D4
Pranoto's Art 47 G4
Prasada Villa 25 J5
Prasanthi Hospital 51 A4
Prasyda, Hotel 19 J2
Pratama Fitness 39 J3
Prawita, Hotel 14 E7
Pregina, Restaurant 23 L8
Premier Surf Camp, Hotel 25 G5
Presidential Palace of Tampak Siring, The 73 K2
Prestige Bali, Hotel 19 K2
Prima Agung, Hotel 56 F5
Prima Agung, Restaurant 56 F5
Prima Galleria Cafe 15 G8
Prima Medika Hospital 21 K5
Prima Rasa Pangan 16 D4
Prima Rasa, Restaurant 23 K4
Prima Tours 53 J3
Prima, Hotel 23 L8
Primebizz, Hotel 11 H4
Princess Benoa Beach Resort, Hotel 33 K2
Princess Nusa Dua, Hotel 33 K2
Pringga Juwita, Hotel 46 D3
Prisciliani, Hotel 26 E8
Procon Indah, Hotel 25 G6
Prodia (Gatot Subroto) 29 G2
Prodia (Ngurah Rai Bypass) 38 C1
Prodia (Jl. Raya Sesetan) 21 L3
Prologue 46 D4
Prudential 38 D1
PT. Ayu Orchid 15 G1
PT. Bali Foam Nusa Megah 16 A6
PT. Bali Mina Utama 12 D6
PT. Bali Mista 19 L4
PT. Bali Trisna Pertiwi 32 F6
PT. Bhanda Ghara Reksa 32 E1
PT. Canning Indonesian Products 21 L1
PT. D Classic 25 J7
PT. Data Info 22 A3
PT. Djarum 16 C4
PT. Evata 19 K5
PT. Gabe International 32 E2
PT. Gapura Angkasa 11 J5
PT. Gilontas Indonesia 12 D6
PT. Ivo 10 F4
PT. Kalimas 23 K8

PT. Lintas Antar Nusa 16 F8
PT. Maruki International 14 F8
PT. Mitrais 11 G4
PT. Paris Bali 16 A6
PT. PNM 22 C4
PT. Puri Amartha Phala 26 D7
PT. Saka Agung Abadi 30 B2
PT. SC Enterprises 19 J3
PT. Sinarmas Multifinance 11 G2
PT. Sucofindo 21 L7
PT. Valencia Intan Permata 19 L5
Pualam Homestay 50 C2
Puas, Restaurant 56 E5
Public Bathing Pool 50 D3
Puja Mandala 38 F4
Pujasari, Restaurant 10 F4
Puji Bungalow 46 D3
Pulau Bali, Hotel 28 E7
Pulau Sakura, Restaurant 17 M2
Pulau Tenang Bali, Hotel 26 B7
Pulestis Beach, Hotel 53 G4
Pullman Bali Legian Nirwana, Hotel 14 C5
Pulu Bungalow 46 F6
Pulukan, Restaurant 68 B2
Puncak Pesona, Restaurant 36 D7
Pundi Bank 21 L2
Pundi-Pundi, Restaurant 46 E7
Pupuk Kaltim 23 K5
Puputan Monument 51 D6
Pura Agung Petilan 30 B4
Pura Arjuna Metapa 49 K7
Pura Bakungan 92 B6
Pura Balai Agung 72 F3
Pura Balangan 35 G3
Pura Bale Agung 32 D4
Pura Batu Belig 45 L3
Pura Batu Bolong 25 H8
Pura Batu Karu 46 F1
Pura Batu Klotok 66 E7
Pura Batu Kuring 109 L4
Pura Batu Madan 109 L4
Pura Batu Pageh 43 K8
Pura Beji 101 K3
Pura Belanjong 17 J4
Pura Buruan 23 J5
Pura Campuan Windu Segara 31 H7
Pura Candi Narmada 15 G8
Pura Candidasa 53 J7
Pura Celangi 35 G2
Pura Dalem (Bebalang, Bangli) 54 D8
Pura Dalem (Gianyar) 50 B5
Pura Dalem (Kuta) 14 D8
Pura Dalem (Lovina Beach) 52 F3
Pura Dalem (Sanur Kaja) 23 K4
Pura Dalem (Sanur) 17 L4
Pura Dalem (Sawan) 101 M5
Pura Dalem (Sidan, Gianyar) 65 M2
Pura Dalem (Sukawati) 65 J8
Pura Dalem (Ubud) 47 G3
Pura Dalem Agung Parang Tegal 46 D7
Pura Dalem Air Jeruk (Sukawati) 65 J8
Pura Dalem Bias Tugel 39 M5
Pura Dalem Cemara 13 L3
Pura Dalem Cungkub 54 E4
Pura Dalem Desa Pakraman 47 L3
Pura Dalem Kahyangan 13 L1
Pura Dalem Kampial 38 E5
Pura Dalem Lan Prajapati 24 D5
Pura Dalem Lukluk 64 B5
Pura Dalem Muter 30 C5
Pura Dalem Nyuhgading 69 M3
Pura Dalem Penataran (Sesetan) 16 B7
Pura Dalem Penataran (Nusa Dua) 38 D6
Pura Dalem Penataran Ped. 108 F1
Pura Dalem Pengembak 17 H5
Pura Dalem Penunggekan 54 C7
Pura Dalem Perancak 18 C1
Pura Dalem Puri 47 H4
Pura Dalem Purwa 54 B3
Pura Dalem Setra 33 K3
Pura Dalem Slaungan 54 E2
Pura Dalem Susunan Wadon 13 K2
Pura Dalem Tengkulung 33 K4
Pura Dalem Ubud 46 D2
Pura Demak 20 F5
Pura Desa (Dauh Puri Kaja) 28 E6
Pura Desa & Pura Puseh 32 D4
Pura Desa Adat Bualu 39 G4
Pura Desa Lan Puseh 47 G1
Pura Desa Ubud 46 E3
Pura Dukuh Sorin Karang Boma 37 K5
Pura Gajah Sesetan 21 L7
Pura Gede Luhur Batungaus 63 H8
Pura Geger 45 M2
Pura Geria Selang 77 L1
Pura Geria Tanah Kilap 15 G7
Pura Gili Kencana 93 G1
Pura Goa Gong 37 H6
Pura Gubug Tamblingan 99 G8
Pura Gunung Kawi Sebatu 87 J8
Pura Gunung Lebah 46 B2
Pura Gunung Payung 44 F6
Pura Gunung Sari 47 J3
Pura Hyang Tiba 65 H4
Pura Jagad Dalem Pagerwesi 39 H4
Pura Jagadnata 101 H5
Pura Jagat Natha 29 G7
Pura Jagat Tirtha 11 H6
Pura Jagatnatha (Puja Mandala) 38 F4
Pura Jati 88 C3

Pura Karang Boma 45 J5
Pura Kayangan Tuban 11 J6
Pura Keboedan 49 K6
Pura Kehen 54 E1
Pura Khayangan 17 G2
Pura Krobokan 73 K6
Pura Ksatria Dalem 10 D5
Pura Kulat 40 B4
Pura Lamun 39 K5
Pura Luhur Batu Karu 85 H6
Pura Luhur Batu Ngaus 24 A3
Pura Luhur Serijong 62 B2
Pura Luhur Ulun Siwi 24 D4
Pura Luhur Uluwatu 40 A5
Pura Manik Tirtha 54 D2
Pura Maospahit 28 E6
Pura Marajan Agung 46 F2
Pura Masceti 72 F5
Pura Masuka 42 F8
Pura Meduwe Karang 102 B3
Pura Merta Sari 17 J5
Pura Nambangan 28 D7
Pura Nataran Agung 54 D4
Pura Pabean 94 E2
Pura Padang Sakti 31 G6
Pura Padma Sari 28 B8
Pura Panataran Cempango 54 D3
Pura Panti Pasek Gelgel 39 H5
Pura Pasek Desa 65 H5
Pura Pegareman 11 J2
Pura Penataran Sari 15 M1
Pura Penataran Sasih 49 J6
Pura Penataran Topeng 65 J4
Pura Petitenget 19 G6
Pura Pojok Batu 103 H4
Pura Prapat Nunggal 15 M8
Pura Puncak Mundi 108 F4
Pura Pusa 52 B6
Pura Puseh (Bangli) 54 D3
Pura Puseh (Nusa Penida) 109 K3
Pura Puseh (Selemadeg) 70 B2
Pura Puseh (Ubud) 46 F1
Pura Puseh Desa Culik Kauh 90 E5
Pura Pusering Jagat 49 K6
Pura Rajan 54 D4
Pura Sadha 64 B4
Pura Sakenan (Serangan Island) 13 J1
Pura Sakenan (Tampak Siring) 87 K8
Pura Samuan Tiga 49 L7
Pura Samuh 39 K2
Pura Saren Agung 46 F3
Pura Segara (Jl. Segara Ayu, Sanur) 23 L6
Pura Segara (Lovina Beach) 52 E3
Pura Segara Desa Adat Kedonganan 32 C4
Pura Segara Nata 39 L6
Pura Segara Sawangan 45 L3
Pura Segara Tigawasa 52 C2
Pura Siwa Dampati 23 K6
Pura Sukamerih 72 F3
Pura Taman Ayun 64 B3
Pura Taman Ayungi 31 H7
Pura Taman Manik Mas 102 D3
Pura Taman Saraswati 46 E2
Pura Taman Sari 51 F6
Pura Tanah Lot 63 G7
Pura Tegal Wangi 36 A1
Pura Tegeh Kuripan 105 L3
Pura Telaga Waja (Ngurah Rai Airport) .. 11 G7
Pura Telaga Waja (Ubud) 73 H5
Pura Teluk Biu 88 F2
Pura Tunggak Tiying 13 H6
Pura Ulun Danu 48 D3
Pura Ulun Danu Balian 99 L5
Pura Ulun Danu Batur 105 M6
Pura Ulun Danu Bratan 99 M8
Pura Ulun Siwi 32 C5
Pura Yeh Gangga 72 C3
Pura Penataran Pande 47 J5
Pure Villa 26 D3
Pureland, The 46 F4
Puri Agung 51 D6
Puri Agung Indah, Hotel 30 C5
Puri Agung Jagatnatha 57 D4
Puri Agung Palace (Amlapura) 55 E4
Puri Agung Palace (Gianyar) 50 D7
Puri Agung Peliatan 47 H8
Puri Agung Tabanan 51 D2
Puri Agung, Hotel 47 H8
Puri Alam Bali, Hotel 98 F7
Puri Alam Dewata, Hotel 49 J7
Puri Alit, Hotel 28 E6
Puri Anantha, Hotel 29 M8
Puri Angsa, Hotel 25 M8
Puri Anom GH 17 K4
Puri Anyar 51 D6
Puri Aries, Hotel 90 F5
Puri Arjuna, Hotel 68 B3
Puri Arjuna, Restaurant 68 B3
Puri Artha, Hotel 46 F8
Puri Asih, Hotel 14 D8
Puri Asri 2, Hotel 47 G7
Puri Asri Bungalow 46 F5
Puri Asri Petulu, Hotel 49 H2
Puri Ayodya Museum 53 G3
Puri Ayu Cottages 46 D6
Puri Ayu, Hotel 21 M2
Puri Bagus Lovina, Hotel 100 F6
Puri Bagus, Hotel 53 M7
Puri Bali Homestay, Hotel 53 G7
Puri Bali Resort, Hotel 40 D6

Building Index

Building Index

Puri Bali Utama, Hotel 30 B4
Puri Bali, Hotel 53 G3
Puri Bali, Restaurant 14 C5
Puri Bamboo, Hotel 32 C3
Puri Baru Ponjok Batu, Hotel ... 103 H4
Puri Bawana, Hotel 25 K4
Puri Bedahulu, Hotel 100 E6
Puri Bendesa II Resort & Spa 43 3G
Puri Bening Hayato, Hotel 50 D2
Puri Bidadari, Hotel 19 G5
Puri Bukit Mas Art 49 H8
Puri Bunga Inn, Hotel 11 G5
Puri Bunga, Hotel 48 D1
Puri Bunga, Restaurant 52 C3
Puri Dalem, Hotel 46 F7
Puri Dalem, Hotel 23 K4
Puri Desa Gede 49 G7
Puri Dewa Bharata, Hotel (Nakula) 14 D2
Puri Dewa Bharata, Hotel (Raya Uluwatu) .32 C7
Puri Dibia, Hotel 14 E8
Puri Dukuh HS, Hotel 27 G8
Puri Dukuh, Hotel 19 L3
Puri Duyung, Hotel 19 K8
Puri Ganesha Villas, Hotel 94 C2
Puri Gatsu Indah, Hotel 27 L2
Puri Gede & Puri Kertasura Palaces ... 55 E4
Puri Gopa, Hotel 17 L4
Puri Hiromi, Hotel 17 L2
Puri Indah Bali, Hotel 28 F5
Puri Indah, Hotel 108 C1
Puri Indra Prasta, Hotel (Jalan Nelayan) ... 25 J7
Puri Indra Prasta, Hotel (Raya Uluwatu) ... 32 C6
Puri Jimbaran, Hotel 32 D8
Puri Kangin, Hotel 51 E6
Puri Kawan Sejahtera Hospital .. 30 C2
Puri Kedaton, Hotel 29 J7
Puri Kelapa, Hotel 23 L6
Puri Kelodan 51 E7
Puri Kosala, Hotel 32 C5
Puri Lukisan Museum 46 E2
Puri Lumbung, Hotel 98 F7
Puri Madawi, Hotel 18 F4
Puri Madha, Hotel 90 D2
Puri Maharani, Hotel 30 D3
Puri Mandhara, Hotel 53 M3
Puri Manggala, Hotel 100 D8
Puri Mango, Hotel 23 L6
Puri Manik Sari, Hotel 52 F2
Puri Mesari, Hotel 17 J5
Puri Naga, Hotel (Jalan Padma) ... 14 B2
Puri Naga, Hotel (Raya Petulu) .. 49 G3
Puri Nusa Indah 2, Hotel 29 M5
Puri Nusa Indah, Hotel (Waribang) ... 30 D6
Puri Nusa Indah, Hotel (WR Supratman) . 29 K5
Puri Nusantara, Hotel 11 H5
Puri Oka Beach, Hotel 53 K7
Puri Pandan, Hotel 53 H7
Puri Pudak, Hotel 53 M7
Puri Puri Kecil, Hotel 19 K6
Puri Raharja Hospital 29 J5
Puri Rahayu Cottage 102 D3
Puri Rai, Hotel 67 L4
Puri Raja, Hotel 14 C3
Puri Rama, Hotel 14 E7
Puri Ratu GH 20 B2
Puri Rena, Hotel 102 D3
Puri Royan Villa, Hotel 32 C4
Puri Royan, Hotel 21 H5
Puri Sading, Hotel 23 L8
Puri Sani, Hotel 46 A3
Puri Sanih Cottages 102 D3
Puri Santrian, Hotel 17 L5
Puri Sanur, Hotel 23 J6
Puri Saraswati 51 D7
Puri Saraswati Bungalows 46 E2
Puri Saren Agung, Hotel 46 F3
Puri Saron, Hotel (Kerobokan Kaja) .. 27 H2
Puri Saron, Hotel (Seminyak) 14 B2
Puri Saron, Hotel (Ubud) 49 M5
Puri Saron, Hotel (Ubung) 28 A2
Puri Segara Village 40 C4
Puri Sejuk, Hotel 24 C4
Puri Sherazade, Hotel 26 E7
Puri Shop 46 D6
Puri Singsing, Hotel 98 B2
Puri Soewiring, Hotel 17 J4
Puri Suar, Hotel 23 L6
Puri Sunny, Hotel 99 H7
Puri Suranadi, Restaurant 22 F4
Puri Tamu, Hotel 36 E4
Puri Tanah Lot, Hotel 14 D5
Puri Tasik Madu, Hotel 52 E3
Puri Temple, Hotel 25 H6
Puri Tempo Doeloe, Hotel 23 K8
Puri Tina, Hotel 53 L7
Puri Tirta, Hotel 49 H2
Puri Uluwatu Villas 40 B4
Puri Uluwatu Villas, Hotel 40 B1
Puri Widiana, Hotel 46 F3
Puri Wirata Dive Resort 90 D1
Puri Wirata Resort 91 J6
Puri Wisata, Hotel 14 D2
Puri Wulandari, Resort & Spa ... 72 F5
Puri Yuma, Hotel 16 E5
Puri, Hotel 28 F7
Puridea 31 G5
Purimas 3, Bakery 21 G5
Purist Villas & Spa, The 49 G3
Purna Sari 48 D8

Purnama Beach 65 K7
Purnama, Hotel (Dewi Sita) 46 E4
Purnama, Hotel (HOS Cokroaminoto) ... 28 D3
Purnama, Hotel (Raya Lovina) ... 52 E3
Puro Blanco, Hotel 18 E2
Purpas Silver 46 E4
Pusat Study Rusia 30 E2
Puskesmas (Jimbaran) 11 H8
Puskesmas (Prerenan) 25 H3
Puskesmas (Sesetan) 16 B4
Puskesmas Kuta Selatan 39 H5
Puspa 46 F5
Puspa Rama, Hotel 53 M3
Puteri, Hotel 26 D6
Putra Bali, Hotel 54 D6
Putra I Made Market 21 M8
Putra Padi, Hotel 46 F7
Putra Salahin, Hotel 49 H8
Putri Ayu, Villa 36 B7
Putri Dewata, Hotel 46 E8
Putu Bali, Hotel 19 G4
Putu GH 25 M8
Putu Putra, Hotel 47 G5

Q

Q, Hotel 14 F8
Quadri Foglio, Hotel 26 C7
Quantum 21 L5
Queen 2, Hotel 21 K3
Queen's of India, Restaurant 33 K7
Queen/Ratu, Hotel 21 L2
Queens of India, Restaurant 10 F3
Quest, Hotel 11 H4
Quick Silver, Hotel 12 E6
Quiksilver (Legian) 14 D5
Quiksilver (Ubud) 46 E4

R

R&R Bali Bed & Breakfast, Hotel 25 H6
Radiantly Alive 47 G4
Radio Gema Merdeka 30 D3
Radja, Restaurant 14 C2
Rahayu Bungalow 46 F5
Rahayu, Shopping 28 F2
Rahmat, Hotel 47 J1
Rai, Hotel 21 L3
Rai, Restaurant 33 K2
Raja Dive Center 52 D2
Raja Gardens, Hotel 19 J8
Raja Warung 39 A8
Raja's, Restaurant (Nusa Dua) .. 39 K3
Rajawali Mart 33 K4
Rajawali, Restaurant 17 L3
Rama Beach, Hotel 10 E4
Rama Candidasa Resort 52 D8
Rama Garden, Hotel 14 C4
Rama Japanese, Restaurant 14 E5
Rama Ocean View, Hotel 53 H7
Rama Phala, Hotel 46 F8
Rama Rama, Villa 36 B7
Rama Shinta, Hotel 53 K7
Rama Shinta, Shopping 20 E5
Rama Tours 11 J4
Rama Villas 17 H5
Rama, Hotel 30 C4
Ramada Bintang Bali Resort, Hotel ... 10 E3
Ramada Resort Benoa, Hotel ... 33 K2
Ramada Resort Camakila 14 B3
Ramayana, Hotel (Jl Danau Tamblingan) .. 17 L2
Ramayana, Hotel (Jl Singosari – Kuta) ... 14 D8
Rambo Homestay, Hotel 41 H1
Rambut Indah Wig Factory 47 K4
Rambutan Boutique, Hotel 53 G3
Ramos Alma Pottery 19 K2
Ramos Cafe 31 G5
Ranadi Villa 19 K7
Randy's, Restaurant 23 L7
Ranggon Bali, Restaurant 100 F6
Rani Hotel & Spa, The 10 F3
Rara Sari 46 F4
Rasa Dua, Hotel 33 K2
Rasa Sayang, Hotel 33 K4
Rasa Sayang, Restaurant (Sunset Road) ... 15 G6
Rasa Senang, Restaurant
   (Jl Danau Tamblingan) 23 L8
Rasa Sayang, Restaurant (Jl. T. Umar) ... 21 G6
Rasmiyasa, Hotel 21 L3
Ratatouille, Restaurant 23 L7
Ratih, Hotel 49 H2
Ratna Beach, Hotel 23 L6
Ratna Jaya, Hotel 57 D2
Ratna, Hotel 14 E8
Ratnasari, Hotel 29 H5
Rattan Resto (Amadeus), Hotel ... 52 F2
Ratu Ayu, Hotel 96 F3
Ratu Bali, Restaurant 23 L6
Rauli, Hotel 19 G3
RAV, Café 33 K1
Ray Sandy 48 E3
Ray, Hotel 53 J2
Raya, Hotel 28 F8
RC Villas 19 H7
Red Camellia 46 F4
Red Canvas, The 39 L3
Red Door Bali, Hotel 25 G3
Red Rocket, Restaurant 47 J4
Redikon 38 E2
Redlotus 47 H4
Regent, Hotel 17 M4
Reina, Hotel 19 K2

Reinhold, The, Hotel 26 F5
Reki, Hotel 24 D4
Rektorat UNUD 37 G5
Rela, Hotel 57 B4
Remede Spa 39 J7
Rena's Silver 46 D7
Rendezvous, Hotel 27 H4
Rendezvousdoux, Restaurant ... 47 G4
Renon Arcade 22 C4
Renon Market 22 F5
Renon Palace 22 E3
Renon, Restaurant (Jl. Ki Hajar Dewantara) 22 E2
Renon, Restaurant (Raya Puputan) .. 22 D4
Rent-a-Car 11 J5
Reptile Park 72 C6
Reservoart 19 K6
Residence Seminyak, The, Hotel .. 19 H5
Resort Prima 53 L7
Respati, Hotel 23 L7
Restaurant at the Legian, The .. 19 G6
Restu Bali, Hotel 14 E6
Retreat, The, Hotel 34 F6
Retro, Café 23 L8
Rhadana, Hotel 14 F7
Rhipidura Bungalows 94 C2
Rian Bagus, Hotel 17 J4
Rice Fields & Vista (Jatiluwih) .. 85 K6
Rice Terraces (Tegal Lalang) 73 H4
Rich Prada, The, Hotel 35 G4
Rich Stone 19 K3
Richard Meyer Culture 19 H4
Ridas, Café 33 K2
Rijasa, Hotel 76 D2
Rindu Rasa, Restaurant 39 H2
Rini, Hotel 52 F3
Rio Helmi 46 E2
Ripcurl (Kayu Aya) 19 H6
Ripcurl (Sunset Road) 15 G5
Ripcurl (Wenara Wana) 46 E5
Risata Bali Resort, Hotel 10 E4
Rishi Resort, The 53 H7
Rishi Villa, The 36 B8
Rishi, The, Hotel 19 J2
Rita, Hotel 17 L2
Ritual Bali, The, Hotel 40 A3
Ritz Carlton, Hotel 45 K4
Rivavi, Hotel 14 D5
River Cafe 47 L6
Riviera House, Hotel 25 M7
Rizka, Restaurant 47 H4
RM Sitha, Restaurant 53 M3
Rock Bali, Hotel 26 C5
Rock Canggu, Hotel 25 M6
Rock Sanur 17 J4
Rococo Gallery 46 D2
Rofa Galleria, Hotel 14 F3
Roja's 1, Hotel 46 E2
Romeo, Hotel 34 D6
Rona 47 H5
Rona GH 47 H5
Rona, Hotel 25 H5
Rona's, Hotel 47 G6
Roof Garden, Restaurant 46 D2
Rooms at Villa Gunung 26 B7
Rosani, Hotel 14 D5
Rose, Restaurant 14 D6
Rosso Vivo Dine & Lounge, Restaurant .. 14 C7
Rouge, Restaurant 46 D3
Roy Jaya Motor 32 C6
Royal Amertha, Hotel 94 E2
Royal Bali Beach Club, Hotel ... 32 D4
Royal Bali Beach Club, The, Hotel .. 32 B7
Royal Bali Celadon 19 K2
Royal Beach, Hotel 19 J8
Royal Brunei Airlines 11 J5
Royal Kamuela, Hotel (Nusa Dua) .. 39 K6
Royal Kamuela, Hotel (Ubud) ... 46 D6
Royal Santrian, The, Hotel 33 L8
RRI (Denpasar) 29 K7
RRI (Jl. Gajahmada, Singaraja) .. 57 E4
RRI Singaraja 53 H3
RSAD Udayana Hospital 21 M1
RSCH 21 G5
RSU Negara 56 C4
RSUD (Amlapura Hospital) 55 D2
Ruci 49 G7
Rudana Museum & Gallery 49 G8
Rudi Hadisuwarno Spa 17 H4
Rudy, Hotel 25 M7
Ruko (Jl. Diponegoro) 21 L3
Ruko Griya Amanda 22 B2
Ruko Kuta Berlian 14 E8
Ruko Royal Sunset 15 G7
Ruko Shanti 23 J3
Ruko Udayana 29 G8
Rumah Bajan, Hotel 25 K3
Rumah Bali, Hotel 33 K5
Rumah Cahaya, Hotel 48 D3
Rumah Makan Berkah, Hotel ... 67 K3
Rumah Matise, Hotel 24 E5
Rumah Nancy, Hotel 52 F8
Rumah Potong Hewan (Abatoir) .. 16 B5
Rumah Reposado, Hotel 19 G3
Rumah Roda, Restaurant 46 E1
Rumah Sehat Terapy 47 G4
Rumah Shiraz, Hotel 26 B6
Rumah Siam 26 B6
Rusty Indo Warehouse 11 G3
Ryoshi, Restaurant (Hanoman, Ubud) .. 46 F7
Ryoshi, Restaurant (Raya Seminyak) ... 14 C2

S

S'cape, Hotel 23 L7
S&G 19 K6
SA Cafe 10 E4
Sabana, Hotel 25 H1
Sadar Mosque 21 M7
Sado 49 G7
Sadra 49 H8
Safari, Restaurant 57 C4
Safin Inn, Hotel 19 K6
Sagitarius Inn, Hotel 46 E6
Sagitarius Shop 46 E6
Sahabat, Hotel 19 J4
Sahadewa, Hotel 46 F7
Sahaja, Restaurant 19 H2
Sahita, The, Hotel 24 B4
Sails, Restaurant 91 K6
Sajak, Hotel 26 B6
Saka Dindu, Hotel 57 B4
Sakala, Restaurant 33 K2
Sakanaya Fish Market 19 L7
Sakova, Hotel 25 M5
Sakti, Hotel 26 D6
Sakuntala Massage 53 H3
Sakura 21 J3
Sakura, Restaurant 17 M2
Sam Gee Tang, Restaurant 23 K8
Sam Sally, Hotel 46 F7
Sama Cottages 46 D3
Sama Sama, Hotel 91 H5
Sama Sama, Restaurant (Nusa Dua) ... 38 C1
Sama Sama, Restaurant (Sanur) .. 17 K4
Sama Sama, Shopping 46 B2
Sama Suka, Restaurant 31 M2
Samabe Bali Resort & Villas 45 J5
Samaya Courtyard, The, Hotel .. 19 H6
Samaya Ubud, Hotel 48 B5
Samaya, The, Hotel 19 G6
Samdadad Village 48 F3
Samhita, Hotel 46 D3
Sami Sami, Restaurant 35 L1
Samitha Bali 19 M5
Sampurna, Hotel 92 A5
Samsara, Hotel (Jalan Legian) .. 14 E6
Samsara, Hotel (Lasmana Oberoy) .. 19 G6
Samsat 22 C3
Samudera, Restaurant 14 C4
Samudra Beach Cottages 52 B2
Sanathana FM 20 E8
Sanctuario Luxury Hotel & Spa .. 31 H5
Sanctus, The, Hotel 40 D7
Sanda Butik Villas 84 D6
Sanda Day Spa 39 H4
Sandat Mas, Cottage 40 D2
Sandat, Hotel 14 E7
Sandhya, Hotel 25 G7
Sandi Phala, The, Hotel 10 C4
Sandipani 30 C5
Sang Spa (Jembawan) 47 G5
Sang Spa (Wenara Wana) 46 E6
Sanga, Hotel 25 H5
Sanggar Surya Art 32 E3
Sanggingan, Hotel 48 E3
Sangkar, Restaurant 41 J8
Sanglah Bird Market 21 L4
Sanglah Market 21 L4
Sanglah Public Hospital 21 K4
Sanglah, Hotel 21 L3
Sania's House, Hotel (Denpasar) .. 28 F4
Sania's House, Hotel (Ubud) 46 F4
Sania's, Hotel 46 E4
Sanidata, Hotel 19 G3
Sanjiwani Hospital 50 B4
Sanjiwani, Hotel 47 H5
Sankara 39 L3
Sankara, Hotel 25 J8
Sansil, Hotel 24 D5
Santai Canggu, Hotel 18 E2
Santai Segar, Restaurant 69 H5
Santai, Hotel (Amed) 91 J6
Santai, Hotel (Bumbak) 26 C6
Santai, Hotel (Jalan Danau Tamblingan) . 17 L2
Santi Sari, Hotel 93 L3
Santi Silver 46 E2
Santi, Hotel 46 E2
Santi, Restaurant 32 B4
Santika Beach, Hotel 10 E3
Santika Siligita, Hotel 39 H6
Santika Wijaya 16 A6
Santika, Hotel 14 F7
Santo Paulus Catholic Church .. 26 C2
Santo Yoseph School 21 L3
Santosa 21 J3
Santra Putra, Hotel 48 D4
Sanur Agung, Hotel 23 K3
Sanur Art Market 23 K7
Sanur Ayu, Hotel 23 K7
Sanur Beach Market (Jl. Pantai Sindhu) .. 23 L6
Sanur Beach Market (Jl. Hang Tuah) .. 23 L4
Sanur Beach Villa 17 L3
Sanur Beach, Restaurant 23 L6
Sanur Billiards 23 K5
Sanur Hobby Center 23 J5
Sanur Indah, Hotel 23 J5
Sanur Karaoke 17 K4
Sanur Paradise Plaza Suites, Hotel .. 17 L2
Sanur Paradise Plaza, Hotel 23 L4
Sanur Pharmacy 23 J6
Sanyas Suites, Hotel 19 L4

Sanyas, The, Hotel 19 H4
Sapphire Duty Free 23 K7
Saputra Bungalows 52 A5
Sara Residence, Hotel 14 E3
Saraswati, Hotel 53 J3
Saren GH 26 E5
Saren Indra, Hotel 46 D8
Sari Agung, Hotel 25 K7
Sari Agung, Restaurant 33 L8
Sari Amerta Batik 30 F1
Sari Beach Inn, Hotel 14 B4
Sari Beach, Hotel 19 G7
Sari Bundo, Restaurant (Jl. Danau Poso) .. 17 K4
Sari Bundo, Restaurant
    (Jl. Ki Hajar Dewantara) 22 E2
Sari Bundo, Restaurant (Raya Uluwatu) 32 D3
Sari Bunga, Hotel 14 B2
Sari Cafe 57 E3
Sari Dharma Hospital 21 L3
Sari Jaya, Hotel 52 D8
Sari Kembar, Restaurant 20 B4
Sari Organic, Restaurant 48 F3
Sari Rasa, Restaurant 57 D4
Sari Ratu, Restaurant 31 L2
Sari Sanur, Hotel 23 L7
Sari Segara Resort, Hotel 32 C3
Sari Textile 20 B3
Sari Tour 23 J6
Sari Utama Cottage 19 J8
Sari Wangi, Hotel 48 F2
Sari Warta Boga, Restaurant 15 H1
Sari Yasa Samudra, Hotel 14 C7
Sari, Hotel 49 G7
Sari, Restaurant (Tabanan) 71 K5
Sari, Restaurant (Tanjung Benoa) 33 K6
Sari, Villa 36 B7
Sarinande Beach Inn, Hotel 19 J8
Sarita Tour 30 D2
Sarong, Restaurant 19 H5
Sartya, Hotel 53 J2
Sasana Budaya Art Center 54 E2
Sasec 29 H2
Sasec Laundry 32 E5
Sasrabahu, Hotel 53 H7
Sate Bali 19 G6
Sate House, Restaurant 21 H6
Sate Penyu 14 E5
Satelindo 27 L2
Sativa, Hotel 17 L4
Satria Art Market 28 F6
Satria Mahottama Statue 54 D4
Satria, Restaurant 30 D3
Satrya Ayu, Hotel 27 L3
Satya, Hotel 53 K3
Savvoya, Hotel 19 L6
Sawah Alam Lodge, Hotel 49 G7
Sawangan, The, Hotel 45 H5
Saya, Hotel 90 E2
Sayan Ayu 48 D3
Sayan Dewata, Hotel 48 C4
Sayan Terrace, Hotel 48 C3
Sayang Lansia Clinic 31 H5
Sayang Maha Mertha, Hotel 14 D5
Sayang Sanur, Hotel 23 L8
SC, Restaurant 14 E7
Scala Bed & Beyond, Hotel 26 D4
School of Tourism (Udayana University) ... 36 F5
Scruffy Murphy's, Hotel 36 D7
Scuba Seraya Resort 90 D3
SD Negeri 1 Ubud 46 E4
SD Negeri 3 Pejeng Kawan 47 M4
SD Saraswati 5 .... 30 C4
SDN 1 (Semarapura) 51 D6
SDN 1 Benoa 39 G3
SDN 1 Kerobokan Kaja 26 F1
SDN 1 Pedungan 21 G8
SDN 1 Prerenan 25 H3
SDN 1 Sesetan 21 L6
SDN 1 Tanjung Benoa 13 G8
SDN 1 Tibubeneng 26 D1
SDN 1 Tonja 29 K2
SDN 1 Ungasan 43 J3
SDN 11 (Legian) 14 D4
SDN 11 Denpasar 22 F4
SDN 11 Pedungan 15 K6
SDN 11 Pemecutan 28 D8
SDN 11 Sesetan 16 A3
SDN 12 Sanur 23 K4
SDN 13 Pamecutan 15 G2
SDN 13 Sesetan 16 D5
SDN 14 Kesiman 30 B4
SDN 14 Pedungan 21 G7
SDN 16 Dauh Puri 20 F7
SDN 17 Kesiman 31 H5
SDN 17 Pemecutan 28 D8
SDN 18 Padang Sambian 20 C4
SDN 18 Sesetan 16 B2
SDN 19-20 Pemecutan 20 F1
SDN 2 Batu Bulan 31 G1
SDN 2 Canggu 25 J6
SDN 2 Kedewatan 48 E1
SDN 2 Kutuh 44 B3
SDN 2 Pecatu 34 D8
SDN 2 Pedungan 21 J7
SDN 2 Pemecutan 20 F6
SDN 2 Prerenan 25 J1
SDN 2 Sanur 23 J4
SDN 2 Ungasan 43 J4
SDN 2,5,8 Sesetan 16 B4
SDN 21 Dauh Puri Kauh 21 J3

SDN 26 Pemecutan 28 B8
SDN 27, 28, 31 Pemecutan 20 F2
SDN 28 Dangin Puri 29 J6
SDN 29 & 30 Dangin Puri 22 B2
SDN 3 Ketewel 31 M4
SDN 3,4,7 Kampung Baru 57 F2
SDN 32 Pemecutan 20 F1
SDN 4 Dauh Puri 28 F4
SDN 4 Panjer 22 C7
SDN 4 Pecatu 41 L5
SDN 4 Pemecutan 28 D6
SDN 4 Sesetan 16 E3
SDN 4 Sumerta 29 L7
SDN 4,9,13 Sanur 17 K2
SDN 5 Kesiman 30 C5
SDN 5 Panjer 16 E1
SDN 5 Pedungan 16 B6
SDN 6 Kesiman 29 M4
SDN 6 Kutuh 44 A3
SDN 6 Sanur 23 J4
SDN 6 Tanjung Benoa 33 K7
SDN 6 Tuban 11 H5
SDN 7 Sesetan 21 M8
SDN 9 Jimbaran 38 A1
SDN 9 Sesetan 16 F4
SE Supermarket (Jalan Malboro) 20 F6
SE Supermarket (Jalan Pulau Bungin) 21 H8
SE Supermarket (Raya Tohpati) 30 E3
Sea Breeze Cabins, Hotel 52 E3
Sea Safari Cruises, Hotel 12 E5
Sea Side, Restaurant 32 B2
Sea View, Restaurant 32 B2
Seaside Cottages 53 G8
Seaview Villa Sanur 30 F8
Secret Point Huts, Hotel 108 B3
Sedana Merta Market 26 D2
Sedana Yogya, Hotel 57 E4
Sedasa Lodge, Hotel 25 M7
Sederhana, Hotel 51 D3
Sederhana, Restaurant (Denpasar) 21 J3
Sederhana, Restaurant (Kuta) 14 F8
Segar, Restaurant (Singaraja) 57 D2
Segar, Rumah Makan (Amlapura) 55 E5
Segara Agung, Hotel 17 M4
Segara Bayu, Hotel 25 M5
Segara Beach, Hotel 10 F1
Segara Beach, Restaurant 14 C8
Segara Biru, Restaurant 14 F8
Segara Cafe Bali, Restaurant 23 L3
Segara Clinic 23 L6
Segara Condhotel, The 33 K1
Segara II, Restaurant 57 D3
Segara Mandala, Hotel 56 F5
Segara Village, Hotel 23 L6
Segara Wangi Homestay, Hotel 53 G7
Seiryu, Hotel 19 J8
Sejuk, Hotel 19 G3
Sekar Ayu Inn, Hotel 46 C2
Sekar Nusa, Hotel 45 K1
Sekar Orchid, Hotel 53 M7
Sekar Sari, Hotel 10 F4
Sekar Sejagat, Spa 38 A1
Sekar Taman II, Hotel 19 H8
Sekar Tanjung Antiques 23 K4
Sekolah Tinggi Ilmu Komputer Indonesia .. 22 B8
Sekolah Tinggi Pariwisata Bali 38 A8
Sekuta Condo Suite, Hotel 23 J8
Selang Resort 91 L7
Selera Kuring, Restaurant 14 E3
Selera Nusantara, Restaurant 39 G4
Semana Resort 48 B7
Semar 11 J2
Semara Husada Hospital 51 D6
Semara Luxury Villa 42 E8
Semara Ratih 47 H2
Semara Resort 19 G5
Semarajaya Museum 51 D6
Semarapura, Hotel 24 A3
Semat, Hotel 25 L6
Sembahan Treatment 48 F3
Semen Gresik 27 K4
Semen Tonasa 27 J2
Seminyak Market 19 H7
Seminyak Square 19 H6
Seminyak Suite, The, Hotel 14 C2
Seminyak Village Resort 19 J6
Seminyak, The, Hotel 19 G7
Sena, Hotel 57 E6
Senang, Hotel 25 H5
Seng Hong Bio Temple 57 L1
Seniman, Restaurant 46 F3
Seniwati 46 F3
Senja, Hotel 26 B8
Sense, Hotel 19 G6
Sentral, Hotel 19 G6
Sequislife (Gatot Subroto Bypass Timur) .. 30 C2
Sequislife (Jl. Raya Puputan) 22 F4
Serai, Hotel 19 J2
Serangan Inn II 67 L4
Seraphim Art 46 D6
Serela, Hotel 14 F5
Serena Villas Bali 19 K7
Serenity Eco GH 25 J8
Serenity, Hotel 25 J8
Serenity, Restaurant 23 K7
Seri Suites, The, Hotel 19 H2
Seri Villas, The 19 G5
Seriska 2, Hotel 17 J4
Seroni, Hotel 46 F4
Seruni, Hotel 27 H2

Seseh Beach, Hotel 24 C4
Seseh Serasi, Hotel 24 C4
Setia Tour 17 J4
Setra Gede Bualan Kampial 38 E5
Seven Angels Villa 38 C1
Seven Garden, Hotel 19 J7
Seyu, Restaurant 52 E2
Shaga 14 E2
Shakuntala, Restaurant 46 F4
Shaliman Boutique 46 F7
Shalimar, Hotel 24 E5
Shamira, Hotel 25 J6
Shana, Hotel 46 F4
Shanti Graha 21 M4
Shanti Private, Hotel 26 C6
Shanti Residence, The, Hotel 45 H5
Shanti, Hotel 25 M7
Shanti, Villa 23 M8
Sheppy's, Restaurant 14 D5
Sheraton Bali Kuta, Hotel 14 C7
Shinta Bali Hotel & Spa, Hotel 32 D8
Shinta Chrisna 30 C3
Shinta Dewata 30 E2
Shita Bali Hotel & Spa 37 G2
Shiva House, Hotel 46 F5
Shopping Center 51 E7
Shore Inn, Hotel 24 D4
Shorea Beach Resort, Hotel 92 F2
Shunda, Hotel 28 F2
Si Doi, Hotel 14 D6
Siadja, Gallery 65 H3
Siddharthas, Hotel 46 A2
Sidharta Badminton 19 M4
Sienna Villas 14 C2
Sika 48 E3
Silco Cargo 14 F5
Silk Road 46 F6
Silk Weaving 65 L3
Siloam Hospital 15 G6
Silq Private Residences, Hotel 19 J4
Simona Oasis & Spa, Hotel 25 J4
Simpang Ampek, Restaurant 21 G6
Simpang Inn, Hotel 14 D6
Sin Sin, Hotel 19 J1
Sinar 11 J4
Sinar Abadi 20 D8
Sinar Alami 30 D7
Sinar Bali, Hotel 14 C3
Sinar Bank (Jl. Debes, Tabanan) 51 E3
Sinar Bintang 23 H7
Sinar Dunia 27 J2
Sinar Indah Bungalows 14 D3
Sinar Mas (Gatot Subroto) 29 H2
Sinar Mas (Letda Tantular) 22 C3
Sinar Nusantara Indah 30 F5
Sindhu Beach Market 23 M7
Sindhu Bhrata Inn, Hotel 53 K7
Sindhu Mertha Suite, Hotel 17 J4
Sing Ken Ken, Hotel 14 B2
Sing Sing Waterfall 98 C2
Singa Ambararaja Statue 57 E7
Singa Pizza 52 D3
Singambara 47 G5
Singaraja Hospital 57 D6
Singosari, Hotel 97 J3
Sinteg Bungalow 46 A6
Siputih Gallery 22 E1
Sirocco, Hotel 18 E3
Sitara Padi, Hotel 26 A8
Siti, Hotel 49 G7
Siwa Plaza 28 D6
Siwa Ratih Dance Stage 47 H4
Six Point, Restaurant 23 K6
Sky Garden Lounge, Restaurant 14 E7
Slashrock Office & Store 19 L6
SLB 32 F8
SMA Dwijendra 29 J7
SMA Nasional 22 B5
SMA PGRI 51 B7
SMA PGRI 6 .... 22 E2
SMAN 1 (Denpasar) 29 J6
SMAN 1 Kuta Selatan 43 M3
SMAN 1 Negara 56 F5
SMAN 1 Semarapura 51 B8
SMAN 1 Singaraja 57 D4
SMAN 1 Ubud 49 G3
SMAN 2 Denpasar 21 M4
SMAN 2 Kuta 32 E4
SMAN 2 Singaraja 57 C8
SMAN 3 (Denpasar) 29 K5
SMAN 3 Singaraja 57 F1
SMAN 4 Denpasar 21 G1
SMAN 5 (Sesetan) 16 D4
SMAN 6 Denpasar 23 H5
SMAN 7 (Denpasar) 29 J6
SMAN PGRI 1 Denpasar 21 M4
SMAN PGRI 2 Denpasar 21 G1
Smart Comfort Batu Jimbar, Hotel 17 L2
Smile Shop 46 F2
SMK Prashanti Nilayam 11 H2
SMK Saraswati 30 D5
SMK Tenas 22 B4
SMK TI Bali Global Denpasar 22 D6
SMKN 1 (Denpasar) 28 E2
SMKN 1 Kuta 38 C3
SMKN 1 Kuta Selatan 38 C2
SMKN 2 (Sesetan) 16 D4
SMKN 3 (Sanur) 17 J3
SMKN 3 Singaraja 57 F4
SMKN 4 (Denpasar) 29 L7

SMP Ganesa Denpasar 16 A3
SMP Muhammadiyah 1 .... 20 F7
SMP Muhammadiyah 3 .... 20 F1
SMP Pancasila 26 B3
SMP Pertiwi 29 H6
SMP PGRI 1 .... 21 G2
SMP PGRI 2 .... 29 L4
SMP PGRI 4 Denpasar 16 A5
SMP SMA Dharma Wiweka Denpasar 15 M2
SMP Wisata 23 K6
SMPN 1 (Denpasar) 29 G7
SMPN 1 Kuta 10 F4
SMPN 1 Semarapura 51 D7
SMPN 1 Singaraja 57 D3
SMPN 1 Tabanan 51 E2
SMPN 10 (Denpasar) 28 F3
SMPN 11 Denpasar 16 E8
SMPN 2 Kuta Selatan 43 J4
SMPN 3 (Denpasar) 29 J6
SMPN 3 Kuta Selatan 33 K3
SMPN 4 (Denpasar) 28 C6
SMPN 6 Denpasar 16 B3
SMPN 7 Denpasar 21 G2
SMPN 8 (Denpasar) 29 L4
SMPN 9 Denpasar 17 L1
SMSR Art High School 46 A1
Sobat, Restaurant 20 D7
Sobek Bina Utama 17 K4
Sobek Rafting 48 D2
Soejach, PT 20 B1
Sofitel Bali Nusa Dua Beach Resort, Hotel . 39 K3
Sofitel, Hotel 25 H6
Sogo 39 K5
Soho, Restaurant 19 J6
Soka Indah, Restaurant 62 B2
Soka Tours 22 F3
Sokasati, Hotel 29 M5
Sol Paradise, Hotel 10 F1
Solaluna Beach, Hotel 91 H5
Soldier Statue 23 G4
Somer Hill, Hotel 40 C2
Sonni Puteri, Hotel 38 C1
Sony Shop 47 H3
Sopa, Restaurant 46 F5
Soraya Villa 29 K8
Sorga Beach, Hotel 14 C5
Sorga Nusa Dua, Hotel 33 K2
Sosro 15 G5
Soto Ayam Surabaya (Ngurah Rai Bypass) . 16 B6
Soto Ayam Suroboyo (Veteran) 29 G6
Sound of the Sea, Hotel 24 E5
Source Bali, The, Hotel 26 C3
Soverdi International School 11 G5
Spa at The Bale, The 39 H8
Spa at the Legian, The 19 G6
Spa Hati 47 J3
Spa on The Rocks 35 J1
Spa, The 41 K8
Space at Bali, Hotel 19 J7
Spaghetti Jazz Club 14 D2
Spanish Consulate 39 L4
Spartacvs, Hotel 19 G5
Spasion 38 D2
Spazzio, Hotel 14 E5
Spice Beach Water Sport 52 E3
Spice Dive 52 D3
Spice, Restaurant 33 L7
Spies House 46 B2
Spirit Art 19 M4
SPN Police School 57 A4
Sport Center 55 D4
Sports Station 46 E5
Spring Villa 25 H5
Spunky's, Restaurant 53 J3
SR 29 K2
Sraya Bali Style 23 J2
Sri Artha Homestay, Hotel 52 F7
Sri Devi Villas 14 F4
Sri Hamerta Boga, Restaurant 56 F4
Sri Homestay, Hotel 53 M2
Sri Kusuma, Hotel 14 D7
Sri Partha (Denpasar) 29 K5
Sri Partha Bank (Amlapura) 55 B6
Sri Partha Bank (Bangli) 54 C7
Sri Partha Bank (Negara) 56 D5
Sri Partha Bank (Singaraja) 57 D5
Sri Partha Bank (Tabanan) 51 F3
Sri Phala, Hotel 23 K4
Sri Ratih Cottages 46 B3
Sri Ratu, Hotel 14 D4
Srikandi 39 H5
Srikerthi Market 20 C5
Sriwijaya Air PK-CKM B733 .... 32 E4
Sriyana Homestay, Hotel 40 C1
St Mikael's 14 B1
St. Regis, Resort Residences 39 J7
Stadium Cafe 14 D8
Stadium Cafe & Flapjaks 17 L5
Stalls 17 M2
Star Furniture 19 M5
Star, Restaurant (Jl. Danau Tamblingan) ... 17 M2
Star, Restaurant (Setiabudi) 14 F7
Starbucks (Jl. Danau Tamblingan) 23 L8
Starbucks (Raya Ubud) 46 E3
Starbucks (Teuku Umar) 21 J5
Stargate, Restaurant 46 E2
Starlight, Hotel 53 H2
Starry House, Restaurant 23 L8
State Prison of Kerobokan 19 L4
State Temple 50 C4

Building Index

Steak Cok, Restaurant........................21 G5
STIE Triatma Mulya..........................27 H1
Stiff Chilli, Restaurant.......................17 M4
STIKES Bali (Tukad Balian)...................22 F8
STIKES Bali (Tukad Pakerisan).............22 B8
Stiki Indonesia................................16 D1
STIKOM..21 G5
STIKOM BALI...................................22 B4
STIMI Handayani..............................21 L5
STMIK Primakara..............................22 E8
STMIK STIKOM Bali.............................20 F6
Stone Gate....................................36 F7
Stones, The, Hotel............................14 C5
Street Cafe, Restaurant......................23 L7
Street Life, Hotel.............................19 J6
Street Theatre................................36 F7
STSI...16 B3
Studi Tas.....................................39 L4
Studlo 13.....................................49 H3
Studio Perak..................................46 F4
Suar Tur......................................30 D4
Suara Ombak, Hotel...........................34 D6
Suargan Temple...............................48 D2
Suarmas, Hotel................................28 C2
Suarti..46 E4
Subak Sari Boutique, Hotel...................18 E2
Subak Tabalo..................................66 F1
Subaliku, Hotel...............................19 J5
Suci Homestay, Hotel..........................53 L3
Suci Sari Jaya................................28 F8
Sudamala, Hotel...............................17 K4
Sudana, Hotel.................................46 F4
Sudirman Agung Mall..........................21 M4
Sudirman Mosque..............................21 M2
Sugars Villa..................................49 G2
Sukawati Art Market...........................65 H6
Sukma Sari....................................27 H3
Suku, Restaurant..............................33 L7
Sukun, Hotel..................................17 L4
Sulawesi Art Shop.............................19 M5
Sulendra.....................................47 G6
Suli, Hotel...................................29 H5
Suluban Surfing...............................40 B1
Suly Resort & Spa.............................49 H7
Suma, Gallery.................................49 G7
Suma, Hotel...................................53 J3
Suman Tour....................................23 L7
Sumatra Kayu, Hotel..........................25 M1
Sumatra, Hotel................................18 F3
Sumatra, Restaurant..........................20 B4
Sumbar Rasa, Restaurant......................55 E4
Sumber Hidup, Restaurant.....................47 G4
Sumber Rasa, Restaurant......................51 E6
Sun Boutique, Hotel...........................15 G4
Sun Island, Hotel (Dewi Sartika)..............10 F2
Sun Island, Hotel (Goa Gong)..................37 J7
Sun Royal, Hotel..............................14 F4
Sun Villa.....................................46 F1
Sunari Villas & Spa Resort....................53 H3
Sunari, Gallery................................48 E2
Sunarta, Gallery...............................48 E1
Sunarta, Hotel................................46 F2
Sunda Kelapa, Restaurant.....................21 H5
Sundara Bali..................................32 A8
Sundaram's, Hotel.............................34 D6
Sungai Seafood, Restaurant...................11 H4
Sungai Tinggi, Hotel..........................24 E6
Sungu Resort & Spa, The.......................46 B3
Sunia Loka, Hotel.............................94 C2
Sunia, Hotel..................................25 L6
Sunny Blow, Hotel.............................48 E2
Sunrise Dive Center...........................52 D2
Sunrise Dive Ctr..............................52 E3
Sunrise, Restaurant...........................23 L4
Sunset Ayu Bungalow...........................53 J3
Sunset Ayu, Restaurant........................53 H3
Sunset Condotel, Hotel........................14 E5
Sunset Hill Villa..............................48 F2
Sunset Indah..................................15 G5
Sunset Mansion Bali, Hotel....................19 L6
Sunset Point..................................19 K6
Sunset Residense, Hotel.......................14 E2
Sunset Villa..................................36 C8
Sunset, The, Hotel............................14 F5
Sunshine Bungalows...........................91 J6
Sunti, The, Hotel.............................48 F7
Super Walet...................................11 H4
Super Yess....................................20 B5
Superman, Restaurant.........................52 E3
Suputra Pondok Wisata, Hotel................52 F7
Sura, The, Hotel..............................19 H6
Sura's, Restaurant............................46 F2
Surabaya, Restaurant.........................63 L4
Suranadhi, Hotel..............................29 K7
Surati, Hotel.................................14 C2
Surawadhi II, Hotel...........................28 F7
Surf Camp, Hotel (Munduk Catu)..............25 H7
Surf Camp, Hotel (Raya Pantai Pererenan) 24 F5
Surf Shop.....................................14 E6
Surfer Girl...................................39 L3
Surfers Paradise..............................32 E2
Suriwathi, Hotel..............................14 D4
Surya Abadi, Hotel............................26 B3
Surya Asri, Hotel.............................56 C5
Surya Baru Motor..............................30 B2
Surya Damai, Hotel............................18 F2
Surya Dive Center.............................17 L4
Surya Husada, Hospital (Denpasar)...........21 K5
Surya Husada, Hospital (Nusa Dua)..........39 G5
Surya Indah Motor............................30 C2

Surya Jaya Offset.............................22 D1
Surya Jaya Sakti..............................19 M4
Surya Villa...................................36 B8
Surya, Hotel (Negara).........................56 E5
Surya, Hotel (Gilimanuk).....................92 A5
Sushi Hana, Restaurant........................14 F3
Sushi Q, Restaurant...........................21 G6
Sushi Tei, Restaurant (Dewi Sri)..............14 E3
Sushi Tei, Restaurant (Sunset Road)..........15 G5
Swan Inn, Hotel...............................46 E3
Swara Mandera, Hotel.........................49 H2
Swasti Eco Cottages...........................48 F7
Swasti Homestay, Hotel........................48 E7
Swasti, Restaurant............................46 D8
Swastika 1, Bungalows.........................23 L7
Swastika I, Restaurant........................23 L7
Swastika, Hotel...............................17 L2
Swastika, Restaurant..........................23 L8
Swedish & Finnish Consulates.................23 L6
Sweet Corner.................................19 K6
Swell, Restaurant.............................40 B1
Swimming Pool "Taman Segara Madu"...........25 L3
Swiss Belhotel Bay View, Hotel...............38 E3
Swiss Belhotel, Hotel.........................19 J4
Swiss-Belhotel Rainforest, Hotel.............15 G5
Swiss-Belinn..................................19 L7
Swiss-Belresort Watu Jimbar, Hotel..........23 K8
Symon Studio.................................46 B1

T

Ta Chi Cottages, Hotel.......................108 B1
Tabanan Hospital..............................51 E2
Tabanan Market................................51 D3
Tabanan Prison................................51 D2
Tabanan, Hotel................................51 E3
Tabungan Negara Bank.........................21 L3
Taco Casa & Grill.............................46 E8
Taco Casa, Restaurant........................19 J3
Taipan Village................................19 H7
Takapit Car Service...........................15 H1
Taksu, Hotel..................................17 K4
Talaga Spa...................................14 E3
Talenta.......................................19 K7
Talisa, Hotel.................................19 J4
Talisman, Restaurant..........................49 J7
Taliwang (Batu Riti), Restaurant.............99 M8
Taliwang Baru, Restaurant....................21 K3
Taliwang Bersaudara, Restaurant.............14 F6
Taliwang, Restaurant..........................51 E3
Tam's..32 C7
Tama...48 E3
Taman Agung, Hotel...........................17 L2
Taman Ahimsa, Hotel..........................24 B4
Taman Arum, Hotel............................65 H3
Taman Bali Raja...............................73 M7
Taman Bali, Hotel (Lovina Beach)............53 H2
Taman Bali, Hotel (Seminyak)................19 K7
Taman Bebek, Hotel...........................48 C3
Taman Bhagawan, Hotel.......................33 K6
Taman Ciung Wanara..........................50 B7
Taman Dewi Sri, Hotel........................94 C2
Taman Gilimanuk, Restaurant................92 A6
Taman Indrakila, Hotel.......................48 E3
Taman Lily's, Hotel...........................52 F3
Taman Mutiara Apartment.....................15 G3
Taman Nusa, Hotel.............................66 A4
Taman Rahasia, Hotel.........................48 D4
Taman Rosani, Hotel..........................19 H4
Taman Sakti, Hotel............................49 G3
Taman Sari Marine Sport......................33 K1
Taman Sari Market (Jalan Pulau Bungin)....21 H7
Taman Sari Market (Raya Kerobokan).........19 K3
Taman Sari Royal Heritage Spa,.............38 D3
Taman Sari Villa & Spa, Hotel...............32 C6
Taman Sari, Hotel.............................94 C2
Taman Sari, Hotel (Negara)...................56 D4
Taman Sari, Hotel (Sanur)....................23 J6
Taman Sari, Restaurant (Negara)............56 D4
Taman Sari, Spa (Tanjung Benoa)............33 K7
Taman Selini, Hotel...........................94 C2
Taman Semadi Para Atma Temple
  (Pura Dalem)................................52 F6
Taman Suci, Hotel............................21 J1
Taman Wana Villas & Spa......................79 H2
Taman Wana, Hotel............................18 F3
Taman Wisata, Hotel..........................29 H2
Tamba Market.................................29 M2
Tambo..19 K4
Tambora, Hotel................................28 E8
Tamu Seseh, Restaurant.......................24 D4
Tamukami, Hotel..............................23 L7
Tanadewa Luxury Villas & Spa, Hotel.........38 B1
Tanah Bali, Villa..............................36 C7
Tanah Gajah, Restaurant......................49 J7
Tanah Merah Resort & Gallery...............49 J1
Tanaya's, Restaurant..........................14 E6
Tandeg, Hotel.................................26 B4
Tandjung Sari, Hotel..........................17 M1
Tangga, Hotel................................24 F6
Tangkas......................................47 G4
Tangku, Hotel................................47 H5
Tanju Bali, Hotel.............................24 A3
Tanjung Alam, Hotel..........................52 C2
Tanjung Benoa Watersport....................32 F8
Tanjung Bungkak..............................22 F2
Tanjung Lima, Hotel..........................14 E3
Tanjung Mekar, Hotel.........................33 K2
Tanjung Pinang...............................11 H3
Tanjung Sari, Hotel...........................23 M7
Tankis, Hotel.................................48 E3

Tantra & Raka, Gallery........................65 G3
Tao Li, Restaurant............................45 K3
Tao, Restaurant...............................33 K2
Tapis...32 B5
Tara Cottages................................102 E3
Tarita (Ngurah Rai Bypass)....................15 G7
Tarita (Raya Padang Luwih)...................27 H2
Taruna Jaya, Hotel............................51 E3
Taruna, Homestay.............................94 D2
Taspen..22 B3
Tati Photo....................................29 G6
Tawakal.......................................22 A4
Taxa, Hotel...................................14 F5
Taxi Service..................................46 B2
Tea Tree Spa..................................10 E4
Teba House, Hotel.............................46 F6
Tebeska......................................47 G7
Technical Faculty (Udayana University).......37 H4
Teduh, Hotel..................................26 E8
Tegal Bemo Terminal..........................28 E8
Tegal Cupek Residence, Hotel................26 D6
Tegal Harum Market...........................21 G2
Tegal Sari, Hotel.............................46 E8
Tegeh Sari Temple.............................32 A8
Teges Temple..................................27 J8
Tegun Folk Art Gallery........................46 F5
Tegun Ngurah Rai Bypass......................22 E4
Teko, Restaurant..............................22 E4
Telaga Naga, Restaurant......................17 L3
Telaga Restaurant & Bar......................25 K8
Telaga Wangi Villas...........................25 L8
Telaga, Restaurant (Nusa Dua)...............33 K5
Telkom.......................................22 C3
Telkom (Jl. Gajah Mada, Singaraja)...........57 D3
Telkom (Jl. Raya Puputan, Denpasar).........22 B3
Telkom (Jl. Teuku Umar, Denpasar)...........21 L3
Telkom (Lovina Beach).........................53 G3
Telkom (Raya Uluwatu)........................32 D4
Telkom Unit Pengelolaan Network............43 K3
Telkomsel....................................22 E2
Telkomsel (Jl. Diponegoro, Dauh Puri).......21 L2
Temples, Durga Statue........................65 J2
Ten Pin Bowling...............................23 L5
Tenang, Hotel.................................18 F4
Tenun Ikat Balinusa...........................30 C4
Tepe Villa Lux.................................52 F3
Tepi Kali, Hotel...............................25 H5
Tepi Laut, Restaurant.........................39 M4
Tepi Laut, Hotel...............................24 D5
Tepi Sawah, Hotel.............................49 G7
Terang Bulan Cottages.........................47 J8
Terazo, Restaurant............................46 E3
Terazza Martini, Restaurant..................17 K5
Teresa, Hotel.................................25 J8
Terminix.....................................11 J5
Terrace, Hotel.................................52 E8
Terrace, Restaurant...........................39 G7
Terracotta, Restaurant........................23 L8
Tete Homestay, Hotel..........................40 C2
Thai Express..................................10 F3
Thailand Embassy.............................22 F4
Thalassa, Hotel...............................25 J4
Thalassa, Spa.................................33 K4
The Duck Nutz, Restaurant....................23 L7
The Glass House, Restaurant..................23 L7
The Heart of Bali, Restaurant................33 K7
The Tree, Restaurant..........................33 K5
Think Pink Nails..............................19 H4
Thomas Homestay, Hotel......................40 D1
Three Brothers Amed, Restaurant............91 H5
Three Mogkeys Villas..........................40 C2
Three Monkeys, Restaurant...................17 L1
Tia, Restaurant................................17 K4
Tiara (Gatot Subroto Barat Bypass)..........27 H2
Tiara (Raya Kuta).............................14 F6
Tiara Dewata Shopping Center...............29 G8
Tiara Grosir Shopping.........................28 E4
Tiara Husada..................................11 H5
Tiara Soputan.................................20 D7
Tiaranusa, Villa..............................37 J6
Tibu Indah, Hotel.............................26 D2
Ticket Office.................................50 B3
Tiga Samudra, Hotel..........................26 C6
Tigadis Villa..................................36 E7
Tiing Gading Bungalows.......................47 G6
Tiing Gading Sanjiwani, Hotel...............47 G6
Tika...30 D5
Timbis Paragliding............................44 D7
Timboel......................................49 H2
Timur Jaya....................................20 B5
Tinjaya, Hotel (Medewi, Pekutatan)..........68 A2
Tinjaya, Hotel (Tabanan).....................51 A3
Tino 2.......................................46 D2
Tino MM......................................46 E3
Tirarella Beach, Hotel........................53 M7
Tirta Ayu Swimming Pool......................31 G7
Tirta Bali, Hotel..............................40 F7
Tirta Buana Swimming Pool...................54 B4
Tirta Empul...................................73 K2
Tirta Ening Agung, Hotel......................17 K3
Tirta Lestari, Hotel...........................29 G4
Tirta Mas.....................................32 C3
Tirta Naga, Hotel.............................19 H7
Tirta Sari Dance Stage........................47 J5
Tirta Sari, Hotel..............................94 D2
Tirta Suni Cave...............................94 E2
Tirtarum Villas Bali...........................25 J7
Tirtha Gangga................................76 D2
Tirtha Luhur, Hotel...........................40 F7
Tirtha Uluwatu, Hotel.........................40 F7
Tis, Hotel....................................56 D5

Tisna..46 F5
Titi Batu Cafe................................30 D7
Titi Sedana, Restaurant......................91 J6
Titi Warung..................................48 D5
Titimas, Gallery..............................65 G3
Titin, Hotel..................................19 J2
TJ's, Restaurant..............................14 D7
Tjampuhan, Hotel.............................46 B2
Tjendana Villas, Hotel........................38 C2
TK Widya Kumara.............................26 F1
TK's, Restaurant..............................23 L6
TKP PPDS 1...................................21 K5
TNI-AD Hospitals.............................57 E4
TNT Courier..................................32 E1
Toga Mas.....................................21 L4
Togog..11 H2
Toke Cafe....................................52 F8
Toko Family..................................53 J7
Toko Gemino.................................53 J7
Tokoku.......................................27 K2
Tom Ton Garment Factory....................20 D8
Tom yum, Restaurant.........................14 D7
Tony Marindo Seasport.......................33 K2
Tony's Villas.................................19 G5
Top FM.......................................30 D6
Top Hill Court...............................37 H7
Top Hill Villas...............................41 J3
Topeng 1 & 2, Hotel..........................25 M6
Topeng Bar...................................52 F7
Topeng Dance................................73 H4
Topi Inn, Hotel...............................67 L4
Topi Kopi....................................14 C3
Tosa...28 B2
Toshiba Service Center.......................30 C4
Toto...48 E2
Touch Terminal, Hotel........................90 D2
Tour & Travel................................56 D5
Tourism College..............................48 D3
Town House, Hotel............................14 D7
Toya Villa....................................90 D1
Toya, Spa....................................38 F3
Toyota (Gatot Subroto Barat Bypass).........28 D3
Toyota (HOS Cokroaminoto)..................28 E3
Toyota (Imam Bonjol)........................15 G2
Toyota (Ngurah Rai Bypass)..................17 K2
Toyota (Sunset Road)........................14 E2
Toyota Rent-a-Car...........................32 E1
Tra, The, Hotel...............................25 K7
Tradisi Villas.................................91 H5
Traditional Balinese Healing Center..........47 G4
Traditional Market............................56 B6
Tragia (Nusa Dua)............................39 G4
Tragia (Semarapura)..........................51 D6
Trans Resort Bali, The........................19 K6
Tratoria da Marco, Restaurant...............17 L5
Trattoria, Restaurant.........................19 J6
Travel.......................................39 L3
Tresnajaya Bungalow.........................91 J6
Tresni, Restaurant............................22 D2
Trevelly.....................................108 B3
Trijata Hospital..............................29 H5
Trikaya......................................31 J4
Triniti, Restaurant............................21 J4
Trio Cafe.....................................49 H2
Trio, Hotel...................................22 F1
Trisna SS.....................................31 K4
Trisna, Hotel.................................100 F6
Trolley Market................................32 D4
Trophy, The, Hotel............................17 K5
Tropical Bale, Hotel..........................48 E2
Tropical Bale, Restaurant.....................48 E2
Tropical Bali, Hotel...........................30 E7
Tropical Pool & Spa...........................17 K3
Tropical, Restaurant
  (Bali Collection, Nusa Dua)................39 M3
Tropical, Restaurant
  (Jl. Pantai Mengiat, Nusa Dua)............39 J6
Tropical, Restaurant (Ubud).................46 E3
Tropicana Cottege, Hotel....................19 L8
Tropis Club..................................52 F3
Tropis Living.................................52 D3
Truth..46 F5
Truth Shop...................................46 F5
TS Suites, Hotel..............................14 D2
Tuban Plaza..................................11 J4
Tuban Seafood...............................11 H4
Tude's Home Stay, Hotel......................46 F6
Tude's, Restaurant...........................17 K5
Tugu, Hotel..................................25 H7
Tukad Alit, Hotel.............................26 E8
Tulamben Bali, Hotel.........................90 D2
Tulamben Wreck Divers Resort..............90 D2
Tulasi Dewi Spa..............................46 E7
Tulip, Restaurant.............................19 H3
Tunas Jaya...................................17 J4
Tune, Hotel (Jalan Arjuna)...................14 B2
Tune, Hotel (Jalan Pantai Kuta).............14 D8
Tunjung Mas Bungalows.....................46 F8
Tunjung Sari Spa.............................33 C7
Tunjung, Restaurant.........................48 C7
Turmak, Restaurant..........................46 E4
Turtle Center.................................16 F8
Turtle Park...................................33 H3
Turtle Water Park............................13 K1
Tusita, The, Hotel.............................10 F4
TVRI Denpasar................................22 E2
TVS...30 C2
Twilight Bungalows..........................108 B3
Twin Islands Condotel, Hotel................39 H7
Twin Spring, Hotel...........................25 K5

U

Ubud Art Market 46 E3
Ubud Bungalow 46 E6
Ubud Canti, Hotel 46 F6
Ubud Ceramics 46 F4
Ubud Cliff Villas 49 J7
Ubud Clinic 46 C2
Ubud Dedari Villas 49 K7
Ubud Explorer 46 F6
Ubud Garden Spa, Hotel 46 D3
Ubud Green Resort 49 G2
Ubud Hanging Garden, Hotel 72 F2
Ubud Inn, Hotel 46 E6
Ubud Kaos 47 G2
Ubud Palace 46 F3
Ubud Point 46 E5
Ubud Premium 14 E4
Ubud Property 47 J4
Ubud Sari Health Resort 46 E1
Ubud Terrace Bungalow 46 D6
Ubud Terrace, Gallery 46 D6
Ubud Valasindo 46 D2
Ubud Village 46 E5
Ubud Village Resort & Spa, The 48 F7
Ubud, Hotel 46 F2
Ubung Terminal 28 D2
UC Silver 30 F2
UD Agus 27 K5
Udary 31 J5
Udayana Resort 91 K6
Udayana University (Jimbaran Campus) .. 37 H4
Udayana University (Singaraja Campus) .. 57 D7
Udayana University (Sudirman Campus) .. 21 M3
Udayana University Hospital 37 H3
Udayana University Stadium 36 F4
Udiyana Painting 30 D2
Ufo Electronic 21 H5
Ugly Duckling, Hotel 23 L7
Ujung Water Palace (Taman Sukasada) .. 76 F5
Ujung, Villas 36 D4
Ulam Sari, Restaurant 22 E2
Ulam, Restaurant (Jl. Pratama) 39 J2
Ulam, Restaurant (Jl. Pantai Mengiat) .. 39 J6
Ulin Villa & Spa 19 J6
Ulina, Hotel 27 G1
Ultimo, Restaurant 19 J6
Ulun Ubud Resort Hotel 48 E2
Ulundanu, Restaurant 99 M8
Uluwatu (Bali Collection, Nusa Dua) 39 L3
Uluwatu (Jalan Danau Tamblingan) 17 L1
Uluwatu (Jalan Legian) 14 F7
Uluwatu (Jl. Danau Tamblingan, Sanur) .. 23 L8
Uluwatu Cottages 40 C1
Uluwatu Handmade 46 E5
Uluwatu Peak, Hotel 42 C6
Uluwatu Surf Villas 40 B2
Uma Dauh, The, Hotel 25 M1
Uma Girasole, Hotel 24 F5
Uma Kaya Market 22 E7
Uma Sari Cottage 46 D4
Uma Ubud, Hotel 48 E2
Uma, The, Hotel 26 C6
Umah Gran, Hotel 49 J7
Umah Pesisi, Hotel 24 D5
Umah Peter, Hotel 25 G5
Umah Putih, Hotel 26 C2
Umah Tunduh, Hotel 40 B3
Umala's Stable, Hotel 19 H2
Umalas Equestrian Resort 19 H2
Umalas Lestari, Hotel 19 J2
Umalas Residence, Hotel 19 H2
Umalas, Hotel 19 K2
Umasari, Restaurant 23 K3
Umaseni, Hotel 29 K1
Umasri Bali, Hotel 26 B8
Umbu Art 19 M4
Un's, Hotel 14 D6
Un's, Restaurant 14 E8
Undagi Handycraft 20 C4
Under the Volcano 1, Hotel 50 C2
Under the Volcano 2, Hotel 50 D2
Ungasan Bay Villas, Hotel 36 C7
Ungasan, Hotel 36 C6
Unik Cargo 17 J4
United Colors, Hotel 26 B2
Universitas Pendidikan Nasional
  (Sidakarya) 16 D2
Universitas Pendidikan Nasional (Panjer) .. 22 B5
University Hindu Indonesia 30 B1
Universo 19 K6
Uno, Restaurant 39 M3
Unud Lodge 37 H3
UOB Buana Bank (Gatot Subroto Bypass) .. 29 H2
UOB Buana Bank (Jl. Diponegoro) 21 L3
UOB Buana Bank
  (Jl. Wahidin Sudirohusodo) 28 E7
Upadi Wellness 46 F8
Uppala Hills (U/C), Hotel 38 C8
Uppala, Hotel 26 C6
UPT PSTKP Bali 11 L1
Urock 21 G5
US Embassy 23 G3
Utama, Bank 47 H6
Utama, Hotel 25 H3
Utami Collection 20 F6
Uyah Amed, Hotel 91 G5
Uyah Resto 14 E4

V

Valbury 21 J4
Valentino Aromatic 37 L2
Vamelo, Hotel 25 M5
Van Mandri GH 26 F5
Varennes I & II, Hotel 26 B8
Varon Village 20 D5
Vasanti, Hotel 19 G4
Vayatour 23 K7
Venna, Hotel 24 B3
Venna, Villa 24 B3
Venue, The 39 L3
Versus, Silver & Mahima 46 D4
Veteran Monument 37 M2
Veterinary Faculty (Udayana University) .. 37 J3
Veterinary Medicine, Udayana University .. 21 L8
Viceroy Bali, Hotel 49 H3
Victoria, Hotel 26 D8
Victory 19 M5
Vidi Boutique, Hotel 37 L2
Viena Beach Cottage 91 K6
Vihara Buddha Dharma 14 E2
Vihara Buddha Guna 38 F4
Vihara Buddha Sakyamuni 27 L6
Viking 2, Hotel 21 J4
Viking, Hotel 21 L2
Vikko Dera, Hotel 25 J3
Vila Adenium, Hotel 36 C6
Vila Hanani, Hotel 32 B5
Vila Kedidi, Hotel 25 H7
Vila Sasih, Hotel 31 G2
Vilastra Dive 33 L8
Villa & Spa, Hotel 32 C3
Villa 8 .... 19 K6
Villa Agung Beach Inn 53 M2
Villa Agung Khalia 49 K3
Villa Air Bali Resort 19 J5
Villa Alamanda 49 K8
Villa Alba Bali Dive Resort 90 D2
Villa Albia 19 J1
Villa Alea 43 J6
Villa Amatoa 25 H4
Villa Ambangan 36 B7
Villa Ambra 24 E5
Villa Amour 19 M7
Villa Anandi 19 G3
Villa Anggrek 19 L7
Villa Angle's 19 H5
Villa Anjani 52 B8
Villa Apsara 19 L8
Villa Aquamarine 91 L7
Villa Arya 48 D7
Villa Asoka 25 J6
Villa Atas Ombak 18 E3
Villa Ava Bali 19 J5
Villa Awang Awang 49 J1
Villa Aya 19 H6
Villa Ayu 19 K4
Villa Azzalea, Hotel 32 C4
Villa Ba Jabula 24 D2
Villa Bali Asri 19 J7
Villa Bali Balik 19 G5
Villa Baliana 14 C3
Villa Balquisse, Hotel 32 C7
Villa Bamboo 19 L6
Villa Batu, Hotel 32 B5
Villa Beji Indah 48 E7
Villa Bendega 25 J7
Villa Berawa 18 D1
Villa Bhagawan 48 E3
Villa Bidadari 44 A7
Villa Bintang 48 F2
Villa Biu Biu 35 J2
Villa Bu Nunie 36 D7
Villa Bukit Jati 47 M4
Villa Bukit Pujian 1 .... 36 B7
Villa Bukit Ubud 48 E2
Villa Bunde 19 J4
Villa Cactus 14 F4
Villa Cantik & Villa Sayang 19 G5
Villa Cantik Tresna 19 M8
Villa Capung 41 H3
Villa Cempaka 46 D4
Villa Chandra 19 J7
Villa Chimera 19 H7
Villa Cinta 25 K4
Villa Coco 14 C2
Villa Coraffan 25 K5
Villa De Daun 14 E6
Villa Dhyan 48 C4
Villa Diana 14 D3
Villa Diana Bali 14 D3
Villa Disana 91 H5
Villa Echo 14 F4
Villa Elegancia Bali 19 J6
Villa Elsa 52 B2
Villa Emanjo 44 B3
Villa Famille 19 H1
Villa Gad 19 J7
Villa Gajah Putih 18 D2
Villa Gala 47 G2
Villa Hai 25 K8
Villa Harmony 19 G3
Villa Hibiscus 17 J4
Villa Hitu 14 D2
Villa Hugo 19 H5
Villa Ida 91 L7
Villa Imogiri 48 F1
Villa Impossible 34 C7

Villa Indah 48 D1
Villa Indalia 19 K8
Villa Ininda Ligaya 19 M6
Villa Jago 18 C1
Villa Jalak 25 M6
Villa Jalan Jalan 48 F7
Villa Jayana 19 M6
Villa Jepun 48 E2
Villa Jerami 19 L7
Villa Joan 25 G5
Villa Jodie 19 J6
Villa Julie 19 L6
Villa Kaira 18 C1
Villa Kalani & Villa Bumbak 26 B8
Villa Kalyana, Hotel 32 C7
Villa Kania, Hotel 36 D7
Villa Karang 44 A7
Villa Karang Putih 44 B7
Villa Karisa 19 K8
Villa Kayu 19 H5
Villa Kayu Putih 18 E3
Villa Kecapi 19 H5
Villa Kelapa 53 G3
Villa Kendil 19 K5
Villa Kirey, Hotel 15 L6
Villa Ko 36 D7
Villa Koi 18 F4
Villa Kresna Boutique Suites 19 H8
Villa Kubu Pesisi 19 H6
Villa Kubu Seminyak 14 C2
Villa Kumala Putra 19 L6
Villa Kunang Kunang 47 H3
Villa La Sirena 4 .... 14 A1
Villa Latitude Bali 44 B7
Villa Lumbung 19 H5
Villa Lylah 14 D3
Villa Mahita 37 J7
Villa Mandalay, Hotel 63 K8
Villa Mandi 46 A7
Villa Manggis 25 J5
Villa Manis 19 M6
Villa Markisa Tauchen, Restaurant 90 F3
Villa Massilia 19 J7
Villa Mathis 26 B8
Villa Mawar 26 B4
Villa Max 19 L7
Villa Melati 48 C1
Villa Melhuni 49 K1
Villa Morlowe 81 H6
Villa Naga Laut 14 E3
Villa Naga Maya 14 C3
Villa Naga Taksaka 36 B7
Villa Naree 18 E2
Villa Nirwana 48 D4
Villa Nisaka Niwasa 17 H5
Villa Noah 36 D7
Villa Omsi 17 M1
Villa Onga 26 B8
Villa Pacung 49 G2
Villa Panca 19 J7
Villa Pantai Bali 53 G8
Villa Pantai Biru 18 F6
Villa Pantai Karang 23 M8
Villa Paya Paya 19 J5
Villa Pelangi 19 J6
Villa Pemandangan Laut 17 H5
Villa Pipit 24 F5
Villa Pisang Mas 14 C2
Villa Plenilunio 41 G8
Villa Pondok Bambu 16 E5
Villa Pulu 14 E3
Villa Puri Ayu 17 K5
Villa Puri Balangan 36 B7
Villa Puri Bawana 25 H6
Villa Puri Camas 48 C3
Villa Putih 19 H6
Villa Rama 53 H7
Villa Ratnasari 90 D2
Villa Rent 36 C8
Villa Rumah Manis 14 D2
Villa Rumi 19 J7
Villa Sabandari 47 K3
Villa Sama Sama 36 A6
Villa Sami Sami 36 C8
Villa Sampanye 19 L6
Villa Sancita 49 G1
Villa Santa Mandala 48 E1
Villa Santai 25 H3
Villa Saraswati (Petitenget) 19 M6
Villa Saraswati (Ubud) 48 D1
Villa Sari Bumi 93 K4
Villa Sari Bumi, Hotel 93 K4
Villa Sarna 49 H2
Villa Sarsana 26 C1
Villa Sasoon 53 K7
Villa Scena, Hotel 38 F3
Villa Semana 46 E7
Villa Seminyak 14 D2
Villa Senja 19 H3
Villa Senyum 25 K8
Villa Seraya 77 G5
Villa Shanti 17 M1
Villa Sinar Cinta GH 91 G5
Villa Skye Dee 14 E4
Villa Sonia 48 F7
Villa Soul 18 F2
Villa Sukawati 47 J1
Villa Taman Dayu 25 H5
Villa Taman Ganesha 53 G3
Villa Taman Perancak 25 K7

Villa Tanjung Mas 17 H4
Villa Tari 18 E2
Villa Teman 52 F3
Villa Teras Singa 36 C8
Villa Terima Kasih 36 A6
Villa the Beji 25 M8
Villa Travis 19 G3
Villa True Colors 14 E3
Villa Turkuaz & Efes 14 E2
Villa Ultimo 36 B8
Villa Uma Sapna 19 J7
Villa Uma Soca 49 G8
Villa Umah Abah 19 J5
Villa Wanakerta 48 E7
Villa Willy 19 H5
Villa Wisnu 18 E3
Villa Zen Tao 14 F3
Villa Zig 25 L7
Village Market 39 H4
Village, Restaurant 47 H5
Villarossa 53 L7
Villas Sales & Rental 38 F3
Villas Sunset, The 19 L8
Villas, The 19 L7
Villaveeta 26 E8
Vinly Villa Bali 14 F2
Violette Villas 14 E5
Vira, The, Hotel 10 F4
Virgo Dive Center 33 K3
Vista Express 23 K4
Viva Lavi Building 19 L6
Volcano Beach, Hotel 91 H5
Volcano Discotheque 53 K3
Voyager Boutique Creative Retreat, Hotel .. 25 J6

W

W Barwa 49 G8
W Brekele, Hotel 18 D2
W Retreat & Spa, Hotel 18 F4
W. Hardja 49 H7
Waeni's Sunset View, Hotel 91 J6
Wahana, The, Hotel 26 B5
Wahyu Dana, Hotel 52 C2
Wahyu, Hotel 46 E4
Wahyu, Spa 38 C1
Waka Di Ume Resort 48 F2
Waka Gangga, Resort 62 F5
Waka Louka Cruises 12 E5
Waka Namya, Hotel 46 E7
Waka Nusa, Resort 108 B2
Walet Utama 11 H4
Wali Beach 32 B1
Wangaya Hospital 28 F5
Wantilan I 10 F5
Wantilan II 10 F4
Wantilan III 10 F4
Wapo KKN, Restaurant 23 K5
Wardani Boutique 46 E5
Waribang Residence 30 C6
Waringin, Hotel 24 E6
Warisan Casa 32 E2
Warisan Living 19 K4
Warisan, Restaurant 19 K4
Warmadewa University (UNWAR) 30 B7
Warna Kusuma 47 H4
Waroeng Ethnic, Restaurant 19 G3
Waroeng Surya, Hotel 40 B2
Warsa's Garden, Hotel 46 E6
Warsi Bungalow 46 E4
Warta Puspita, Hotel 28 C3
Warta, Hotel 28 E3
Warung Anda 53 G4
Warung 115 Bandung, Restaurant 20 D5
Warung 39 .... 19 M7
Warung 66 .... 14 D7
Warung Agung 17 L4
Warung Agung
  (Jl. Pratama, Tanjung Benoa) 39 H3
Warung Arema 16 C6
Warung Ayu Sari, Hotel 67 K4
Warung Bali 33 K4
Warung Bamboo (Buleleng) 100 F6
Warung Bandung 14 E4
Warung Banyuwangi 19 H4
Warung Batavia (Kunti2) 19 M7
Warung Batavia (Raya Kerobokan) 19 K5
Warung Bebek D'uma 17 G2
Warung Betutu 52 D3
Warung Biah Biah 46 F4
Warung Bintang Karaoke 53 M3
Warung Blanjon 17 K4
Warung Bodag Maliah 48 E3
Warung Bu Kardi 11 H3
Warung Bu Kris 20 E5
Warung Bu Novi, Hotel 67 K4
Warung Bu Wahyu, Hotel 67 K4
Warung Bubur Ayam 21 J4
Warung Bucu, Restaurant 31 H5
Warung Coco, Hotel 14 E6
Warung D'sawah 19 K3
Warung Dayu's 31 L2
Warung Dewi Ayu 17 L2
Warung Dolphin 53 J2
Warung Dukuh 18 F2
Warung Enak 46 E8
Warung Gossip 19 L3
Warung Gula 52 E2
Warung Ibu Jaya 15 G3
Warung Jaan 19 L3
Warung Jamur 22 B7

Warung Jawa 32 E8
Warung Jepun Bali 52 E2
Warung Jerman 22 F4
Warung Kak Rebo 30 F2
Warung Kalimantan 14 E1
Warung Kampung, Restaurant 22 E2
Warung Ketut 17 L4
Warung Khas Bali 32 D4
Warung Kodok 48 B5
Warung Kolega 19 H4
Warung Kopi Bali 52 E2
Warung Lawar 49 H8
Warung Liku 14 F3
Warung Litut 19 L2
Warung Madiun 10 F6
Warung Mahkota 21 L5
Warung Mak Beng 23 L3
Warung Makan Untung 11 G3
Warung Mimpi 19 K8
Warung Mina, Restaurant 47 J4
Warung Mina, Restaurant 23 L6
Warung Murah (Jalan Arjuna) 14 B2
Warung Murah (Jalan Legian) 14 C3
Warung Muslim 11 G4
Warung Muslim Bu Abi 11 K6
Warung Nasi Bali 32 D1
Warung Nasi Warna 19 L1
Warung Nikmat 16 B2
Warung Nyoman
(Jl. Pratama, Tanjung Benoa) 33 K6
Warung Nyoman, Restaurant 23 K3
Warung Ocha 19 L8
Warung Ole 20 E3
Warung Padang 14 D4
Warung Pade Demen 32 C1
Warung Padi 26 B7
Warung Pencar 30 E7
Warung Pojok 23 K6
Warung Pulau Kelapa 48 D3
Warung Putu 53 M2
Warung Raos Bu Mel 11 G3
Warung Rasso 19 M3
Warung Rasta 53 M2
Warung Red Rice 48 D4
Warung Riska 53 G4
Warung Rumpi's 19 J5
Warung Saji Rasa 14 E2
Warung Sanji 48 E3
Warung Satria 29 G6
Warung Schnitzel 47 G3
Warung Sinartha 52 F7
Warung Sobat 1 .... 18 F3
Warung Sobat 2 .... 19 L3
Warung Sopo Nyono 11 G6
Warung Taman 23 L6
Warung Taulan 19 L1
Warung Teges 49 G7
Warung Wardani 28 F6
Warung Yan 53 G4
Warung Yogya 14 C4
Warwick Ibah Luxury Villas & Spa 46 C2
Warwick, Hotel 46 A3
Waskita 29 M8
Water Blow 39 M5
Water Garden, The, Hotel 52 F7
Water Sport Dive Center 33 L6
Watering Hole, Hotel 23 L4
Waterworld Watersport Shop 38 C1
Watu Jimbar Kondotel, Hotel 17 L1
Wawa Wewe Rock, Hotel 91 J6
Wawa Wewe Two, Hotel 91 J6
Wayan, Restaurant 23 L8
WBL, Restaurant 21 K3
Wena, Hotel 46 F4
Wenara Bali Bungalows 46 D7
Werdhapura, Hotel 23 M8
Werdhi Shop 46 F4
Westin Resort, The 39 K4
Westin Ubud Resort & Spa, The 48 D7
White Lotus Lodge, Hotel 48 C5
White Rock, Café 39 G4
White Rose, Hotel 14 E6
White Villas, The 47 G2
Whitesand, Restaurant 23 L6
Whitney, Hotel 46 B4
Wibawa Spa, The 46 E6
Wicala Guesthouse 49 L7
Wida, Hotel 14 D5
Widi 19 L7
Widuran, Restaurant 20 F6
Widya Batik 49 G1
Widya Kusuma Wood Carvings Museum .. 48 E7
Widya's, Hotel 23 K5
Widyas Luxury, The, Hotel 27 H6
Wijaya, Hotel 57 B5
Wika's, Restaurant 34 D7
Wild Palm Villa 17 J5
Wilsana Villas 19 G6
Win Art Photography 26 C2
Wine House 19 K4
Wine Shop 46 F8
Winotosastro, Hotel 29 M8
Wira Bali, Hotel 102 F3
Wira Pada, Hotel 56 E5
Wira Pada, Restaurant 56 E5
Wirama, Restaurant 38 F3
Wirasana Rent a Car 23 K4
Wirasatya Building 21 M2
Wiratha's Bungalows 53 H7
Wiratni 29 G5

Wisata 21 Theatre 28 E7
Wisata Cottages 48 E3
Wisma Bahari, Hotel 17 L4
Wisma Indovision 21 L2
Wisma Lansia Dewi Kunti 31 H5
Wisma Ritra 32 E2
Wisma Sari, Hotel 29 G8
Wisma Tanjung 21 K2
Wisma Tirta Yastra, Hotel 50 D2
Wismaya, Gallery 65 G3
Wisnu Dive Center 53 J3
Wisnu Foundation 19 L2
Wisnu Plaza 36 F7
Wito, Hotel 29 H6
Wola, The, Hotel 14 E1
Wolas Villa & Spa, The 19 M8
Woles Villas, The 14 E5
Wong Solo, Restaurant 22 E2
Wood Carving 65 J4
Wood Fossil 19 K2
Wooden Masks 65 G5

X

Xanadu Village Resort 19 M7
Xhotel Trade 53 M3
XL Center 20 F6

Y

Y Resort Umalas 26 D5
Yaan Toya Art Studio 19 L4
Yamasari 47 J2
Yamayuri, Restaurant 23 L7
Yani Craft Center 49 H2
Yani, Hotel 16 B6
Yanie's, Restaurant 14 D5
Yarama Cottages 46 F7
Yayasan Dharma Kerti Husada 32 D3
Yayasan Kupu-Kupu Bali 47 G3
Yeye's, Restaurant 34 B8
Yoga Baan, The 47 G7
Yoga Homestay, Hotel 53 J3
Yohana Spa 47 G4
Yoniko 20 C5
Yoyo, Hotel 18 F3
Yuam, Hotel 32 C4
Yubi, The 19 G5
Yudha 49 H2
Yudha Mandalatama Independence Monument
.... 57 D2
Yudhistira 31 K2
Yulia Village Inn, The 46 E5
Yulia, Hotel 14 D8
Yuliati House, Hotel 47 G5

Z

Zappa Bali, Hotel 26 D6
Zappaz, Restaurant 19 H6
Zelie, Hotel 18 E2
Zen Inn, Hotel 67 M4
Zen Resort 52 F1
Zen Villas 17 L2
Zero Six, Restaurant 10 E4
Zhumira, Hotel 19 J4
Zigis Studio One, Restaurant 52 E2
Ziva Honeymooners Villas 19 J6
Ziva, Hotel 14 C2
Zoe Villa 25 K7
Zolima, Villa 69 L6
Zonatri 21, Restaurant 20 E5
Zoo, Restaurant 23 L8
Zoom Bali 23 J6

Places Index

A

Aan 66 C3
Aas 91 L8
Ababi 76 D2
Abang 76 E1
Abang (Abang Songan) 88 D4
Abang (Batu Riti) 85 M2
Abang (Trunyan) 88 E3
Abang Dukuh 88 E3
Abang Kaler 76 E1
Abang Kelod 76 E1
Abang Songan 88 D6
Abang Tudinding 88 D5
Abangan 73 G5
Abasan (Dangin Puri) 29 G7
Abasan (Padang Sambian Kelod) 19 M1
Abasan (Pangkung Paruk) 96 F4
Abasan (Sangsit) 101 L4
Abasan (Singapadu Tengah) 65 G5
Abian Base 14 F6
Abian Base (Gianyar) 50 D8
Abian Base (Mengwi) 64 B6
Abian Base Kaja Kauh 65 L3
Abian Base Kelod Kauh 50 D8
Abian Calak 73 L7
Abian Canang 67 K2
Abian Jero 76 E2
Abian Kapas Kaja 29 K5
Abian Kapas Kelod 29 L6
Abian Kapas Tengah 29 L6
Abian Kuta 11 H2

Abian Lalang 71 L7
Abian Luang 86 C6
Abian Nangka Kaja 29 M3
Abian Nangka Kelod 29 M4
Abian Seka 65 H4
Abian Semal 48 F8
Abian Soan 76 C4
Abian Tegal 21 H6
Abian Timbul 15 H1
Abian Tiying Kaja 75 M5
Abian Tiying Kelod 75 M5
Abian Tubuh 30 A5
Abian Tuwung 63 L3
Abian Tuwung Kelod 63 L4
Abing (Batunya) 86 C4
Abing (Persiapan Sulangai) 86 D6
Abiyan Tiying 75 J5
Abuan (Kintamani) 87 K3
Abuan (Susut) 73 L5
Abuan Kangin 87 K3
Abuan Kauh 73 L5
Adat Dangin Yeh 101 L4
Adat Dauh Yeh 101 L4
Adegan 108 E3
Adegan Kangin 108 E3
Adegan Kawan 108 F2
Adeng 71 M6
Adnya Sari 79 G3
Agantaka 64 F5
Agung 64 D3
Air Anakan 79 J8
Air Jeruk Beach 65 J8
Air Kuning 80 E8
Akah 66 D3
Aktha 31 J3
Alang Kajeng 64 B3
Alang Kajeng Gede 28 E8
Alas 62 D2
Alas Angker 101 K7
Alas Arum (Payangan) 71 M4
Alas Harum (Bungkulan) 101 M3
Alas Harum (Kalianget) 97 L2
Alas Jero 71 M7
Alas Kedaton 63 L2
Alas Ngandang 74 E1
Alas Pengembunan 71 M7
Alas Perean 71 M4
Alas Pujung 87 J4
Alas Sandan 71 M4
Alas Sari 103 G3
Alas Tunggal 75 J7
Alasan 72 D4
Alengkong 106 D6
Alis Bintang 73 M2
Alit Saputra Field 51 F2
Amankila 67 L3
Amartha Sari 90 E6
Ambang 84 B3
Ambang (Banjar) 97 L2
Ambengan (Ayunan) 72 C7
Ambengan (Kamasan) 66 E6
Ambengan (Peguyangan Kangin) 64 E7
Ambengan (Pejukutan) 109 K5
Ambengan (Penuktukan) 106 C3
Ambengan (Persiapan Pangsan) 72 D2
Ambengan (Petulu) 47 J2
Ambengan (Rendang) 74 E6
Ambengan (Sayan) 48 B8
Ambengan (Sengekerta) 64 E2
Ambengan (Sesetan) 16 A5
Ambengan (Sukasada) 99 J2
Ambengan (Ubung Kaja) 64 C7
Ambengan Kebon 99 K2
Ambyar Sari 78 E2
Amed 91 G5
Amed Beach 91 G5
Amerta Sari (Panca Sari) 99 M5
Amerta Sari (Pegayaman) 99 L2
Amlapura 55 C5
Amo 73 G3
Ampadan 70 D4
Ampel (Karang Asem) 55 C4
Ampel (Pejukutan) 109 K5
Amplas 71 J2
Ancak 38 B5
Anchor Wreck, Dive Site 92 F1
Ancut (Kertha Mandala) 90 F7
Ancut (Sebudi) 75 H4
Ancut (Tianyar Barat) 106 F5
Angan Sari 105 K1
Angan Tiga 86 E6
Angas 108 F3
Angga Sari 79 G3
Angga Sari Kaja 83 L5
Angga Sari Kelod 83 L6
Anggabaya 64 E6
Anggar Kasih (Medahan) 65 L5
Anggar Kasih (Sanur Kaja) 23 K5
Anggrek 81 K7
Anggungan 72 E4
Anggungan Dauh 72 E4
Angkah Gede 70 C5
Angkah Munduk 70 C5
Angkah Pondok 70 C4
Angkah Tegeh 70 C5
Angkal 109 J3
Angkasa Pura I 32 F8
Angkeb Canging 64 A3
Angkeh Canging 64 B2
Angkling 65 L1

Anglikan 71 G7
Angsa 97 K7
Angseri 85 M5
Anjingan 66 C5
Anom 70 C6
Anta 109 H6
Antagana Kaja 70 D5
Antagana Kangin 70 E5
Antagana Kelod 70 D6
Antap (Panjer) 21 M6
Antap (Selemadeg) 62 C2
Antap Dajan Sema 62 C1
Antap Dajan Telabah 62 D1
Antap Delod Sema 62 C2
Antap Gawang 69 K1
Antap Kaja 22 A5
Antap Kangin 22 B5
Antap Kelod 62 C2
Antapan 86 C5
Antapura 103 M6
Antepan 108 F6
Antiga 67 J4
Antiga Kelod 67 L4
Antosari 70 C7
Antugan (Blah Batuh) 65 J4
Antugan (Jehem) 74 B4
Anturan 53 L3
Anyar (Air Kuning) 80 E8
Anyar (Anturan) 100 F7
Anyar (Baluk) 80 B6
Anyar (Carang Sari) 72 E4
Anyar (Dangin Tukad Aya) 80 E6
Anyar (Kalopaksa) 97 H5
Anyar (Kerobokan) 26 D5
Anyar (Kuta) 11 G2
Anyar (Marga) 72 B5
Anyar (Penatahan) 85 H8
Anyar (Perean Tengah) 72 D2
Anyar (Sakti) 108 D2
Anyar (Selumbung) 67 M2
Anyar (Sembung) 72 C6
Anyar (Senganan) 85 M4
Anyar (Sobangan) 72 C7
Anyar (Tegal Badeng Barat) 80 B7
Anyar (Tukad Mungga) 53 M4
Anyar (Tunjuk) 71 L5
Anyar Anyar 64 D7
Anyar Gede 32 C4
Anyar Kaja 26 D4
Anyar Kaja (Penyaringan) 81 H6
Anyar Kelod 26 D5
Anyar Kelod (Penyaringan) 81 H7
Anyar Sari 78 F4
Anyar Sari Kangin 78 F4
Anyar Tembles 81 H7
Anyar Tembles Kaja 81 H7
Anyar Tengah 81 H7
Aper 66 C6
Aper 66 E3
Apit Yeh (Bangli) 86 B5
Apit Yeh (Gunung Salak) 70 F4
Apit Yeh (Munduk Temu) 83 L7
Apit Yeh (Patemon) 97 J3
Apit Yeh (Sepang Kelod) 83 H3
Apit Yeh (Wana Giri) 70 E4
Apit Yeh Kaja 67 M2
Apit Yeh Kelod 67 M2
Apit Yeh Pondok 70 F5
Apuan (Batu Riti) 86 B6
Apuan (Singapadu) 65 G5
Apuan (Susut) 73 L6
Apuan Kaja 73 L5
Apuan Kelod 73 L6
Apuh (Lodtunduh) 65 G4
Apuh (Sebatu) 87 K5
Arca 68 C1
Arma open Stage 48 F7
Arum 92 B5
Asah 52 A4
Asah (Bantiran) 83 M2
Asah (Belimbing) 84 F7
Asah (Gobleg) 99 G5
Asah (Kertha Mandala) 91 G8
Asah (Munduk) 99 H7
Asah (Pedawa) 98 C6
Asah (Pempatan) 88 F7
Asah Badung 83 G4
Asah Dulu 90 D7
Asah Duren 68 D1
Asah Kaja 71 L2
Asah Kelod 71 K3
Asah Kelod Kauh 99 H4
Asah Munduk 99 G5
Asah Panji 99 J3
Asah Teben 90 E6
Asah Tegeh 70 E1
Asah Tepi 99 G5
Asak Kangin 76 D7
Asem (Bengkel) 84 D1
Asem (Jineng Dalem) 101 K5
Aseman 26 C3
Aseman (Abian Semal) 64 D2
Aseman (Pupuan Sawah) 70 F4
Aseman (Sedang) 64 E4
Aseman Kangin 26 C3
Aseman Kawan 26 B3
Asih 92 A6
Asri 92 A5
Asta Buana 20 F3
Aster Villas 35 G6

Astina 57 E5
Atuh 84 D2
Auman 86 D3
Auman Dajan Semu 69 L2
Auman Delod Semu 69 L3
Awan (Awan) 105 J6
Awan (Batu Kandik) 109 G6
Awen Lelateng 80 C7
Awen Mertasari 56 B8
Ayah 73 G4
Ayunan 72 C7

B

Babahan 85 L8
Babahan Kanginan 71 L1
Babahan Kawah 71 L1
Babahan Tengah 71 L1
Babakan 27 G2
Babakan (Beneng) 63 L7
Babakan (Blah Batuh) 65 K3
Babakan (Cau Belayu) 72 D4
Babakan (Duda) 75 H6
Babakan (Gegelang) 67 J4
Babakan (Mambang) 62 F2
Babakan (Nyitdah) 63 J5
Babakan (Panji Anom) 100 F6
Babakan (Purwakerthi) 91 G5
Babakan (Sambangan) 101 G6
Babakan (Selemadeg) 70 E7
Babakan (Sukawati) 65 J6
Babakan (Wana Giri) 70 F2
Babakan Kangin 64 C3
Babakan Kawan 64 C3
Babakan Sari 22 F3
Baban 73 M7
Babung 66 F5
Bada 86 F5
Badak Sari 29 K8
Badak Sari 22 C1
Badeg Dukuh 75 J3
Badeg Kelodan 75 J4
Badeg Tengah 75 J3
Badegede (Antosari) 70 C7
Bading Kayu 69 H2
Badung (Ayunan) 64 C1
Badung (Bungkulan) 101 L3
Badung (Gulingan) 64 B3
Badung (Lukluk) 64 C5
Badung (Melinggih) 72 F3
Badung (Pejaten) 63 J5
Badung (Sibang Gede) 64 D5
Badung Cemetery 28 D8
Badung Tengah 72 C7
Baha 64 B1
Bahel 90 C2
Baingin 98 A3
Bajangan 98 A2
Bajera 70 D7
Bajera Belayu 63 M2
Bajera Kaja 70 D7
Bajera Kangin 70 D7
Bajera Kelod 70 D7
Bajera Pagebegan 63 M2
Bajera Tengah 70 D7
Bajing 66 E2
Bakalan 89 L3
Bakas 66 B4
Bakas Kangin 66 B4
Bakbakan 73 K8
Bakbakan Kanginan 73 L8
Bakisan 63 L1
Bakti Sebaga 57 A7
Bakul 30 D1
Bakul 65 G8
Bakung (Beratan) 101 J6
Bakung (Manggis) 67 L1
Bakung Sari 42 E2
Bakungan 105 G1
Balangan Beach 34 F3
Balangan Pratama 35 J3
Bale Agung (Jegu) 71 K4
Bale Agung (Kayu Putih) 98 E7
Bale Agung (Kerobokan) 101 K4
Bale Agung (Munggu) 63 J7
Bale Agung (Paket Agung) 57 E8
Bale Agung (Serampingan) 70 D7
Bale Agung (Timuhun) 66 C1
Bale Agung (Unggahan) 97 J6
Bale Agung (Yeh Embang) 81 K7
Bale Agung Kaja 101 K3
Bale Banjar Tuban Geriya 11 J6
Bale Gede 90 E6
Bale Kembar 39 H4
Bale Punduk Kaler 76 F3
Bale Punduk Kelod 55 F1
Bale Timbang 84 B7
Baledan 108 F3
Balega Kanginan 65 K4
Balen Pasar 64 D5
Baler Bale Agung (Baler Bale Agung) .. 56 D3
Baler Bale Agung (Tegal Cangkring) .. 81 G6
Baler Pasar (Menanga) 74 E5
Baler Pasar (Mendoyo Dangin Tukad) .. 80 F7
Baler Setra 82 C7
Baleran 63 J4
Bali Aga Village 88 E2
Bali Arum 17 G3
Bali Arum Jimbaran 37 J4
Bali Bird Park 64 F6
Bali Camel Safari 45 K5

Bali Kencana Resort I 43 J1
Bali Kencana Resort II 43 J2
Bali Mangrove Park 16 C8
Bali Mangrove Park 13 G1
Bali Marine Sports 17 L4
Bali Reptile Park 64 F6
Bali Safari and Marine Park 65 M5
Bali Zoo Park 65 G5
Balian Beach 69 L7
Balimbing 76 C1
Balina Beach 67 M3
Balong Gede 28 E5
Balong Menak 28 E5
Baluk 80 B6
Baluk Dua 80 C6
Baluk Rening Beach 79 H8
Baluk Satu 79 L8
Balun 28 E6
Ban 89 J1
Banda (Saba) 65 J6
Banda (Takmung) 66 C6
Bandung (Gunaksa) 66 F5
Bandung (Munggu) 63 K7
Bandung (Pandak Bandung) 63 K5
Bandung (Siangan) 65 K1
Bangah 86 B5
Bangal 69 L1
Bangan 101 D6
Bangbang 74 D7
Bangbang Biaung 75 J6
Bangbang Kaler 74 D6
Bangbang Kawan 74 E5
Bangbang Kembar 41 M6
Bangbang Pande 74 E5
Bangbang Tengah (Bangbang) 74 D6
Bangbang Tengah (Rendang) 74 F5
Bangbung Pegat 106 D6
Banggras 55 D5
Bangkang 57 B7
Bangket 34 F7
Bangkiang Jaran 69 K4
Bangkiang Mayung 71 G7
Bangkiang Sidem (Gobleg) 98 F5
Bangkiang Sidem (Gunung Salak) .. 70 F5
Bangkiang Sidem (Penarungan) ... 64 C2
Bangkiang Sidem (Penatahan) 71 K3
Bangkiang Sidem (Peninjoan) 74 E5
Bangkiansidem 48 F1
Bangkilesan 65 G3
Bangkled 74 B1
Bangle 91 H8
Bangli (Bangli) 54 B5
Bangli (Yeh Embang Kangin) 81 M7
Bangli (Yeh Sumbul) 82 A6
Bangsing 84 D5
Bangun Lemah Kangin 73 L7
Bangun Lemah Kawan 73 L7
Bangun Liman 65 J3
Bangun Urip Kaja 109 G5
Bangun Urip Kelod 109 G5
Banjar 97 L3
Banjar Alas 62 F2
Banjar Angkan 66 B6
Banjar Anyar (Kediri) 63 L3
Banjar Anyar (Panji) 99 H2
Banjar Asem 97 G3
Banjar Bali 57 D3
Banjar Balu 63 L3
Banjar Jawa 57 D4
Banjar Sakti 48 F1
Banjar Sari 97 M6
Banjar Tegal 57 D7
Banjar Tegehe 97 L3
Banjar Tengah 56 C5
Banjaran 64 C2
Banjaran Anyar 70 C6
Bantang 105 K3
Bantas (Belandingan) 106 D6
Bantas (Dauh Yeh Cani) 64 C2
Bantas (Gobleg) 98 D6
Bantas (Kerambitan) 62 F4
Bantas (Manukaya) 73 K1
Bantas (Peguyangan Kangin) 64 E7
Bantas (Selemadeg) 70 F7
Bantas (Suwug) 101 M6
Bantas Bale Agung 70 F7
Bantas Kaja 64 E4
Bantas Kelod 64 E5
Bantas Tengah Kaja 70 F7
Bantas Tengah Kelod 62 F1
Bantiran 84 B3
Banua 87 J3
Banyan Estate 19 G2
Banyu Asri 57 C6
Banyu Asri Dua 57 A5
Banyu Asri Satu 57 B6
Banyu Asri Skip 57 A4
Banyu Atis 98 D7
Banyu Atis Kaja 98 D7
Banyu Atis Kelod 98 D7
Banyu Atis Tengah 98 D7
Banyu Biru 79 J8
Banyu Biru Kangin 79 K7
Banyu Biru Kauh 79 J7
Banyu Campah 67 G2
Banyu Poh 94 F2
Banyu Seri 98 C6
Banyu Wedang 93 K3
Banyualit 53 J2
Banyualit Beach 53 K2

Banyuning (Abang) 91 L7
Banyuning (Singaraja) 57 F4
Banyuning Barat 57 F4
Banyuning Indah 101 J5
Banyuning Selatan 101 J5
Banyuning Tengah 101 J5
Banyuning Timur 101 J5
Banyuning Utara 101 H4
Barat Jalan 99 K1
Barong Dance & Kecak Dance Show .. 30 D6
Baru (Batu Riti) 86 B3
Baru (Pulukan) 68 B2
Baru (Tua) 86 B8
Baruna Sari 57 E2
Basa 71 M6
Basang Alas Kangin 76 F1
Basang Alas Kawan 76 F1
Basang Ambu 73 K2
Basang Tamiang 64 G4
Basanga 87 M4
Basangkasa 19 L7
Bat Cave, Dive Site 93 G1
Batan Ancak 49 H8
Batan Asem 64 C6
Batan Buah 30 B4
Batan Buah (Beraban) 63 H6
Batan Buah (Dauh Yehcani) 64 C2
Batan Buah (Tangguntiti) 62 E2
Batan Duren 63 L6
Batan Nyuh (Marga) 71 M7
Batan Nyuh (Pemecutan Kelod) ... 21 G5
Batan Nyuh (Sudimara) 63 G5
Batan Nyuh Kaja 76 F3
Batan Nyuh Kaler 71 M7
Batan Nyuh Kelod 71 M7
Batan Nyuh Kelod (Karang Asem) .. 55 E1
Batan Poh (Pandak Gede) 63 K5
Batan Poh (Sanur Kaja) 23 K4
Batan Tanjung 63 J7
Batan Wani 71 M7
Batang (Culik) 90 E5
Batang (Menanga) 75 G3
Batang Asah 105 J3
Batang Tingkad 106 A6
Batih 106 A4
Batu (Mengwi) 25 H2
Batu (Mengwi) 63 M2
Batu Abah 109 L6
Batu Agung 80 E6
Batu Agung (Gerokgak) 95 L4
Batu Aji (Batu Bulan Kangin) 65 G7
Batu Aji (Kerambitan) 71 J8
Batu Aji Kaja 63 J1
Batu Aji Kawan Kaja 71 H7
Batu Aji Kawan Kelod 71 H7
Batu Aji Kelod 63 J1
Batu Ampin 75 M5
Batu Bara 69 H4
Batu Bayan 48 A2
Batu Belig 18 F3
Batu Belig Beach 18 E4
Batu Bidak 27 G3
Batu Bintang 21 K3
Batu Bolong 20 C4
Batu Bolong Beach 25 G8
Batu Bulan 65 G7
Batu Bulan Kangin 65 H7
Batu Culung 27 G3
Batu Dawa Kaja 90 C3
Batu Dawa Kelod 90 D3
Batu Dinding 106 F7
Batu Dingding 99 L1
Batu Gaing 63 H7
Batu Gede 67 K1
Batu Giling 90 B2
Batu Guling 109 G5
Batu Gunung 77 G2
Batu Jimbar 17 M1
Batu Kaang 105 G7
Batu Kambing 85 J8
Batu Kandik (Denpasar Barat) 64 B7
Batu Kandik (Nusa Dua) 109 G5
Batu Kapal 83 K5
Batu Kelabit 90 E2
Batu Keseni 91 L8
Batu Lantang 86 D5
Batu Layah Beach 35 H2
Batu Lompeni 107 H6
Batu Lumbang (Antap) 70 B8
Batu Lumbang (Les) 106 C2
Batu Lumbang (Sangeh) 72 D5
Batu Lumbang (Ubud) 49 K8
Batu Lumbung 108 F7
Batu Madeg (Besakih) 75 G2
Batu Madeg (Nusa Penida) 108 E5
Batu Madeg (Tista) 90 E7
Batu Madeg Kaja 108 E5
Batu Madeg Kelod 108 E4
Batu Mandeg 98 F6
Batu Mas 29 H8
Batu Megaan 83 L1
Batu Mejan Beach 25 G7
Batu Mekaem 64 C7
Batu Melang 108 B2
Batu Meling 108 D6
Batu Meyeh Kauh 106 E5
Batu Mulapan Kangin 109 H1
Batu Mulapan Kauh 109 H2
Batu Niti 90 F3
Batu Nunggal 109 H1

Batu Palah 105 H2
Batu Paras 64 C8
Batu Pulu 100 F7
Batu Ringgit 107 L8
Batu Ringgit Kelod 107 L7
Batu Riti (Batu Riti) 86 B4
Batu Riti (Kerambitan) 63 H2
Batu Riti Kaja 63 G2
Batu Riti Kelod 63 G3
Batu Riti Tengah 63 G3
Batu Sangian 63 H4
Batu Sari (Bongkasa) 72 E6
Batu Sari (Sangeh) 72 D6
Batu Sari (Ubud) 48 A1
Batu Sesa (Candi Kuning) 99 M8
Batu Sesa (Menanga) 74 F4
Batu Talen 108 A2
Batu Tampih Kangin 63 G6
Batu Tampih Kawan 63 G5
Batuan 65 H5
Batuan Kaler 65 H4
Batung Ajeg 102 D4
Batung Anten 86 D6
Batungsel 84 D5
Batungsel Kaja 84 D5
Batungsel Kelod 84 D5
Batunya 86 C3
Batur (Batu Bulan) 64 F7
Batur (Batur Utara) 105 L6
Batur (Peguyangan Kaja) 64 D6
Batur Hening 64 E2
Batur Natural Hot Springs 50 D2
Batur Sari (Bitera) 65 K2
Batur Sari (Mengwitani) 63 M4
Batur Selatan 105 M6
Batur Tengah 88 B3
Batur Utara 105 L6
Baung 48 C5
Bayad (Kedisah) 73 J2
Bayad (Melinggih Kelod) 72 F4
Bayad (Sembiran) 103 G6
Bayan 86 C8
Bayuh (Nusa Penida) 109 H3
Bayuh (Ungasan) 42 F4
Bayung Cerik 87 J2
Bayung Gede 87 L2
Bayview Villa Residences 38 C2
BDC 17 K4
Bebalang (Bangli) 73 M5
Bebalang (Bebalang) 54 C8
Bebalang (Kawan) 54 D6
Bebali 62 C2
Bebandem 76 B4
Bebayu 90 F5
Bebengan 64 A6
Bebetin 102 B7
Bebetin Kaja Kangin 102 B8
Bedauh 72 D4
Bedegul 71 K3
Bedha 63 H4
Bedil (Baha) 72 C8
Bedil (Sukawati) 65 H5
Bedugul (Batunya) 104 B8
Bedugul (Bungaya) 76 D4
Bedugul (Rendang) 74 F5
Bedulu 49 L8
Bedulu Palace 49 K7
Begawan (Melinggih Kelod) 72 E4
Begawan (Pedungan) 21 H7
Beja (Kuwum) 71 M6
Beja (Lalang Linggah) 69 K6
Beji (Bungaya) 76 D5
Beji (Munduk) 98 F7
Beji (Pangeragoan) 69 G4
Beji (Sangsit) 101 K3
Bekul 16 E2
Bel 89 K3
Belah 86 C8
Belahan 87 L8
Belalang 63 H6
Belalu 109 G6
Belaluan (Dangin Puri Kauh) 29 G6
Belaluan (Singapadu Tengah) 65 G5
Belanban 72 B3
Belancan 105 K8
Belandingan 106 C6
Belang (Sembung) 72 B6
Belang (Singapadu Kaler) 64 F3
Belanga 105 G6
Belanjong 17 J4
Belantibah 70 E1
Belantih 105 G5
Belatung (Menanga) 75 G4
Belatung (Pandak Gede) 63 K5
Belatung (Senganan) 85 M7
Belatung Lengis 96 E5
Belatungan 83 K7
Belawan 64 D2
Belebet 108 E3
Belege 65 K4
Belimbing 106 C2
Belimbing Anyar 84 D8
Belimbing Desa 84 D8
Belimbing Tegal 84 D8
Belingkang 106 C6
Belo 89 K3
Belok (Belok) 104 F8
Belok (Kayu Bihi) 74 C2
Belok Sidan 86 F1
Belong (Ban) 89 K3

Belong (Batu Riti) 63 H2
Belong (Belumbang) 62 F4
Belong (Karang Asem) 55 E2
Belong (Manggis) 67 L2
Belong (Patemon) 97 J3
Belong (Sanur Kaja) 23 J4
Belong (Taro) 87 J6
Belong (Ulakan) 67 K3
Belong Danginan 88 D5
Belong Dauhan 88 D4
Beluangan 72 D2
Belubuh 77 J3
Beluhu 88 D7
Beluhu Kangin 90 C1
Beluhu Kauh 90 C2
Belulang (Kapal) 64 B5
Belulang (Mengesta) 85 L8
Belulang (Senganan) 83 J2
Belulang Selatan 85 K7
Beluluk 71 G7
Belumbang 62 F3
Belumbang Kaja 62 F3
Belumbang Kelod 63 G3
Belumbang Tengah 62 F3
Beluran 26 F3
Belusung 64 D6
Bena Sari 77 J3
Benana Kaja 71 L4
Benana Kelod 71 K5
Benawah Kangin 73 K5
Benawan Kawan 73 K6
Benaya 64 D7
Benben 106 C3
Benbiyu 64 D6
Bencingah 74 F5
Bendul (Jegu) 71 K4
Bendul (Semarapura Tengah) 66 D4
Bendung Mambal 64 E3
Bendungan Soka 70 D6
Bendungan Tukad Unda 51 E5
Beneh Kawan 72 D8
Benekasa 75 G6
Benel 79 K6
Beneng 66 C4
Beng (Carang Sari) 72 E4
Beng (Gianyar) 50 C4
Beng (Marga) 72 B5
Beng Kaja Kangin 65 L2
Beng Kaja Kauh 65 L2
Beng Kelod Kangin 50 D5
Beng Kelod Kauh 50 C5
Beng Selatan 71 L6
Beng Utara 71 L6
Bengan 74 D6
Bengkala 102 B5
Bengkala Kaja 102 B5
Bengkala Kelodan 102 B5
Bengkel (Alas Angker) 101 K7
Bengkel (Antosari) 70 B7
Bengkel (Bebetin) 102 B7
Bengkel (Bengkel) 98 D7
Bengkel (Busung Biu) 98 C7
Bengkel (Gegelang) 67 J5
Bengkel (Kediri) 63 H5
Bengkel (Padangbai) 67 K4
Bengkel (Sumerta Kelod) 29 L7
Bengkel (Timpag) 71 G6
Bengkel (Wongaya Gede) 85 H8
Bengkel Gede 63 H5
Bengkel Kawan 63 H5
Bengkel Kelod 67 K5
Beniti 84 D8
Benoa 38 B6
Beraban (Beraban) 63 H6
Beraban (Dauh Puri Kauh) 21 H4
Beraban (Kediri) 63 H6
Beraban (Selemadeg) 62 E4
Beraban Kauh 62 D3
Berangbang 80 C4
Beratan (Beratan) 57 F8
Beratan (Patemon) 97 J3
Beratan (Yeh Kuning) 80 F8
Berawa Salak 79 J8
Berawan Tangi 79 G6
Berawan Tangi Kaja 79 G5
Berawan Tangi Kelod 79 G6
Berawan Tangi Taman 79 H6
Berembeng 70 D8
Bergong 101 L6
Beringkit (Mengwitani) 64 B4
Beringkit (Peken) 63 M1
Bernasi 63 M6
Bersela 73 H2
Bersih 64 D6
Berteh 72 C3
Besakih 75 G2
Besakih Kangin 75 G2
Besakih Kawan 74 F2
Besan 67 G4
Besan Kanginan 67 G4
Besan Kawan 67 G4
Besan Kelodan 67 G4
Besang 76 D2
Besang Kangin 66 D4
Besang Kawan 66 D4
Besang Tengah 66 D4
Bestala 97 M6
Betanha 55 E5
Betelan 98 C8
Beteng 83 K5

Betiting 73 L7
Bhuana Merta 20 F2
Bhuana Sari (Dangin Puri Kaja) 29 G4
Bhuana Sari (Kayu Putih) 98 D2
Bhuana Sari (Tegal Kerta) 20 F1
Bhuana Sari (Wana Giri) 99 K5
Bias (Abang Tudinding) 88 D5
Bias (Abang) 76 D2
Bias (Besakih) 74 F2
Bias (Kampung Islam Kusamba) 67 G6
Bias Lantang Kaler 90 F5
Bias Lantang Kelod 90 F6
Bias Tugel Beach 67 L4
Biaung (Kesiman Kertha Langu) 31 G4
Biaung (Ped) 108 E2
Biaung (Penebel) 71 M2
Biaung (Penatih Dangin Puri) 65 G8
Biaung Beach 31 H6
Biaung Indah Candra Asri 65 H8
Biaung IndahCandra Asri 31 J4
Biaung Kaja 71 M2
Biaung Kelod 71 M3
Biaung Tengah 71 M2
Bijih 102 E4
Bila (Batu Ringgit) 89 M3
Bila (Klumbu) 109 G3
Bila (Kubu Tambahan) 102 C6
Bila Kanginan 102 C5
Bila Kawanan 102 C6
Biluk Poh 81 G7
Biluk Poh Kangin 81 G7
Bilukan 87 L5
Bina Arta 84 D3
Binaria Beach 52 F2
Bindu 64 E3
Bindu Tingas 64 E3
Bingin (Batu Kandik) 109 G6
Bingin (Culik) 90 E5
Bingin (Galungan) 104 C2
Bingin (Kampung Islam Kusamba) 67 G6
Bingin (Pecatu) 34 E8
Bingin Banjah 52 A3
Bingin Beach 34 D6
Binoh Kelod 28 C1
Binong 72 B7
Binyan 105 G7
Biotasak 87 G7
Bird Park 37 H7
Bitera 65 K2
Bitra 49 M7
Biya 65 K5
Biyan 88 B5
Black Sand Beach 67 H6
Blah Batuh 65 J4
Blah Kiuh 72 D8
Blah Pane Kaja 66 A4
Blah Pane Kelod 66 A4
Blah Tanah 65 H4
Blangsinga 65 J4
Blaslantang 77 K3
Blaslantang Kangin 77 K3
Blimbing Sari 78 F2
Blok Alpukat 35 G4
Blok Arjuna 42 D2
Blok Dahlia 35 G6
Blok Exclusive Housing Glof 35 G5
Blok James Cook Village 35 J5
Blok Merpati 43 K2
Blok Natural Residential 35 H8
Blok Nuri (Bali Kencana Resort) 43 K2
Blok Nuri (Pecatu Indah Resort) 35 J8
Blok Orange Village 42 B1
Blok Residential Exclusive Glof 35 G5
Blok Sahadewa 42 C2
Blok Sirsak 35 H4
Blue Corner 108 C1
Blue Ocean Beach 14 A3
Blumbang 64 C3
Bluncing 66 F2
Bodong 108 F2
Bokong 66 E5
Bokong Kaja 66 E5
Bolangan (Babahan) 85 L7
Bolangan (Kayu Putih) 98 E7
Bon 104 F6
Bon Agung 98 B7
Bon Dalem 103 K5
Bon Dalem Kaja Kangin 103 K5
Bon Dalem Kaja Kauh 103 K5
Bon Dalem Kelod Kangin 103 L5
Bon Jaka 87 J7
Bon Nyuh 73 K6
Bongan (Tabanan) 63 J4
Bongan (Tegal Mengkeb) 62 E2
Bongan Cina 83 K4
Bongan Cina Kaja 83 K5
Bongan Gede 63 J4
Bongan Kauh Kaja 63 J4
Bongan Lebah 63 K4
Bongan Munduk 63 J3
Bongan Nyawa Kangin 63 J4
Bongan Nyawa Kawan 63 J4
Bongan Pala 63 J3
Bongan Tengah 63 J4
Bongkang 102 B5
Bongkasa 48 A4
Bongli 71 J2
Bonian 69 M8
Bono 65 K3
Bono Kaja 65 K3

Bono Kangin 65 K3
Bono Kelod 65 K4
Bontihing 102 C7
Bontihing Kanginan 102 C7
Bontihing Kawanan 102 C7
Bonyoh 87 L3
Botanic Garden 49 G2
Botanic Gardens 47 G3
Botanical Gardens/Kebun Raya 85 L1
Br. Bekul's Cemetery 16 D1
Brahmana (Sangeh) 72 D6
Brahmana (Sawan) 102 B6
Brahmana (Sibetan) 75 M6
Brahmana Bukit 54 D1
Brahmana (Sibetan) 54 D3
Brahmana Pande 54 D3
Branjingan 62 E2
Brawa 18 D2
Brawa Beach 18 C2
Brongbong 96 E3
Buading 63 L6
Buagan 20 F5
Buahan (Buahan) 86 E8
Buahan (Kedisan) 88 C4
Buahan (Payangan) 86 E8
Buahan (Tabanan) 71 L7
Buahan Kaja 71 L6
Buahan Kelod 71 L7
Buahan Tengah 71 L7
Buaji 65 G7
Buaji Anyar 30 B8
Buaji Sari 29 M7
Bualu 39 G4
Bualu Indah 39 H5
Buana Anyar 30 B7
Buana Asri 28 A7
Buana Indah 20 E4
Buana Kerti 97 K5
Buana Kubu 20 E2
Buana Mas Indah 20 D2
Buana Permata Hijau 20 D1
Buana Santi 20 D1
Buana Sari (Penarukan) 101 J4
Buana Sari (Pinggan) 106 B6
Buana Sari (Wana Giri) 99 J5
Buangga 72 E3
Buayang (Culik) 90 E6
Buayang (Dawan Kelod) 66 F5
Buayang (Kayu Bihi) 88 C7
Bubuan 96 C3
Bubung 88 D4
Bubung Klambu 88 B3
Bucang 108 E4
Bucu (Darmasaba) 64 C5
Bucu (Nongan) 74 E6
Bucu (Semarapura Tengah) 51 C6
Budaga 51 B7
Budakeling 76 C3
Budamanis 67 G1
Budapaing 76 E3
Budeng 80 D7
Buditirta 73 K7
Buduk (Bengkel) 63 H5
Buduk (Mengwi) 63 L7
Buduk (Sengekerta) 64 F2
Buduk (Ubud) 48 C7
Buffalo Races 80 C6
Bugal 107 G6
Bugbug 76 C8
Bugbugan 88 A3
Bugbugan Kaja 85 L5
Bugbugan Kelod 85 M6
Bugis 16 E8
Bugis 13 K2
Bugis Cemetery 16 E5
Bugis Suwung 16 D6
Buitan 67 M3
Bujaga 74 E6
Bujak 83 H5
Bukian (Nongan) 74 E7
Bukian (Payangan) 87 G8
Bukian (Pelaga) 86 E2
Bukian Kaja 73 H1
Bukih 87 J1
Bukit (Jineng Dalem) 101 K5
Bukit (Karang Asem) 77 G2
Bukit (Kutampi) 109 H3
Bukit (Pelaga) 86 D4
Bukit (Sukadana) 107 J6
Bukit (Tampak Siring) 73 K3
Bukit Batu (Ambengan) 99 J2
Bukit Batu (Samplangan) 65 M2
Bukit Buwung 30 A4
Bukit Catu 99 M8
Bukit Hijau 36 C5
Bukit Jangkrik 50 F4
Bukit Jimbaran 36 E4
Bukit Juet 67 M1
Bukit Kaber 77 G2
Bukit Kangin 76 C6
Bukit Kauh 76 B5
Bukit Kelod 77 G3
Bukit Mungsu Indah 86 B1
Bukit Pratama 37 H5
Bukit Sakti 97 J4
Bukit Sanggulan Indah 63 L2
Bukit Sari (Pengulon) 96 C3
Bukit Sari (Sidan) 65 M2

Bukit Sari (Songan B) 106 E6
Bukit Satu 75 M8
Bukit Seni 103 H7
Bukit Tabuan 77 G2
Bukit Telu 98 D8
Bukit Tengah 76 C6
Bukit Tumpeng 69 K5
Bukit Tungtung 106 E6
Bukti 102 F3
Bulada 98 F1
Bulakan (Gobleg) 98 E6
Bulakan (Tukad Sumaga) 96 E4
Bulakan Dua 106 D4
Bulakan Kangin 99 G8
Bulakan Kauh 98 F7
Bulakan Satu 106 D3
Bulangan 72 C4
Bulian 102 C5
Buluh (Batu Kandik) 109 G6
Buluh (Guwang) 65 H7
Buluh (Songan A) 106 E5
Buluh (Tangkup) 66 F2
Buluh (Tukad Sumaga) 96 E4
Bumbak 26 B8
Bumi Asa 89 H2
Bumi Asri 21 K5
Bumi Banten 21 K3
Bumi Jimbaran Asri 36 F6
Bumi Kerthi 21 J4
Bumi Santi 21 K5
Bumi Sari 21 K5
Bumi Werdhi 21 J5
Bun 29 G7
Bunderan Gatsu 29 H2
Bunga 89 G4
Bunga Mekar 108 E4
Bungan Kapal 71 M4
Bungaya (Bebandem) 76 C5
Bungaya (Klungkung) 66 D4
Bungaya Kangin 76 D4
Bungbungan 66 C1
Bungbungar 72 B5
Bungkil 109 F6
Bungkuan 73 M2
Bungkulan (Sawan) 101 M3
Bungkulan (Seraya) 77 K6
Bungkulan Indah 101 L3
Bungli 86 F7
Bungsu 64 F5
Buni 14 D8
Bunteh 87 G5
Buntu 77 J3
Buntu Sari Tempekan Pesanggaran 16 A6
Bunut (Cempaga) 74 B6
Bunut (Trunyan) 89 G2
Bunut Bolong 82 E7
Bunut Panggang 52 C4
Bunut Puhun (Bantas) 70 D7
Bunut Puhun (Penatahan) 71 H3
Bunutan (Bunutan) 91 J8
Bunutan (Kedewatan) 72 F5
Bunutan (Payangan) 86 B8
Bunutan (Seraya Barat) 77 J4
Bunutan (Tua) 86 B8
Buntin (Bangli) 66 A3
Buntin (Bunutin) 87 G2
Buntin (Kintamani) 87 G2
Buntin (Taman Bali) 73 M7
Bunyah (Sukadana) 89 L3
Bunyuh (Perean) 72 C2
Buruan (Blah Batuh) 65 J2
Buruan (Buruan) 65 K3
Buruan (Penebel) 71 K5
Buruan (Sanur Kaja) 23 K5
Buruan (Tampak Siring) 73 K3
Buruan Kaja 71 K4
Buruan Kelod 71 L5
Buruan Tengah 71 L5
Busana 64 E5
Busana Kaja 64 C1
Busana Kelod 64 C2
Bustegeh 40 C5
Busung Biu 97 L6
Busung Biu Kaja 97 M7
Busung Biu Kelod 97 L6
Busung Biu Tengah 97 L6
Busungyeh Kangin 28 C8
Busungyeh Kauh 28 C8
Butbaris 106 B5
Butterfly Park 71 K6
Butus 76 C1
Buu 87 J4
Buungan 74 A4
Buwit 63 K6
Buwit Kaja 63 K6
Buwit Tengah 63 K6
Buyan 74 E3
Buyuk 109 G1

C

Cabe 64 D6
Cacab 71 M2
Cacah 108 E5
Cagaan 49 L3
Calik 109 H4
Calo 73 K1
Caluk Kauh 76 D7
Campuan 26 F6
Campuhan 46 B1
Candi Baru 50 B7

Candi Geha 90 B2
Candi Kesuma 78 F6
Candi Kuning 104 A7
Candi Kuning Dua 85 M1
Candi Kuning Satu 99 M7
Candi Permai 52 E7
Candi Tebing Kalebutan 49 K5
Candidasa 52 F6
Candidasa Beach 53 H8
Candra Asri 31 J4
Canggu 25 J5
Canggu Asri 25 L7
Canggu Permai 25 M5
Canggu Surfing 25 H8
Cangi 65 H4
Cangkup (Rejasa) 71 J4
Cangkup (Wana Giri) 70 E4
Cangwang 91 G7
Cantel 70 B4
Cantung 90 A1
Canyon Wreck, Dive Site 94 C1
Carang Sari (Banjar Angkan) 66 C1
Carang Sari (Petang) 72 D4
Carik (Gadungan) 71 G6
Carik (Puhu) 87 H7
Carik (Tista) 63 G2
Carik Padang 63 M4
Caruban 109 H5
Catholic Community 79 H3
Catu 106 F5
Catuk Kangin 76 E7
Catur 104 F5
Catur Panca 21 K2
Cau 72 B2
Cau Belayu 72 C6
Cave Point, Dive Site 92 F1
Cavehouse 108 C1
Cebaang 65 L4
Ceblong 101 M7
Cebok 73 J3
Cegeng 66 E4
Cekeng 74 A5
Cekik (Berembeng) 70 D8
Cekik (Gilimanuk) 92 A6
Ceking 106 E4
Celagi (Denbantas) 71 L7
Celagi (Padang Kerta) 76 E3
Celagi (Seraya Barat) 77 J3
Celagi (Tianyar) 89 G1
Celagi (Unggahan) 97 J6
Celagi Bantar 103 L5
Celagi Basur 36 F3
Celagi Batur 103 K5
Celagi Gendong 28 E8
Celagi Landan 109 J3
Celatiga 67 G2
Celuk (Abang) 76 E2
Celuk (Benoa) 39 H3
Celuk (Buruan) 65 K3
Celuk (Celuk) 65 H6
Celuk (Dalung) 64 B7
Celuk (Kapal) 64 B4
Celuk (Melinggih Kelod) 72 F4
Celuk (Panjer) 21 M5
Celuk (Sangsit) 101 K4
Celuk Agung Beach 53 L2
Celuk Buluh 53 J4
Celuk Kangin 63 G4
Celuk Kawan 63 G4
Celuk Negara 55 D5
Celukan Bawang 96 D3
Cemadik 49 M1
Cemagi (Serampingan) 70 D8
Cemagi (Seseh) 24 B3
Cemara 84 F2
Cemara Agung 20 F2
Cemara Indah 26 D7
Cemenggaon 65 H6
Cemenggon 64 C2
Cemlagi 109 K6
Cempaga (Bangli) 54 C8
Cempaga (Banjar) 98 C4
Cempaka (Lumbung) 70 B6
Cempaka (Pikat) 67 H5
Cemulik 108 D3
Cengiling 35 L6
Cengkilung 64 E6
Cengkog 64 C1
Cengolo 63 G4
Cenigahan 105 J2
Cening Sari 16 C2
Ceningan Kangin 108 C2
Ceningan Kawan 108 C2
Ceningan Reef Surf Break 108 B2
Cepag 71 K4
Cepaka (Cepaka) 63 L6
Cepaka (Gadungan) 71 G5
Cepaka (Kapal) 64 B4
Cepaka (Pangyangan) 68 E3
Cepaka (Pupuan Sawah) 70 F4
Cepaka Dalung 63 M7
Cepik 71 L4
Cepik Kelod 71 L4
Cepunggung 74 E6
Ceramcam 29 L4
Chandra 21 M2
Cheningan Channel 108 C2
Cheningan Wall 108 C2
Chinese Cemetery 48 B2
Chris's Garden, Dive Site 94 D2

Cibukan 70 E5
Cibulik 88 F7
Cice 64 A5
Cingan 74 B4
Circus Waterpark 11 G4
Close Encounters, Dive Site 94 D1
Congkang 98 D3
Coral Garden, Dive Site (Menjangan) 92 F1
Corot (Cempaga) 98 C4
Corot (Dencarik) 97 M3
Crystal Bay 108 C3
Crystal Marine Sports 17 M4
Cubang 108 E3
Cucukan 65 M5
Culagcalig 64 B4
Culik 90 F6
Cupel 80 A6
Curah 63 H3
Cutcut 89 K2
Cutcut Kangin 89 L2
Cutcut Kelod 89 K2

D

Dada Putih 83 J5
Dadia (Babahan) 85 M8
Dadia (Taman Bali) 73 M7
Dadia Puri 73 M8
Dajan Bingin 64 C5
Dajan Ceking 83 K7
Dajan Margi (Nagasepaha) 101 K7
Dajan Margi (Sari Mekar) 101 J6
Dajan Margi (Silang Jana) 99 M2
Dajan Pangkung 104 C2
Dajan Peken (Mengwitani) 63 M4
Dajan Peken (Penarungan) 64 C2
Dajan Peken (Sembung) 72 B5
Dajan Peken (Seririt) 98 J3
Dajan Peken (Tabanan) 63 K2
Dajan Peken (Timpag) 71 H6
Dajan Pura 98 B4
Dajan Rurung (Banjar Asem) 97 G3
Dajan Rurung (Batu Bulan Kangin) 65 G7
Dajan Sema 70 C5
Dajan Tangluk 29 M4
Dakdakan 63 L4
Dalam 75 K7
Dalang Anyar 71 G4
Dalang Desa 71 G3
Dalang Pondok 71 H3
Dalang Tengah 71 G3
Dalem (Agantaka) 64 F5
Dalem (Gumbrih) 68 F4
Dalem (Kayu Putih) 98 D6
Dalem (Kerobokan) 101 K4
Dalem (Pejaten) 63 J5
Dalem (Sinabun) 101 K5
Dalem (Songan A) 106 C7
Dalem (Tianyar) 107 G6
Dalem (Tista) 83 J4
Dalem Kaja 101 K3
Dalung 64 B7
Dalung Kaja 64 B7
Dalung Permai 26 F1
Dama 63 M8
Dama Karya 74 D5
Damai 16 D5
Dangin Bengin 72 C5
Dangin Berawah 80 D8
Dangin Jalan (Guwang) 65 J7
Dangin Jalan (Kelating) 62 F4
Dangin Jelinjing 63 H6
Dangin Labak 48 E7
Dangin Marga 80 F8
Dangin Margi (Bulian) 102 D5
Dangin Margi (Pemaron) 100 F6
Dangin Margi (Pidpid) 76 C1
Dangin Margi (Tampekan) 97 M3
Dangin Numa 63 L6
Dangin Pangkung (Antosari) 70 D7
Dangin Pangkung (Kekeran) 63 M5
Dangin Pangkung (Kelating) 62 F5
Dangin Pangkung (Pekutatan) 68 D3
Dangin Pangkung (Tista) 63 G3
Dangin Pangkung Jangu 81 G5
Dangin Pasar 74 F5
Dangin Peken (Penarungan) 64 C3
Dangin Peken (Seririt) 97 J2
Dangin Pura (Depeha) 102 E6
Dangin Pura (Tiga Wasa) 98 D3
Dangin Puri Kaja 29 H3
Dangin Puri Kangin 29 J6
Dangin Puri Kauh 28 F5
Dangin Puri Kelod 22 B2
Dangin Sema (Baha) 63 L7
Dangin Sema (Bebandem) 76 C2
Dangin Sema (Karang Asem) 55 E6
Dangin Tangluk 29 M5
Dangin Tukad Aya 80 E6
Dangin Yeh (Abian Base) 64 B6
Dangin Yeh (Bungkulan) 101 L3
Dapdap Tebel 106 D4
Daren 69 L6
Darma Kaja 71 K5
Darma Saba 64 D5
Darma Santi 64 D7
Darma Tengah 71 K6
Darma Tiaga 65 J3
Darma Winangun 107 H6
Darma Winangun Dua 107 H6
Darma Winangun Kangin 107 J6

Darma Winangun Satu 107 H6
Darma Yasa 64 B3
Darmaji 89 H3
Dasong 73 G2
Datah 90 D6
Datah Kelodan 90 E6
Datengan 63 L7
Dauh 76 C1
Dauh Jalan 62 F4
Dauh Labak 48 E8
Dauh Marga 80 F7
Dauh Margi (Bulian) 102 C5
Dauh Margi (Pemaron) 100 F6
Dauh Margi (Tirtasari) 98 C6
Dauh Margi (Tunjung) 102 F5
Dauh Munduk 101 M3
Dauh Pala 51 B2
Dauh Pangkung (Pajahan) 83 M4
Dauh Pangkung (Pekutatan) 68 C3
Dauh Pangkung (Tista) 63 G3
Dauh Pangkung (Ume Jero) 98 D8
Dauh Pangkung Jangu 81 G7
Dauh Pasar 81 G7
Dauh Peken (Kaba-Kaba) 63 L5
Dauh Peken (Penarungan) 64 C2
Dauh Peken (Seririt) 97 J3
Dauh Peken (Tabanan) 51 C3
Dauh Pungkung 77 G4
Dauh Pura (Depeha) 102 E5
Dauh Pura (Panji) 101 G7
Dauh Pura (Tiga Wasa) 98 C3
Dauh Puri 21 K2
Dauh Puri Kaja 28 F6
Dauh Puri Kauh 21 H4
Dauh Puri Kelod 21 K4
Dauh Puseh 41 L5
Dauh Rurung 63 H6
Dauh Siong 69 M4
Dauh Tangluk 29 M5
Dauh Tukad (Penglatan) 101 J5
Dauh Tukad (Tenganan) 76 B6
Dauh Uma (Batuan Kaler) 65 G4
Dauh Uma (Bitera) 65 L2
Dauh Waru 80 D6
Dauh Yeh 63 K6
Dauh Yeh Cani 64 D2
Dauma 76 E3
Daup 105 J4
Dausa (Bantang) 105 J3
Dausa (Padang Kerta) 76 D3
Dawan 66 F5
Dawan Kaler 67 G4
Dawan Kelod 67 G5
Dawas 26 E1
Daya 89 H4
Debantas 71 L8
Deep Reef, Dive Site 94 D2
Dehan 108 F5
Delod Bale Agung 63 M3
Delod Berawah 80 F7
Delod Bingin 64 C6
Delod Bung 66 F6
Delod Ceking 69 M5
Delod Margi (Nagasepaha) 101 K7
Delod Margi (Sari Mekar) 101 J7
Delod Margi (Silang Jana) 101 L8
Delod Padonan 25 H4
Delod Pangkung (Budeng) 80 E7
Delod Pangkung (Sukawati) 65 H5
Delod Pasar 64 D1
Delod Peken (Kendran Penataran) 57 F6
Delod Peken (Keramas) 65 L5
Delod Peken (Mengwitani) 64 B4
Delod Peken (Tabanan) 51 D2
Delod Peken (Timpag) 71 H7
Delod Pempatan 63 M5
Delod Pempatan
   (Mendoyo Dangin Tukad) 80 E7
Delod Pura 98 B4
Delod Puri 63 K4
Delod Ruing 63 K2
Delod Rurung (Antosari) 70 C7
Delod Rurung (Batu Bulan Kangin) 65 G7
Delod Rurung (Dajan Peken) 51 C2
Delod Rurung (Pangkung Paruk) 96 F3
Delod Sema (Buwit) 63 K6
Delod Sema (Kekeran) 63 M5
Delod Sema (Lumbung) 70 C6
Delod Sema (Serampingan) 70 D8
Delod Sema (Seraya Barat) 77 H3
Delod Setra 82 B8
Delod Tangluk 65 H6
Delod Tukad 16 C3
Delod Tunon 65 H5
Delod Uma 63 K6
Delod Wates 75 M7
Delod Yeh 63 M5
Demulih (Bangli) 54 A4
Demulih (Susut) 73 M4
Demung 63 K3
Denbantas 71 K8
Dencarik 97 M3
Denjalan 65 G5
Denkayu Baleran 64 B2
Denkayu Delodan 64 B2
Denpasar 21 J3
Dentiyis 65 H5
Denuma (Kukuh) 71 M8
Denuma (Tengkudak) 71 K2

Denyeh 64 D6
Depeha 102 F6
Depo Pertamina 67 K3
Dero Jehem 74 B4
Desa (Agantaka) 64 F5
Desa (Bungaya) 76 C5
Desa (Kayu Putih) 98 E7
Desa (Subagan) 76 D5
Desa (Sudaji) 101 M7
Desa Anyar 69 M6
Desa Dukuh 90 B2
Desa Tengah 76 C4
Dewa Nyoman Batuans
   Community of Artists 49 G7
Dewasana 80 A4
Dharma Jadra 53 M3
Dharma Kerti 100 E6
Dharma Semedi 100 F7
Dharma Yasa 100 F7
Dingin Pangkung 63 L6
Diponegoro Mega Complex 21 K1
Dirgahayu 64 D3
Diving-WW II "The Liberty" Wreck 90 E1
Diving-WW II The Liberty Wreck............ 90 D1
Dlodblumbang 73 J3
Dlotyeh Kangin 67 G3
Dlotyeh Kawan 66 F3
Dlundungan 107 H7
Dlundungan Pasar 107 H7
Dolphin Statue 52 F3
Double Six Beach 14 A2
Dream Wall, Dive Site 92 F1
Dreamland Beach 34 E4
Drop Off 90 E2
Dualang (Kaba-Kaba) 63 L5
Dualang (Peguyangan Kaja) 64 D6
Dualang (Sibang Gede) 64 D4
Duda 75 J6
Duda Timur 75 K7
Duda Utara 75 K5
Dujung Kaja 87 I8
Dukuh 29 L2
Dukuh (Abian Base) 63 M6
Dukuh (Belalang) 63 H6
Dukuh (Bunutin) 73 M7
Dukuh (Dalung) 63 M7
Dukuh (Dauh Peken) 51 B2
Dukuh (Karang Asem) 76 D4
Dukuh (Kelating) 62 F4
Dukuh (Kenderan) 73 H5
Dukuh (Kubu) 90 B2
Dukuh (Mundeh) 69 L3
Dukuh (Nyalian) 66 B2
Dukuh (Nyambung) 63 K5
Dukuh (Padang Kerta) 55 A4
Dukuh (Pejaten) 63 J4
Dukuh (Penebel) 71 L2
Dukuh (Rendang) 74 F6
Dukuh (Sangkan Gunung) 74 F6
Dukuh (Sibetan) 75 L7
Dukuh (Sudaji) 101 M7
Dukuh (Susut) 54 B1
Dukuh (Tiying Gading) 70 D5
Dukuh (Trunyan) 88 E3
Dukuh Buahan 71 L8
Dukuh Bukit Gandang 76 E3
Dukuh Gede 63 G2
Dukuh Geria 47 M5
Dukuh Kawan 47 M6
Dukuh Kuning 71 M2
Dukuh Merta Jati 16 D3
Dukuh Pesirahan 16 A2
Dukuh Pulu Kaja 70 F8
Dukuh Pulu Kelod 62 F2
Dukuh Pulu Tengah 70 F8
Dukuh Sari 16 B3
DukuhKangin 49 K6
Dukun Sampih 76 E1
Dundungan 109 H6
Dungkap Dua 109 G6
Dungkap Satu 109 G6
Dupuan 63 M3
Duren 109 G5
Duren Taluh 70 D2
Dusun Bali International 42 B2
Dusun Chiyoda Town 35 K6
Dusun James Cook Village 35 H5
Dusun Neue Potsdam 35 H4
Dusun Parisian Village 35 H6
Dusun Trafalgar Square Estate............... 35 J4

E

Eco Dive 91 H6
Eel Garden, Dive Site........................ 92 E1
Eha 73 K4
Eka Adnyana 107 H5
Eka Dharma 22 C1
Eka Paksi 21 L2
Ekasari 79 G3
Ekasila 21 L2
Emerald Bay 90 E2
Empalan 85 L8
Enjung Sangiang 52 C3
Euro Dive 91 G5

F

Finish Rafting 48 C2
Fishing Village 67 G6

G

Gablogan 70 D8
Gado Gado Beach 19 H8
Gadon 26 F4
Gaduh (Gianyar Area) 64 B5
Gaduh (Sesetan) 16 B1
Gadungan (Gadungan) 71 G6
Gadungan (Kelusa) 73 H3
Gaga 73 M6
Gagah 73 H3
Gahing 108 E5
Gajah Mina Beach 69 L7
Gaji 64 B7
Galiang 74 F1
Galih 75 L2
Galiran (Bakti Sebaga) 101 G6
Galiran (Tembuku) 74 B5
Galiran Kaler 55 B5
Galiran Kelod 55 L8
Galiukir Kaja 84 A7
Galiukir Kelod 83 M7
Galungan 104 C2
Gamat Bay 108 C2
Gambang (Jineng Dalem) 101 K6
Gambang (Mengwi) 64 B2
Gambang (Munggu) 63 K7
Gambang (Seraya Barat) 77 H3
Gambih 86 F6
Gambuh 98 E2
Gambuk 84 B5
Gamongan (Kaba-Kaba) 63 L6
Gamongan (Selemadeg) 70 E6
Gancam 66 A1
Gandongan 96 E4
Ganggasari 64 B4
Ganter 63 M3
Garba 75 M5
Garden Land Residence 38 E5
Garuda Wisnu Kencana Cultural Park ... 36 F7
Gata 86 F5
Gatot Subroto Permai 28 B3
Gde Jeroan 64 C4
Gde Umah Anyar 64 C5
Gebagan 74 B2
Gede (Abian Base) 64 B6
Gede (Akah) 66 D4
Gede (Batuan) 65 H5
Gede (Kerobokan) 26 F5
Gede (Muncan) 75 G5
Gede (Subagan) 55 A8
Gede Sengguan 64 C7
Gede's Reef, Dive Site 94 D1
Gegadon 64 A5
Gegaran 64 B1
Gegelang (Antiga) 67 J3
Gegelang (Beraban) 63 J6
Geger Sawangan Beach 45 L3
Gejuh 109 H5
Gelagah (Kutampi) 109 H3
Gelagah (Payangan) 71 M4
Gelagah Linggah 105 K6
Gelagah Puwun 63 M5
Gelgel 65 L4
Gelogor (Antapan) 86 D4
Gelogor (Bantas) 70 F7
Gelogor (Lodtunduh) 65 G3
Gelogor (Pemecutan) 28 E8
Gelogor (Pikat) 67 H4
Gelogor Carik 15 G5
Gelulung 65 H6
Gelumpang (Karang Asem) 55 C1
Gelumpang (Sukawati) 65 J6
Gelunggang 70 B2
Geluntung Kaja 72 B4
Geluntung Kelod 71 M5
Geluwung 74 D1
Gembalan 66 D2
Gemeh 28 F8
Gempinis Kangin 71 G2
Gempinis Kauh 71 G2
Gentah 103 J8
Genteng 55 B7
Gentong 49 J1
Gerana 72 D5
Gerebek 102 F5
Gerenceng 28 E6
Geretek 106 D3
Geria (Ayunan) 72 C7
Geria (Batuan) 65 H5
Geria (Culik) 90 F5
Geria (Kawan) 54 D5
Geria (Melinggih) 72 F3
Geria (Menanga) 74 E5
Geria (Nyalian) 66 B3
Geria Ciwa 65 H5
Geriana Kangin 75 K6
Gerih 65 G5
Gerobog 77 G5
Gerokgak (Buleleng) 95 L4
Gerokgak (Tabanan) 51 D3
Gerokgak (Sempidi) 64 B6
Gerokgak Gede 51 D4
Gerokgak Tengah 51 D3
Gerombong 62 E3
Gerontang 43 K8
Gesing 98 E8
Gesing Dua 84 E1
Gesing Satu 84 E1

Gesing Tiga 98 F8
Getakan 66 B4
Getas 89 M3
Getas Kangin 65 K3
Getas Kawan 65 K3
Getas Keja 107 G6
Getasan Kauh 72 E3
Getasan Tengah 72 E3
Gianyar 50 C6
Gilimanuk 92 A5
Gingsir 66 D4
Giri Hill Terrace 38 B5
Giri Kesuma 72 F2
Giri Loka (Munduk) 99 M6
Giri Loka (Panca Sari) 99 H7
Giri Puspa 37 M3
Giri Sari 41 H6
Gisnu 70 F2
Gitgit (Bakbakan) 73 L8
Gitgit (Gitgit) 99 K3
Gitgit Waterfall 99 K2
Global Village 38 D4
Goa 49 K7
Goa Gajah (Elephant Cave) 49 K7
Goa Garba 49 M5
Goa Lawah Beach 67 M3
Goa Lawah/Bat Cave Temple 67 J6
Goa Raksasa 65 G2
Gobleg 98 E6
Gomongon 76 F2
Gondol 95 G3
Gondol Beach 95 J3
Gong 64 B4
Goris 93 L4
Goris Kelod 93 L4
Graha Kerti 16 D4
Graha LivaKerta Langu 31 G3
Graha Nusa Dua 32 C8
Graha Santi 28 B8
Grand Bali Beach, The, Golf Course 23 L5
Green Bowl Surfing Area 43 L8
Griya (Banyu Poh) 94 E2
Griya (Tampak Siring) 73 K3
Griya Alam Pecatu 34 F5
Griya Alam Pecatu 42 C2
Griya Bali 19 M3
Griya Bali - Intan Permai 19 L4
Griya Dana 16 D4
Griya Mandiri 37 L3
Griya Nuansa Pratama 37 J4
Griya Nuansa Raya 26 D1
Griya Nusa Damai 37 L1
Griya Permata 36 C8
Griya Sanga Magening 23 H5
Gubat 49 M6
Gubug 63 H3
Gubug Baleran 63 H3
Gubug Belodan 63 H3
Guliang 49 L5
Guliang Kangin 65 M1
Guliang Kawan 73 M8
Gulingan (Antosari) 70 C6
Gulingan (Darma Saba) 64 D5
Gulingan (Mengwi) 64 B3
Gulingan (Sanur) 23 J6
Gulinten 91 G7
Gumasih 64 D3
Gumbrih 68 F3
Gumicik 31 L4
Guming 64 D2
Gunaksa (Ababi) 76 C1
Gunaksa (Cempaga) 54 E2
Gunaksa (Kenderan) 73 H4
Gunaksa (Klungkung) 66 E5
Guniyang 70 E5
Gunung (Abian Semal) 64 D2
Gunung (Batu Bulan) 65 G7
Gunung (Peguyangan Kaja) 64 D6
Gunung (Penatih Dangin Puri) 64 F7
Gunung (Penebel) 71 L2
Gunung (Tenganan) 76 C5
Gunung (Ubud) 48 A1
Gunung Agung 107 K7
Gunung Bau 105 H7
Gunung Biau 75 G5
Gunung Buduk 63 M7
Gunung Ina 97 J4
Gunung Jawi 83 H6
Gunung Kawi 73 K2
Gunung Lebah 88 E8
Gunung Merta 83 J5
Gunung Pande 63 L7
Gunung Rata 66 C3
Gunung Salak 70 F6
Gunung Sari (Mengwitani) 64 B4
Gunung Sari (Padang Sambian Kaja) 64 C7
Gunung Sari (Pemogan) 15 J1
Gunung Sari (Sepang Kelod) 83 G3
Gunung Sari (Seririt) 98 B6
Gunung Sari (Tegal Linggah) 99 G2
Gunung Sari (Temukus) 98 B3
Gunung Sari (Yangapi) 74 C2
Gunung Sari Desa 85 K6
Gunung Sari Uma Kayu 85 K5
Gunung Sekar (Kayu Putih) 98 F2
Gunung Sekar (Pohsanten) 80 F4
Gunung Siku 71 M8
Guwang 31 L3

H

Heron & Egret Resting Area 49 H2
Historic Site 90 B8
Hitbhuana 28 E1
Holy Spring 87 J8
Holy Waringin Tree 72 D7
Hot Spring (Banjar) 97 L4
Hot Spring (Penebel) 71 K3
Hot Spring (Wana Giri) 99 J4
Hot Spring Belulang 85 L8

I

Ideran 98 D7
Impossibles Beach 34 C6
Insakan 98 E5
Intaran 49 L6
Ipah 75 G6
Ipil 70 F7
Isoh (Klumbu) 109 G3
Iseh (Sidemen) 75 H7
Istana Regency 16 B5

J

Jaang 86 E7
Jaba Jero 11 G2
Jaba Pura (Kutuh) 44 B5
Jaba Pura (Padang Sambian Kelod) 20 C5
Jabe Jero 64 F5
Jabon 66 E5
Jadi Babakan 71 L8
Jadi Desa 63 L2
Jadi Pesona 16 A4
Jadi Pesona Barat 21 M7
Jaga Pati 64 F6
Jaga Raga 101 M5
Jaga Satru 63 L4
Jaga Tamu 71 G8
Jageperang 65 M2
Jakatebel 62 E3
Jalanbau 73 M3
Jambe 27 G4
Jambe Baleran 51 B1
Jambe Belodan 51 B2
Jangkahan (Batu Aji) 71 J7
Jangkahan (Biaung) 71 M2
Jangkahan (Kayu Bihi) 74 B3
Jangu 75 J7
Jarak 109 G6
Jarat 101 J4
Jasan 87 K7
Jasi Kaler 76 E5
Jasi Kauh 76 E6
Jasri 65 K4
Jati (Kedisan) 88 C3
Jati (Sebatu) 87 J6
Jati Luwih 85 K6
Jati Luwih Kangin 85 K6
Jati Luwih Kawan 85 K6
Jatituhu 89 H3
Jawa Barat 57 D4
Jawa Timur 57 D4
Jaya Giri 29 H8
Jaya Giri 22 B1
Jaya Maruti 105 L5
Jayakarta 31 J3
Jebaud 63 M2
Jegu 71 K4
Jegu Pande 71 K4
Jegu Tegal 71 K5
Jegu Tengah 71 K4
Jehem 74 C6
Jehem Kaja 74 B6
Jehem Kelod 74 C7
Jelai 63 G4
Jelantik 86 B7
Jelantik Kali Bukbuk 86 C7
Jelantik Kelodan 86 B7
Jelantik Kuri Batu 66 D6
Jelantik Mamoran 66 D6
Jeleka 65 H5
Jelekungkang 66 A3
Jelijih 84 C8
Jelijih Lebah 70 F6
Jelijih Pondok 70 F6
Jelijih Tegeh 70 E7
Jematang 21 J2
Jembong 98 E6
Jembrana 70 E8
Jemeluk 91 H5
Jemeluk Bay 91 H5
Jemeng 72 D4
Jempanang 104 E7
Jempeng 72 E5
Jempinis 25 J2
Jenagung 92 A5
Jenah 64 E6
Jenati 106 B4
Jepun 109 J2
Jero 101 K4
Jero Agung (Kalopaksa) 97 H4
Jero Agung (Kamasan) 66 D6
Jero Gusti 101 M3
Jero Kapal 66 D6
Jero Margi 101 M3
Jeroan (Abian Base) 63 M5
Jeroan (Buduk) 63 L7
Jeroan (Patemon) 97 J3
Jeroan (Selemadeg) 70 E7
Jimbaran Baru 32 C7

Jimbaran Carik 19 H7
Jimbaran Wild Beach 36 A1
Jineng Dalem 101 K5
Joanyar 97 L3
Joanyar Kajanan 97 L4
Joanyar Kelodan 97 K3
Juga 65 H3
Jugul 75 M2
Jujuk 67 G6
Jukung Dive 91 G5
Jukutpaku 64 F2
Julah 103 J5
Julingan 109 J6
Jumbayah 63 M4
Jumenang 77 G2
Jumpai 66 E7
Jumpai Kanginan 66 E7
Jumpai Kawan 66 E7
Jungjungan 73 H5
Jungseri 76 C3
Jungut 65 H5
Jungut Batu 108 C1
Jungutan 75 M6
Juntal (Kaba-Kaba) 63 L5
Juntal (Tinga-Tinga) 96 D3
Juntal Kangin 90 B1
Juntal Kauh 90 B2
Jurang Asri 64 D7
Jurang Aya 109 H3
Jurang Pahit 109 G2
Juwet 72 D1
Juwuk 90 D6
Juwuk Bali 73 M4
Juwuk Legi 86 C3
Juwuk Manis (Alas Angker) 101 M7
Juwuk Manis (Duda Timur) 75 K7
Juwuk Manis (Karang Asem) 55 B2
Juwuk Mas 99 M6

K

Kaba-Kaba (Kediri) 63 L6
Kabakaba (Selemadeg) 70 D8
Kabetan Kaja 73 L6
Kabetan Kelod 73 L7
Kacagbalung 77 J2
Kacang Raya 51 F8
Kadewatan 69 K3
Kadewatan Anyar 48 D2
Kaja (Renon) 23 G4
Kaja Dua 108 C1
Kaja Jati 37 J6
Kaja Satu 108 C1
Kalah 49 G7
Kalang Anyar (Banjar Asem) 97 G3
Kalang Anyar (Datah) 90 D6
Kalang Anyar (Jehem) 74 C3
Kalang Anyar (Jimbaran) 32 D6
Kalang Anyar (Seraya Barat) 77 H3
Kalang Anyar (Sudimara) 63 G4
Kalang Sari 90 D6
Kaler (Gegelang) 67 J4
Kaler (Seraya Barat) 77 H3
Kaler (Tusan) 66 B5
Kaleran (Bungbungan) 74 C8
Kaleran (Manduang) 66 C3
Kaleran (Yehembang) 81 L6
Kali Akah 79 L8
Kali Anyar 67 J2
Kali Asem 52 D4
Kali Bandan 98 D8
Kali Bayang 72 B2
Kali Sada 96 F3
Kali Ungu Kaja 29 G5
Kali Ungu Kelod 29 G6
Kali Untu Dua 57 B4
Kali Untu Satu 57 C5
Kalibukbuk 53 G2
Kalibul 26 D2
Kalibul Kangin 26 D1
Kalibul Kawan 26 C2
Kalopaksa 97 H4
Kamasan (Klungkung) 66 D6
Kamasan (Tabanan) 51 E2
Kambang 48 B5
Kampial Indah 38 C6
Kampial Permai 38 C7
Kampial Residence 2 .... 38 B5
Kampung Anyar (Bukit) 77 G2
Kampung Anyar (Kampung Anyar) 57 C3
Kampung Baru 57 E2
Kampung Bugis 57 C2
Kampung Gegel 66 G6
Kampung Islam Kusamba 67 G7
Kampung Jawa 28 F4
Kampung Kajanan 57 D3
Kampung Singaraja 57 F7
Kancil 26 E5
Kandulatas 99 H2
Kangin Dua 108 C2
Kangin Luan 101 M5
Kangin Satu 108 C2
Kangin Teben 101 M5
Kangkaang 90 E6
Kangkang 25 J1
Kangkid 102 D6
Kapal (Mengwi) 64 B4
Kapal (Sukawati) 65 G7
Kapas Jawa 84 B2
Kapit 66 B3

Karang 94 E2
Karang Anyar (Candidasa) 52 D5
Karang Anyar (Denpasar) 29 H2
Karang Anyar (Kubu) 107 L8
Karang Anyar (Sanding) 73 J5
Karang Anyar (Sibetan) 75 L6
Karang Asem (Amlapura) 55 E6
Karang Asem (Sengkidu) 76 A7
Karang Beach 17 M1
Karang Bilis 109 L5
Karang Bromo 40 E6
Karang Cermen 55 F3
Karang Dadi 66 F7
Karang Dalem Dua 72 F5
Karang Dalem Satu 72 F5
Karang Dawa 108 D5
Karang Gede 109 K5
Karang Jung 72 B5
Karang Langko 55 D6
Karang Sari (Denpasar) 29 G3
Karang Sari (Ekasari) 78 F3
Karang Sari (Suana) 109 J3
Karang Sari (Sukadana) 107 K6
Karang Sasak (Bukit) 77 G2
Karang Sasak (Tegal Linggah) 76 F3
Karang Sekong 55 A6
Karang Suling 64 C6
Karang Suung Kaja 74 D5
Karang Suung Kelod 74 D5
Karang Suwung (Melinggih) 72 F3
Karang Suwung (Pedungan) 21 K7
Karipan 63 L3
Karipan Kaja 63 L3
Karipan Kelod 63 L3
Karma 99 M6
Karya Dharma 16 C4
Karyanadi 97 K5
Karyasari (Belimbing) 84 E8
Karyasari (Perean Tengah) 72 D3
Kastala 76 B4
Katiklantang 46 A8
Katimemes 63 G4
Katulampa Kaja 79 K6
Katulampa Kelod 79 J6
Katung 87 J3
Kauh Teben 101 M4
Kauhluan 101 M5
Kauman 97 J2
Kauripan (Awan) 105 H6
Kauripan (Pering) 65 J5
Kauripan (Sedang) 64 F4
Kawan (Bakas) 66 B4
Kawan (Bakbakan) 73 L8
Kawan (Kawan) 54 C5
Kawan (Manggis) 67 M2
Kawan (Mas) 65 H3
Kawan (Muncan) 75 G5
Kawan (Patemon) 97 J3
Kawan (Petandakan) 101 K7
Kawan (Saba) 65 J5
Kawan (Tampak Siring) 73 J3
Kawanan (Julah) 103 J5
Kawum 97 K6
Kayang 74 B4
Kayangan 64 E7
Kayehan 66 F4
Kayu Ambua 87 M6
Kayu Aya 107 K8
Kayu Bihi 74 B4
Kayu Kapas 105 K7
Kayu Mas Kaja 29 G7
Kayu Mas Kelod 29 H8
Kayu Padi (Besakih) 75 G2
Kayu Padi (Pupuan) 84 B3
Kayu Padi (Songan B) 106 C6
Kayu Puring 84 C3
Kayu Putih (Banjar) 98 D7
Kayu Putih (Bungaya Kangin) 76 B4
Kayu Putih (Kayu Putih) 98 E2
Kayu Putih (Sangga Langit) 95 K5
Kayu Putih (Sukasada) 98 E2
Kayu Putih Kelod 95 K5
Kayu Selem 106 E6
Kayu Sugih 96 E5
Kayu Tulang 25 M2
Kebalian 65 J6
Kebayan (Abian Base) 63 M6
Kebayan (Nyambung) 63 K5
Kebebeng 80 F7
Kebek 87 G7
Kebibil 63 H6
Kebon (Bajera) 70 D7
Kebon (Baler Bale Agung) 56 C2
Kebon (Blah Batuh) 65 J4
Kebon (Kedisah) 73 H3
Kebon (Kertha Mandala) 90 E6
Kebon (Nyitdah) 63 J5
Kebon (Pandak Gede) 63 J6
Kebon (Peninjoan) 74 D4
Kebon (Sampalan Tengah) 66 F5
Kebon (Sidemen) 75 G8
Kebon (Sulahan) 73 L3
Kebon (Tangguntiti) 62 E2
Kebon Agung 98 B7
Kebon Ayar 70 E2
Kebon Bantiran 70 E2
Kebon Bukit 77 G3
Kebon Cepaka 70 E2
Kebon Jero Kangin 83 L7
Kebon Jero Kauh 83 K7

Kebon Kaja (Balege) 65 K4
Kebon Kaja (Kebon Padangan) 84 B6
Kebon Kangin 74 D3
Kebon Kauh 74 D2
Kebon Kelod (Balege) 65 K4
Kebon Kelod (Kebon Padangan) 84 B6
Kebon Kuri Kelod 30 B7
Kebon Kuri Lukluk 29 M6
Kebon Kuri Mangku 30 B6
Kebon Kuri Tengah 30 B6
Kebon Padangan 84 B6
Kebon Sari 57 E2
Kebon Tumpalan 70 E2
Kebung 67 H2
Kecag Balung 77 J2
Kecak Dance 47 H2
Kecak Fire & Trance Dance 47 G3
Kecicang Bali 76 D5
Kecicang Indah 76 D4
Kecicang Islam 76 D4
Ked 87 H8
Kedampal (Babahan) 85 L8
Kedampal (Datah) 90 B6
Kedampal (Dauh Yehcani) 72 C8
Kedampal (Mengesta) 71 L1
Kedaton (Jl. W.R. Suptratman) 30 B5
Kedaton (Jl. Waribang) 30 D7
Kedaton (Sumerta Kelod) 29 K7
Kedaton (Tonja) 29 J1
Keden 31 M1
Kedese 95 L5
Kedewatan 48 C3
Kediri 63 K4
Kedis 84 B1
Kedis Kaja 98 B8
Kedis Kauh 97 M8
Kedis Kelod 98 B8
Kedisan (Kedisan) 88 C3
Kedisan (Kintamani) 88 C3
Kedisan (Tegal Lalang) 73 J2
Kedisan (Yehembang Kauh) 81 K5
Kedisan Kaja 73 J2
Kedisan Kelod 73 J2
Kedok Darsana 55 E5
Kedonganan 32 C2
Kedua (Baha) 72 C8
Kedua (Peguyangan Kangin) 64 E6
Kedui 74 C5
Kedungdung 74 F3
Kedungu 63 H6
Keduran 103 J7
Kehen 30 B3
Kejanan 103 K7
Kekeran (Agantaka) 64 F5
Kekeran (Busung Biu) 97 M7
Kekeran (Mengwi) 63 M5
Kekeran (Penatahan) 71 K4
Kekeran (Selanbawak) 72 B6
Kekeran Kanginan 97 M7
Kekeran Kauhan 97 M7
Kelabang Moding 73 G5
Kelaci 71 M5
Keladian (Besakih) 74 F1
Keladian (Dangin Tukad Aya) 80 E6
Kelagi 72 B4
Kelakah 76 D1
Kelakahan Gede 63 K6
Kelakahan Kangin 63 K6
Kelakat 88 C6
Kelampuak 102 E6
Kelan Abian 32 D1
Kelan Desa 11 H5
Kelandis (Denpasar) 29 J8
Kelandis (Pakisan) 104 E1
Kelapa Balian 80 B7
Kelating 62 F5
Kelating Beach 62 E5
Kelau 83 M5
Kelecung 62 D2
Kelembang Kaja 71 J4
Kelembang Kelod 71 J4
Kelepekan 63 L8
Keliki (Keliki) 73 G4
Keliki (Munggu) 63 J7
Keliki (Penuktukan) 106 B2
Keliki Kawan 73 G4
Kelingkung 65 G3
Kelisih 107 G6
Kelod Dua 108 C2
Kelod Kauh 103 K5
Kelod Kuta 103 K5
Keloncing 85 J8
Kelungah 66 F2
Kelupak 70 C4
Kelurahan Anturan 53 M4
Kelurahan Kali Asem 52 D3
Kelusa 73 G4
Kelusu 49 M5
Kemasan 63 K2
Kembang 80 A6
Kembang Kencana 29 M2
Kembang Merta (Candi Kuning) 99 M7
Kembang Merta (Penglumbaran) 87 M7
Kembang Rejasa 83 J3
Kembang Sari (Blahkiuh) 72 D7
Kembang Sari (Satra) 105 G2
Kembang Sari (Warna Sari) 79 J3
Kembang Tebel 97 H4
Kembangan 86 B7
Kembengan 66 A5

Kemenuh 65 G4
Kemenuh Kangin 65 J4
Kemenuh Kelod 65 J4
Kemetug Desa 70 F4
Kemetug Kanciana Kaja 70 F2
Kemetug Kanciana Kelod 70 F2
Kemoning (Puncak Sari) 83 K3
Kemoning (Tukad Aya) 79 K4
Kemulan 64 F5
Kemuning Kaja 51 C6
Kemuning Kelod 51 C7
Kendal 106 E5
Kenderan 73 H5
Kendran Penataran 57 E6
Kengetan 64 F3
Kepisah (Pedungan) 21 K7
Kepisah (Sumerta Kelod) 29 L7
Kepitu 73 H5
Kepuh (Mendoyo Dauh Tukad) 80 F6
Kepuh (Peguyangan) 64 D7
Keraman 64 D2
Keramas 65 L5
Kerambitan 63 G3
Kerandan 28 D7
Keranjangan 73 L1
Kereteg 66 B4
Keridan 85 M7
Kerobokan (Kelurahan) 27 G5
Kerobokan (Kerobokan Kelod) 19 L4
Kerobokan (Loloan Barat) 56 C7
Kerobokan (Mekar Sari) 86 C6
Kerobokan (Munggu) 63 K7
Kerobokan (Sawan) 101 K4
Kerobokan (Sengan) 83 J4
Kerobokan Beach 18 F5
Kerobokan Kaja 27 G3
Kerobokan Kelod 19 K3
Kerta (Payangan) 87 H4
Kerta (Petang) 86 D7
Kerta (Wana Giri) 70 E3
Kerta Buana (Batur Selatan) 105 L7
Kerta Buana (Tianyar Tengah) 107 G5
Kerta Budi 105 M6
Kerta Graha 30 C2
Kerta Jiwa 30 F3
Kerta Kawat 94 F2
Kerta Nadi (Denpasar) 28 C2
Kerta Nadi (Rangdu) 97 K5
Kerta Pascima 33 J1
Kerta Petasikan 16 F5
Kerta Raharja 16 F4
Kerta Sari (Padang Kerta) 76 D3
Kerta Sari (Panjer) 22 C5
Kerta Sari (Peguyangan) 64 D7
Kerta Sari (Sidakerta) 16 E2
Kerta Usada 16 E4
Kerta Warah Kangin 76 E2
Kerta Warah Kawan 76 E2
Kerta Bhuana 29 H4
Kertha Bhuana Kaja 29 H4
Kertha Bumi 29 K5
Kertha Darma 28 B7
Kertha Jati 28 B5
Kertha Langu 30 D4
Kertha Lestari 16 F5
Kertha Lestari 42 F5
Kertha Mandala 90 E7
Kertha Pura (Kesiman Kertha Langu) ... 30 D4
Kertha Pura (Pemecutan) 28 B6
Kertha Sari 28 B5
Kertha Yasa 32 D3
Kesambahan Kaja 85 K6
Kesambahan Kelod 85 K7
Kesambi (Jati Luwih) 85 K7
Kesambi (Kerobokan) 27 G5
Kesambi (Kesiman Kertha Langu) 30 F5
Kesambi Kembar 35 G3
Kesian 65 M4
Kesianan 72 E2
Kesiman 29 M5
Kesiman Kertha Langu 30 F3
Kesiman Palace 30 A5
Kesiman Petilan 30 A4
Kesimpar 75 H3
Kesimpar Kaler 90 D7
Kesimpar Kangin 90 D8
Kesimpar Kelod Dulu 90 D8
Kesimpar Kelod Teben 90 D8
Kesiut 71 J6
Kesiut Kangin 71 J6
Kesiut Kawan Kaja 71 J6
Kesiut Kawan Kelod 71 J6
Kesiut Tengah Kaja 71 J6
Kesiut Tengah Kelod 71 J6
Kesuma Jati 29 M5
Kesuma Sari 34 E6
Kesuma Sari Beach 17 M5
Ketadan 71 L3
Ketapang (Jimbaran) 32 C3
Ketapang (Lelateng) 56 B6
Ketapang (Pangambengan) 80 B8
Ketapang Kangin 109 H1
Ketapang Kauh 109 H1
Ketapang Muara 80 C8
Ketapian Kaja 29 L5
Ketapian Kelod 29 L6
Ketewel (Singaraja) 101 J5
Ketewel (Sukawati) 31 M1
Ketewel Beach 31 M4
Ketima 71 G3

Ketiman 79 J6
Ketuk 67 J3
Ketuketug 101 K5
Ketutug 56 E6
Kiadan 86 E2
Kiduling Kreteg 75 G2
Kihkian 76 E1
Kikian (Pupuan Sawah) 70 D4
Kikian (Sidemen) 75 G7
Kikian (Sulahan) 73 M2
Kikik 71 M5
Kintamani 105 L6
Kirana 21 M2
Klatakan 78 C1
Klau 84 B4
Klempung 74 C3
Kloncing 101 K4
Klotok Beach 66 D7
Klumbu 108 F3
Kodok 67 K3
Kolega 89 J1
Komala 76 C3
Kombading 80 C7
KompiangSujana Stadium 28 A6
Komplek BI 22 B7
Komplek TNI (Pendem) 56 E3
Komplek TNI Yon Raider 900 .... 57 C6
Kontrak 85 M3
Koreteg 76 A4
Kori Nuansa Jimbaran 37 K5
Kosala 32 F6
Kreneng 29 H6
Kreneng Kaja 29 H6
Kresek 75 M5
Kubakal 74 D2
Kube 84 C3
Kubu (Bangli) 74 B5
Kubu (Kubu) 107 L8
Kubu (Pegayaman) 99 L2
Kubu Alit 32 C2
Kubu Anyar (Kubu Tambahan) 102 B3
Kubu Anyar (Pacung) 103 J5
Kubu Beach 35 J2
Kubu Jati 101 J4
Kubu Kanglu 90 C1
Kubu Kelod 101 M2
Kubu Kili 101 M7
Kubu Pangi 75 L4
Kubu Pratama Indah 15 G3
Kubu Salia 105 L2
Kubu Suih 74 C3
Kubu Tambahan 102 B3
Kubu Tambahan Kaja Kangin 102 C3
Kubur 31 M3
Kuburan Kapal, Dive Site 94 D1
Kuda 87 L4
Kuhum 76 E2
Kukuh (Kerambitan) 63 G3
Kukuh (Lalang Linggah) 69 L6
Kukuh (Marga) 71 M8
Kukuh Kangin 63 H2
Kukuh Kawan 63 G2
Kukuh Kelod 63 H3
Kukul Batu 71 G3
Kulat 40 D3
Kulekan 73 J4
Kulub 73 K4
Kulub Batu 65 G2
Kumedesa 106 C5
Kumkeladi 71 H4
Kumuh 74 C5
Kunci 98 C3
Kundalini 97 H3
Kuning 64 B7
Kuning 66 A2
Kunyit 74 F2
Kupang 71 L2
Kupe 74 E6
Kuripan Kangin 66 C6
Kuripan Tengah 66 C6
Kurubaya 64 G4
Kusambi 77 L1
Kusia 102 B7
Kuta 14 E7
Kuta Bali (Biaung) 71 M4
Kuta Bali (Sibetan) 75 M6
Kuta Beach 14 C8
Kuta Dalem 105 L4
Kuta Permai 11 J2
Kuta Raga 48 A6
Kuta Undisan 74 B3
Kutampi 109 H3
Kutri (Buruan) 65 G5
Kutri (Singapadu Tengah) 65 J2
Kutuh (Kintamani) 103 L8
Kutuh (Kuta) 44 B3
Kutuh (Kutuh) 105 L1
Kutuh (Ubud) 48 D4
Kutuh Kaja 49 H3
Kutuh Kaja (Samsam) 71 J8
Kutuh Kelod 47 H2
Kutuh Kelod (Samsam) 51 A1
Kutup 72 C3
Kutupang 70 B8
Kuum (Marga) 72 A7
Kuwum Ancak 71 M7
Kuwum Anyar 71 M6
Kuwum Kumambal 71 M6
Kuwum Tegal Linggah 71 M6

Kuwun (Banyu Atis) 98 C7
Kuwun (Sembung) 72 C4
Kwanji (Dalung) 64 B7
Kwanji (Sempidi) 64 B7

L

La Stella Bali 37 M2
Laba Amarta 97 G5
Laba Sari (Abang) 90 F5
Laba Sari (Kalopaksa) 97 G4
Labak (Anturan) 100 E7
Labak (Timpag) 71 H6
Labanangga 96 F4
Labuan 67 K4
Labuan Sait 41 G1
Labuan Sait Beach 34 B7
Labuhan Aji 98 B2
Labuhan Lalang 93 H4
Lacerations Surf Break 108 B1
Ladalang 63 M2
Laga Kaler 90 C7
Laing 63 K5
Lakah 97 M4
Lalang Gading 83 L6
Lalang Linggah 69 L6
Lalang Linggah Kangin 69 M7
Lalang Pasek 63 L6
Laleng 70 E4
Lambing (Mambal) 64 E3
Lambing (Sibang Kaja) 64 E4
Lampu 104 F4
Landih 88 B7
Langgahan 87 G3
Langgahan Kangin 87 H3
Langgahan Kauh 87 G3
Langkan 88 C6
Langki 109 H6
Langon 64 B5
Langsat 74 F5
Langudu Kangin 63 G6
Langudu Kawan 63 G6
Lantang Bejuh 16 B2
Lantang Hidung 65 H6
Lantang Katik 75 G8
Lap Lapan 49 G3
Lapangan Lumintang 28 F2
Lapangan Padang Galak 30 E5
Lapangan Pratu Gentir 25 J1
Laplap 64 F7
Laplap Kauh 64 F7
Laplap Kelod 65 G7
Laplap Prya 64 F7
Laplap Sengguan 64 F7
Laplap Tengah 64 F7
Lateng (Dausa) 105 J3
Lateng (Sibang Kaja) 64 D4
Lateng (Sukawana) 105 M2
Lawak 104 F7
Leba 72 D3
Lebah (Dajan Peken) 51 C2
Lebah (Datah) 90 D6
Lebah (Dencarik) 97 L3
Lebah (Keramas) 65 L5
Lebah (Marga) 71 M5
Lebah (Purwa Kerthi) 91 G6
Lebah (Sekumpul) 102 C8
Lebah (Semarapura Kangin) 51 E6
Lebah (Sukadana) 107 J6
Lebah (Susut) 54 A3
Lebah (Suwug) 101 L6
Lebah (Tista) 63 G3
Lebah (Ubud) 49 K7
Lebah (Ume Jero) 98 E8
Lebah A 87 G8
Lebah B 73 G2
Lebah Mantung (Pangkung Paruk) 97 G5
Lebah Mantung (Sari Mekar) 101 J7
Lebah Pangkung 63 M3
Lebah Sari (Bungaya) 76 C5
Lebah Sari (Gulingan) 64 B3
Lebah Sari (Mambal) 64 D4
Lebah Seri 97 J6
Lebah Siung 100 F7
Lebak 53 L4
Lebak Suren Delod Sema 70 C7
Lebak Suren Satu 70 C7
Lebah 29 J6
Lebih (Asah Duren) 82 E7
Lebih (Gianyar) 65 M4
Lebih (Sebudi) 75 H3
Lebih Beach 66 A8
Lebih Duur Kaja 65 M4
Lebih Duur Kelod 66 A7
Lebu Anyar 66 E4
Lebu Babakan 66 E3
Lebu Bungbungan 66 F4
Lebu Gede 66 E4
Ledok 82 C8
Leg 86 F6
Legian 14 C4
Legian Beach 14 B4
Legian Kaja 14 C3
Legian Kelod 14 E5
Legian Tengah 14 D4
Legombang Indah 31 K4
Lekok 66 E5
Lelangon 28 F6
Lelateng 56 C6
Lemaya 104 C2
Lembean 87 H2

Lembeng Beach 31 K5
Lembongan 108 B2
Lembongan Kaja 108 B2
Lembongan Kangin 108 B2
Lembongan Kawan 108 B2
Lembongan Kelod 108 B2
Lemodang 80 D8
Lempuyang Kaja 91 G8
Lempuyang Kelod 91 G8
Lemukih 104 C3
Lenganan 70 D6
Lepang Beach 66 C7
Lepang Kangin 66 C7
Lepang Kawan 66 C7
Les (Pecatu) 40 D2
Les (Tejakula) 106 B3
Les Kanginan 106 B3
Les Kawanan 106 B2
Lesek 77 K2
Let 87 K5
Leyan 91 K6
Leyan Dua 91 K6
Leyan Tiga 91 J6
Liligundi (Bebandem) 76 B3
Liligundi (Liligundi) 57 F8
Liligundi (Ubung Kaja) 64 C7
Limbur Sari 70 F3
Limo 109 G2
Limo Kelod 109 G3
Lingga Beach 57 A3
Lingga Sana 76 B2
Lingga Wana 90 F7
Linjong 87 M5
Lipah 86 D7
Lipah Bay 91 K6
Liplip 79 L7
Lobong 48 D7
Lodsema (Singapadu Kaler) 65 G5
Lodsema (Taro) 73 H1
Lodtunduh 65 G4
Loji 68 B2
Loka Serana 49 M5
Loloan 68 B1
Loloan Barat 56 C7
Loloan Timur 56 E7
Longan 23 J5
Longsegeha 101 K7
Losan 66 C6
Lotus Garden 30 D2
Lovina Beach 53 G4
Luah 66 F1
Luahan 105 H5
Lubang Nagaloka 85 J1
Luglug 31 K3
Luhur 67 K4
Lukluk 64 C5
Lumajang 71 H8
Lumbanan 99 J1
Lumbuan 73 M1
Lumbung (Selemadeg) 70 C5
Lumbung (Tegal Lalang) 73 J3
Lumbung Kauh 70 A4
Lumbung Sari 29 G3
Lumintang 28 E3
Lungsiakan 48 D1
Lusuh Kangin 75 H6
Lusuh Kawan 75 H5
Luwus 86 C8

M

Mabi 105 H4
Macang (Batu Madeg) 108 F5
Macang (Sibetan) 76 A4
Madan 95 J4
Madangan Kaja 73 L5
Madangan Kelod 73 L6
Madenan 103 J8
Madenan Kelodan 103 K7
Mahsa Tama Graha 26 B2
Majangan 86 F5
Majapahit 79 K8
Maju Kauh 109 J2
Malet Gede 87 L5
Malet Gusti 87 M6
Malet Kuta Mesir 87 L6
Malet Seri Batu 87 M6
Malet Tampak Siring 87 L7
Malet Tengah 87 L5
Malibu Point 109 L5
Malkangin 51 D2
Malmundeh 63 L4
Mambal 64 D3
Mambal Kajanan 64 D3
Mambang 62 F2
Mambang Celuk Kaja 70 F8
Mambang Gede 62 F2
Mambang Kaja 70 F8
Mambang Tengah 70 F8
Manasa 101 L5
Manca Warna 73 K4
Mancak 101 M3
Mancingan (Manukaya) 73 K2
Mancingan (Penglumbaran) 87 M7
Mandala Sari 21 M4
Mandala Wangi Asri 16 C2
Mandala Wisata 64 A3
Mandar 80 A7
Manduang 66 C3
Mandul (Luwus) 86 D8
Mandul (Panji) 101 H8

Mandung 71 H8
Manekaji 89 H2
Mangenu Anyar 69 J1
Manggan 74 E6
Manggis 67 L2
Manggis Sari 83 G6
Mangguh 87 J2
Mangku 67 K2
Mangkuning 73 K3
Mangrove, Dive Site 92 F1
Manigunung 72 B6
Manik 75 G5
Manik Aji 74 D4
Manik Liyu 105 H8
Manik Saga 21 M4
Manik Tawang 73 L2
Manikan 65 H7
Manikyang 70 F5
Manis Tutu 80 A3
Manjan 86 C7
Manta Point 108 F7
Mantri 77 G4
Mantring (Petak Kaja) 73 L4
Mantring (Tampak Siring) 73 K2
Manuk 73 L3
Manukaya 87 K8
Manukaya Anyar 73 K2
Manukaya Let 73 K1
Manuksesa 104 D1
Manut Negara 28 A7
Manyar 31 M3
Maos 109 H2
Marga 72 A5
Marga Bingung 49 L7
Marga Jati 28 D3
Marga Sari 84 D3
Marga Sengkala 65 K2
Marga Telu 70 C4
Marga Tengah 87 J3
Margaya 14 F3
Marine Reserve 53 K7
Marta Gangga 64 C7
Mas (Bedulu) 49 M8
Mas (Mas) 49 H8
Mas (Sayan) 48 C6
Masceti Beach 65 M6
Masean 80 F4
Masean Kelod 80 E4
Masem Budi Karya 105 M7
Maspait 65 L4
Matahari Terbit Beach 23 L3
Mawan 108 E5
Mawang 87 H5
Mawang Kaja 65 G4
Mawang Kelod 65 G4
Mawar Kangin 96 E4
Mawar Kauh 96 E4
Mayong 97 L6
Mayungan 101 M6
Mayungan Anyar 86 C3
Mayunganlet 86 C3
Medahan (Blah Batuh) 65 L4
Medahan (Kemenuh) 65 H4
Medahan (Medahan) 65 L4
Medewi 82 B8
Medewi Surfing Beach 68 B3
Medura 17 K1
Megati 70 E7
Megati Kaja 70 F7
Megati Kelod 70 F7
Mekar Buana 28 A8
Mekar Manis 28 D5
Mekar Sari (Abang) 76 E2
Mekar Sari (Batu Riti) 86 C7
Mekar Sari (Denpasar) 28 E2
Mekar Sari (Laba Sari) 90 F5
Mekar Sari (Manis Tutu) 79 L4
Mekar Sari (Perancak) 80 C8
Mekayu 69 K6
Melaka 98 E3
Melang 88 E2
Melanting (Banjar Tegehe) 97 L4
Melanting (Banyu Poh) 94 E3
Melanting (Padangbai) 67 K5
Melaya 78 E4
Melaya Krajan 78 E3
Melaya Pantai 78 D4
Melaya Tengah Kaja 78 E3
Melaya Tengah Kelod 78 D3
Melaya Tengah Krajan 78 E2
Melayang 49 J2
Meliling 71 G7
Meliling Kangin 71 G8
Meliling Kawan 71 G7
Melinggih 72 F3
Melinggih Kelod 72 F4
Melit 73 J2
Menagung 98 D6
Menak (Penyabangan) 66 A6
Menak (Temesi) 95 H3
Menang 66 B2
Menanga 74 E4
Menanga Kangin 74 E4
Menanga Kawan 74 E4
Menasa 97 L3
Mendek 70 E3
Mendira 52 A8
Mendira Beach 52 C8
Mendoyo 81 G7
Mendoyo Dangin Tukad 80 F7

Mendoyo Dauh Tukad 80 F6
Menega (Jimbaran) 32 C4
Menega (Loloan Timur) 80 D6
Menesa (Benoa) 38 C7
Menesa (Darma Saba) 64 D5
Menesa (Pedungan) 21 J7
Mengandang 104 E3
Mengani 87 G1
Mengening 24 C1
Mengening Beach 24 B4
Mengesta 85 K7
Mengiat Beach 39 L6
Menguntur 31 G1
Mengwi (Mengwi) 64 B3
Mengwi (Sibang Kaja) 64 E4
Mengwitani 63 M4
Menjangan 93 J3
Mentigi 109 H1
Menunggul 70 E5
Menyali 102 B6
Menyali Kanginan 102 A5
Menyali Kawanan 101 M6
Merangen 66 E6
Meranggi (Denpasar) 29 M2
Meranggi (Muncan) 75 G5
Meranggi (Padang Kerta) 76 D4
Meranggi (Pandak Badung) 63 K4
Merenggeng 109 G6
Mergan 51 B8
Merita 90 E5
Merta Buana 20 D2
Merta Jaya 28 C6
Merta Sari (Buwit) 63 J6
Merta Sari (Loloan Timur) 56 D7
Merta Sari (Patas) 95 M5
Merta Sari (Pujungan) 84 D4
Merta Sari Kelod (Loloan Timur) 80 D7
Merta Sari Kelod (Patas) 95 M4
Merta Yasa 28 D3
Mertasari Beach 17 J6
Mertha Rauh 29 H4
Mertha Rauh Kaja 29 J3
Merthanadi 29 J6
Mesahan 105 G2
Metakih 108 F3
Metra Kaja 74 C4
Metra Kelod 74 C5
Metra Tengah 74 C4
Metulis 67 G5
Mijil 74 F7
Mincidan 66 E4
Minggir (Batu Nunggal) 109 H2
Minggir (Gelgel) 66 E6
Moding 79 G5
Moding Kaja 79 H4
Moncal 107 G6
Mongan 71 K3
Monkey Forest (Marga) 63 M2
Monkey Forest & Pura Bukit Sari (Sangeh) 72 D6
Moon of Pejeng 49 L7
Mountain View 88 B3
Moyo Permai 16 A3
Muaya Beach Café Area 32 A7
Muding Indah 27 H4
Muding Kelod 27 H6
Muding Mekar 27 H6
Muding Sari 27 H4
Muding Tengah 27 H5
Mudita 65 J6
Mukti 65 G5
Muku 74 E6
Mukus 88 C5
Muliawan 28 B8
Muluk Babi 72 D6
Mulung 73 K6
Mumbi 87 K6
Mumbul (Jimbaran) 37 M2
Mumbul (Sibetan) 75 M6
Mumbul Garden 38 B4
Munang Maning 21 H3
Muncan (Abian Base) 64 B5
Muncan (Muncan) 75 G5
Muncan Kaja 75 G5
Mundak Sekar 102 C5
Mundeh (Kediri, Nyambung) 63 L5
Mundeh (Selemadeg) 69 M3
Mundeh Kangin 70 B1
Mundeh Kawan 70 A1
Munduk (Air Kuning) 80 E8
Munduk (Bajera) 70 D6
Munduk (Banjar Tegehe) 97 L3
Munduk (Banjar) 98 E7
Munduk (Dangin Tukad Aya) 80 E6
Munduk (Kali Akah) 79 L7
Munduk (Lovina Beach) 53 K3
Munduk (Mendoyo Dangin Tukad) ... 80 F6
Munduk (Munduk Bestala) 97 M5
Munduk (Munduk) 98 E7
Munduk (Siangan) 73 K7
Munduk (Tegal Badeng Timur) 80 B7
Munduk (Timpag) 71 H6
Munduk Andong Kaja 85 M3
Munduk Andong Kelod 86 B4
Munduk Anggrek 81 K6
Munduk Anggrek Kelod 81 K7
Munduk Anyar 81 H4
Munduk Anyar Kelod 81 H5
Munduk Asem 80 A6
Munduk Bayur 79 G2
Munduk Bestala 98 B6

Munduk Catu 63 G2
Munduk Damping 86 D6
Munduk Dawa 71 G2
Munduk Gawang 69 K1
Munduk Gedang 70 B3
Munduk Juwet 71 H3
Munduk Kelod 97 K6
Munduk Kemoning 80 E5
Munduk Kendung 79 L5
Munduk Kunci 99 G1
Munduk Lingker 93 M5
Munduk Lumbang 85 M5
Munduk Malang 71 G4
Munduk Mengenu 83 J6
Munduk Ngandang 83 K6
Munduk Pakel 71 H5
Munduk Ranti 79 H7
Munduk Sari (Pengulon) 96 B3
Munduk Sari (Sukadana) 107 J7
Munduk Sekar 101 M4
Munduk Seming 85 G1
Munduk Seming Kaja 85 H2
Munduk Temu 83 L5
Munduk Temu Kaja 83 L3
Munduk Temu Kelod 83 L5
Munduk Tengah 83 H6
Munduk Tiying 86 E5
Munduk Tumpeng 79 M5
Munduk Tumpeng Kelod 79 M6
Munduk Waru 80 E3
Munduk Waterfall 99 G6
Mundukulan 70 E8
Munggal 71 M8
Munggu (Mengwi) 63 K7
Munggu (Selemadeg) 70 E7
Munggu Gulingan 64 B2
Munggu Kaja Kangin 63 K7
Munggu Mengwi 63 M2
Mungguna 51 A5
Mungsengan 104 F6
Munti Desa 107 G5
Munti Gunung 106 F6
Muntig (Selat) 75 J5
Muntig (Tulamben) 90 D4
Muntig Kaja 90 D4
Muntig Kelod 90 C4
Musi 95 J4
Musung Kaja 73 J5

N

Naga Sari 70 B5
Nagasepaha 101 K7
Nagi 49 H3
Nangan Kaler 74 E6
Nangka (Budakeling) 76 B2
Nangka (Lemukih) 104 C3
Nangka (Sembiran) 103 G6
Napoleon Reef, Dive Site....... 94 D1
Negara Town 56 C5
Negara (Sempidi) 64 C6
Negari (Negari) 66 B7
Negari (Semarapura) 64 C6
Negari (Singapadu Tengah)...... 65 G5
Nelayan Beach 25 H8
Nesa 66 B6
Ngayor 84 D8
Ngayor Kaja 84 C8
Ngelinti Kangin 106 F6
Ngelinti Kauh 106 E6
Ngenjung Sari 73 L8
Ngimba 67 K5
Ngis (Manggis) 76 B5
Ngis (Riang Gede) 71 J5
Ngis (Tembok) 106 F4
Ngis Kajanan 76 B5
Ngis Kelod 76 F1
Ngis Kelodan 76 A3
Ngoneng 80 F6
NgurahRai Stadium 29 H6
Niki Mutiara Estate 28 D1
Nongan 74 E7
Nungnung 86 D3
Nungnungan Anyar 86 E4
Nusa Dua 39 K4
Nusa Dua Beach 39 K1
Nusa Mara 81 M6
Nusa Penida 108 E4
Nusa Puri 44 D2
Nusa Sakti 79 G4
Nusa Sari 78 F3
Nusa Sari Kelod 78 F4
Nusu 107 K7
Nyalian (Bangli) 54 E4
Nyalian (Banjar Angkan)........ 66 B3
Nyalian Kelodan 66 B3
Nyambu 63 L4
Nyambung 63 K5
Nyamping 66 E5
Nyampuan 62 E3
Nyanglad 84 D7
Nyanglan 74 D7
Nyanglan Kaja 74 D7
Nyanglan Kelod 66 C1
Nyangnyang Surfing 40 C7
Nyanyi 63 J7
Nyatnyatan 71 G6
Nyawah 105 H4
Nyelati 72 B5
Nyeleket 71 K4
Nyitdah 63 J5

Nyuh (Lemukih) 104 B3
Nyuh (Toyopakeh) 108 E1
Nyuh Gading 69 M3
Nyuh Tebel 76 C7
Nyuhkuning 48 E7
Nyuling (Pitra) 71 L3
Nyuling (Tumbu) 76 F4

O

Oberoi 19 J6
Ogang 74 F7
Old Manta Point 108 D6
Ole 71 M5
Oongan 29 J2
Open Air Stage 49 H7

P

Paang 64 F7
Paang Kaja 64 E7
Paang Kelod 64 F7
Paang Tebel 64 D7
Paang Tengah 64 F7
Pabean 29 M5
Pabean Sangsit 101 K3
Pacing 71 J7
Pacung (Ubud) 49 M6
Pacung (Bakbakan) 65 K1
Pacung (Batu Aji) 71 J7
Pacung (Batu Riti) 86 C4
Pacung (Belalang) 63 H6
Pacung (Sangeh) 72 D5
Pacung (Senganan) 85 M7
Pacung (Tejakula) 103 J5
Pacung (Wana Giri) 70 E4
Pacung Selat 72 D7
Pacut 71 J5
Padang (Kerobokan) 26 E6
Padang (Punggul) 72 E7
Padang Aji Kangin 75 G5
Padang Aji Kawan 75 H5
Padang Aji Tengah 75 H5
Padang Aling 72 D4
Padang Asri 20 B1
Padang Bali 63 M7
Padang Bulia 99 K1
Padang Galak 31 G7
Padang Galak Beach 23 L1
Padang Indah 20 C1
Padang Keling 101 J6
Padang Kerta 76 D3
Padang Lestari 27 H8
Padang Linjong 25 K3
Padang Padang Beach 34 B7
Padang Sambian Kaja 64 C8
Padang Sambian Kelod 20 C6
Padang Sari 106 F6
Padang Sigi 73 J5
Padang Sumbu Kaja 20 B6
Padang Sumbu Kelod 20 A7
Padang Tawang 63 L7
Padang Tegal Kaja 46 F5
Padang Tegal Kelod 46 E6
Padang Tegal Mekar Sari 46 F5
Padang Tegal Tengah 46 E5
Padang Tunggal Kangin 75 J7
Padang Tunggal Kauh 75 J7
Padangan Kaja 84 C5
Padangan Kelod 84 C6
Padangasah 89 J2
Padangasah Satu 89 J1
Padangbai 67 L5
Padangbai Indah 67 K4
Padapdapan 49 K4
Padi Dive Center 17 K4
Padpadan (Pengotan) 87 M3
Padpadan (Petak Kaja) 73 K5
Pagan Kaja 29 J6
Pagan Kelod 29 J7
Pagan Tengah 29 J7
Pagending 63 M7
Pagi 85 M7
Pagpagan 41 G4
Pagubugan 67 L1
Pagutan (Banjar Angkan) 66 B6
Pagutan (Sukawati) 64 F7
Pagutan Kaja 64 F7
Pagutan Kelod 64 F7
Pajahan (Pajahan) 84 B4
Pajahan (Wana Giri) 70 F2
Paka 84 D6
Pakel (Gegelang) 67 J4
Pakel (Sampalan Tengah) 66 E5
Pakel (Tangkup) 66 E1
Paken 101 K3
Paket Agung 57 E7
Paketan 105 M4
Pakilen 72 B7
Pakisan 102 D6
Pakse Bali 66 E5
Pakse Bali Kanginan 66 E5
Pakse Bali Kawan 66 E5
Paku 109 H5
Pakuaji 70 B2
Pakudansih Dua 75 G6
Pakudansih Satu 75 G5
Pakudui 73 H2
Pakuseba 87 H6
Pala Giri 30 E1
Pala Linggah 79 G3

Pala Rejo 79 H2
Palak (Besakih) 75 G3
Palak (Keramas) 65 L4
Palak (Sukawati) 65 J6
Palasan Tumbu 76 F4
Palbesi 95 L5
Paleg 89 H1
Palengkong 93 K4
Palikala 74 F2
Palisan 106 B2
Pamedilan 80 E6
Pamenang 63 L2
Pameregan 28 E7
Pamesan (Kalopaksa) 97 J3
Pamesan (Ketewel) 31 L1
Pamesan (Pejaten) 63 H5
Pamongan Kaja 21 G7
Pamsam 101 M3
Panaban 76 F2
Panataran Bujak 83 H5
Panca Bhinneka 33 J1
Panca Darma 63 M4
Panca Jaya 64 B3
Panca Sari 99 L6
Panca Seming 80 F3
Panca Warga 63 M3
Panca Yasa 63 M3
Pancak Kertha 28 B8
Pancak Kertha 20 F1
Pancar Dawa 80 D4
Pancean 63 J7
Pancingan 67 G6
Pancoran (Busung Biu) 97 L6
Pancoran (Kamasan) 66 D6
Pancoran (Mundeh) 69 M4
Pancoran (Panji Anom) 99 H1
Pandak Bandung 63 K5
Pandak Gede 63 J5
Pandan (Selulung) 105 G4
Pandan (Tulamben) 90 C3
PandanHarumStage 53 H7
Pande (Abian Semal) 64 D2
Pande (Beng) 50 C4
Pande (Benoa) 39 H5
Pande (Blah Batuh) 65 J4
Pande (Cempaga) 54 D2
Pande (Dawan Kaler) 67 G5
Pande (Gubug) 63 H4
Pande (Kampung Islam Kusamba).. 67 G7
Pande (Kediri) 63 L4
Pande (Kelating) 63 K5
Pande (Kenderan) 73 J4
Pande (Manggis) 67 L2
Pande (Mengwi) 63 M2
Pande (Pedungan) 21 K6
Pande (Pejeng) 49 K6
Pande (Peliatan) 47 J5
Pande (Rendang) 74 E6
Pande (Renon) 23 G5
Pande (Sayan) 64 F1
Pande (Semarapura Kelod Kangin).. 51 F7
Pande (Semarapura Kelod) 66 E5
Pande (Sumerta Kaja) 29 K6
Pande (Suwat) 73 K5
Pande (Temesi) 66 B6
Pande Galiran 51 D7
Pande Mas 14 D6
Pande Mas (Kamasan) 66 D6
Pande Pemaron 63 K7
Pande Sari 76 B4
Pandean (Mengwi) 63 M2
Pandean (Munggu) 63 K7
Pane 64 D5
Panek 89 J1
Panempahan 87 L7
Paneraga 97 J4
Pangambengan 80 B7
Pangayehan 24 C1
Pangedan Kaja 69 M2
Pangedan Kelod 69 M2
Pangejaran 105 G3
Pangembunga Sari 48 B4
Pangembungan (Batu Bulan) 64 F6
Pangembungan (Bongkasa) 48 A5
Pangembungan (Tampak Siring) .. 73 J5
Pangembungan (Tegal Jadi) 71 L7
Pangeragoan 69 H5
Pangeragoan Dangin Tukad 69 H5
Pangeragoan Dauh Tukad 69 H4
Panggung 103 H7
Panggung Gayung 79 M6
Panggung Gondang 80 E6
Pangi 75 K4
Pangi Kangin 67 G5
Pangi Kawan 67 G5
Pangi Tebel 67 K4
Pangiangan Kangin 73 M1
Pangiangan Kawan 73 L1
Pangiyahan 107 G5
Pangkot 108 E3
Pangkung (Belatih) 105 H4
Pangkung (Pandak Gede) 63 K5
Pangkung (Pejaten) 63 H5
Pangkung Anyar 108 F5
Pangkung Apit 81 H4
Pangkung Buluh Kangin 79 K7
Pangkung Buluh Kauh 79 J7
Pangkung Dedari 78 E4
Pangkung Gayung 80 D3
Pangkung Gedu 108 E6

Pangkung Jajang 79 J6
Pangkung Jelati 81 M6
Pangkung Karung 63 H3
Pangkung Karung Kangin 63 J3
Pangkung Karung Kawan 63 H3
Pangkung Kunyit 83 K5
Pangkung Langkuas 71 G5
Pangkung Languan 81 M7
Pangkung Languan Mekar 81 M7
Pangkung Lubang 81 H5
Pangkung Manggis 79 M7
Pangkung Medaan 82 C7
Pangkung Nyuling 63 M2
Pangkung Panes 79 H8
Pangkung Paruk 97 G4
Pangkung Selepa 82 B8
Pangkung Tanah Kangin 78 F2
Pangkung Tanah Kauh 78 E2
Pangkung Tibah 63 H6
Pangkung Tibah Baleran 63 H5
Pangkung Tibah Belodan 63 G6
Pangkung Tibah Selatan 63 H6
Pangkungkwa 81 J6
Panglan (Kapal) 64 C3
Panglan (Ubud) 49 L5
Panglipuran 74 B5
Pangsan 72 D2
Pangsut 73 L2
Pangusari 98 D4
Pangyangan 68 E3
Paninjoan 74 D5
Panjahan 83 M8
Panji 101 G7
Panji Anom 99 H1
Panji Kelod Kauh 101 G7
Panjingan 106 B2
Pantai Sari 32 C4
Pantai Soka 62 B2
Panthi Giri 44 C4
Panti (Bantang) 105 J2
Panti (Kayu Putih) 98 E3
Panti (Kediri) 63 K4
Panti (Kuwum) 71 M7
Panti (Pandak Gede) 63 J6
Panti (Sanur Kauh) 23 H6
Panti Gede 28 D6
Panti Sari 28 E6
Panti Sari (Pemogan) 15 J1
Papaan 66 E5
Papung 76 C4
Paradise House Reef 90 E2
Pararudan 32 C4
Paregge 63 M2
Parekan 64 D5
Parigi 70 C3
Pasangbe 72 D3
Pasangkan Anyar 75 K6
Pasar (Gumbrih) 68 F3
Pasar (Kintamani) 105 L6
Pasar (Lovina Beach) 53 K4
Pasar (Nusa Sari) 78 E3
Pasar (Pekutatan) 68 B2
Pasar (Yeh Embang Kauh) 81 K8
Pasar Delod 48 A2
Pasar Kalisari 53 G3
Pasar Ratu 53 G3
Pasar Swadaya 20 B7
Pasdalem (Balege) 65 L4
Pasdalem (Gianyar) 50 D8
Pasek (Aan) 66 C3
Pasek (Jagapati) 64 F6
Pasek (Jimbaran) 32 D4
Pasek (Kubu Tambahan) 102 B3
Pasekan (Abian Base) 63 M5
Pasekan (Abian Tuwung) 63 M4
Pasekan (Buduk) 63 M6
Pasekan (Dajan Peken) 51 D1
Pasekan (Dawan Kaler) 67 G4
Pasekan (Kaba-Kaba) 63 L5
Pasekan (Ketewel) 31 M1
Pasekan (Munggu) 63 K7
Pasekan (Sembung) 72 B5
Pasekan (Tembuku) 66 B1
Pasekan Kaja 63 M6
Pasekan Tengah 63 M6
Paselatan 90 F4
Pasih Batu Telu Seraya Beach .. 77 J4
Pasih Pejongan Beach.......... 77 H5
Pasti 63 J6
Pasut (Banyu Seri) 98 C6
Pasut (Mundeh Kangin) 70 B3
Pasut (Pangeragoan) 83 H7
Pasut (Tibu Biyu) 62 E4
Pasut Beach 62 D4
Pasut Katiasa 101 K7
Patah 75 L7
Patas (Gerokgak) 95 M5
Patas (Taro) 87 J6
Pateluan 65 M2
Patemon 97 J3
Patolan 65 K5
Pau 66 C4
Pauman 77 H3
Pausan 87 G3
Pawitra 97 H3
Payan 70 B8
Payangan (Depeha) 102 E5
Payangan (Marga) 71 M3
Payangan (Payangan) 72 F3

Places Index

Payangan Kaja 71 M3
Payangan Medi 71 M3
Payangan Tengah 71 M3
Payogan 48 E1
Payuk 74 D6
Payung Bangkah 71 H7
Payungan 66 D2
Pebantenan 99 J2
Pebuahan 79 H7
Pecatu 41 K5
Pecatu Indah Resort 35 J6
Pecatu Kangin 41 L6
Pecatu Kauh 41 M5
Ped 108 E1
Pedahan Kaja 89 G1
Pedahan Kaja Desa 106 F6
Pedahan Kelod 107 G6
Pedawa 98 D5
Pedlungan 15 L1
Pedungan Kaja 21 H6
Pegadungan 101 K8
Pegametan 93 M3
Pegatepan 66 D6
Pegayaman (Sukasada) 99 K2
Pegayaman (Temukus) 98 A2
Pegending 51 B5
Pegentengan 97 M5
Pegeringsingan 76 C6
Pegesangan 65 M2
Pegok 16 B3
Pegongan 48 A1
Pegubugan Kangin 71 H5
Pegubugan Kauh 71 H5
Peguyangan (Astina) 57 E6
Peguyangan (Batu Madeg) 108 F6
Peguyangan (Denpasar Utara) ... 64 D7
Peguyangan Kaja 64 D6
Peguyangan Kangin 64 E7
Pejarakan 93 K4
Pejaten 63 J5
Pejenengan 98 D7
Pejeng 49 L5
Pejeng (Rendang) 75 G4
Pejeng Kaja 73 J6
Pejeng Kangin 49 M1
Pejeng Kawan 49 K5
Pejeng Kelod 49 M6
Pejengan 73 H4
Pejukung 107 G6
Pejukutan 109 J5
Pekambingan 28 F8
Pekandalas 66 B3
Pekandelan (Abian Base) 50 C8
Pekandelan (Akah) 66 D4
Pekandelan (Batuan) 65 H5
Pekandelan (Culik) 90 F6
Pekandelan (Kerambitan) 63 G3
Pekandelan (Kukuh) 71 M8
Pekandelan (Nyalian) 66 B3
Pekandelan (Pemecutan Kelod) ... 20 E6
Pekandelan (Sading) 64 C6
Pekandelan (Sanur Kaja) 23 K3
Pekandelan (Sanur Kauh) 23 H7
Pekandelan (Semarapura Kelod) ... 51 C7
Pekandelan (Sibang Gede) 64 D5
Pekandelan (Ubud) 49 L7
Pekandelan Kaja 71 H2
Pekandelan Kelod 71 H2
Pekarangan (Batu Riti) 86 B3
Pekarangan (Nyuh Tebel) 76 B6
Pekarangan (Padang Kerta) .. 76 D2
Pekarangan (Pelaga) 86 D2
Pekem 29 J5
Peken (Aan) 66 C3
Peken (Bakas) 66 B4
Peken (Benoa) 39 H4
Peken (Gelgel) 66 E6
Peken (Panca Sari) 99 L6
Peken (Peken) 71 M8
Peken (Renon) 22 E5
Peken Baleran 64 B4
Peken Jelodan 64 B5
Pekundelan 55 E4
Pekutatan 68 C2
Pekuwon 54 E2
Pekuwudan 65 H6
Pelaga 86 E2
Pelagan 64 E6
Pelak Tiying 88 B7
Pelambengan 25 M7
Pelapuan 98 B7
Pelasa 14 E6
Pelem Gede 71 H8
Peliatan (Kelusa) 73 G4
Peliatan (Kerobokan) 26 D6
Peliatan (Ubud) 47 H7
Pelilit Asah 109 K6
Pelilit Kubu 109 K6
Pelita Sari 21 K2
Peludu 87 K1
Pemalukan 64 D7
Pemamoran 14 E7
Pemangkalan 64 C8
Pemanis 71 M2
Pemanis Kelod 72 A2
Pemaron (Buleleng) 100 F6
Pemaron (Munggu) 63 K7
Pemaron (Patemon) 97 J4
Pembuangan 21 M6
Pembungan 66 B1

Pemebetan 64 B4
Pemecutan 28 D8
Pemecutan Kaja 28 E5
Pemecutan Kelod 21 G4
Pemedilan 28 D7
Pemeteran 88 E6
Pemijan 72 D6
Pemijian 72 D4
Peminge 39 J7
Peminge Baru 39 G7
Pemogan 15 K1
Pemogan Kaja 15 K1
Pempatan (Baha) 63 L7
Pempatan (Batungsel) 84 D5
Pempatan (Munggu) 63 K7
Pempatan (Pempatan) 74 E3
Pempetan 72 C5
Pemudungan 84 E7
Pemuhunan 75 G5
Pemutaran 85 M1
Pemuteran 94 C2
Pemuteran Beach 94 D2
Penaga (Peninjoan) 74 C3
Penaga (Sakti) 108 E3
Penaga Gunung Sari 74 C2
Penaga Landih 88 C7
Penangkidan 108 D4
Penarukan (Peninjoan) 74 D4
Penarukan (Singaraja) 101 J4
Penarukan (Timuhun) 66 B2
Penarukan Kelod 62 F4
Penarukan Tengah Kelod 63 G4
Penarungan (Mengwi) 64 C3
Penarungan (Singaraja) 101 J4
Penasan 66 C5
Penatahan (Penebel) 71 K3
Penatahan (Susut) 73 M4
Penatahan Kaja 71 K3
Penatahan Kelod 71 K3
Penataran (Batuan) 65 G5
Penataran (Mundeh) 69 L2
Penataran (Tista) 83 H6
Penatih 64 F7
Penatih Dangin Puri 64 F7
Pende (Sayan) 48 C5
Pende (Taman Bali) 73 M7
Pendem (Alas Angker) 101 L6
Pendem (Bebetin) 102 B7
Pendem (Dalung) 64 B7
Pendem (Karang Asem) 55 E2
Pendem (Muncan) 75 G5
Pendem (Ped) 108 F1
Pendem (Pejukutan) 109 K5
Pendem (Pendem) 56 F2
Pendem (Tukad Aya) 79 J5
Pendukuan 74 E5
Penebel 71 L2
Penebel Kaja 71 L2
Penebel Kelod 71 L3
Peneca 72 F4
Peneka 73 K2
Penelokan 88 B4
Penendengan 73 L2
Peneng 86 C7
Penenjoan 64 D5
Penestanan 46 B2
Penestanan Kaja 46 A2
Penestanan Kelod 46 A4
Penestanan Young Artists 48 D5
Pengabetan (Baha) 64 B2
Pengabetan (Kuta) 14 D6
Pengadangan 64 B4
Pengajaran 79 M6
Pengajaran Kaler 79 M5
Pengaji 72 F4
Pengalu 87 H4
Pengalusan 89 J5
Pengambangan 65 G7
Pengangalon 67 K5
Penganggahan 85 J8
Pengastian 23 L5
Pengastulan 97 J2
Pengaud 109 J2
Pengawan 75 M7
Pengayasan 17 H3
Pengayehan (Gubug) 63 H4
Pengayehan (Munggu) 63 K7
Pengedan Kaja 69 M2
Pengejeroan 66 D1
Pengembunan 71 M7
Pengembungan 25 G4
Pengenderan 32 D3
Pengending 63 M7
Pengererengan Kaja 70 B6
Pengererengan Kelod 69 M7
Pengesan 70 E3
Penggakrajeng 90 F4
Pengiasan 48 A8
Pengiasan (Dauh Puri Kauh) .. 21 J3
Pengiasan (Mengwi) 63 M3
Penginuman 92 A6
Penginyahan 87 G6
Penginyan 98 B7
Pengipian 19 M5
Pengiyakan 105 G2
Penglatan 101 K6
Penglatan Kajanan 101 K5
Penglatan Kelodan 101 J5
Penglumbaran 54 A2
Penglumbaran Kangin 74 A3

Penglumbaran Kawan 87 M8
Pengosekan 46 E8
Pengosekan Kaja 48 F7
Pengosekan Kelod 48 F8
Pengotan 88 B6
Pengubengan Kangin 19 L3
Pengubengan Kauh 19 L2
Pengubungan (Depeha) 102 D5
Pengubungan (Duda) 75 K6
Pengukuh 64 E7
Pengulon 96 C3
Pengumbahan 94 B2
Penida 65 H5
Penida Kaja 74 C6
Penida Kelod 74 C6
Penikit 86 E5
Penina 108 C3
Peninjoan 74 D5
Peninjoan (Batuan) 65 H5
Peninjoan (Peguyangan Kangin) .. 64 E7
Peninjoan (Sampalan Tengah) .. 66 E5
Penuktukan 106 B3
Penuktukan Kawanan 106 C3
Penulisan (Batu Aji) 71 J7
Penulisan (Medahan) 65 L4
Penulisan (Tunjung) 102 F5
Penusuan 73 H5
Penutuk 108 E4
Penyaban 109 J7
Penyabangan (Gerokgak) 95 H3
Penyabangan (Kerta) 87 H6
Penyabangan (Penyabangan) .. 95 H3
Penyaitan 28 C7
Penyalin 51 A1
Penyancangan 109 H6
Penyarikan (Benoa) 39 H5
Penyarikan (Kekeran) 63 M5
Penyaringan (Penyaringan) ... 81 H7
Penyaringan (Sanur) 17 H1
Penyebah 87 M4
Penyembahan 73 K5
Penyucuk 72 C3
Penyungsungan 106 C5
Peradi 106 E5
Perampas 97 M5
Perancak Beach (Kerobokan) .. 18 B1
Perancak Beach (Negara) 80 D8
Perang Anggungan 64 C5
Perang Lukluk 64 C5
Perang Sada 65 J5
Perang Sari Kaja 75 K5
Perang Sari Kelod 75 L5
Perang Sari Tengah 75 L5
Perasi Kaler 76 E6
Perasi Kelod 76 E7
Perasi Tengah 76 E6
Perean 72 C3
Perean Tengah 72 D3
Pererenan Beach 24 E6
Pererenan Bunut 99 K3
Pergan 72 C3
Pergung 81 G7
Perian 87 L5
Perikyukti 71 K6
Pering (Bakas) 66 B4
Pering (Kuta) 14 D7
Pering (Pering) 65 K5
Pering Kanginan 65 K5
Permata Giri Estate 38 B3
Permata Nusa Dua 38 F5
Persiapan 81 J6
Persiapan Pangsan 86 E8
Persiapan Sulangai 86 D5
Pertigaan 83 K3
Pertima 76 E6
Pertukangan 56 C5
Perum "Kuta Family" 19 L5
Perumahan Candra Ditya 30 F2
Perumahan Puri Citra Pratama .. 19 M3
Perumahan Taman Yasa 38 B4
Perwata Sari 79 H3
Perwira 29 J8
Perwira 22 B1
Pesaban 66 D1
Pesaban Kaler 74 D7
Pesaban Kangin 66 D1
Pesaban Kawan 66 D1
Pesagi (Jungutan) 75 L3
Pesagi (Rejasa) 71 H4
Pesalakan (Jimbaran) 32 D5
Pesalakan (Pejeng Kangin) ... 49 M1
Pesalakan (Tuban) 11 G5
Pesanggaran 16 A6
Pesangkan Anyar 75 K7
Peselatan 88 D6
Pesinggahan (Dawan) 67 H6
Pesinggahan (Pekutatan) 68 B2
Pesinggahan Kanginan 67 H6
Pesuguhan 77 H4
Pesurungan 67 G7
Petak (Bebalang) 66 A2
Petak (Gianyar) 73 L6
Petak (Pejeng Kaja) 73 J6
Petak (Taman Bali) 73 M6
Petak Kaja 73 K4
Petanahan 80 E5
Petanahan Kaja 80 E5
Petandakan 101 K7
Petang 86 D8

Petangan 43 M4
Petangan Gede 64 C7
Petapan 63 J8
Petapan Kaja 81 G5
Petapan Kelod 81 G6
Petapan Persidi 81 H6
Petiga 72 B3
Petiga Kangin 72 B3
Petiles 70 C6
Petingan 27 G4
Petitenget 19 H6
Petulu 49 H2
Petulu Desa 49 H1
Petung 88 B4
Piakan 64 D4
Pidada 109 J3
Pikad 108 D4
Pikah 64 D1
Pikat (Dawan) 67 G5
Pikat (Tirta Gangga) 76 C2
Pilan 87 H5
Piling 74 F4
Piling Kanginan 71 K2
Piling Kawan 85 K8
Pilisang 63 L5
Pinda (Pering) 65 K5
Pinda (Saba) 65 J6
Pinge 86 B7
Pinggan 106 C6
Pinjul 73 H5
Pipitan 25 L3
Pisang Kaja 87 K5
Pisang Kelod 87 K5
Pisiatin 77 G4
Pitik 15 K1
Pitra 71 L3
Piuh 72 D3
Playground Surf Break 108 B1
Poh (Budakeling) 90 B7
Poh (Pohbergong) 101 L6
Poh Asem 97 L5
Poh Bergong 101 L6
Poh Gading 64 D7
Poh Gending Kangin 71 L3
Poh Gending Kawan 71 L3
Poh Kembar 96 E3
Poh Manis 64 F5
Poh Santen 80 F6
Poh Tegeh 88 D7
Pojok 13 M1
Pokas 65 J4
Police Station 47 J3
Pondoh 73 L4
Pondok (Beraban) 62 D3
Pondok (Gadungan) 71 G6
Pondok (Peguyangan Kaja) ... 64 D7
Pondok (Petandakan) 101 K6
Pondok (Wana Giri) 99 J6
Pondok Batu 96 F6
Pondok Gebang 85 K7
Pondok Indah Anyelir 29 M6
Pondok Joan 85 L7
Pondok Kaha Kaja 108 D4
Pondok Kaha Kelod 108 E4
Pondok Kelod 108 E4
Pondok Purnawira 20 C1
Pondok Tegal Indah Permai .. 20 C5
Pondok Temukuaya 62 E3
Ponggang 87 G7
Ponjok 109 H3
Ponobolian 67 G1
Pos 1, Dive Site 92 F1
Pos 2, Dive Site 93 G1
Poyan 86 D8
Praja 74 D4
Prangi 76 E3
Prapat 108 E1
Prapat Kelod 108 E1
Prasan 89 J4
Pratama 65 M3
Prembon 108 E5
Prerenan 25 H4
Presatriyo 67 G6
Pringalot 74 E5
Protestant Community 78 F2
Puakan (Taro) 87 J5
Puakan (Tengkudak) 71 J2
Puana 80 B6
Puaya 65 H5
Pucak Sari (Puncak Sari) 83 K2
Pucak Sari (Warna Sari) 79 H4
Pucang 89 K4
Pucangan 74 B2
Pucuk 71 G7
Pudeh 102 F7
Pugutan 71 M7
Puguyan 66 B6
Puhu 87 G7
Pujinan 84 C1
Pujung Kelod 73 J2
Pujungan (Pupuan) 84 D4
Pujungan (Tianyar) 107 G6
Pukuh 87 M3
Pukuh Satu 87 M2
Pulaki Reef, Dive Site 94 E2
Pulangan Baru 109 H4
Pule (Kawan) 54 D6
Pule (Pempatan) 88 F7
Pulenanga 105 K4
Pulesari Kawan 74 E4

Pulu 106 C6
Pulukan 82 C8
Pulukpuluk (Pecatu) 41 G7
Pulukpuluk (Tengkudak) 71 J2
Pulung 54 B8
Pulungambang 64 D7
Pulungan Batu 80 E4
Pumahan (Alas Angker) 101 L7
Pumahan (Biaung) 85 M8
Pumahan (Gitgit) 99 K2
Pumahan (Senganan) 86 A8
Pumnan 73 G2
Puncak Sari (Busung Biu) 83 K2
Puncak Sari (Denpasar) 29 G4
Puncak Sari (Mundeh) 69 K3
Puncak Sari (Penatahan) 85 H8
Punduh Kulit 64 D7
Punduh Lo 101 L3
Punduh Sangsit 101 M3
Punduk Dawa 67 G5
Punduk Paku 85 M7
Pundung 86 E8
Punggang (Kali Asem) 98 C2
Punggang (Sanda) 84 B7
Punggul 72 E7
Pungkukan 96 D3
Pungutan 67 G2
Punia 75 G7
Punjuhan 86 C8
Pupuan (Pupuan) 84 C3
Pupuan (Suana) 109 J3
Pupuan (Tegal Lalang) 87 K6
Pupuan Dua 106 C6
Pupuan Satu 106 C5
Pupuan Sawah 70 E4
Pura (Kali Asem) 98 D2
Pura (Sebudi) 75 H3
Pura Agung 54 B5
Pura Batukaru 85 H6
Pura Kanginan 54 C4
Pura Luhur Beratan 86 A1
Pura Penataran Sasih & Moon of Pejeng .. 49 L6
Pura Ulun Danu Bratan.................... 86 A1
Puregae 88 F7
Puri 28 E7
Puri Bendesa 43 H2
Puri Bukit 54 D1
Puri Dencarik 54 D5
Puri Desa Gede 49 G7
Puri Gading 36 C5
Puri Kampial 38 C5
Puri Kencana Asri 20 D5
Puri Mumbul Permai......................... 37 L2
Puri Nusa Dua 38 F3
Puri Sembadha Canggu 26 C1
Puring 71 H2
Purna Desa (Siangan) 73 K7
Purna Desa (Suwat) 73 K7
Purnama Asri 64 D7
Purnama Beach 65 K7
Purnayasa 102 E5
Purwa 97 J2
Purwa Kerta 64 D3
Purwa Kerthi 90 F5
Purwa Santi 33 K1
Purwayu 76 F1
Puseh (Abang Songan) 88 C5
Puseh (Agantaka) 64 F5
Puseh (Batu Bulan Kangin) 65 H7
Puseh (Kediri) 63 L4
Puseh (Pedungan) 21 H7
Puseh (Pejeng) 49 K5
Puseh (Perean) 72 C2
Puseh (Tista) 83 J5
Puseh (Tuwed) 79 G6
Puseh Kangin 23 H5
Puseh Kauh 23 H6
Puseh Pengalasan 64 C5
Puspa Jati 98 B7
Puspa Sari 84 D4
Putra Bali Hill 38 E5
Putulu Gunung 73 H6
Putung (Besakih) 75 G2
Putung (Duda Timur) 75 L7
Putung (Menanga) 74 E3
Putus 66 F5

R

Raden (Luwus) 86 C8
Raden (Tua)....................................... 86 C8
Raketan 48 B2
Rame 67 G6
Ramuan 109 H7
Rangdu (Medoyo Dauh Tukad)........ 80 F6
Rangdu (Seririt) 97 K5
Rangdu Kaja 97 K5
Rangdu Kelod 97 K5
Rangkan 65 J7
Rarangan 101 M7
Rata 108 F4
Ratna Bhuana 29 J5
Rawa 97 K5
Raya Kampial 44 E2
Real Estate Taman Mumbul............ 38 D3
Rejasa 71 J5
Rejasa Kaja 71 J5
Rejasa Kelod 71 J5
Rendang 74 F5
Rendang Kelod 74 F6
Rendang Tengah 74 F5

Rendetin 102 D6
Rening 79 J8
Rening Cupel 80 A6
Rening Kelod 80 A6
Renon (Denpasar) 22 E5
Renon (Gerokgak) 95 L5
Renon Kelod 22 F6
Reptile Park 72 C6
Residential Exclusive 34 F4
Riang Ancut 71 J8
Riang Gede 71 K7
Riang Kaja 71 K6
Riang Kauh 71 J6
Riang Kelod 71 K7
Riang Kubu 71 K6
Riang Lodsema Gede 71 J7
Riang Tengah 71 J7
Rice Fields & Vista 85 K6
Rice Terraces 90 E8
Rice Terraces 73 H4
Rijasa Beach 62 B3
Ringdikit 97 K4
Ringdikit Kajanan 97 K5
Ringdikit Kelodan 97 J4
Roban (Bitera) 65 K2
Roban (Kelusa) 73 G4
Roban (Siangan) 73 K7
Robokan 64 B8
Royal Garden Residence 38 C3
Rubaya 90 D1
Rukun 68 F3
Runuh Kubu 101 J7

S

Saap 105 J7
Saba (Pandak Gede)......................... 63 J5
Saba (Penatih) 64 E7
Saba (Saba) 65 J5
Sabang 105 H5
Sabi 101 M6
Sablong 81 M8
Sacred Monkey Forest Sanctuary ... 46 D7
Sacret Bay, Dive Site 92 B5
Sadewa 73 M7
Sadimara 76 E2
Sading 64 C6
Sading Sari 20 E6
Sadnya Sari 79 G2
Sagah 68 E2
Saganing Waterfall 108 D5
Sagara 65 J8
Sai 84 B4
Saih 64 D6
Saiman 92 A6
Sakah (Batuan Kaler) 65 H4
Sakeh 63 G4
Sakenan Baleran 51 E2
Sakenan Belodan 51 D3
Sakih 65 H7
Saksak 75 J5
Sakti 108 D3
Sala (Abuan) 73 L4
Sala (Pejeng Kawan) 47 M3
Salak (Batu Madeg) 108 E5
Salak (Keliki) 73 G4
Salang 109 G4
Salen 108 E5
Salepa 68 B1
Salia 84 D2
Salt Panning 91 G5
Sama 21 J7
Sama Geria 74 C5
Sama Undisan 74 C6
Samantha Residences 38 B3
Samarutha 87 H6
Sambangan 101 H7
Sambi Renteng 106 C3
Sambian Pengayehan 71 H7
Sambian Pondok 71 H7
Sambian Tengah 71 H6
Sambian Undagi 71 H6
Samblong 80 E7
Samoja 84 B3
Sampalan 109 H1
Sampalan Kelod 66 E6
Sampalan Tengah 66 E5
Sampiang 50 D6
Samping Buni 21 H3
Samplangan 50 F6
Samsam 63 H2
Samsam Dua 63 H2
Samsam Satu 63 J2
Samsaman Alas 63 H2
Samsaman Kaja 70 C4
Samsaman Kelod (Kukuh) 63 H2
Samsaman Kelod (Lumbung) 70 C4
Samu 64 E3
Samuan Kangin 72 E4
Samuan Kawan 72 D5
Samuan Tiga 49 L7
Samudra Kuta Place Football Field .. 14 F8
Samuh (Candidasa) 53 K5
Samuh (Pempatan) 88 E6
Samuh Kelod 53 M6
Samuh Kelod 76 D8
Samuh Tengah 76 D8
Sanda (Sanda) 84 D6
Sanda (Satra) 105 H2
Sanda (Selulung) 105 H4
Sandakan 86 E5

Sandan (Bangli) 85 M5
Sandan (Wongaya Gede) 71 J2
Sandan Danginyeh 71 L6
Sandan Dauhyeh 71 K6
Sandan Lebah 71 K6
Sandan Pondok 71 L5
Sandan Teger 71 K5
Sanding (Gianyar) 65 K1
Sanding (Tampak Siring) 73 J5
Sanding Biangbasa 73 J5
Sanding Bitra 73 J5
Sanding Gianyar 73 J5
Sanding Serongga 73 J5
Sandingan 83 M8
Sandy Slope, Dive Site 92 F1
Sangambu 105 J1
Sangburni 102 C7
Sangeh 72 D6
Sangga Agung 21 G2
Sangga Langit 95 K4
Sanggem 74 F7
Sangging (Abian Base) 65 L3
Sangging (Akah) 66 D3
Sangging (Dawan Kelod) 66 F5
Sangging (Kamasan) 66 D6
Sangging (Kelating) 62 F4
Sanggulan 51 F4
Sangiang 63 M5
Sanging 64 E4
Sangka Buana 51 B6
Sangkabah 84 B5
Sangkan Aji (Talibeng) 66 E3
Sangkan Aji (Tembuku) 74 C5
Sangkan Gunung 74 F7
Sangkar Agung 80 E7
Sangket 101 H7
Sangketan 71 H2
Sangkungan 66 E2
Sanglah 21 L5
Sanglah Barat 21 K5
Sanglah Timur 21 L4
Sanglah Utara 21 K4
Sangluh 67 H5
Sanglung 102 E5
Sangsana 106 F7
Sangsit 101 K3
Sangut 72 E4
Sangyangan 24 E1
Sangyangapi 76 B4
Sanih 101 K5
Sanlangki 104 D4
Santal 97 L5
Santhi Karya 43 K2
Santi 75 J5
Sanur 17 K1
Sanur Beach 17 M3
Sanur Beach 23 M4
Sanur Kaja 23 J4
Sanur Kauh 17 J2
Sapat 73 H5
Sapiah 97 K5
Sapta Bumi 20 E2
Sarang Burung Walet Cave 108 B2
Saraseda 73 K2
Sarasidi 71 H7
Saraswati 29 L2
Saren (Kerta) 87 G4
Saren (Nongan) 74 E7
Saren (Sibang Kaja) 64 D4
Saren Anyar 76 C3
Saren Jawa 76 C3
Saren Kaler 74 E7
Saren Kangin 76 C3
Saren Kauh 76 C3
Saren Kelod 74 D7
Saren Tengah 74 E7
Sarga 65 G5
Sari (Bestala) 97 M6
Sari (Bungkulan) 101 M3
Sari (Gumbrih) 69 G4
Sari (Pengastulan) 97 J2
Sari (Sesetan) 16 E3
Sari (Talibeng) 66 F3
Sari (Ubung) 28 C1
Sari Asri 37 L1
Sari Buana 20 F2
Sari Jimbaran 32 F7
Sari Kaja 99 L6
Sari Kaya 42 F4
Sari Kuning 79 H4
Sari Kuning Tulung Agung 79 J5
Sari Mekar (Buleleng) 101 J6
Sari Mekar (Katung) 87 J4
Sari Mekar (Ringdikit) 97 K5
Sari Merta 66 C6
Sari Tengah 99 L6
Sarin Buana 70 F1
Sarnih 102 E3
Sasih (Ketewel) 65 G8
Sasih (Panjer) 22 C4
Satra (Kintamani) 105 H2
Satra (Klungkung) 66 D6
Satra Kangin 66 D6
Satra Kawan 66 D6
Satria (Blah Batuh) 65 J4
Satria (Bungkulan) 101 M3
Satria (Mas) 65 H2
Satria (Pelapuan) 98 B7
Satria (Penarukan) 101 J4

Satria (Pendem) 56 D3
Satung 72 E2
Sawa Gunung 49 M4
Sawah (Bebandem) 76 D3
Sawah (Pedungan) 21 H7
Sawah (Wana Giri) 70 E3
Sawan (Sawan) 102 B6
Sawan (Siangan) 49 M4
Sawan Kanginan 102 B6
Sawan Kawanan 102 B6
Sawangan Kaja 45 H2
Sawangan Kelod 45 H3
Sawe 80 E4
Sawe Rangsasa Kelod 80 E4
Sayan 48 C5
Sayan Baleran 72 B7
Sayan Delodan 64 B1
Sayan Ridge 48 C1
Sayan Ridge 72 F6
SD, Diving Site 108 E1
Sebali 73 G6
Sebatu 87 J8
Sebau 91 G6
Sebonipil 109 G3
Sebual 80 E6
Sebudi Denpasar 29 L8
Sebudi (Selat) 75 H4
Sebuluh 108 E5
Sebunibus 108 D3
Sedahan (Gulingan) 64 B3
Sedahan (Munggu) 63 K7
Sedana Merta 28 D2
Sedang 64 F4
Sedewa 66 A2
Sedihing Dua 109 J7
Sedihing Satu 109 J7
Sedit (Bebalang) 54 A8
Sedit (Taman Bali) 73 M5
Segah 74 E7
Segara (Padangbai) 67 L4
Segara (Tuban) 10 E4
Segara Katon 55 E7
Segara Mukti 95 J4
Sege 91 G8
Sekaan (Bangbang) 74 D6
Sekaan (Sekaan) 87 L3
Sekar (Banjar) 97 L4
Sekar (Gunung Sari) 98 B7
Sekar (Kali Asem) 98 D2
Sekar (Munduk Bestala) 97 M6
Sekar (Nongan) 74 D7
Sekar Dadi 87 M3
Sekar Gula 86 C6
Sekar Gunung Kaler 76 F2
Sekar Gunung Kelod 76 F2
Sekar Kangin 16 E3
Sekar Kejula 81 K6
Sekar Mukti (Belok) 104 E8
Sekar Mukti (Persiapan Pangsan) .. 72 E2
Sekar Panca Sari 80 F5
Sekar Sari (Banyu Seri) 98 B5
Sekar Sari (Kampung Baru) 57 F2
Sekar Sari (Selat) 98 F2
Sekar Taji (Sekartaji) 109 H7
Sekar Taji (Wanasari) 71 L6
Sekumpul 104 B3
Sekunjeng 87 H3
Selabih Pangkong Kuning 69 H5
Selabih Tengah 69 J5
Selabih Wana Sari 69 J5
Selalang 77 H3
Selanbawak 72 B7
Selanbawak Kaja 72 B5
Selanbawak Kelod 72 B6
Selang 91 K6
Selangambu 71 G7
Selantang 86 F2
Selasih 86 F7
Selasih Beach 24 D5
Selat (Balege) 65 K4
Selat (Banjar Angkan) 66 B6
Selat (Buahan) 66 F6
Selat (Klungkung) 66 D3
Selat (Mengwitani) 64 B4
Selat (Perean Tengah) 72 C4
Selat (Samplangan) 65 L1
Selat (Sangeh) 72 D6
Selat (Selat) 75 H6
Selat (Siangan) 73 K7
Selat (Sidan) 73 L8
Selat (Sobangan) 72 C7
Selat (Sukasada) 98 F2
Selat (Tegak) 66 D3
Selat Kaja 75 J6
Selat Kaja Kauh 73 L3
Selat Kelod 75 J6
Selat Nyuhan 73 L2
Selat Peken 73 L3
Selat Tengah 73 L3
Selati 65 M1
Seledumi 75 H5
Seleksek 83 M3
Selemadeg 70 E7
Selemadeg Bale Agung 70 E6
Selemadeg Kaja 70 E6
Selemadeg Kelod 70 E7
Selingsing Kaja 63 H2
Selingsing Kelod 63 H2
Selisihan 66 C2
Selisihan Kangin 66 C2

Selisihan Kawan 66 C2
Seloding 71 M3
Selokah 83 L1
Selombo 103 L5
Selonding 41 J6
Seloni 90 F6
Selulung 105 G3
Selumbung 75 M8
Selumbung Kaleran 75 M8
Selumbung Kanginan 75 M8
Selumbung Kelodan 75 M8
Selumbung Tengah 75 M8
Sema (Bitera) 50 A5
Sema (Bungkulan) 101 M3
Sema (Kediri) 63 L4
Sema (Melinggih) 72 F3
Sema (Patemon) 97 J3
Sema (Pering) 65 K5
Sema (Saba) 65 J5
Sema (Sangsit) 101 L3
Sema (Suwat) 73 K6
Sema Agung 66 C5
Semaga 64 F7
Semaja 70 C6
Semana 48 B8
Semanik 86 D1
Semarapura 51 C5
Semarapura Kaja 66 D4
Semarapura Kangin 51 E6
Semarapura Kauh 51 B6
Semarapura Kelod 51 C7
Semarapura Kelod Kangin .. 51 E8
Semarapura Tengah 51 D5
Semate 64 B5
Semawang 17 K4
Semaya 109 K4
Sembahan 46 F1
Sembiran 103 H6
Sembiran Kanginan 103 J6
Sembiran Kawanan 103 J6
Sembung (Lumbung) 70 B6
Sembung (Mengwi) 72 C5
Sembung (Taman Bali) 73 M6
Sembung (Tegal Cangkring) . 81 H6
Sembung Dua 106 E4
Sembung Gede 71 H8
Sembung Merangi 71 H8
Sembung Sari 22 E3
Sembung Satu 106 E4
Sembuwuk 73 J5
Semebaung 49 M8
Semer 26 E8
Semila Jati 28 C5
Seming (Kerta) 87 G4
Seming (Klumbu) 108 F2
Semingan 72 B3
Seminyak 19 J8
Semoan 86 F8
Sempidi (Abian Semal) 64 D1
Sempidi (Mengwi) 64 C6
Sempidi Kangin 64 C7
Semseman 66 E1
Semut 42 4C
Senangka 108 E3
Senapahan 63 L2
Sendang Dalam 94 D2
Sendang Luar 93 M4
Sendang Pasir 94 B1
Senganan (Penebel) 85 M6
Senganan Kangin 85 M6
Senganan Kawan Kaja 85 M6
Senganan Kawan Kelod 85 M6
Sengguan (Abian Base) 64 B6
Sengguan (Baha) 63 M6
Sengguan (Bitera) 50 A5
Sengguan (Dawan Kaler) 67 G5
Sengguan (Gumbrih) 68 F3
Sengguan (Kaba-Kaba) 63 L5
Sengguan (Munggu) 63 K7
Sengguan (Nyitdah) 63 J5
Sengguan (Penarungan) 64 C3
Sengguan (Semarapura Kangin) 51 E5
Sengguan (Sibang Gede) 64 D5
Sengguan (Singapadu) 65 G5
Sengguan (Tonja) 29 K1
Sengguan Kangin 50 C7
Sengguan Kawan 50 D6
Sengguang 63 M6
Sengkaduan (Sekaan) 87 L4
Sengkaduan (Taro) 87 K4
Sengketan 70 E3
Sengkidu 52 A6
Sengliding 66 C3
Sengon 99 H7
Sente 67 G5
Sentral Kangin 109 G2
Sentral Kawan 108 F2
Sepang 83 H3
Sepang Kelod 83 H4
Serahi 105 K5
Serai 87 M7
Serampingan 70 D7
Serampingan Kaja 70 E7
Serampingan Kelod 70 F8
Serangan (Mengwi) 63 M3
Serangan (Serangan Island) . 13 L1
Serangan Dukuh 13 K2
Serangan Kaja 16 F7
Serangan Kaja 13 L1
Serangan Kawan 16 F8

Serangan Peken 16 F8
Serangan Peken 13 L1
Serangan Pojok 16 F8
Serangan Tengah 16 F8
Serangan Tengah 13 L1
Serangeh 108 F2
Serason 71 L3
Seraya 90 E3
Seraya (Antiga) 67 K3
Seraya (Bakti Sebaga) 57 A8
Seraya (Karang Asem) 77 H3
Seraya Barat 77 G4
Seraya Timur 77 K1
Seribupati 72 C5
Seririt 97 J3
Serokadan 73 M6
Serong 68 F4
Serongga 65 I4
Serongga Dua 106 C7
Serongga Gede 63 H3
Serongga Kaja 65 L3
Serongga Kelod 65 M4
Serongga Kemenuh 63 H3
Serongga Pondok 63 H3
Serongga Satu 106 C7
Serongga Tengah 65 L4
Serutang 97 J5
Sesana 76 C4
Sesandan Kangin 70 F4
Sesandan Kauh 70 F5
Seseh 24 D4
Seseh (Singapadu) 65 G5
Seseh Beach 24 D5
Sesetan 16 B3
Sesetan Kaja 21 L6
Setra Pemogan Cemetery 15 J5
Shipwreck Surf Break 108 B1
Siakin 106 B4
Sianga 102 E5
Siangan 73 K7
Sibak 72 C5
Sibang (Jagapati) 64 F5
Sibang (Sangeh) 72 D6
Sibang Gede 64 D5
Sibang Kaja 64 D4
Sibetan 75 M6
Sidakarya 67 G1
Sidakarya 16 E3
Sidan (Belok) 86 F3
Sidan (Sidan) 65 M2
Sidaparna 74 C3
Sidayu 101 J4
Sidayu Nyuhaya 66 C7
Sidayu Tojan 66 D7
Sidem Bunut 54 F2
Sidemen 67 G2
Sidetapa 98 B4
Sigar 74 E7
Sigaran (Jegu) 71 K4
Sigaran (Mambal) 64 E3
Sigaran (Sedang) 64 E4
Siih 73 K5
Siladan (Siangan) 73 K7
Siladan (Taman Bali) 73 M6
Siladarma (Mengwitani) 63 M4
Siladarma (Tejakula) 103 M6
Silagading Dua 106 C3
Silagading Satu 106 D3
Silagading Tiga 106 D4
Silakarang 64 F3
Silang Jana 99 L1
Silayukti 26 E5
Siligita 38 F5
Silungan 65 G4
Sima 29 K4
Simpang Pasedahan 52 D7
Simpang Sari 37 G3
Simpang Tohpati 30 D3
Simpang Ubung 28 D3
Simpangan 63 H5
Simpangban 107 H7
Sinabun 101 K5
Sinalud 98 E2
Sindhu Beach 23 M6
Sindhu Kaja 23 L7
Sindhu Kelod 17 L1
Sindhu Kelod 23 L7
Sindu Bali 75 G7
Sindu Islam 75 G7
Sindu Jiwa 48 B6
Singapadu 65 G6
Singapadu Kaler 64 F4
Singapadu Tengah 65 G5
Singaperang 87 G4
Singaraja 57 D5
Singarata 74 E5
Singekerta 48 D7
Singgi 23 J5
Singkung 99 M1
Sinjuana 63 J7
Sintrig 64 E4
Siyut 66 B7
Siyut Beach 66 B7
Snorkeling Spots 91 G5
Sobangan 72 C7
Sobangan Gede 72 C7
Sogra 75 K3
Sogsogan 24 D4
Sogsogan Beach 24 C5
Soka Beach 62 B2

Soka Kaja 70 C8
Soka Kanginan 85 L6
Soka Kawan 85 L6
Sombang 79 H4
Sompang 108 C4
Song Bintang 40 C4
Song Layung 73 K5
Song Londak 73 M1
Songan 77 K3
Songan A 106 D7
Songan B 106 D7
Soyar 109 H6
Spring 108 E5
Srijati 64 E5
Sriteja 86 F6
Suana 109 K4
Subagan (Candidasa) 52 C6
Subagan (Subagan) 55 C6
Subamia 71 K8
Subamia Ambalambal 71 K7
Subamia Bale Agung 71 K8
Subamia Dencarik 71 K7
Subamia Kelong 71 K8
Subang 97 J4
Subaya 103 M8
Subilang 73 G1
Subuk 97 M8
Suci (Dauh Puri Kangin) 28 F8
Suci (Tejakula) 103 L5
Suda 63 K4
Sudaji 101 M7
Sudaji Kaja Kauh 101 M8
Sudamukti 84 C2
Sudihati 105 L6
Sudimara 63 G5
Sudimara Kaja 63 G5
Sudimara Kelod 63 G5
Suka Dana 107 K7
Suka Luwih 75 J4
Sukadarma 103 L5
Sukaduka 65 J4
Sukahati 67 H6
Sukahed 66 E3
Sukajati (Gobleg) 99 G5
Sukajati (Taman) 72 E6
Sukarama 105 L6
Sukarkejula 81 K6
Sukarkejula Kelod 81 K7
Sukasada 101 J6
Sukawana (Kintamani) 105 L3
Sukawana (Selat) 75 H6
Sukawati (Bedulu) 49 M7
Sukawati (Selemadeg) 70 E7
Sukawati (Sukawati) 65 H6
Sukra 76 D3
Sukun 108 F5
Sulahan 73 M2
Sulang 66 E5
Sulang Kangin 66 E5
Sulang Kawan 66 E5
Sulangai 86 D5
Sulanyah 97 K3
Suluban 40 C3
Suluban Beach 40 A1
Suluban Surfing 40 B1
Sumampan 65 H3
Sumber Batok 92 F4
Sumber Kelampok 92 E5
Sumber Kesambi 93 M4
Sumber Kima 93 L4
Sumber Sari 78 D2
Sumbul 81 M8
Sumega 97 J6
Sumerta 29 L5
Sumerta Cemetery 29 L4
Sumerta Kaja 29 K5
Sumerta Kauh 29 J7
Sumerta Kelod 29 L8
Sumping 70 C4
Sumuh 21 H5
Sunantaya Kaja 71 M2
Sunantaya Kelod 71 M2
Sungiang Sari 29 L8
Sunia 64 B1
Sunting 87 M4
Suraberata 69 L7
Suradadi 70 D3
Suralaga 63 L3
Surga 97 H5
Surya Dive Center 17 L4
Susuau 55 D2
Susuk 103 K5
Susut (Buahan) 72 F2
Susut (Muncan) 74 F5
Susut (Susut) 73 L3
Susut (Tua) 86 B7
Susut Kaja 73 L3
Susut Kelod 73 L4
Suter 88 D5
Suukan 74 F3
Suwat 73 K6
Suwat Kaja 73 K6
Suwat Kelod 73 K7
Suwitrayasa 67 G6
Suwug 101 L6
Suwug Kajanan 101 L6
Suwug Kelodan 101 L6
Suwung Batan Kendal 16 C5
Suwung Kangin 16 F3
Swakarya Baru 21 M3

Swalegiri 66 C3
Swastika 68 E3

T
Tabah 72 E6
Tabanan 51 C2
Tabang 102 C7
Tabin 88 B5
Tabog 98 E7
Tabola 67 G1
Tabu (Selat) 66 D3
Tabu (Songan A) 106 B6
Tabu (Tangkup) 66 E2
Tabuanan 109 H7
Tagtag Kelod 28 F1
Tagtag Tengah 28 F1
Taguan 72 D7
Tainsiat 29 G5
Tajen Dauyeh 71 L3
Tajen Jeroan 71 M3
Tajen Pane 71 M3
Tajen Sodahan 71 L4
Tajun 102 F6
Taked Kelod 105 G3
Takedan 66 D2
Takmung 66 C6
Takmung Kangin 66 D6
Takmung Kawan 66 C6
Talaga 75 L7
Talangpati 86 C4
Talibeng 66 F3
Taman (Abian Semal) 72 E6
Taman (Bedulu) 49 L7
Taman (Bestala) 97 M6
Taman (Dangin Tukad Aya) .. 80 E5
Taman (Darma Saba) 64 D6
Taman (Desa Taman) 48 A2
Taman (Gubug) 51 A4
Taman (Karang Asem) 55 D2
Taman (Kayu Putih) 98 F7
Taman (Munduk) 98 F7
Taman (Penatih Dangin Puri) 64 F7
Taman (Penebel) 71 L2
Taman (Penyabangan) 95 G3
Taman (Sanur) 23 K6
Taman (Seraya) 77 J2
Taman (Tuwed) 79 G6
Taman Bakas 74 B7
Taman Bali 66 A3
Taman Bali Raja 73 M7
Taman Darma 75 G5
Taman Graha Permai 37 L3
Taman Griya 37 K3
Taman Kaja 46 F1
Taman Kelod (Jehem) 54 F7
Taman Kelod (Tembuku) 74 B8
Taman Kelod (Ubud) 46 F2
Taman Kertha Nadhi 19 K5
Taman Kota Denpasar 28 F2
Taman Laut 108 D2
Taman Mulia 2 Residences .. 32 D7
Taman Mumbul 38 D2
Taman Mumbul Indah 38 D4
Taman Sakura 36 B5
Taman Sari (Banyu Seri) 98 B6
Taman Sari (Batungsel) 84 E4
Taman Sari (Dangin Puri Kaja) 29 G5
Taman Sari (Delod Peken) ... 51 E3
Taman Sari (Kampung Baru) . 57 F1
Taman Sari (Mengwitani) 63 M4
Taman Sari (Munduk Bestala) 97 M6
Taman Sari (Pandak Gede) ... 63 K6
Taman Sari (Sesetan) 16 C4
Taman Sari (Sulanyah) 97 K3
Taman Sari (Tianyar Barat) . 106 F4
Taman Sari Anyar 63 K3
Taman Sari Dua 106 F5
Taman Sari Kangin 84 F3
Taman Sari Satu 106 F5
Taman Sekar (Kediri) 63 K3
Taman Sekar (Sading) 64 C7
Taman Suci 16 D3
Taman Surodadi 63 L3
Taman Tanda 86 B2
Taman Tengah 74 B7
Taman Wirasaba 19 K4
Taman Yang Batu 29 H8
Taman Yangbatu 22 A1
Tambak 102 B2
Tambak Asa 87 J7
Tambak Sari (Kampung Baru) 57 E1
Tambak Sari (Kapal) 64 B5
Tambakan 104 E4
Tambau Kelod 29 M1
Tambau Tengah 30 B2
Tamblang 102 C6
Tamblang Kaja Kangin 102 D6
Tamblang Kaja Kauh 102 C6
Tamblang Kelod Kauh 102 C6
Tamblingan 99 G7
Tambrah 66 C5
Tambunan 74 D5
Tameng 65 H6
Tamiga Gede 76 D3
Tampak Gangsul 28 F5
Tampak Karang 86 B6
Tampak Kerep 63 M7
Tampak Siring 73 K3
Tampak Siring Kelodan 73 K3
Tampekan 98 A3

Places Index

Tampuagan (Karang Asem) 55 D5
Tampuagan (Peninjoan) 74 D5
Tanah Ampo (Jungutan) 75 L5
Tanah Ampo (Manggis) 67 L3
Tanah Aron 75 M2
Tanah Bang 63 L3
Tanah Barak 77 L1
Tanah Bias (Kedisah) 73 J3
Tanah Bias (Toyo Pakeh) 108 E1
Tanah Daa 105 L4
Tanah Embut 105 H1
Tanah Gambir 105 G2
Tanah Lengis 76 D1
Tanah Lot 63 H7
Tandang Buana Sari 105 L6
Tandeg 26 B4
Tangeb 98 A3
Tangga Yuda 48 C3
Tanggahan Anyar 65 M1
Tanggahan Gunung 73 M3
Tanggahan Pekan 73 M2
Tanggahan Talang Jiwa 73 M7
Tanggahan Tengah 73 M6
Tanggu Wisia 97 K3
Tangguan 105 G5
Tangguntiti 30 F4
Tangguntiti (Selemadeg) 62 E3
Tangguwisia 97 K3
Tangi 80 B6
Tangi Kelod 80 B7
Tangi Miyeh 80 C4
Tangis 83 M6
Tangkas (Gelgel) 66 E6
Tangkas (Kenderan) 73 J4
Tangkas (Susut) 73 M3
Tangkid 102 D6
Tangkup (Bukian) 72 F3
Tangkup (Kedisah) 73 H3
Tangkup (Pupuan) 87 K6
Tangkup (Sidemen) 66 E2
Tangkup Anyar 66 E3
Tangkup Desa 66 E3
Tanglad 109 J6
Tangsub 65 H6
Tangtu 30 F6
Tanjung (Batu Kandik) 109 G5
Tanjung (Gumbrih) 69 G3
Tanjung Benoa 33 J2
Tanjung Benoa Anyar 33 J2
Tanjung Benoa Tengah 33 J1
Tanjung Bungkak Kaja 29 M8
Tanjung Bungkak Kelod 22 E1
Tanjung Bungkak Satu 29 M7
Tanjung BungkakKelod 29 M8
Tanjungan 105 H3
Tapesan 63 M3
Taro 87 H7
Taro Kaja 87 H7
Taro Kelod 87 H7
Tarukan 49 L2
Tarukan (Mas) 65 H3
Tatag (Guwang) 65 J7
Tatag (Manukaya) 87 K8
Tatag (Rejasa) 71 J4
Tatag (Sampalan Tengah) 66 E5
Tatag (Sibang Gede) 64 E5
Tatag (Taro) 87 H8
Tatag Beringkit 71 M8
Tatag Seminyak 19 L8
Tatag Wirasanthi 14 E1
Tatasan Kaja 29 K2
Tatasan Kelod 29 J4
Tatiapi Kaja 49 K5
Tatiapi Kelod 49 J5
Tauka 76 E3
Tauman (Kekeran) 63 M5
Tauman (Sembung) 72 B5
Tauman (Tenganan) 76 C7
Teba 32 D5
Teba Rejo 48 B1
Tebanding 102 C2
Tebe 109 K6
Tebejero 63 K6
Tebesaya 47 H4
Tebongkang 48 C8
Tebuana (Sukawati) 65 H6
Tebuana (Taro) 87 J5
Tedung 65 L4
Tega 29 J2
Tegak 66 D2
Tegak Gede 81 L8
Tegal (Baha) 64 C2
Tegal (Bebalang) 54 D8
Tegal (Bubunan) 97 K5
Tegal (Guwang) 65 H6
Tegal (Jimbaran) 32 E5
Tegal (Kubu Tambahan) 101 M3
Tegal (Kukuh) 71 M7
Tegal (Kuta)........................ 14 E8
Tegal (Nyitdah) 63 J5
Tegal (Pering) 65 K5
Tegal (Sangsit) 101 K3
Tegal (Tegal Lalang) 73 H4
Tegal Abian Base 50 E8
Tegal Agung 21 H1
Tegal Ambengan 63 G3
Tegal Asah (Sanur Kaja) 23 J5
Tegal Asah (Tembuku) 74 C5
Tegal Asih (Dangin Tukad Aya)...... 80 E6
Tegal Asih (Puncak Sari)............ 83 K3

Tegal Badeng 80 C6
Tegal Badeng Barat 80 B6
Tegal Badeng Timur 80 C6
Tegal Baleran 51 B2
Tegal Belodan 51 B3
Tegal Besar 66 C7
Tegal Besar Beach 66 C7
Tegal Bingin 65 H2
Tegal Buah 20 B1
Tegal Bunder 92 D5
Tegal Cangkring 81 G7
Tegal Cantel 80 F7
Tegal Dukuh Anyar 21 H2
Tegal Gede 21 J2
Tegal Gundul 25 M8
Tegal Harum 20 F2
Tegal Jadi 71 M7
Tegal Jaya 27 H1
Tegal Juuk 73 K1
Tegal Kanbin 21 H2
Tegal Kauh 64 C7
Tegal Kawan 28 C8
Tegal Kawan 21 H1
Tegal Kepuh 63 K6
Tegal Kerta 28 B8
Tegal Kontang 69 M4
Tegal Kuning 48 C1
Tegal Kuwalon 29 K4
Tegal Lalang (Kawan) 54 E5
Tegal Lalang (Tegal Lalang) 73 H4
Tegal Langlangan 90 E4
Tegal Langon 28 D8
Tegal Langon 21 J1
Tegal Lantang (Ban) 89 J3
Tegal Lantang (Denpasar) 20 C4
Tegal Lantang (Pengulon) 96 C3
Tegal Lantang (Ubud) 49 G2
Tegal Lantang Kaja 20 B3
Tegal Lantang Kelod 20 C4
Tegal Lenga 96 F3
Tegal Lingah 65 K2
Tegal LInggah (Denpasar) 28 D7
Tegal Linggah (Karang Asem) 76 F3
Tegal Linggah (Kertha Mandala).... 90 E7
Tegal Linggah (Menanga) 75 G3
Tegal Linggah (Panji Anom) 98 F1
Tegal Linggah (Pinggan) 106 B6
Tegal Linggah (Sempidi) 64 B7
Tegal Linggah (Sukasada) 100 F7
Tegal Linggah (Tegal Linggah) 55 F2
Tegal Linggah Kaja 71 J4
Tegal Linggah Kelod 71 J4
Tegal Linggah Pondok 71 J4
Tegal Mas 76 D5
Tegal Mengkeb 62 D3
Tegal Mengkeb Kaja 62 D2
Tegal Mengkeb Kelod 62 D3
Tegal Mengkeb Tengah 62 D2
Tegal Narungan 72 C7
Tegal Panti 90 C1
Tegal Payang 87 K7
Tegal Saat (Kapal) 64 B5
Tegal Saat (Tampak Siring) 73 J5
Tegal Sari (Banjar Tegal) 57 E7
Tegal Sari (Bondalem) 103 K5
Tegal Sari (Padang Sambian) 27 M4
Tegal Sari (Panjer) 21 M5
Tegal Sari (Patas) 96 B3
Tegal Sari (Sulanyah) 97 K3
Tegal Sari (Sumber Kima) 93 L4
Tegal Sari (Tangguwisia) 97 K3
Tegal Sari (Tegal Harum) 27 M8
Tegal Sari (Tianyar Barat) 106 F4
Tegal Sari Kelod 95 M5
Tegal Sari Satu 106 E4
Tegal Seka 71 H5
Tegal Selat 72 D6
Tegal Suci (Kubu) 74 B6
Tegal Suci (Sebatu) 87 K6
Tegal Suci (Tampak Siring)......... 73 K3
Tegal Tamu 65 G5
Tegal Temu Kaja 62 F4
Tegal Temu Kelod 62 E4
Tegal Ulung 65 J5
Tegal Wangi (Bakas) 66 B4
Tegal Wangi (Denpasar) 28 A7
Tegas 71 H4
Tegayang Kaja 71 J3
Tegayang Kauh 71 J3
Tegayang Kelod 71 J3
Tegeh (Denpasar) 27 G5
Tegeh (Angseri) 86 B5
Tegeh (Selat) 75 J5
Tegeh Sari 29 J1
Tegeha (Batuan) 65 G5
Tegeha (Pakisan) 102 D7
Tegeha (Sempidi) 64 B6
Tegehe 31 G1
Tegenan 74 F4
Tegenungan 65 J4
Teges (Beraban) 62 E3
Teges (Pempatan) 88 E8
Teges Kanginan 49 H7
Teges Kawan 49 H7
Teges Kelod 50 C7
Tegil Kiuh 95 H4
Teguan 48 A4
Tejabukit 83 M3
Tejakula 103 M6
Tejakula Kanginan 103 M6

Tejakula Kawanan 103 L6
Tejakula Kelodan 103 M5
Tejakula Tengah 103 M6
Tektek 64 D7
Tektekan 109 K6
Tekumas Village 52 B3
Telabah (Batu Bulan) 64 F7
Telabah (Sukawati) 65 J6
Telaga (Batu Nunggal) 109 G1
Telaga (Busung Biu) 97 K7
Telaga (Telaga) 97 K7
Telaga Kaleran 76 E8
Telaga Kelodan 76 D8
Telaga Tengahan 76 E8
Telaga Tunjung Kaja 71 H6
Telaga Tunjung Kelod 71 H6
Telaktak 108 C1
Telanga 64 D6
Telembal 88 A3
Telengah 75 H7
Telengan 67 H2
Telengis 63 G5
Telepud 73 J1
Telugtug 72 E3
Telukbiu 88 F3
Telun Buana 75 J3
Telun Wayah 67 G2
Telun Wayah Betenan 67 G2
Telun Wayah Duuran 67 G2
Telutug (Padang Kerta) 76 D3
Telutug (Sibetan) 75 M6
Temacun (Kuta) 14 E7
Temacun (Mekar Sari) 86 C7
Temaga (Talibeng) 66 E4
Temaga (Tiga) 87 M6
Temakung 89 J3
Tembau 71 M5
Tembiyak 42 D7
Tembok 106 E3
Tembuku 74 C7
Tembuku Bakas 74 C7
Tembuku Kaja 74 C6
Tembuku Kawan 74 C7
Temen (Manukaya) 87 L7
Temen (Sulahan) 87 L8
Temesi 65 M3
Tempat Pembuangan Sampah Akhir (TPA)
  Suwung 16 C7
Tempek Kelahan 87 K4
Tempek Kelod 102 B3
Temple Garden, Dive Site (Pemuteran) 94 C1
Temple Hill Private Estates 36 E3
Temple Point, Dive Site 93 G1
Temple Wall, Dive Site 94 C2
Temudewi 42 B4
Temukaya (Rejasa) 71 J4
Temukuaya (Tangguntiti) 62 E2
Temukus (Asah Duren) 68 D1
Temukus (Banjar) 98 B2
Temukus (Besakih) 75 H3
Tenaon 101 L7
Tengading 67 K4
Tengah (Abian Base) 63 M5
Tengah (Abian Semal) 72 D8
Tengah (Akah) 66 D4
Tengah (Antosari) 70 C7
Tengah (Banjar Jawa) 57 D5
Tengah (Banjar Tegehe) 97 L3
Tengah (Batuan) 65 H5
Tengah (Bedulu) 49 K8
Tengah (Blah Batuh) 65 K4
Tengah (Darma Saba) 64 D5
Tengah (Datah) 90 D6
Tengah (Dawan Kaler) 67 G5
Tengah (Gobleg) 98 E6
Tengah (Gumbrih) 68 F3
Tengah (Kalopaksa) 97 H3
Tengah (Kenderan) 73 J4
Tengah (Ketewel) 65 H7
Tengah (Kukuh) 71 L8
Tengah (Lodtunduh) 65 G2
Tengah (Manduang) 66 D4
Tengah (Manggis) 67 L2
Tengah (Marga) 71 M5
Tengah (Mendoyo Dangin Tukad) .. 80 F6
Tengah (Nongan) 74 E7
Tengah (Nyanglan) 74 D7
Tengah (Padang Kerta) 76 D3
Tengah (Peguyangan) 64 D7
Tengah (Punggul) 72 E7
Tengah (Renon) 22 F5
Tengah (Saba) 65 J5
Tengah (Sedang) 64 E4
Tengah (Selat) 66 D2
Tengah (Sesetan) 21 M7
Tengah (Sibang Kaja) 64 D4
Tengah (Sibetan) 75 M6
Tengah (Sidakarya) 16 E3
Tengah (Sidemen) 75 G7
Tengah (Sinabun) 101 K5
Tengah (Singekerta) 48 C7
Tengah (Sobangan) 72 C7
Tengah (Sobangan) 72 C7
Tengah (Subagan) 55 A8
Tengah (Sulang) 66 F5
Tengah (Suwat) 73 K5
Tengah (Tampak Siring) 73 K3
Tengah (Tegal Badeng Barat) 80 B6
Tengah (Tegal Badeng Timur) 80 B7
Tengah (Tegal Cangkring) 81 H7

Tengah (Tegal Lalang) 73 H4
Tengah (Temukus) 98 B2
Tengah (Tenganan) 76 C7
Tengah (Timuhun) 66 C2
Tengah (Ubung) 28 D1
Tengah (Ulakan) 67 L3
Tengah (Yeh Kuning) 80 E8
Tengah Belayu 71 M8
Tengah Kaler 64 B3
Tengah Kangin 47 H7
Tengah Kauh 47 H8
Tengah Kelod 64 B3
Tengah Lukluk 64 C5
Tengah Sempidi 64 B7
Tenganan 76 C6
Tenganan Kanginan 76 C6
Tenganan Kauhan 76 C6
Tengeh 64 B7
Tenggang 77 H4
Tengipis 87 G5
Tengkudak 71 K2
Tengkulak 49 J8
Tengkulak Kaja Kangin 49 J8
Tengkulak Kaja Kauh 49 J7
Tengkulak Kelod 65 H2
Tengkulak Mas 65 H3
Tengkulung 33 K4
Tenten 21 G4
Teras Ayung 29 L1
Terora 33 K5
Teruna (Blah Batuh) 65 J4
Teruna (Bunutin) 73 M7
Teruna (Siangan) 73 K8
Teruna (Taman Bali) 73 M7
Teruna (Ubud) 47 H6
Terusan 56 B7
Tetelan 78 F5
Tewel 48 C8
The Rock Garden & Karang Lestari, Dive Site
  .... 94 D2
Threads of Life 46 E1
Tiangan 105 G4
Tianyar 107 H5
Tianyar Barat 107 G5
Tianyar Tengah 107 G5
Tiapi 49 M6
Tiba Kauh 72 F4
Tibu Belang Kaler 81 J5
Tibu Belang Kelod 81 J6
Tibu Belang Tengah 81 J6
Tibu Beneng 26 D1
Tibu Biyu 62 E4
Tibu Biyu Kaja 62 E4
Tibu Biyu Kelod 62 E4
Tibu Dalem 84 D3
Tibu Laka Bali 76 F3
Tibu Laka Sasak 76 F3
Tibu Langgang 81 J4
Tibu Poh 62 F3
Tibu Sambi 81 L7
Tiga 87 M7
Tiga Kawan 87 M7
Tiga Wasa 98 D3
Tigaron 107 K7
Tihingan 66 C5
Tihingan Kangin 76 A3
Tihingan Kauh 76 B3
Tihingan Tengah 76 A3
Tihingsaka 76 A2
Tiingpuan 73 J1
Timbrah 76 D6
Timbul (Bungaya) 76 D5
Timbul (Kedis) 97 M8
Timbul (Pupuan) 87 K7
Timpag 71 H7
Timuhun 66 C2
Timur Jalan 99 L2
Tindih 90 D5
Tinga Tinga 96 C3
Tingas 74 C1
Tingas 104 D7
Tinggar Sari 84 A1
Tinggar Sari Kanginan 97 M8
Tinggar Sari Kauhan 97 M8
Tinggi 68 B2
Tingjajang 108 E3
Tingkat Batu 74 C6
Tingkih Kerep 71 J3
Tinjalas 77 K2
Tinungan 86 B7
Tinyeb 56 A4
Tireman 70 A7
Tireman Kangin 70 B6
Tireman Kelod 70 B7
Tirta Gangga 76 D2
Tirta Kesuma 79 G5
Tirta Sari 98 C6
Tista (Abang) 90 E8
Tista (Busung Biu) 83 H5
Tista (Kerambitan) 63 G3
Tista Tengah 90 E7
Titab 97 L7
Titigalar 86 B3
Titih 64 B4
Titih Kelod 28 F8
Titih Tengah 28 F7
Tiying Gading 70 D5
Tiying Gading Desa 70 D5
Tiying Jangkrik 76 F3
Tiying Tali 76 E2

Tiying Tali Kaler 76 E2
Tiying Tali Kelod 76 F2
Tiying Tukul Puri 25 K1
Tiyingan (Bukian) 73 G2
Tiyingan (Pelaga) 104 D8
TNI AL 16 C5
Togah 66 B1
Togoh 66 C1
Tohjiwa (Nyambung) 63 L5
Tohjiwa (Talibeng) 66 E4
Tohjiwo 86 C4
Tohpati (Abian Semal) 64 E2
Tohpati (Banjar Angkan) 66 C1
Tohpati (Bungaya Kangin) 76 C3
Tohpati (Denpasar) 30 E2
Tohpati (Karang Asem) 55 C5
Tohpati (Ubud) 48 A7
Tohpati Kangin 74 C7
Tohpati Kawan 74 C7
Tojan 66 D6
Tojan Kaler 66 D6
Tojan Kelod 66 D6
Tongtongan 107 H7
Tonja (Denpasar) 29 J1
Tonja (Tabanan) 63 H3
Toya Bungkah 50 C2
Tuyo Pakeh 108 E2
Traditional Village (Kubu) 74 B5
Traditional Village (Pengotan) . 88 A6
Trijuta 64 D3
Triwangsa (Bakbakan) 73 L8
Triwangsa (Beng) 50 D4
Triwangsa (Bitera) 50 A6
Triwangsa (Bungaya Kangin) ... 76 C3
Triwangsa (Bungaya) 76 D5
Triwangsa (Jagaraga) 101 M5
Triwangsa (Kelusa) 73 G3
Triwangsa (Kenderan) 73 J4
Triwangsa (Samplangan) 50 E8
Triwangsa (Siangan) 73 K8
Triwangsa (Suwat) 73 K6
Triwangsa (Tegal Lalang) 73 H4
Triwangsa Bersela 73 G3
Triwangsa Keliki 73 G4
Triwangsa Kelusa 73 G3
Triwangsa Macang 76 B4
Triwangsa Sebali 73 G5
Triwangsa Sibetan 75 M6
Truna Sari 28 F3
Trunyan 88 F2
Tua 72 B2
Tuakilang Baleran 71 K8
Tuakilang Belodan 63 K1
Tuban 10 F3
Tuban Gerya 11 G5
Tubanan 66 D6
Tubuh (Batu Bulan) 65 G7
Tubuh (Blah Batuh) 65 K4
Tubuh (Manduang) 66 C4
Tugu, Diving Site 108 F1
Tuka (Dalung) 63 M7
Tuka (Perean) 72 C3
Tukad Aya 79 H7
Tukad Batuan 47 L5
Tukad Buah 77 K2
Tukad Bungbung 76 C2
Tukad Jasan 47 K4
Tukad Juwuk 99 H4
Tukad Mas 47 J8
Tukad Mungga 100 F7
Tukad Pule 95 K4
Tukad Saang 109 J5
Tukad Sabuh 75 K5
Tukad Sumaga 96 E4
Tukad Sumage 106 A2
Tukad Telantung 47 L1
Tukad Tiis 77 K2
Tulad 109 G4
Tulamben 90 D2
Tulamben Marine Reserve........ 90 E2
Tulamben Marine Reserve 90 E2
Tulang Ampiang 64 D7
Tulang Apiang 28 C6
Tulang Nyuh 66 D2
Tulikup 66 A6
Tumbu 76 F4
Tumbu Kaler 76 F4
Tumbu Kebon 76 F4
Tumbu Kelod 76 F4
Tuminggal 76 F2
Tumpek 76 E2
Tunas Mekar 79 K5
Tunas Sari 107 H5
Tundak 86 C7
Tundun Penyu 36 B7
Tunggal Sari 51 C3
Tunglangan 71 M4
Tunjuk 71 L5
Tunjuk Selatan 71 L6
Tunjuk Tengah 71 L5
Tunjuk Utara 71 M5
Tunjung 102 F6
Tunon 64 E2
Tunoon 19 G2
Turtle Center 16 F8
Turtle Conservation 80 C8
Turtle Water Park 16 E8
Tusan (Banjar Angkan) 65 J4
Tusan (Blah Batuh) 66 B5
Tusan Kangin 66 B5

Tusan Kawan 66 B5
Tutung 90 E2
Tuwed 79 G6
Tuwug 74 F6

U
Ubud (Carang Sari) 72 E2
Ubud (Gianyar) 46 F4
Ubud Kaja 46 D2
Ubud Kelod 46 D3
Ubud Tengah 46 E2
Ubung (Denpasar) 28 C1
Ubung (Jimbaran) 32 D4
Ubung (Penebel) 71 L2
Ubung (Sempidi) 64 B6
Ubung Kaja 64 C7
Ubung Kaja Kangin 64 C7
Udayana Golf Diving Range 23 H4
Udayana Permai 37 G6
Ujung 29 L3
Ujung Beach 77 G6
Ujung Desa 76 F5
Ujung Desa Bali 76 F5
Ujung Desa Islam 76 F5
Ujung Pesisi 77 G5
Ulakan (Rendang) 74 F6
Ulakan (Ulakan) 67 K3
Ulapan 72 F2
Ulapan Dua 72 D7
Ulapan Satu 64 D1
Ularan 97 J5
Ulian 87 H1
Ulumabadung 64 C3
Ulumsul 66 E5
Ulundanu 106 D6
Ulundesa 63 J6
Uluwatu 40 B4
UluwatuBeach 34 A7
Uma (Duda) 75 H6
Uma (Kapal) 64 B4
Uma (Seririt) 97 J3
Uma Anyar (Bebalang) 73 M6
Uma Anyar (Pejeng Kawan) 49 J1
Uma Anyar (Petak) 73 L6
Uma Bali 72 B4
Uma Basa 84 D1
Uma Bian 63 M1
Uma Buluh 26 B2
Uma Candi 63 M7
Uma Dawa 49 M3
Uma Desa 64 E6
Uma Diwang 71 M8
Uma Diwang Kangin 71 M8
Uma Diwang Kawan 71 M8
Uma Dui 20 C6
Uma Gunung 64 B6
Uma Kepuh 63 M7
Uma Klungkung 64 B7
Uma Kuta 49 M2
Uma Padi 74 D4
Uma Sari (Dangin Puri Kaja) 29 G4
Uma Sari (Kerobokan) 19 J3
Uma Sari Kangin 75 H6
Uma Sari Kauh 75 H6
Uma Seka 70 D6
Uma Sendi 98 C2
Uma Tegal 63 M6
Umah Anjar (Darma Saba) 64 D6
Umah Anjar (Mambal) 64 E2
Umah Anyar (Lukluk) 64 C6
Umah Anyar (Penarungan) 64 D3
Umalas 19 H2
Umalas Kangin 19 J2
Umalas Kauh 19 H2
Umanyar (Ababi) 76 C2
Umanyar (Belimbing) 84 E7
Umanyar (Nyalian) 66 A3
Umbalan 74 C5
Ume Anyar 97 H3
Ume Jero 84 E1
Ume Jero Kaja 84 E1
Ume Jero Kangin 84 E1
Ume Kaja 83 G4
Ume Ngandang 98 C7
Ume Poh 86 B5
Ume Salakan 66 C6
Umopoh 64 C2
Umpeng 41 J2
Undagi 64 D3
Undisan (Payangan, Puhu) 87 H7
Undisan (Tembuku) 74 D7
Undisan Kaja 74 D6
Undisan Kelod 74 D7
Undisan Panca Sari 74 D6
Ungasan 43 J4
Ungasan Kaja 43 H2
Ungasan Kangin 43 K4
Ungasan Kauh 43 J4
Ungasan Kelod 43 J5
Ungasan Permai 43 K2
Ungasan Simpang 43 G1
Unggahan 97 J6
Unggahan Kangin 97 J6
Unggahan Kauh 97 J6
Untalan 75 M3
Untaluntal 64 B7
Unusan 98 E6
Utu 85 L7

V
View (Kedewatan) 48 D1
View (Labuan Sait Beach) 34 B7
View (Sayan) 48 C4
Views (Gianyar) 65 M2
Views (Seririt) 97 M6
Villa Kuta Regency 11 H3
Volcanic Lake (Lake Batur) 88 D2

W
Wahaprasta 105 L7
Wali 81 K7
Waliang 76 E1
Wana Giri (Kintamani) 105 L7
Wana Giri (Selemadeg) 70 F2
Wana Giri (Sukasada) 99 L5
Wana Giri (Ungasan) 42 F3
Wana Giri (Wana Giri) 70 F2
Wana Keling 86 C5
Wana Sara 63 H4
Wana Sara Kaja 63 J4
Wana Sara Kelod 63 H4
Wana Sari (Denpasar) 28 F4
Wana Sari (Ekasari) 79 H2
Wana Sari (Kintamani) 105 L8
Wana Sari (Sidemen) 75 H7
Wana Sari (Tabanan) 71 K6
Wana Sari (Talibeng) 66 F3
Wana Sari (Tohpati) 74 C8
Wana Sari Baleran 71 K6
Wana Sari Belodan 71 L6
Wana Sari Tengah 71 L6
Wanayu (Bedulu) 49 L8
Wanayu (Tiying Gading) 70 D3
Wangaya Kaja 28 F5
Wangaya Kelod 28 F6
Wangaya Tengah 28 F6
Wangbung 65 J7
Wangkal 70 E2
Wangsian 66 E2
Wani (Abang) 76 E2
Wani (Gadungan) 71 G6
Wani (Serampingan) 70 E8
Warga Sari 79 G3
Waringin 88 E7
Warna Sari 79 G4
Warna Sari Kelod 79 G4
Waru (Buahan) 88 B4
Waru (Gesing) 84 F2
Waru (Kutampi) 109 G3
Waru (Serampingan) 70 E8
Waru Kaja 85 G2
Waterbom Park 10 F2
Waterfall (Sukawati) 65 J5
Wates (Datah) 90 C7
Wates (Tanglad) 109 K7
Wates Kaja 75 K6
Wates Kangin 75 K7
Wates Tengah 75 K6
Werdi Bhuana 72 C7
White Water Rafting 48 C1
Widyasari 57 F2
Wijaya Kusuma 57 C5
Wijaya Kusumah 42 E6
Wira Satya 17 G4
Wiradarma (Kintamani) 105 L5
Wiradarma (Mengwitani) 63 M4
Wirabuana (Sukasada) 99 L3
Wirasana 23 J4
Wirasatya (Dauh Puri) 21 M2
Wisma Nusa Permai 38 D5
Wongaya Beban 85 L7
Wongaya Bendul 85 J8
Wongaya Gede 85 J8
Wongaya Kaja 85 J7
Wongaya Kangin 85 J8
Wongaya Kelod 85 J8
Yadnya Kerti 97 J5

Y
Yang Api (Abian Tuwung) 63 M3
Yang Api (Manduang) 66 D3
Yang Api (Muncan) 75 G6
Yang Api (Tembuku) 74 C4
Yang Api (Undisan) 74 C6
Yang Batu Kangin 22 B2
Yang Batu Kauh 22 A1
Yangloni 47 M8
Yeh Anakan 97 H3
Yeh Bakung 69 K6
Yeh Basang 102 D5
Yeh Bau Dua 106 E4
Yeh Bau Satu 106 E3
Yeh Biu 96 B3
Yeh Buah 81 J7
Yeh Bung 77 G5
Yeh Bungan 75 M5
Yeh Embang 81 K7
Yeh Embang Kangin 81 K7
Yeh Embang Kauh 81 K7
Yeh Gangga 62 F5
Yeh Kali 77 H4
Yeh Kayu 69 L4
Yeh Ketipat 99 L5
Yeh Kori 75 L3
Yeh Kuning (Pekutatan) 68 D3
Yeh Kuning (Yeh Kuning) 80 E8
Yeh Lebah (Pangyangan) 68 E2
Yeh Lebah (Yeh Embang Kauh) 81 K5

Yeh Lesung 102 E5
Yeh Maled Kaja 62 F3
Yeh Maled Kelod 62 F3
Yeh Malet 67 J5
Yeh Mampeh 106 A7
Yeh Mas 96 E4
Yeh Mecebur 81 J5
Yeh Mekecir 80 F6
Yeh Mempeh Waterfall 106 A3
Yeh Panas (Pemuteran) 94 C2
Yeh Panas (Songan A) 106 D7
Yeh Poh 67 L1
Yeh Pulu Rock Carvings 49 K8
Yeh Satang 81 M7
Yeh Sibuh 69 K2
Yeh Silah 69 M5
Yeh Sumbul 81 M8
Yeh Tengah 73 G4
Ycha 75 H4
Yoh 87 M4
Yonif 900/Raider 11 H5
Yuwuk Manis Kaja 83 G7
Yuwuk Manis Kelod 83 G7